THE LIFE AND TRIALS
OF ROGER CLEMENS

The Life and Trials of Roger Clemens

Baseball's Rocket Man and the Questionable Case Against Him

Hansen Alexander

McFarland & Company, Inc., Publishers
Jefferson, North Carolina

LIBRARY OF CONGRESS CATALOGUING-IN-PUBLICATION DATA

Names: Alexander, Hansen, author.
Title: The life and trials of Roger Clemens : baseball's rocket man and the questionable case against him / Hansen Alexander.
Description: Jefferson, North Carolina : McFarland & Company, Inc., Publishers, 2017. | Includes bibliographical references and index.
Identifiers: LCCN 2016054327 | ISBN 9781476665764 (softcover : acid free paper) ∞
Subjects: LCSH: Clemens, Roger. | Pitchers (Baseball)—United States—Biography. | Baseball players—United States—Biography. | Athletes—Drug use—United States. | Steroid abuse—United States. | Doping in sports. | Governmental investigations—United States.
Classification: LCC GV865.C54 A54 2017 | DDC 796.357092 [B] —dc23
LC record available at https://lccn.loc.gov/2016054327

BRITISH LIBRARY CATALOGUING DATA ARE AVAILABLE

ISBN (print) 978-1-4766-6576-4
ISBN (ebook) 978-1-4766-2594-2

© 2017 Hansen Alexander. All rights reserved

No part of this book may be reproduced or transmitted in any form or by any means, electronic or mechanical, including photocopying or recording, or by any information storage and retrieval system, without permission in writing from the publisher.

Front cover: Roger Clemens in his final year with the Red Sox, 1996 (courtesy National Baseball Hall of Fame Library, Cooperstown, New York)

Printed in the United States of America

McFarland & Company, Inc., Publishers
 Box 611, Jefferson, North Carolina 28640
 www.mcfarlandpub.com

For Bill Bugli,
a tough critic, a tough coach, a loving father,
a religious man who never swore,
and a .400 hitter

Table of Contents

Acknowledgments ix
Introduction 1

1. The Self Invention of Roger Clemens 11
2. The Consistency of Roger Clemens 20
3. The Passive Injector 41
4. Keeping Up Appearances with George Mitchell 52
5. Evidence? What Evidence? 66
6. Roger Clemens' Last Brawl with the Baseball Writers 77
7. An Investigation of the Investigation 98
8. Clemens Gets Clobbered in Congress 104
9. The Desperados 116
10. The Mysterious Mister McNamee 126
11. Squeezing McNamee 140
12. The Trial That Wasn't 148
13. A Prosecutor's Dream Jury 158
14. Rusty Hardin's Comfort Zone 176
15. The Government's Double-Edged Swords 186
16. When the Evidence Told Roger Clemens' Side of the Story 195
17. A Theory of the Case 207
18. At Home in Houston 223
19. Roger Clemens, Family Man 227

Chapter Notes 231
Bibliography 252
Index 255

Acknowledgments

The one-sided coverage by the press and the politically-inspired prosecution by the government against Roger Clemens stunned me. First and foremost the lack of fairness appalled me. I had been inspired as a boy to become a lawyer after reading the biography of Samuel Leibowitz, who had defended the Scottsboro Boys, young African American men who had been falsely accused of rape in Alabama in the 1930s.[1] This is not to suggest, however, that the pursuit of Clemens was comparable to the terrible injustice committed against the young men in Alabama.

What I learned in almost a decade of researching, interviewing, and writing this book is that what people believe has little to do with evidence and ideas and more to do with their own personal needs.

From a writing standpoint, one technique has intrigued me from the beginning: logical analysis. My friend Annette Gordon-Reed used it so effectively in her landmark book, *Thomas Jefferson and Sally Hemings*, an allegation of the relationship between Jefferson and his slave later proved by DNA analysis, that I was determined to employ it in my own investigation of the Roger Clemens case. That technique dominates this book.

For informational assistance, I am indebted to Gus Gustafson of the College Baseball Hall of Fame in Waco, Texas.

Thanks to my life-long friend, and favorite receiver when we played football, Jim Coffin, for editing this very complex book. In addition, Jim has an MS in biochemistry from Cornell and proved a valuable asset in breaking down the DNA evidence discussed in the trial and other scientific information.

My friend George Vecsey, whom I consider the best sportswriter ever, and have given that opinion in many venues, blessed me to use the book's opening quote from one of his articles. He also corrected mistakes I had made in the chapter on Clemens's relationship with baseball writers, even though I was extremely tough on those writers and even though he was skeptical of my theories regarding the PED charges against Clemens. Indeed George and I have disagreed about the Clemens case for years and will probably continue to do so as long as we live.

In addition, I want to thank the following people for help and encouragement in putting this book together: Karen Valentine Slawson, Jeff Hearron, Mike Trout, Suzanne Haliburton, Bill Little, Cliff Gustafson, Rob Bennett, Lenny Sturner, Desmond Whitaker, Sarah Einstein, David Rabinowe, Dave Pomes, Jim Carey, the late Jeremy Still, Carlyon Hayes, Joe Daraskevich, Tim Taliaferro, Jim Kay, Pam Walker, and Nakia James-Jenkins.

My father, Bill Bugli, a former sportswriter, talked me out of becoming one when I was fifteen and therefore protected me from a life of poverty. This allowed me to develop the objectivity to launch this assault on the imperfections of baseball writing.

My wife Taube Cyrus suffered years of my commandeering of the sole computer in our one-room New York apartment, and without her extraordinary understanding and patience, this book could not have been written. The computer crashed in the autumn of 2013 and I lost everything, including the Clemens manuscript. An expensive, diagnostic claw back was performed to recover Roger Clemens' story.

"Now the old warrior has come back from a few short months of off-season retirement to give his hometown team some new hope. Clemens came down with a brutal virus Saturday night and was trudging around without the chesty swagger of old.... It was a masterly 'Perils of Pauline' performance, with Clemens battling his rustiness, the residual effects of the virus, a foxhole in front of the pitching mound and his own onrushing forty-two years. The burly old master showed how to eke out a victory on patience and brains and gall."—George Vecsey

Introduction

"Roger Clemens is in George's box. Roger Clemens is coming back. Oh my goodness gracious," said Yankees radio announcer Suzyn Waldman, only the third woman in Major League history to serve as a full-time color commentator. "Of all the dramatic things I've ever seen, Roger Clemens is standing right in George Steinbrenner's box announcing he is back." To be sure, it was literally under the bright lights, albeit the natural lights of a blazing afternoon sun on a May Sunday in the Bronx, which shined on the old Yankee Stadium. Television lights and microphone were turned on in the private suite of one of baseball's most controversial and successful baseball owners. "Well, they came and got me out of Texas," Clemens said into the microphone, and the crowd roared. So big a character in the history of baseball was Roger Clemens that the announcement was almost literally true. Nine years earlier, Yankees owner George Steinbrenner, not a young man by any means, had flown down to Clemens' Houston home to recruit him and even lifted weights with Clemens in the effort. Clemens signed with the Toronto Blue Jays, however, that winter, polishing off two more Cy Young Awards, before Steinbrenner got his man by trading for him in 1999. Clemens proved crucial in pitching the Yankees to World Series titles in 1999 and 2000. Later that day in 2007, Clemens told reporters, "I'm coming back to do the only thing they know how to do with the Yankees, and that's win a championship. Anything else is a failure, and I know that."[1] But the 2007 season would not prove to be the happy ending of the Roger Clemens story. Although the desperate Yankees were in the midst of a losing streak and stuck at 13–15, Clemens would help them make the playoffs by winning a Wild Card spot that fall, finishing 94–68. But he struggled to a 7–7 record, his hamstring gave out at the end of the season, and he lasted only 2.1 innings in his final game against the Indians, on October 7, in the playoffs, although he struck out the last batter he ever faced, Victor Martinez. The Indians went on to win the series. More importantly, ahead lay the greatest challenge of his life: To prove that he did not take human growth hormone and anabolic steroids to enhance his pitching performance in the latter part of his career. An allegation had been made in the so-called Mitchell Report, a public relations charade pretending to be an objective investigation.

Roger Clemens played Major League baseball for 24 seasons. Because he won 354 games and lost 184, a superlative winning percentage of .658, ranked third in career strikeouts with 4,672, and won the Cy Young Award for best pitcher seven times, the most ever, many of the game's authorities considered him the greatest pitcher in the century-and-a-half history of the sport. Clemens' ability to throw strikes was so consistent that in years 14–24, his number of walks-per-year was within a hundredth of a percent of what it had been in his first 13 years with the Boston Red Sox: 65.846 to 65.818. He had seven seasons, the first in 1984 and the last in 2007, in which he had a perfect fielding percentage of 1.000.[2] When he retired he was the only pitcher ever to strike out 20 batters in a game twice. He was selected for the Major League All-Star Game 11 times in 15 completely healthy seasons. He ranks seventh all time in games started, 707 and ninth with 354 wins. He was voted AL MVP once, a rarity in an age when each league had its own Cy Young Award for best pitcher. He received MVP votes nine other times. He threw 46 shutouts. And Clemens absolutely dominated modern baseball statistical analysis for a pitcher:

- Base-Out runs saved 771.69, FIRST ALL TIME
- Situational wins saved, 73.2, FIRST ALL TIME
- Win Probability added, 77.7, FIRST ALL TIME
- Base-Out wins saved, 80.7, FIRST ALL TIME
- Adjusted pitching runs, 708, SECOND ALL TIME
- Adjusted pitching wins, 74.3, SECOND ALL TIME

This portrait of Clemens is both a biography and a critical investigation of the criminal prosecution against him for perjury, a case premised on the underlying accusation that he cheated at the sport of baseball by taking performance enhancing drugs. Yet it is also a celebration of baseball.

His story, the saga of an American high school student undrafted by the professional major leagues who became the best player at his position in the last quarter of the twentieth century, is remarkable enough. This book offers a new and different perspective on Clemens' development as a pitcher and his career as a ballplayer. The text will show that Clemens was not a one-trick pony, a "flamethrower" who could only throw a fastball and needed performance enhancing drugs in the second half of his career to maintain his velocity. Rather, Roger Clemens was a control artist who only discovered he had a major-league fastball rather late in his development. As early as Little League, he was a strikeout machine. While earlier coaching intervention had effected an increase in

Clemens' pitching speed,[3] this book reports for the first time that a similar pitching defect in his grip was discovered and corrected in his last semester at the University of Texas, unleashing his devastating curveball. Baseball fans will already be familiar with the split-finger fastball Clemens developed in Toronto in 1997, making him equally unhittable through much of the second half of his career. This book acknowledges, however, that Clemens did experience a *decline* due to age in most endurance categories in pitching, particularly in complete games and innings pitched, in the second half of his career. Clemens' strikeouts-per-year declined from 210.2 from ages 21 to 35 to 168.7 from ages 36 to 44.[4]

Baseball players have always been entertaining, quirky, loyal characters. They are not less so in these pages. Cal Ripken, Jr., and Ken Griffey, Jr., discuss in vivid detail what it was like to bat against Clemens. Casey Stengel, Clemens' alter ego in temperament and manner of speaking, walks around naked in the clubhouse, thumping his chest, venting. Clemens' first manager in Boston, Ralph Houk, spits tobacco juice at the feet of reporters. Jeff Hearron, Clemens' roommate and catcher at the University of Texas, discusses living with Clemens and how he could never get enough to eat and was always hungry in college. Clemens gets into a brawl during his first semester. Cliff Gustafson, the legendary University of Texas coach who ran his team like a Marine drill sergeant, talks about Clemens in school and defends him vigorously against the charge that he would cheat by taking performance enhancing drugs. Clemens' major league catchers, Rich Gedman of the Red Sox, Charlie O'Brien and Darrin Fletcher of the Blue Jays, Jorge Posada of the Yankees, and Brad Ausmus of the Astros, bravely support Clemens against the national condemnation whipped up by the release of the Mitchell Report. O'Brien tells us that Clemens was so against cheating that he would not even throw scuffed baseballs, a time-honored method of bending the rules.

Wade Boggs, Clemens' third baseman in Boston, eats chicken every day and attains the second highest batting average in Red Sox history after Ted Williams. We learn that Williams, like Clemens, grew up without a father figure. Shortstop Spike Owen and pitcher Calvin Shiraldi, University of Texas teammates, are traded to the Red Sox, where they play with Clemens in the 1986 World Series. There is Marty Barrett, the plucky Red Sox second baseman who comes to Clemens' defense against the charge that he asked out of the sixth game of the 1986 World Series after a blister opened up on his pitching hand. Clemens' teammates Andy Pettitte and Chuck Knoblauch provide the reader with the most detailed explanations of *why* they used human growth hormone. David Ortiz, the jolly Falstaff of Boston baseball, provides a fascinating, and logically incomprehensible, explanation of whether he took performance enhancing drugs. Manny Ramirez, a chronic flunker of drug tests, looks like a bullfight clown as he tries to play defense in the shadow of Fenway Park's massive left field wall. Chuck Knoblauch receives approximately ten injections of HGH from Brian McNamee because he cannot make the short throw from second base to first base. The injections help him not at all. Jose Canseco somehow blows through $45 million and turns to accusing everybody but the Pope and Roger Clemens of taking steroids. Jason Giambi takes the Fifth Amendment regarding whether he took anabolic steroids with Canseco in Oakland. In only his second major league season in Pittsburgh, Barry Bonds' teammate R.J. Reynolds states for the record that Bonds is such a great hitter that he will one day put up numbers that nobody will believe. Major League Baseball's own consultant for eyesight says Bonds is the only player tested in 50 years who has perfect vision. Dodgers closer Eric Gagne saves a record 84 consecutive games over three seasons, but in two of the years he does not take human growth hormone. Indeed, an analysis of Major League Baseball's own drug tests show there was not a pervasive use of anabolic steroids or other PEDs in baseball, and the myth of a "steroids era" was mainly an invention of baseball writers desperate to make themselves relevant in the twilight of print journalism. Phil Garner, Clemens' manager with the Houston Astros, analyzes thousands and thousands of pitches thrown by Clemens.

Deep in the foothills of New York's Adirondack Mountains, my mother used to cook what she called *"tutti frutti,"* an eclectic mix of vegetables from our five gardens mixed with whatever inexpensive meat was available. This book is a *tutti frutti* of baseball, dramatic court room confrontations, wildly entertaining and informative footnotes, satires and jokes (both invented and outrageously ripped off from other writers), unapologetic mixed metaphors, careful legal analysis, extensive guesses, opinions and theories about what Clemens' accuser Brian McNamee actually did regarding anabolic steroids and human growth hormone. Was I able to cook worth a damn, I would even have included recipes to entertain you, as does political consultant James Carville, but I didn't want to poison my readers.

In these pages we catch a glimpse of Rusty Hardin, one of America's best trial lawyers. While acknowledging that Hardin's work in defending Clemens was exceptional, I also debunk as nonsensical the myth that the Justice Department's lawyers were inept and thus overwhelmed by Hardin's skills. In prosecuting a weak case that should never have been pressed in the first instance, federal prosecutors pulled out all the stops in a futile effort to obtain a conviction. They even made an extraordinary attempt to sneak in inadmissible hearsay testimony at the first trial, leading to the suspicion that the tactic may have been used by the government to blow up the trial because it did not like the jury, as Rusty Hardin suggested, and were awarded a second bite at the apple to convict

Clemens. The composition of the first jury was very pro defense, while the composition of the jury in the second trial was unusually pro government, by the demographics of the Washington, D.C., jury pool. The lawyer who established her national reputation in this trial was prosecutor Courtney Saleski, the government's go-to attorney on DNA evidence.

In the spring of 1987, after only his first full season in the majors, Roger Clemens became the sole active player to challenge Major League Baseball's collusion to restrain player salaries, walking out of spring training, as a matter of principle, in protest. In 2007, when a private report issued by former Senate Majority Leader George Mitchell on behalf of Major League Baseball accused Clemens of using performance enhancing drugs, Clemens took umbrage. Faced with the alternative of admitting to acts he believed he did not commit and being left alone, or challenging Mitchell's report by protesting his innocence and facing certain prosecution for perjury by a government determined to find a scapegoat for a two-decade failed crusade against performance enhancing drugs in professional sports, Clemens bravely stood up to this crusade, as a matter of principle. In his testimony before the House Committee on Oversight and Government Reform, which will be referred to often in this book as the Waxman Committee after its chairman, California Congressman Henry Waxman, Clemens denied using steroids and performance enhancing drugs. Sure enough, he was selectively prosecuted by the Justice Department. Clemens was tried for perjury, a case motivated and driven by Clemens' refusal to capitulate to the United States government's will.

Indeed, after the hot-tempered Clemens had basically been hounded out of his Houston home by the sports media[5] and forced to defend himself against the charge of taking performance enhancing drugs before Congress in 2008, he and his legal team were warned by congressional staffers that if he challenged the Mitchell Report and said its allegations against him were false, then he would be referred to the FBI for investigation and prosecution by the Justice Department.[6] That is precisely what happened.[7] Congressman Tom Davis, the senior Republican for the House Committee on Oversight and Government Reform and a $1,000 recipient from Major League Baseball's political action committee,[8] admitted subsequently and publicly that it was, in fact, Clemens' challenge to the Mitchell Report, in which "Congress had an investment," which narrowed the focus of the congressional query to just one player, Roger Clemens.[9] Clemens' lawyer, Rusty Hardin, however, said several years after the trial that he did not believe that Congress and the Justice Department worked "hand in glove" with each other to prosecute Clemens.[10] It was therefore, he felt, a case of two separate parts of the U.S. government "with their own fish to fry." Gabe Feldman, professor at Tulane Law School and director of the Tulane

Sports Law Program, estimated that the United States government spent more than $120 million of taxpayer money in its pursuit of Clemens,[11] nearly as much as he earned in 24 years as the highest paid pitcher of his era, $150.6 million.[12] Taxpayer money was used, essentially, in the hunt for witches and ghosts, for at the time this introduction was completed in the winter of 2016, there was no known connection between the use of anabolic steroids, human growth hormone and baseball performance, in spite of the breathless contentions of the sports media. Nor was such a cause and effect likely to be determined any time soon. The science was simply not there to decide one way or the other.

The psychological, political, and social posture of the United States in the 21st century made it all the harder to explain the Roger Clemens prosecution, because Americans were bombarded weekly by television dramas where the defendant was always guilty. Indeed, as a country, we were a long way away from the television episodes of Perry Mason in the 1960s when the defendant was always NOT GUILTY. Americans falsely accused of crimes had become an irritating inconvenience to our way of thinking. F. Lee Bailey, the most famous real defense lawyer of the 1960s, wrote several lucrative books, including the 1971 best seller, *The Defense Never Rests*. By the 21st century, no publisher would bring out his version of the O. J. Simpson case, even though he conducted the textbook cross examination of lead prosecution witness Mark Fuhrman that proved crucial to winning the trial of the century. Bailey was left with publishing it on his own website.[13] Yet one thing had not changed since Perry Mason. Under the American system of justice, the jury was still the fact-finder. This book merely verifies the findings of the Clemens jury.

The case against Roger Clemens for perjury before Congress *sounded* convincing in the one-sided version offered by just one of his more than 40 fitness coaches, Brian McNamee; the nation's press; former senator George Mitchell; Congressman Henry Waxman; and federal prosecutors. Clemens' "best friend," Andy Pettitte, thought Clemens admitted to him once that he took human growth hormone (HGH), although it was not banned by baseball at the time.[14] Brian McNamee said he injected Clemens with anabolic steroids, HGH, and testosterone, and plied him with numerous vitamins and other pills from 1998 to 2001. McNamee gave federal prosecutors needles, syringes, anabolic steroids, cloth, and other items that he claimed to have saved in his basement since 2001, smattered with Clemens' DNA in a steroids solution, according to a lab report. The anabolic steroids and human growth hormone for Clemens might have come from former New York Mets clubhouse attendant Kirk Radomski who, according to Senator Mitchell, simultaneously told Mitchell that he supplied the illegal, performance-enhancing drugs when McNamee was saying the same thing to other Mitchell associates.

Clemens, the government's theory went, had been introduced to anabolic steroids at a pool party at the home of confessed steroids user Jose Canseco. The party had allegedly taken place during the summer of 1998, when Clemens and Canseco played for the Toronto Blue Jays. Upon returning to Toronto, Clemens was said to have pulled a stash of steroids vials out of his pocket in a crowded Blue Jays locker room and discussed their use with Jose Canseco and McNamee, before handing the illegal drugs to Canseco. Soon thereafter, Clemens asked McNamee to inject him with steroids. McNamee claimed he even injected Clemens that summer in St. Petersburg, Florida, when the Blue Jays traveled there to play the Tampa Bay Devil Rays. Two years later, McNamee again joined up with Clemens, now a New York Yankee, claiming he injected Clemens again with HGH and anabolic steroids. McNamee claimed that he administered the injections at Clemens' upper East Side apartment. McNamee said he saved the needles in a Miller Lite can he had salvaged from Clemens' apartment. To show his good will toward Clemens (and perhaps defend himself in a future libel case), McNamee testified that he had tried to warn the Hendricks Agency, who represented Clemens in endorsement deals and salary negotiations, that Clemens would fail the 2003 random drug test due to one of his steroids injections. The logic was simple: By 1996, his last year in Boston, Clemens was "in the twilight of his career," a quote attributed to Red Sox general manager Dan Duquette, perhaps as a negotiating ploy. Brian McNamee was cast as a savior of sorts, able to revive Clemens' career with anabolic steroid and human growth hormone injections given in 1998, 2000, and 2001. Besides, with so many details of locker rooms, clubhouses, Clemens' apartments in Toronto and New York, not to mention the embellishment that sandwiches were served at Canseco's Miami pool party, McNamee *had* to be telling the truth.

As it turned out, Andy Pettitte said he could not remember "specifics about the conversation" wherein Clemens allegedly admitted to taking HGH.[15] Perhaps most importantly, Pettitte did not remember or think of Clemens' alleged use at the time the left-hander took HGH himself,[16] leading to the supposition that Pettitte's memory on the subject was enhanced by Brian McNamee's reminders and spin, particularly because McNamee was with Pettitte when he thought he heard Clemens make the admission, and because Pettitte and McNamee met for the final time in the summer of 2007, only months before their testimony before Congress in February 2008. Therefore, the decisive testimony against Clemens from his purported best friend came down to a vague memory that Clemens *said* he took HGH, instead of setting out convincing details. Although Clemens claimed that he and Pettitte were "very close,"[17] the accumulated evidence suggested otherwise. Actually, the idea that

Clemens and Pettitte were best buddies was debunked by Brian McNamee, of all people, who revealed that he and Pettitte, both the sons of cops, were much closer. Pettitte said of McNamee in 2008, "He's become a good friend of mine."[18] Former Houston Astros manager Phil Garner testified at Clemens' 2012 trial about the relationship between Clemens and Pettitte, "I don't think they spent a lot of time together socially.... They had different life styles."[19] Contrary to public perception, McNamee was not Clemens' go-to guy. Rather, McNamee went in and out of Clemens' life, particularly after McNamee was fired by the Yankees in 2001. His work with Clemens in Texas in the off-season, for example, consisted of only four to seven days per year in the winter.[20] (What was a little shocking, however, was the fact that McNamee worked Clemens out three or four times in 2007[21]— after he had cut a deal with the Feds.) Don Amore and David Heuschkel, who covered Clemens for the *Hartford Courant*, wrote, "Clemens, throughout his long career, has gotten close to very few players.... Clemens keeps his thoughts to himself."[22] Jim Murray, who represented Clemens in endorsement deals, denied that Brian McNamee tried to warn his agency that Clemens might fail a drug test for performance enhancing drugs.[23] When PED supplier Kirk Radomski went to prison, Clemens' agents at the Hendricks Agency asked him to talk to McNamee to find out whether he knew Radomski. Clemens testified before Congress, "I asked him, who is the drug dealer from the Mets? I asked him do you know this guy. He said no. I reported back to Randy Hendricks."[24]

Steve August, the assistant general manager of the Red Sox when the team was considering whether to bring Clemens back after the 1996 season, said at the trial, "I told Mr. Duquette that Roger was at the top of his game," not washed up, and the recommendation he submitted to the team was to resign Clemens.[25] August's evaluation was no doubt influenced by a game Clemens pitched late in that season, on September 18, against the Detroit Tigers, when he tied his own Major League record of 20 strikeouts. However, even Clemens admitted during his 2008 congressional deposition that he was aware of the team's long-standing policy of not signing players his age, 34, to long-term contracts. Clemens said, "I don't think he wanted to give a pitcher of a certain age a deal."[26] The policy went back at least as far as the exile from the Athens of America in 1978 of pitcher Luis Tiant, 37 at the time. If you are curious about Babe Ruth, who had the fourth best earned run average among pitchers in team history as of 2015, 2.19, the Red Sox sent him packing to the Yankees in 1919 when he was only 24. Hall of Fame third baseman Wade Boggs had also been shown the door, also at age 34, after the 1992 season, to be followed in the ensuing years by such Red Sox icons as Mo Vaughn, 30, Nomar Garciaparra, 30, Johnny Damon, 31, Pedro Martinez, 33, Jacoby Ellsbury, 30, and John Lester, 30.[27] The

Red Sox had apparently been operated for decades by 60s radicals who did not trust anybody over 30. The Red Sox did not depart from this long-standing policy until December 2015, when they signed pitcher David Price, age 29, to a seven-year, $217 million contract that will reach to his 37th birthday.[28]

Dr. Bert W. O'Malley, chairman of Baylor College of Medicine's department of molecular and cellular biology, an expert in the physiological effects of anabolic steroid use, examined Clemens' medical records for the period of 1995–2008. Dr. O'Malley found no signature evidence of anabolic steroid use, e.g., elevated blood pressure, acne, increased LDL cholesterol, or decreased HDL cholesterol. "The record is remarkably uniform and devoid of suspicious indications," O'Malley said.[29] Furthermore, Clemens waived his privacy right to keep his 2003 random drug test confidential. His lawyer, Rusty Hardin, gave the test results to Congressman Henry Waxman's House Committee on Oversight and Government Reform in February 2008, where they were summarily ignored, and the test results were mentioned only in passing by Republican senior member Tom Davis in his Minority Report.[30] The results showed that Clemens tested negative for both performance-enhancing drugs and masking agents.[31] Or to put it another way, the Rocket's fuel was clean.

The government's strongest evidence against Clemens at his 2012 trial was his DNA, according to an FBI lab report, found in a vial of steroids solution. Yet DNA evidence had never been "a silver bullet," as former prosecutor Harlan Levy put it in his 1996 book, *And the Blood Cried Out*.[32] Forensic scientist Elizabeth Johnson told *60 Minutes* in May 2003 that "Most people think it's absolute and black and white and infallible. The test has to be performed correctly and interpreted correctly."[33] Errors in DNA testing occur frequently, according to William C. Thompson, Professor and Chairman of the Department of Criminology, Law & Society at the University of California, Irvine. Among a litany of things that can go wrong in DNA testing are the inadvertent transfer of cellular material from one item to another, error in identification or labeling of samples, misinterpretation of test results, and intentionally planting of biological evidence, which the Clemens defense argued. Crime scenes often produce incomplete or partial samples of DNA, limited quantities, degradation of the sample, and presence of contaminants that make it impossible to determine genotypes.[34] A particular problem occurs when evidentiary samples consist of a mixture of materials from different people. That is precisely what happened in the Clemens case. Brian McNamee, or someone else, comingled materials from injecting Clemens, Yankees player Chuck Knoblauch, "other players," and perhaps injections of his son for diabetes, perhaps injections for himself and his wife of anabolic steroids and HGH, and perhaps even of insulin injections for his own diabetes. To confound forensic analysis of this motley admixture even further, McNamee had literally bled on the evidence, apparently from pricking his finger when injecting others, or even perhaps when injecting himself.

Furthermore, his wife contradicted most of his trial testimony related to his handling of these materials, stating that she found needles in a Bud Lite can, not a Miller Lite can, raising the question: Did McNamee dump some of his evidence and add DNA samples, perhaps, as Clemens claimed, from B-12 injections?

Brian McNamee's saving of injection materials may not even have been about Roger Clemens at all, but about Chuck Knoblauch, with whom McNamee shared a controversial night in Miami involving the alleged drugging of a female with a "date rape drug" in a hotel room. Later, McNamee, but not Knoblauch, was seen, according to testimony to police by a hotel security guard, having sex with the woman in the complex pool. The incident in the pool led McNamee's wife to begin divorce proceedings against him. Materials from injecting Knoblauch were in the box of saved materials, although it took several years and the trial until McNamee admitted that fact. McNamee never really had anything to fear from Roger Clemens, who had no knowledge or evidence of McNamee's injections of players and Wall Street gym rats, according to the testimony of both men. Indeed Clemens would long believe McNamee's benign version of whatever happened in the hotel room party and in the pool that night. Whatever did happen that night, Chuck Knoblauch knew about it. He was a threat to Brian McNamee's peace of mind—and always would be.

While it is this lawyer's theory that Brian McNamee fabricated his story to save his own neck, I nowhere argue that I have cracked the case or have provided a definitive answer as to what *actually* occurred. My belief is that like Clemens, McNamee was also a victim of an overly zealous government prosecution. Near the end of this book, I offer my theory to explain McNamee's claims. But a lot of what happened will likely remain a mystery forever. Fair-minded readers may now compare this view of the controversy to others they may have read.

The greatest pleasure in Clemens' life was his children, not baseball, and since his retirement he has enjoyed the development of his four sons and the charity work which mostly is devoted to children.

Roger Clemens now assumes his rightful place alongside Babe Ruth, Ty Cobb, Shoeless Joe Jackson, John McGraw, Casey Stengel, Ted Williams, Billy Martin, Pete Rose, Reggie Jackson, and Barry Bonds in the pantheon of the most talented and controversial men of baseball.

1

The Self Invention of Roger Clemens

There was something both intensely religious and intensely existential about Roger Clemens' developing into the best pitcher of his generation. Like Henry Ford, Clemens was a boy who imagined his own greatness, dreamed of his greatness, declared his greatness, and willed himself to greatness when he did not yet possess the physical attributes to be great. His was a church-going family,[1] which must have played a role in his believing in his vision when nobody else would. He called his baseball skills "the talents God gave me."[2] His youthful boasting, understandably, annoyed a lot of people as he climbed the baseball ladder.

A chubby Little Leaguer in Dayton, Ohio—Clemens would not lose his baby fat until he began lifting weights in high school—he threw a mediocre fastball and had no breaking pitch for all practical purposes.[3] Yet, he was born with perfect pitching control, something that coaches noticed even as early as Little League. He was, therefore always *becoming* a pitcher from grade school until his retirement in 2007. There was no moment in which Roger Clemens stopped this process. Indeed, in the spring of 2012, at the age of 49, he pitched a perfect inning in an alumni-varsity exhibition game at the University of Texas, using his split-finger fastball to strike out two of the three batters, all of whom were more than 30 years his junior. Later that year, shortly after he turned 50, he pitched three scoreless, minor-league innings for the Independent Atlantic League's Sugar Land Skeeters.[4]

In 1978, when he was 15 years old, Clemens moved to Sugar Land, one of the poorer of the southwest Houston suburbs.[5] Later, his mother, in the manner of many American parents of promising athletes, made the sacrifice of moving her family all the way to Spring Branch in the northwest suburbs, another gritty, blue collar enclave, so Roger could play for a perennial powerhouse high school baseball program and its legendary coach, Charlie Maiorana.

Maiorana gave Clemens what all athletes need—structure. Part of the structure was a conditioning program that Clemens would embrace and enhance the rest of his baseball days. The conditioning would evolve into running miles late at night after games, pushing his pitching hand through a bowl of dry rice to strengthen his fingers,[6] doing countless sit-ups, pushups, weight training, crunches and stretching. Clemens' high school teammate, Todd Howey, testified at trial that when other players were out at night, "looking for trouble," Clemens "would be working out."[7] In fact, Howey suggested that Clemens was actually a better football player, a defensive end in high school, than a baseball player.[8] In a photograph of Clemens in his football uniform, helmet off, the longer hair style of 1979 visible, you can see the huge head of the 17-year-old Clemens. Photographs taken of Clemens pitching for the University of Texas, mostly with his baseball cap on, made his face look thinner than it actually was.

Howey testified that Clemens' pitching speed in high school was only in the low 80s.[9] Yet, recalling when he batted against Clemens in college, Howey recalled that Clemens' "fastball was like an aspirin. The guy was destined for greatness, and he acted like it then. And I wished I had believed in him." Mike Capel, who pitched with Clemens at Texas and later pitched for the Chicago Cubs, also played against him in high school.[10] Capel confirmed Howey's account.[11] Capel said Clemens was a pudgy pitcher in high school who was "average." When asked by Rusty Hardin about Clemens' work ethic, however, he replied, "Far beyond most men that large."

> HARDIN: "From high school to now, did Clemens change the way he took care of his body?"
> CAPEL: "No, sir."
> HARDIN: "Ever see a pro athlete work harder?"
> CAPEL: "No, sir."

Clemens' enemies have made much of the fact that he threw only in the low 80s and was the number three starter at Spring Branch. Less mentioned is the fact that the youngster without a decent fastball set the school record with 18 strikeouts in his junior year and broke his own record with 19 his senior year.[12] It is typical, if bizarre, that Clemens' failures throughout his life have been magnified so much that they dwarf his accomplishments. Part of this phenomenon is that he mostly had success. The failures, therefore, were easier to spot, like errors of fact by *The New York Times* or by *CBS News*, conspicuous because of their rarity.

Many have tried to disparage Clemens as being "not a real Texan" because he spent 15 years in Dayton, Ohio. But the idea that Clemens, or the first President George Bush, for that matter, was not a real Texan, never played in the Lone Star State. Texas has historically been a place where the natives welcomed visitors and newcomers with friendly, open arms. Indeed, it was not uncommon for Texans to suggest, at the outset, that visitors move permanently to their state, so proud of it were they and so happy to have new friends. Motivated in part by the encouragement of his oldest brother, who had been a college basketball player, in part by a strong-willed mother, chain-smoking Bess Clemens, who worked three jobs including as a janitor,[13] and who possessed a powerful work ethic, and further motivated by high school coach Maiorana, William Roger Clemens became like a lean Texas Longhorn steer who survived the devastating cycles of drought and flash floods of the Southwest climate: tough and gritty. Texas can mold a man. It molded Bear Bryant's first recruiting class at Texas A&M, the "Junction Boys," who survived a hellish summer camp in Junction, Texas, and just two years later, in 1956, went on to win the Southwest Conference Championship. It molded Roger Clemens into the man who led the Texas Longhorns to the National Championship in the 1983 College World Series.

Shortly before she died from emphysema, Bess Clemens told everybody in her family to "go to work." Roger Clemens followed his mother's orders. Several hours after she died on September 15, 2005, he threw a five-hitter, even with a sore hamstring, as the Astros beat the Florida Marlins, 10–2. Afterwards, he said, "She was my strength, she was my will." Astros general manager Tim Purpura said of his star pitcher, "It's heroic. He understands the meaning of duty. His mother taught him about duty."[14] In a similar example, tennis great Jimmy Connors, another high-strung straight-arrow who did not take drugs, missed his father's funeral because his Dad ordered him to finish a tournament instead of coming home for a funeral.[15] Although it is now commonplace for players and coaches to take time off to witness a child's birth or graduation, to consider in which city to play based on a wife's job or the quality of the school system, such open-mindedness was unheard of in the 1960s, before free agency. Roger Clemens was born in 1962. He pitched on the days his own sons were born.[16]

Bess Clemens fit in with the Texas tradition of strong, independent women such as Anne Armstrong, United States Ambassador to the United Kingdom and the first woman to deliver her party's keynote address when she spoke before the 1972 Republican National Convention[17]; Sissy Farenthold, a 1972 Democratic vice-presidential consideration; Annette Gordon-Reed, the first African American to win the Pulitzer Prize for History[18]; Governor Ann Richards; journalist Molly Ivins[19]; singer Janis Joplin, and actresses Farrah Fawcett and Renee Zellweger. All but Armstrong, Gordon-Reed, and Ivins studied at Clemens' *alma mater*, the University of Texas, and Zellweger was a cheerleader at Katy High School, not far from Clemens' high school in Spring Branch. Joplin left school after a year, and Clemens, a business and finance major,[20] left after his junior year, both to make a lot of money. It was Bess Clemens who convinced Roger to return to college after being offered a contract by the New York Mets in 1981.[21]

Clemens' biological father, William Clemens, a truck driver, apparently abused his wife, Bess. She moved her children away from him when Roger was three months old. William Clemens died in 1981, at age 54,[22] coincidentally the same year that Roger's extraordinary gift was discovered.

If the 15-year-old boy of 1978 was ever going to make it to the Major Leagues, the only way was through perfect control and knowing *how* to get batters out. With only an 82 mile-an-hour fastball at tops, Clemens in fact would not be selected at all in the Major League draft following his senior year in high school.[23] His development from nobody to the most dominant pitcher of his time, at minimum, was similar to a player that he would be linked to in a dramatic confrontation during the 2000 World Series, Mike Piazza, the Hall of Fame catcher. The Dodgers drafted Piazza in the 62nd round, and only as a favor to manager Tommy Lasorda, a friend of Piazza's father. Paid a paltry $15,000 for signing, Piazza nearly quit the game after struggling during his first year at Vero Beach in the Florida State League.[24]

Fortunately, Roger Clemens was also born with a sixth sense, much like Pedro Martinez, the great Montreal Expos and Boston Red Sox pitcher selected to the Hall of Fame in 2015, of guessing what a batter could and would do. Clemens could look a batter in the eyes and guess accurately what the batter expected of him, what pitches caused the batter to flinch. The longer the battle waged on and the more pitches Clemens threw, the better he could outguess the batter. Ken Griffey, Jr., who batted .311 against Clemens,[25] explained: "I was just trying to get him early. He's one of those pitchers as the game goes on, he zones in to how he pitches. If you get him early and get him out, you don't have to worry about him. But he's the kind of pitcher that gets stronger and stronger as the game goes on because he knows what you like and what you don't like and he has a feel for each hitter the second and third time around."[26]

Because Clemens hoisted himself by his own petard, to paraphrase Shakespeare, his conflated and inflated sense of self demanded that each pitch he threw be a matter of life and death; for Clemens—before he could throw a fastball—every pitch from Little League through high school to that dramatic first year of junior college when he discovered his fastball, was a matter of his own survival, his own identity. Without a father most of his life,[27] Clemens created himself out of whole cloth, alone, on the pitcher's mound, a testament to the remarkable possibilities in the world of athletics for upward mobility and personal wealth. Yankees center fielder Bernie Williams, a Clemens teammate on the 1999 and 2000 World Champion teams, summed him up: "He treated every start like the seventh game of the World Series,"[28] an attitude he shared with Cal Ripken, Jr., of the Baltimore Orioles.[29]

Clemens' nemesis, Brian McNamee, used the word "edge" to describe what Clemens sought as a pitcher. Although Clemens himself used that same word in congressional testimony,[30] he was off-base. Clemens did not merely want an edge. He sought what every other pitcher worth his split-finger fastball seeks: total control and domination, and he came as close as any pitcher in the game's history to reaching that goal. In fact, the word used by players who batted against Clemens to describe him was *control*. Athletes define themselves as they were in their initial successes as children. In Clemens' case, he had a weak fastball and thus created himself as a control pitcher. By college he identified with Nolan Ryan, the Texan with a murderous fastball and a vigorous workout regimen.[31] But it was Clemens' own drive and need, not an admiration of Ryan, that motivated him. Clemens played with the competitive fierceness of New England Patriots' Tom Brady. He took defeat with a sense of loss, almost like death, in the mold of the pre-eminent American basketball coach, Bob Knight. That was from whence Clemens' complete control and command on the mound originated. Cal Ripken remembered being startled that even in his rookie season Clemens already felt comfortable and in command.[32] Maintaining control, of course, was part of Clemens' conflict with the baseball media. Clemens understood this conflict and said so to Congress, "People who make false accusations should not be allowed to define another person's life."[33] To Clemens, sportswriters were likewise control freaks who wanted to dictate the narrative and the history of the game. Clemens, on the other hand, believed he was a man who earned his way into Baseball's Hall of Fame and has been robbed of his chance by men who were too pious and rigid for their own good. Many in the sports media, however, saw Clemens as that 1870 Texas stereotype of a "kind of hairy gorilla,"[34] an inarticulate and dangerous Lenny, the retarded farm worker who accidentally squeezes a woman to death in John Steinbeck's classic novel, *Of Mice and Men*.

In the ensuing years, Clemens pitched with a small hamstring tear and a swollen elbow.[35] In his final 1986 regular season start he was hit in the elbow with a line drive against the Orioles. When the swelling went down Clemens pitched game 2 of the World Series against the Mets with the flu, lasting 4⅓ innings, allowing four walks and three runs but was bailed out by Boston hitting in a 9–3 win. And then, of course, in the crucial game 6, a blister opened up on Clemens' pitching index finger, bleeding the Red Sox right out of the World Series.[36] One time in 2001, he convinced manager Joe Torre to pitch him on three hours' sleep when scheduled Yankees starter Adrian Hernandez came down with the flu.[37] So fierce was Clemens that before a Yankees start he would take the hottest whirlpool possible and then have trainer Steve Donahue rub the hottest liniment available on his testicles.[38] Like Mickey Mantle, Clemens "wrapped much of his body in medical tape to hold everything together."[39] Clemens even chewed on a plastic night guard while pitching sometimes so he would not grind his teeth to a pulp.[40]

Clemens' battery mate at the University of Texas, Jeff Hearron, told a similar story.

> It was summer ball in Hutchison, Kansas. I'm catching Roger and he is going through the motions on the mound. In between innings he calls me back to the clubhouse. He told me to slap him on the face. I said, "I'm not gonna' do that." He said, "DO IT." So I slapped him silly, three or four, good, Hollywood slaps. He lets out a big roar and charges back to the bench. He took the mound and put up a bunch of zeros.[41]

Rick Cerone, a catcher for both the Yankees and the Red Sox, said that Clemens "was the most intense, most competitive guy I'd ever played with."[42] Red Sox first baseman Mo Vaughn said, "The worst thing you can do is put a man like Roger in a position to prove something."[43] General Manager Brian Cashman, architect of the two-decade Yankees dynasty that began in 1996, said at trial, "Clemens pulled people together. And he wasn't up for any slackness, either."[44] When asked how competitive Clemens was on a scale of one to ten, Cashman replied, "I could tell you it's a hundred."[45] *Sports Illustrated*'s Jeff Pearlman reported that Clemens "arrived four or five hours before games he wasn't starting, delving into a regimen of film study, fly-ball shagging, wind sprints and stretching."[46] "Clemens would not talk to you the day *before* he pitched," Yankees announcer Michael Kay said on the *YES* network.[47] According to Kay's colleague John Flaherty, who caught Clemens while with the Yankees, Clemens used multiple signs in every game, even if no runners were on base, so batters could not pick up the type of pitch he would throw.[48] Clemens kept detailed journals on hitters and umpires and studied them before every game he pitched.[49] Rather routine, you say, in the 21st century, but in the first half of Clemens' career in the 20th century, players still smoked cigarettes, chewed tobacco, drank large quantities of beer, and were generally not lifting weights or running through the Boston night after games.[50]

The claim made by former Red Sox Manager John McNamara, trying to escape the embarrassment of losing a lead to the Mets in the 1986 World Series, that Clemens asked to be taken out of Game Six when a blister opened up on the index finger of his throwing hand, after 135 pitches, seemed unlikely.[51] If Clemens' ego was as large as the writers claimed, it was likely that Clemens wanted to be on the mound when the Red Sox won their first World Series since 1918, as they had a 3–2 lead in games at the time. Indeed, Red Sox second baseman Marty Barrett, a witness to the exchange as he stood on the mound, said, "Roger absolutely did not ask out of the game. I was right there, and I can swear for a fact that he didn't. But Roger was young and respectful of authority, and he didn't say, 'I want to finish' either. He left it up to John McNamara."[52] In fact, 1986 was Clemens' first full season, as he had been called up during the 1984 season from the minors and underwent shoulder surgery in 1985. McNamara made another improbable claim—that Red Sox pitcher "Oil Can" Boyd was "too drunk for relief work in Game 7."[53]

Former college and professional teammates concurred that "When Clemens got angry, he became unhittable."[54] Former Yankees first baseman Tino Martinez, who was dismissed as hitting coach by the Florida Marlins in 2013 for allegedly being too harsh on young players, said, "A lot of guys go out there and try to be mean, but it doesn't work out because it's not their personality. Roger had it naturally."[55] Without trying to play psychiatrist, it would seem logical that Clemens inherited this meanness on the baseball field from his father, who apparently beat his mother. Clemens himself, with not a little bravado, put it like this: "I'm relentless. I like to pound guys. Challenge power hitters with my fastball.... I want to jiggle their eyeballs."[56] Clemens was driven to play the game with the maniacal intensity of Ty Cobb, John McGraw, Casey Stengel, Babe Ruth, Leo Durocher, Jackie Robinson, and Pete Rose.

Yet in comparison to these other intense players, Clemens kept his temper under control to a remarkable degree over 24 seasons. Most famously, Clemens was tossed in the second inning of game 4 of the 1990 ALCS against the Oakland Athletics. He was so furious at home plate umpire Terry Cooney for handing A's hitter Willie Randolph a walk on five pitches that he swore at Cooney, and then charged Cooney after he was thrown out, and pushed umpire Jim Evans aside trying to get to Cooney. Afterwards he threatened Cooney. As Claire Smith of the New York Times reported after the game, the entire Red Sox team had been feuding with the umpires throughout the entire Series and umpiring crew chief Jim Evans had given Clemens a warning for yelling at first base umpire John Hirchbeck from the Red Sox dugout in the previous game. If anything, the Cooney confrontation was not a one on one with Clemens, but rather a Red Sox team riot, as the Boston bench reacted to Clemens' ejection by throwing water coolers, mounds of sunflower seeds, paper cups and other debris from the dugout as they stormed the field. Clemens' loyal second baseman Marty Barrett was ejected for throwing a water cooler. The chaos lasted a good 15 minutes while Red Sox Manager Joe Morgan and Red Sox catcher Tony Pena heatedly argued with the umpires.

Of all these intense competitors, the one perhaps closest to Clemens in temperament and who shared his difficulty with expressing himself, was Charles Dillon "Casey" Stengel. Don Amore and David Heuschkel wrote of Clemens in the *Hartford Courant*: "His rambling interviews, in which he always seems to be answering a completely different question than the one just asked, is not just a Casey Stengel–like ploy to keep reporters at a distance. He's the same with teammates."⁵⁷ Stengel, filled with rage, confessed later in life, "I was always too aggressive. I made too much trouble."⁵⁸ At his induction into the Baseball Hall of Fame, for managing seven World Series champions, although he was also a .284 lifetime hitter, Stengel thanked the league presidents in his signature raspy voice, for not taking "more of my money when I was obnoxious or expectorated when I shouldn't have."⁵⁹

Like Clemens, Stengel was "assured, confident; sometimes outrageous ... with a "hard, almost brutal streak of reality."⁶⁰ Stengel, like Clemens, was largely influenced by his mother.⁶¹ Both men played football and basketball in high school, Clemens a center/power forward in basketball, a two-way end in football. Stengel was the star guard of the 1909 Kansas City high school basketball champions. He played fullback in the days before helmets. Stengel was hot-tempered and not adverse to fisticuffs with other players,⁶² just as Clemens would resort to throwing a few punches in his day. Clemens entangled himself in a bar room brawl in his first semester at the University of Texas.⁶³ He would later spend 12 hours in jail for resisting arrest after his brother punched a Houston cop.⁶⁴

The Boston press was no kinder to Stengel than it would later be to Clemens. After Stengel was hit by a car before the 1943 season and was fired at its end as manager of the Boston Braves, a columnist for the *Boston Record* declared that "[t]he man who did the most for baseball in Boston in 1943 was [the motorist who ran Stengel down two days before the opening game and kept him away from the Braves for two months."⁶⁵ Of course, Stengel possessed the wit of the one-liner that Clemens lacked. After watching his star pupil Mickey Mantle angrily throw something in the dugout after striking out, Stengel pulled out a bat and said to Mantle, "Here, why don't you bang yourself on the head with this?"⁶⁶ Like Clemens, and like many movie stars, Stengel expressed hostility to photographers and was once arrested for kicking one of them who blocked his view of first base.⁶⁷ Like Clemens, Stengel "was never destroyed by defeat."⁶⁸ Clemens and Stengel spoke almost identically in their roundabout ways. To be fair, public speaking is an ancient art—rhetoric. Most people are, well, average at it, as with any other skill. Stengel and Clemens, on the other hand were below average, to put it more kindly than did the baseball press. Philip Barnett, the Waxman Committee's lead attorney, asked Clemens during his Congressional deposition when he first learned that George Mitchell had sent letters to the Players Association. Clemens responded:

> I don't think—at that point I think they discussed that a lot of the players or none of the players were going down to talk about that. And I think from what I understand, they asked what was it concerning, and they said you basically got to come down and we will tell you about it. We assumed, and I thought that the 2006—it would have been September 2006,

about the Grimsley or the L.A. Times report that I had to get up and you know, obviously deny all those, they came out of nowhere and it brought grief, you know, for a year that I had to deny those, saying it wasn't true, it wasn't true, and it wasn't true. And I believe that's when Randy Hendricks assumed it was about also. If I would have known of what Brian McNamee was stating in the report, I would have been there in a heartbeat.[69]

Compare that to the answer Stengel gave Congress during a 1958 hearing when asked why Major League Baseball wanted to be exempted from the Sherman Antitrust Act:

> I would say I would not know, but I would say the reason they want it passed is to keep baseball going as the highest paid ball sport that has gone into baseball, and from the baseball—angle—I am not going to speak of any other sport. I am not in here to argue about those other sports. I am in the baseball business. It has been run cleaner than any business that was ever put out in the one hundred years at the present time. I am not speaking about television or I am not speaking about income that comes into the ball parks. You have to take that off. I don't know too much about it. I say the ballplayers have a better advancement at the present time.[70]

2

The Consistency of Roger Clemens

Roger Clemens had just turned 18 when he enrolled at San Jacinto Junior College.[1] He arrived at school with what his coach called "genius-level control."[2] He was not yet the bonus baby, fastball pitcher who would become a member of the Boston Red Sox four years hence.

Clemens at the time was merely what the hard-scrabble farmers of the Texas Hill Country called an old-fashioned "cedar chopper," independent contractors who performed the thankless and backbreaking job of chopping down the thickets of cedar trees that dotted the Texas landscape, which were used to make sturdy fence posts for the region's farms. Ironically, the cedar choppers were looked down upon socially in the same manner as the Boston and New York press would eventually look down upon Clemens, as a "hillbilly, rube, hick."[3] This condescending and exaggerated attitude about Texans extended at least as far back as the 1870s when it was said, "The typical Texan ... is a hairy kind of gorilla ... supposed to reside on a horse.... He is expected to carry four or five revolvers in his belt, as he were a sort of perambulating gun rack.... The only time the typical Texan is supposed to be peaceable is after he has killed all his friends, and can find no fresh materials to practice on."[4] Clemens chopped along at San Jacinto in his now-familiar routine. He worked hard. He walked four miles immediately *before* he pitched a game. His coach at San Jacinto, Wayne Graham, unlocked the hidden secret to Clemens' future success.

Wayne Graham first appeared on the scene in the early 1960s as a member of an alleged major league baseball team, the New York Mets, who lost 737 games in their first seven years of existence, winning only 394,[5] a team so inept that its famous manager, the aforementioned Casey Stengel, once quipped, "Can't anybody here play this game?"[6] The Mets were brought in as a replacement National League team for the Giants and Dodgers, who had left New

York for California in 1957. The team even borrowed the orange of the Giants and the blue of the Dodgers, ever after suffering an identity crisis. The Mets and their fans also developed a massive inferiority complex toward the city's more famous team, the Yankees. Graham's footnote to fame was having been part of trades involving two power hitters of the late 1950s and 1960s. One was Frank Thomas, who slugged 286 home runs for such teams as the Pittsburgh Pirates, Chicago Cubs, and New York Mets.[7] The other slugger traded for Graham was Dick Stuart, known as "Dr. Strangeglove" for his poor fielding, who hit 228 home runs, mostly for the Pirates and Boston Red Sox.[8]

Clemens experienced a life-changing moment at San Jacinto similar to Alexander Solzhenitsyn's defeat of cancer in the gulag. In December 1953, doctors told the Russian future Nobel Laureate that he had three weeks to live. "I did not die, however," he recalled. "With a hopelessly neglected and acutely malignant tumor, this was a divine miracle; I could see no other explanation. Since then, all the life that has been given back to me has not been mine in the full sense: it is built around a purpose. That spring ... I deliriously took possession of the life restored to me."[9] Solzhenitsyn felt God-like after his cancer disappeared, and the reprieve gave him the courage to challenge the Soviet authorities at every turn, writing novels and histories that revealed every nightmarish detail of the Russian police state. For Clemens, whose whole identity, work ethic and thought processes were based on the demonstrated fact that he had but a mediocre fastball, the God-like moment occurred when Graham discovered a mechanical defect in the young pitcher's throwing motion. Graham observed that when Clemens threw a fastball, he did not extend his arm completely to "finish" the pitch. Once Graham intervened to correct the defect, Clemens' pitching speed increased to the high 80s, then to the low 90s, and finally to the mid- and upper 90s, an enormous increase in velocity. It was a gift from God."[10] After his year at San Jacinto Junior College, Clemens was drafted in the 12th round of the MLB draft by the New York Mets. Clemens was 18 years old. Clemens agreed to work out at the Astrodome when the Mets came to Houston to play the Astros. After his workout the Mets offered $20,000 and then $40,000 and ended up offering somewhere between $40,000 and $50,000, according to Clemens' memory.

Clemens said, "That was a lot of money, but my mother wanted me to go back to school."[11]

As he became older, Clemens developed other pitches: a nasty slider, split-finger fastball, split-finger changeup, cutter and two-seam fastball. He also carefully scouted lineups to pick and choose which batters he would "pitch around" and which weaker hitters he would "pitch to." Clemens, according to his college coach Cliff Gustafson, "never lost much" on his fastball but used it sparingly in his later years.[12] Clemens was, most of all, a student of the game. He never stopped learning and growing as a pitcher. Julio Franco, who played in the majors until the age of 49, said, "Every year you saw him, you could see the progress. Every time you saw him, he was walking the ladder. Every year you saw him, he was more dominating. He was more fearsome."[13]

Clemens was awarded a baseball scholarship to the University of Texas following an exhibition-game performance when he fanned 14 Longhorns as a San Jacinto pitcher. In Austin, he played under the iron hand of an old-school disciplinarian, Cliff Gustafson. Called "Coach Gus" by his players, Gustafson had grown up on a cotton farm and coached high-school baseball in San Antonio for almost a decade before being called to Austin.[14] He coached at Texas for 29 years, earning the second-most coaching wins in NCAA history. Following his retirement, he operated a ranch outside of Austin, still going strong at age 80. The old coach made clear during a 2011 interview that he was as proud of his players who became successful doctors, dentists, lawyers, teachers, and successful businessmen as he was of those who made it to the majors.

Tall, thin and wiry, Gustafson looked like a casting director's idea of a Texan, wearing a permanent brown tan on his arms and face, weather-beaten from the hot Texas sun. He stage-managed the Texas baseball team in the manner of the New York City Ballet's legendary George Balanchine. Part ballet choreographer, part Marine drill sergeant, Gustafson left no detail to chance. He was a man of restless energy who would get out of bed in the middle of the night and jot down ideas for the next day's game. Gustafson also operated his team like a master puppeteer. Everything was *his* doing. He was not above ordering that his batters take 16 or 20 pitches in a row if the opposing hurler was having control problems. Neither Clemens nor catcher Jeff Hearron called a single pitch the prize prospect threw. Gustafson called every one of them.[15]

The Texas baseball team consisted of highly recruited players who had turned down Major League offers to spend time under Gustafson in his famous and successful program. They were a tough bunch whose favorite recreation was, apparently, rattlesnake hunting. Playing time was at a premium for those players who weren't starters. Jealousy and frustration toward the stars was abundant and palpable. Players made fun of pitcher Calvin Schiraldi, who acted as the team's version of George Hamilton, the Hollywood actor known for his permanent sun tan, as the tall star lay on the grass near the ball field to catch some rays. While admiring Clemens' unmatched workout routine, players questioned his morals after he was charged with stealing another player's sweat pants from a locker and then wearing them in public. The ringleader of the accusers was All-American shortstop Spike Owen, according to a witness. As it turned out, Clemens, known for hell raising and practical jokes with those he trusted, had borrowed the sweat pants of one of his roommates as a practical joke.

Like most pitchers, Clemens possessed a long memory. He decked Owen when he led off for the Seattle Mariners. Owen stated diplomatically, "When he's on the mound, he has no friends."[16]

In investigating Clemens' life, a stunning discrepancy emerged between the stories told about Roger Clemens and the man Roger Clemens. Many, such as the tale that Clemens demanded to pitch the home and road openers in 1982 in order to accept a scholarship to the University of Texas, reported by Jeff Pearlman in his book, *The Rocket That Fell to Earth*, turned out to be urban myths. Cliff Gustafson scoffed ruefully at the suggestion. "Roger did what he was told," stated the stern coach.[17]

A major problem in trying to evaluate Roger Clemens is that people tend to remember the few times he was not outstanding. A contemporary of Clemens at the University of Texas, Steve Campbell, who covered him as a sportswriter for the school newspaper and later reported baseball for the *Houston Chronicle*, remembered Clemens getting shellacked by the University of Texas–Arlington in the spring of 1983, and the overall impression, which many people shared at the time, that Clemens' teammate, Calvin Schiraldi, was a better college pitcher.[18] Schiraldi, in fact, was more dominant than Clemens in 1983, winning 14, losing only two, and sporting a spectacular 1.74 Earned Run Average. Clemens' Earned Run Average (ERA) was actually the worst of the three starters, 3.04, while Mike Capel, with a 13–1 record, was second with a 2.98 ERA.[19] Clemens' 1983 statistics, thus, did *not* appear overly impressive. His won-lost record was 13–5.

A photocopy of what purports to be a Red Sox scouting report on Clemens in 1983, and signed by the Red Sox scout who convinced the team to draft him, Danny Doyle, grades him as having only an average fastball, a below average curve, below average control, average poise, below average baseball instincts, above average aggressiveness, good arm action, a good delivery. The qualifier "purported" is used here because why would the Red Sox have signed in the first round a player with such alleged deficiencies?

Yet consistency was everything in evaluating Clemens, who never pitched a no-hitter or perfect game. His collegiate ERA of 3.04 was remarkably similar to his 24-year Major League ERA of 3.12. In his last year at Texas, he struck out 151 batters in 166 innings and allowed only 22 walks.[20]

In two seasons pitching for the Longhorns, Clemens walked only 56 batters while striking out 241. His cumulative totals were 25 games won, seven lost, six shutouts, and an ERA of 2.62.[21] Yes, he possessed a fierce temper in college: he yelled at umpires when he did not like their rulings; intimidating

Texas' 1983 national championship team included four players who went on to have lengthy major league careers, including Mike Brumley (front row, fifth from left), Bruce Ruffin (back row, fourth from left), Calvin Schiraldi (back row, sixth from right), and Clemens (back row, fifth from right). Backup second baseman Johnny Sutton (front row, fourth from left) became a famous prosecutor as the U.S. attorney for the Western District of Texas. Pitching coach Clint Thomas (middle row, second from right) discovered that Clemens was not throwing his curve ball correctly (courtesy University of Texas).

glares emanated from his raised eyebrows and wide forehead, followed by a step off the mound towards the opposing team's dugout if he heard something he didn't like.

Clemens apparently rooted for the Yankees when he was a kid because he reportedly wore a Yankees cap around campus. The Texas baseball team did not have the visibility of the football players, particularly the massive offensive linemen. Many football players, at lunch time, watched soap operas on the television sets in the Jones Communications Center. Nor did the baseball players have the visibility of members of the vaunted swimming team, many of whom, like Olympic gold medalists Rick Carey and Jill Sterkel, hung out sitting on a high wall in front of the famous tower (Stenkel now works in the University's sports information office).[22] Unlike the famous football training table at Texas that included steaks and other exotic fare, the baseball players ate like regular students. Their scholarships were modest, and they lived on Pell Grants and family donations. Fortunately for Clemens, the in-state tuition at Texas in those days was only a couple of hundred dollars a semester. Clemens' roommate and catcher, Jeff Hearron, who batted .341 in 1983, remembered that they both ran out of scholarship money and practically lived on Ramen noodles at their off-campus apartment. Hearron recalled that the six-foot, four-inch, 205-pound Clemens, who even then possessed enormous shoulders, massive thighs, huge buttocks, and yes, large head, was always hungry. Hearron said that Clemens did not have enough to eat before the final game of the 1983 College World Series against Alabama. Early in the game, Clemens gave up a home run. Hearron recalled what happened next. "Coach Gus came out to the mound and said, 'Roger, what's wrong, son?' Roger said, 'I'm hungry, coach.' To that Coach Gus replied, 'You better get hungry for these hitters.' He pitched a complete game and got the win."[23] And the Longhorns became the 1983 NCAA baseball champions. The team included shortstop Mike Brumley, who hit .298 and later served as a utility infielder for the Cubs, Tigers, Mariners, Red Sox, Astros, and Athletics, where he hit .206 over eight seasons.[24] At the end of the 2013 season, Brumley had served four years as the first base coach of the Seattle Mariners.[25] Freshman second baseman, Billy Bates, who hit .296, would play in the 1990 World Series for the Cincinnati Reds, where he batted a perfect 1.000.[26]

Amazingly, both Hearron and Coach Gustafson harbored false memories of Clemens. "His curve wasn't a true curve," Hearron insisted. "More like a slurve," he joked. Not to be outdone by anyone, especially one of his catchers, Gustafson laughed that Clemens' curve ball at Texas was "unintentionally his off-speed pitch!" Hearron told New York's *Daily News* in 2003, "He didn't have a true slider or curve at Texas. He developed them in pro ball and that splitter is amazing."[27] Not true for the curve ball. What both men had forgotten, and

Gustafson did acknowledge when reminded of it some 30 years later, was "Clemens' second miracle."[28]

In between the time UT-Arlington embarrassed Clemens and the arrival of powerful Arizona State and their freshman superstar, Barry Bonds, for a spring-break weekend series, Texas pitching Coach Clint Thomas discovered a flaw in the way that Clemens gripped the ball on his breaking pitches.[29] Years later, Alabama's Dave Magadan would recall Clemens' "corrected curve ball" when he faced it again in the major leagues with the Seattle Mariners and Oakland Athletics.[30] From that moment forward, Roger Clemens was never again a one-trick pony. As German philosopher Martin Buber once explained it, "Those are great moments of existence when a man discovers his essence or rediscovers it on a higher plane; when he decides anew to become what he is and, as one who is becoming this, to establish a genuine relation to the world; when he heroically maintains his discovery and decision against his everyday consciousness and against his unconscious."[31]

Clemens struck out five Sun Devils on spring-break weekend, allowed no walks, scattered six hits, and pitched a complete-game shutout. He extended his scoreless streak to 27 innings.[32] Future major leaguers Barry Bonds, playing center field instead of left field, and Oddibe McDowell,[33] the night's designated hitter, batted a collective zero-for-eight against Clemens. Center fielder Mike Trent led the Longhorns in their weekend sweep of the Sun Devils by going four-for-eight at the plate with four RBI.[34]

Steve Campbell heard from one scout that Clemens' fastball was too straight. Draft day 1983 showed that other scouts disagreed about Clemens' purported too-straight fastball, or at least Danny Doyle did, when the Boston Red Sox selected Clemens in the first round with the 19th pick.[35] Clemens signed for something close to $120,000 and made $140,000 in 1984, his first season in the majors.[36] The New York Mets then chose Calvin Schiraldi eight selections later with the 27th pick. The Chicago Cubs selected Mike Capel in the 13th round.[37] Believe it or not, years before he did not take anabolic steroids or human growth hormone, Roger Clemens did not always finish games. His closer was a gritty, former football player with the wonderful Texas name of Kirk Killingworth. Although highly effective and efficient as a relief pitcher, 12–3 with an ERA of 2.56 that year,[38] Killingsworth's knees were not quite functional. A common sight late in games included the buckling of one or another of Killingsworth's knees, a collapse to the ground, a trainer rushing to the mound, and the manipulation of Killingsworth's knee back into the joint. This scene repeated itself often. The Seattle Mariners drafted Killingsworth in the seventh round and he gutted it out for six minor league seasons.[39]

Roger Clemens arrived in Boston as a pitching savior on May 15, 1984.

2. The Consistency of Roger Clemens

The key factor in Texas' 1983 College World Series title was a nation-leading earned run average of 2.72. This extraordinary pitching staff included, left to right, future major leaguers Bruce Ruffin, Clemens, and Calvin Schiraldi, as well as closer Kirk Killingsworth, a seventh-round draft pick and former high school football star (courtesy University of Texas).

After a dynasty early in the 20th century, in which they won the World Series five times between 1903 and 1918 (the team was known as the Boston Americans from 1901 to 1907), the Red Sox never won another World Series until the 21st century. The reason was a lack of pitching. Throughout the 20th century, the Red Sox had produced Hall of Fame hitters such as Ted Williams, Carl Yastrzemski, Jim Rice, and Wade Boggs. But they lacked the pitching to put them over the top. When Roger Clemens started his first game for the Red Sox, against the Cleveland Indians, the team had not been to the playoffs in nine years. Although the Red Sox would not win the World Series with Clemens, he did take them to one in 1986. They would make the playoffs four times during his years as baseball's most dominant pitcher.

If age discrimination were a cause of action in baseball, the team would have been liable for much of the 20th century. Most baseball fans were familiar with the team's sale of Babe Ruth to the Yankees, but perhaps not all the details. Ruth's final year with the Red Sox, 1919, was outstanding. He led the league in home runs with 29, drove in 114 runs, and batted .322 while manning the challenges of the high wall in left field at Fenway Park. In addition, he was 9–5 as a pitcher. The Red Sox rewarded the 24-year-old Ruth for this stellar year by selling him to the Yankees for $125,000 in cash and $300,000 in loans. How did Ruth do after that? Well, the next year, 1920, Ruth's homer total jumped from 29 to 54 and his batting average climbed from .322 to .376. In 1921, Ruth further increased his numbers to 59 home runs and a .378 batting average, despite being walked 150 times. And of course, there were other years in which Ruth dwarfed his Boston numbers. In 1923, Ruth's home run total collapsed all the way down to 41, but his batting average ascended to .393 in a year in which he was granted 150 walks. Four years later, Ruth found his home run swing again, belting 60 home runs, hitting .356, and accepting 137 walks.[40]

The handling of Wade Boggs was particularly pertinent and peculiar. The front office in Boston kept Boggs in the minors for six years even though he hit over .300 in five of them. They brought him up to the big team in 1982, where he hit a mere .349. Not only did Boggs have a mustache out of the Deadball Era of the early 20th century, but he had batting averages not seen since that time before the home run became the be all of baseball's obsession. He hit .361 in 1983, .368 in 1985, .357 in 1986, .363 in 1987, .366 in 1988, .330 in 1989, and .332 in 1991. In all, Boggs batted over .300 in 15 of his 18 major league seasons.[41] Boggs experienced a slump, however, in 1992, slipping to .259 with 50 runs batted in. Since he was blessed with extraordinary 20/12 vision, Boggs suspected his eyesight was the problem, and therefore went to an ophthalmologist, who explained that his vision had deteriorated to 20/20 and prescribed contact lenses, which put his eyes back to 20/10.[42] The Red Sox front office obviously knew Boggs had consulted an eye doctor but that apparently did not interfere with their conclusion that his .259 average was indisputable evidence that he had slipped into the twilight of his career at age 34. This twilight thinking among the Boston brass led to Boggs' exile from Boston and his welcome in New York, where his fading twilight prompted him to bat .302, .342, .324, .311, and .292, helping the Yankees earn their first World Series championship in 18 years in 1996.[43]

Mo Vaughn was a bedrock foundation of the Clemens teams in Boston. He batted .337 in 1998, but that statistic was apparently a minor footnote compared to the fact that he had turned 30. In Vaughn's case, he was actually in the twilight of his career, due to chronic back problems, for which he took human growth hormone (HGH) out of desperation. As with other players in this book, HGH proved worthless, and after hitting .281 in his first year of free agency with the Angels, he declined steadily in his last three seasons to finish out at .190 in 2003 with the Mets.[44]

No one represented the resurgent Red Sox of the late 1990s and early 21st century as much as their beloved shortstop, Nomar Garciaparra, who arrived in Boston at the end of the 1996 season and was joined by his college teammate from Georgia Tech, catcher Jason Varitek, late in the 1997 season. Garciaparra hit .323 with 178 home runs and 690 RBI in nine New England summers. His post-season batting averages were mostly extraordinary: .333 in 1998, .417 in the first round of the 1999 playoffs and .400 in the AL Championship Series. In 2003, he batted .300 in the first round and .241 in the Championship Series against the Yankees. Although Garciaparra hit .301 in 2003, he also reached the dreaded Red Sox age of 30, and the twilight thinkers in the front office could not get him out of town fast enough. In ancient Wrigley Field and sedate Dodger Stadium, where Garciaparra played out his final years and married soccer superstar Mia Hamm, he batted .297, .283, .303, .283, .264, and .281. Due to a chronic bad back, he hit double digit home runs only once in his last six years.[45]

Johnny Damon was the clubhouse leader and chief cheerleader, in addition to being a superb leadoff man, of the Red Sox team which broke the 85-year curse in 2004. Two years later, when his contract ran out, Damon was still effective, batting .316 with 75 RBI, and 18 stolen bases. But at season's end, Damon was 31 years old. It was time to go. The Yankees gladly grabbed up such a good leadoff hitter, and Damon batted .285, .270, .303, and .282[46] for Boston's bitter rival, and like Boggs before him, Damon helped the Yankees end a World Series drought, a major catalyst as the Yankees defeated the Phillies in the 2009 Fall Classic.

When Pedro Martinez was traded to the Red Sox in 1997 at the age of 26, he was more or less replacing Roger Clemens as the ace of the staff. He lived up to that job description and established his credentials for the Hall of Fame. In seven years with the Red Sox he was an extraordinary 117–37, a winning percentage of .760, an outstanding ERA of 2.52, and 1,683 strikeouts. In his last year in Boston, 2004, Martinez pitched superbly, going 16–9 with a 3.90 ERA, and struck out 227 batters. Yet he was nearly 33 years old when his contract expired at the end of the season. Fenway Park was not a home for AARP. The Red Sox let him go and the New York Mets welcomed him with open arms. In his first year with the Mets, Martinez was his usual extraordinary self, going 15–8 with a masterful 2.82 ERA and 208 strikeouts. But after that Martinez steadily declined in his last years until a swan song in his final year, 2009, age 37, with the Philadelphia Phillies. Martinez helped the Phillies get into the World Series for the second consecutive year by going 5–1 with a 3.63 ERA in the regular season. He was valiant but wanting in the battle against his old nemesis, the Yankees, going 0–2 with an ERA of 6.30. He struck out 13 batters in ten innings, gave up nine hits, seven runs, and four walks. But he was undone by three homeruns, including a mammoth, two-run blast by Series MVP Hideki Matsui.[47]

Jon Lester was the Red Sox's most dominant left-handed starter since Bruce Hurst. Yet Lester was 30 years old in 2014 and was therefore traded to the Oakland Athletics. His combined numbers for the season were 16 wins, 11 losses, an ERA of 2.46 and 220 strikeouts. Lester signed in the off-season with the Chicago Cubs, rejoining his Red Sox general manager, Theo Epstein, the architect of the end of the Curse. In 2015 Lester went a misleading 11–12 with the Cubs because his ERA was an outstanding 3.34, he struck out 207 batters,[48] and he led the Cubs to their first post-season appearance since 2008, and their first trip to the NL Championship Series since Moises Alou lost a controversial foul ball to an eager fan in the bleachers in 2003 against the Florida Marlins. The Red Sox's failure to resign Lester led to overpaying David Price $31 million a year, beginning with the 2016 season.

In personality, Clemens most resembled Ted Williams among Boston legends. Williams spent his career feuding with both baseball writers and fans. He was a moody, bitter man, whose father had left the family when he was young. Therefore, like Clemens, Ted Williams had essentially grown up without a father. There was no loving Dad to watch Clemens in Little League. No loving Dad to encourage him in high school. Perhaps in search of a father figure, Clemens would revere the legendary players of baseball and the game's history. He ran his fingers over Babe Ruth's monument before every start in Yankee Stadium and kept a baseball of Cy Young permanently lighted in a glass case in his house. Such slights in childhood can be a massive motivator. The antithesis of the 21st-century, self-congratulatory, corporate athlete, Ted Williams hit a home run in the last at-bat of his Hall of Fame career in September 1960. There were no high-fives, no curtain calls with waving arms and tipped cap, no postgame interviews to tell the assembled Red Sox customers they were the greatest fans in the world, no waiting around with tin cup in hand to accept lucrative financial rewards for hitting a home run in his final at-bat. Williams simply rounded the bases, stepped on home plate, disappeared into the Red Sox dugout, and was never seen in a major league lineup again.[49]

As New England's only major league franchise, the Red Sox probably had the most loyal and passionate fans of any region in the United States. The fans were knowledgeable and long-suffering. The 85-year drought of the Red Sox without a World Series championship was usually called "The Curse of the Bambino" because they suffered more than eight decades of disappointment after selling Babe Ruth. However, it could also be called "The Curse of Ingmar Bergman" because the time period more or less coincided with Bergman's life, 1917–2007, and because the brooding angst of Red Sox fans was reminiscent

Like Clemens, Ted Williams (right) was a fiery competitor whose relationship with the media was less than warm (courtesy National Baseball Hall of Fame Library, Cooperstown, New York).

of a Bergman movie. The knowledge of Red Sox fans was certainly enhanced by an extraordinarily long line of talented broadcasters: Curt Gowdy, Ned Martin, Dick Stockton, Sean McDonough, and Joe Castiglione.[50] Ned Martin may have been the second most descriptive baseball announcer ever, after the incomparable Vin Scully, and was also an excellent play-by-play man for Harvard football games on WEEI Radio.

Perhaps Ted Williams's theory of hitting helped explain why Roger Clemens was so difficult to hit. "To be a good hitter, you've got to get a good ball to hit.... If I have to bite at stuff that is out of my happy zone, I'm not a .344 hitter."[51] Clemens' best pitches were his high fastball on the outer part of the plate, which traveled at more than 95 miles an hour (hence the nickname "Rocket"), which he threw early in his career; and his split-finger fastball, which he threw to get strikeouts in the second part of his career beginning in 1997. The split-finger fastball "dives" low and to the outside to right-handed hitters, who comprise the majority of batters. Perhaps only Mike Piazza, the best-hitting catcher of all time, would have called a high and outside fastball "his happy zone."

From 1984 to 1996 Clemens won 192 games, struck out 2,590 batters, averaged 29.4 starts and 213.5 innings per year. Coincidentally, the 192 wins was the same number of wins for the Red Sox by Cy Young, for whom the annual pitching award is named.[52] Most importantly, Clemens' ERA, the best evaluator of a pitcher's performance, was a stingy 3.06 despite subpar years in 1993 and 1995 in which his ERA had climbed to 4.46 and 4.18, respectively.

What made Clemens' pitching results even more remarkable was the fact that he pitched approximately half his games in a hitter's paradise opened in 1912, Fenway Park, a pinball machine that masqueraded as a baseball field. The joke was that an 11-run lead was not safe there. A typical Red Sox disparity in production was illustrated during the summer of 2011, when the Red Sox's team batting average going into August was 50 points higher at Fenway than on the road.[53]

Ralph Houk, a World War II Army major who learned patience as the backup catcher to Yogi Berra and who managed the 1961 Yankees—one of the best baseball teams ever—was Clemens' first skipper in Boston. Houk managed to calm Clemens to a large degree and helped him to focus. Houk was known for spitting tobacco juice on reporters' shoes during post-game interviews, according to a baseball writer of that era.

The Red Sox have never, ever been a dull team, and the squads Clemens played with from 1984 to 1996 were no different. His third baseman, Wade Boggs, who looked like a player from the late 19th century with his wide, drooping mustache, was known for eating chicken before every single game, and for enjoying mistresses on the road. Boggs, during his years with Clemens, became the second leading hitter in Red Sox history after Ted Williams. Boggs's career batting average with the Red Sox, ten points higher than his final percentage, was .338. Ted Williams's career average, all with the Red Sox, was .344.[54] Boggs has a plaque in Cooperstown.

The 1986 team, which should have beaten the New York Mets in the World Series with a three games to two lead, showed both how dependent the Red Sox were on Clemens and how entertaining a crew was employed between the base lines in Fenway Park. Indeed, if a blister had not opened up on the index finger of his pitching hand, Clemens most likely would have finished off the Mets in the final two innings, ended the 1986 World Series in six games, and extinguished the Curse with the team's first World Series win in 68 years. Clemens logged 254 innings, but the other starrers logged a lot less. Oil Can Boyd pitched 214⅓ innings, Bruce Hurst 174⅓, Al Nipper 159, and 41-year-old Tom Seaver, the former Marine on the way to the Hall of Fame, 104⅓. Bob Stanley led the pitching staff with just 16 saves, Joe Sambito had 12, and Clemens's college teammate, Calvin Schiraldi, had 9, all in the stretch run at season's end. Schiraldi, later a high school baseball coach in Texas, imploded in the World Series that fall. By Red Sox standards, and by standards of a team playing in the World Series, the hitting that year was pedestrian. In a league of his own, of course, Wade Boggs hit .357. Jim Rice in left field, as unpopular with the press as Clemens, and who would accumulate much of his Hall of Fame batting statistics as a designated hitter, batted .324, while driving in 110 runs and belting 20 homers. After that, the numbers were less fearsome. Dwight Evans, perhaps the best all-around right fielder of his time, produced a typical year for him, .259 with 26 homers and 97 RBI. Aging ex-Oriole Don Baylor swatted 31 homers as the DH, but his batting average was .238. Starting shortstops Rey Quinones and Spike Owen respectively hit .237 and .183. Second baseman Marty Barrett hit .267, a bit down from later Red Sox star Dustin Pedroia's career .299 average.[55] Barrett would be remembered in baseball history for scoring the winning run in the longest game ever played, 33 innings, when the Pawtucket Red Sox beat the Rochester Redwings, 3–2. Future Hall of Famers Wade Boggs and Cal Ripken, Jr., went 4-for-14 and 2-for-13 respectively.[56] Clemens's loyal catcher and defender, Rich Gedman, hit .267 with 18 homers. Tony Armas, no Fred Lynn defensively in center field, hit .264. And most remembered from that team, aging Bill Buckner, of the gimpy ankles, hit .258 with 16 home runs, probably not enough offense to justify leaving him at first base in the waning outs of Game 6 as Mookie Wilson's puny ground ball rolled through his injured legs and into baseball immortality. Future star left fielder Mike Greenwell hit .314 in only 35 at-bats.

On August 30, 1985, barely a year into his Major League career, Roger Clemens underwent reconstructive surgery to repair the torn rotator cuff in his right shoulder.

Unlike most of the other 40,000 Americans who undergo rotator cuff surgery each year, Clemens' daily routine already included the physical therapy prescribed for recovery: shoulder exercises, weight lifting, running, stretching—all part of a legendary workout routine going back to junior high school and extending more than two decades into his professional career. Indeed, Clemens' workout regimen was one of the most chronicled in the history of baseball, covered in numerous newspaper and magazine articles and television profiles. In the off-season, between November and January, Clemens ran, lifted weights, and did agility drills for five hours each day, and eventually began throwing to ready himself for spring training.[57] In spring training, where pitchers normally throw only a few innings to tune up for the approaching season, Clemens did power sit-ups

The 1986 Boston Red Sox won the American League pennant and seemed on their way to a world championship before the infamous turn of events in Game Six. Clemens (back row, third from right) departed that game with a blister but also with the lead, having thrown seven strong innings. Front row, from left: Jack Burke, Dwight Evans, Don Baylor, Bill Buckner, Joe Morgan, Rene Lachemann, John McNamara, Bill Fischer, Walt Hriniak, Marty Barrett, Jim Rice, and Ace Adams. Middle row, from left: Rich Zawacki, Don Fitzpatrick, Mike Greenwell, Rich Gedman, Dennis "Oil Can" Boyd, Al Nipper, Tom Seaver, Kevin Romine, Ed Romero, Wade Boggs, Rey Quiñones, Jack Rogers, Vince Orlando, and Charlie Moss. Back row, from left: Joe Sambito, Tony Armas, Calvin Schiraldi, Tim Lollar, Steve Crawford, Bob Stanley, Sammy Stewart, Wes Gardner, Bruce Hurst, Clemens, Marc Sullivan, and Dave Stapleton (courtesy National Baseball Hall of Fame Library, Cooperstown, New York).

between innings to burn up extra energy. One time with the Red Sox, he was knocked out early and his wife Debbie drove him to a Little League field, where he threw against a fence for nine imaginary innings.[58] Despite anecdotal contentions that Clemens abandoned his exercise regime in mid-career and became overweight and out of shape, there is in fact no evidence that he ever did so.

The rotator-cuff tear—in just his second major-league season—was the last major injury of Clemens' remarkable 24-year career, for as his Astros teammate Andy Pettitte put it, Clemens "was never injured that much, you know, really." After that 1985 surgery, Clemens pitched the next three years without missing a single start.

The nagging injuries that later caused Clemens to spend time on the Disabled List consisted of groin and hamstring pulls and stiffness in his upper shoulders and lower back, the natural result of a man who stood six-feet-four, eventually weighed 240 pounds, and possessed enormous thighs.

Clemens' remedies for these aches and pains, including a chiropractor for his back, Vioxx, Aleve, Lidocaine and B-12, both orally and via shots, were consistent with the decades-long use of aspirin by sore-armed pitchers.

In contrast, Human Growth Hormone (HGH) was considered a remedy for healing after surgery and for sexual potency—allegedly an issue for Clemens. Anabolic steroids increase strength and muscle mass.

When he retired in 2007, Clemens had won the Cy Young Award seven times, the most ever. He won 354 games and lost 184, a superlative winning percentage of .658. He ranked third in career strikeouts with 4,672. From 2008–2012, the Roger Clemens Award was given to the top NCAA, Division I pitcher. Winners included David Price of Vanderbilt, who was awarded the 2012 American League Cy Young Award while pitching for the Tampa Bay Rays,[59] and who broke the age barrier for long-term contracts in Boston.

Clemens' cumulative numbers in the post-season were not overwhelming. He went 12–8 with an ERA of 3.75. He gave up 7.8 hits per nine innings, 3.2 walks per nine innings and 7.8 strikeouts per nine innings. His strikeout to walk ratio was 2.47.[60] However, these cumulative statistics belied the fact that Clemens actually performed better as the level of difficulty and pressure increased throughout his post-season career. His ERA declined from 4.61 in Division Series games to 3.87 in League Championship Series to a stingy 2.37 in the World Series. His strikeouts per nine innings rose from 7.0 in first-round games to 7.9 in second-round games to 8.9 in eight World Series games. His walks per nine innings declined from 4.2 in first-round divisional play to 2.9 in Championship Series games to 2.2 in the World Series. And Clemens never lost a World Series game. He was 4–4 in Division Series, 5–4 in League Championship Series, and 3–0 in the World Series.

This gritty warrior demonstrated that he was at his best when his back was up against the proverbial wall, when he *was* the team, when he was *needed* the most. He seemed to thrive when it was him against the world. He would reach back and find something extra. Consider that he struck out the most batters when he pitched for the most undermanned teams. In Toronto, where he was essentially a one-man pitching staff, he averaged 281.5 strikeouts a year. In Boston, a franchise that he picked up by its red-and-white baseball hose, he averaged 199.2 strikeouts a year. Where he was *least needed*, as a pitcher for the powerhouse Yankees of the late 1990s and early 2000s, Clemens averaged his lowest strikeouts, 189.2 a year.[61]

Clemens' "me against the world" attitude probably derived from the fact that he was essentially a loner who might have been happier in frontier days as a cowboy on the range. Most of his socializing occurred within his immediate family. To his regret, Clemens did not have a father figure in his life very long, never had a father who came to his games as a child and gave him support and encouragement. As he grew older, he established an independent routine; partly because as a key player, he was mandated to stay in shape and remain focused, and partly the result of not being much of a drinker. When his younger teammates went out and partied on the road, Clemens would often, instead, make solo excursions, driving around a city to see the sights and turning in early at the team hotel. Clemens' loner behavior made it difficult later on for him to defend against public rebuke in the wake of the allegations of steroid use. Clemens' own public relations efforts in defense against these charges were so awkwardly clumsy and ham-handed as to be laughable.

Because Clemens never pitched a no-hitter or a perfect game, his dominance over a generation is understated. In nine of the 24 seasons in which he did not win the Cy Young Award, he was either on the disabled list or pitched only partial seasons. To put it another way, when Roger Clemens was healthy and pitched a full season, or as they say in employment law, was "ready, willing, and able" to work, he won seven Cy Young Awards in 15 years, an astonishing accomplishment.

Clemens possessed the consistency of a Swiss clock. In 21 American League seasons his strikeout-to-walk ratio was 2.96. In three National League seasons in Houston, it was 2.97. Clemens' ability to throw strikes was so regular, in fact, that during the years 14 through 24 of his career, his number of walks-per-year was within a hundredth of a percent of what it had been in his first 13 years in Boston, 65.846 to 65.818.

Clemens achieved this consistency even though the ravages of age eventually affected his durability. In innings pitched and complete games, he declined across the board in years 14 through 24. In 13 years in Boston, Clemens averaged 213.5 innings a year. In 11 seasons in Toronto, New York, and Houston his innings per year fell to 194.6, or two-thirds of an inning less in each game. In the first half of his career he averaged 7.8 complete games, compared to 2.0 in the second half of his career. He pitched shortened seasons in his final two years, throwing only 113⅓ innings in 2006 with Houston and 99 innings with the Yankees in 2007. In addition, Clemens struck out 210.2 batters a year from age 21 through 35, but only 168.8 from age 36 to 44, further evidence of the wear and tear of Father Time. In 2004 Clemens, then 41, became the oldest pitcher ever to start an All-Star Game. He looked like it. Ichiro Suzuki led off the game and doubled. Ivan Rodriguez tripled. Manny Ramirez homered. Clemens retired Vladimir Guerrero and Alex Rodriguez. Jason Giambi reached first base on an error by Jeff Kent, and Derek Jeter singled. Up stepped Alfonso Soriano. Whack. Soriano deposited Clemens's first pitch over the left field wall. After 35 mostly dreadful pitches, Clemens was mercifully lifted from the game.[62] When Clemens pitched the opening game of the 2005 World Series for his hometown Houston Astros against the Chicago White Sox, he was 43 years old, the second-oldest pitcher to start a World Series game, and he pitched like it. He gave up four hits and three runs, and was gone by the third inning.[63]

Baseball writers in 2007 convinced the public that Roger Clemens was washed up by 1996 and that his career was revived by taking anabolic steroids and HGH. The same baseball writers who thought that in 2007 did not think that in 1996. Yet, as they say in baseball, the numbers don't lie. In his supposedly washed-up year of 1996, Roger Clemens matched his game-high strikeout mark of a decade earlier, 20, and led the American League in strikeouts with 257. He also ranked first in the American League in strikeouts per nine innings pitched, 9.532; second in the league in hits allowed per nine innings; and fourth in complete games.

In fact, the widely held view that there was ever a "decline" in Clemens' career was largely a myth. The period most often cited to prove that assertion is 1993–1995, when he won 30 games and lost 26, as he fought through chronic muscle strains in the left side of his back, the back side of his right shoulder, his groin, a briefly inflamed elbow, and a pulled hamstring. Moreover, this period included the longest strike in baseball history. ESPN's TJ Quinn observed that the Feds tried to show Clemens' decline during these years at the trial, "But incredibly, [Gil] Guerrero and the prosecution team seemed unaware that both the 1994 and 1995 seasons were shortened by the historic strike that killed the 1994 World Series. Nor were they aware that Clemens was injured in the late and abbreviated spring training of 1995."[64] This alleged decline during these years was the substance of a nutty study done by two

From 1984 to 1996 Clemens won 192 games, tying Cy Young for most victories among Red Sox pitchers (courtesy National Baseball Hall of Fame Library, Cooperstown, New York).

Wharton professors, and eagerly published by *The New York Times*, that claimed these years were proof that Clemens was in decline and that his return to better pitching when healthy again and armed with the split-finger fastball, was "statistically unusual" and therefore a "spike" in his performance.[65] The 1993 season was arguably Clemens' worst, with an 11–14 record and 4.46 ERA. Yet his strikeouts per nine innings were 7.5, only one strikeout per game under his career average of 8.6. In 1994 he led the major leagues in holding opposing batters to a .204 average. In 1995, he went 10–5, gave up more hits and more walks than usual, but barely missed his 8.6 career average of strikeouts per nine innings, punching out 8.5.

In 1997 Clemens won the Cy Young with his new team, the Toronto Blue Jays, who gave him what was then the largest pitching salary in history, $8.4 million.[66]

Brian McNamee said he arrived with the Blue Jays in the spring of 1998 and injected Clemens after the pitcher struggled early in the year. The problem with McNamee's story was that Clemens' pitching performance without steroids or HGH in 1997 was almost identical to his pitching performance allegedly with anabolic steroids and HGH in 1998. If anything, Clemens' 1998 statistics were slightly worse. In 1997, purportedly without steroids, Clemens made 34 starts, struck out 292 batters, had a 2.05 ERA, and went 21–7, winning the pitching Triple Crown. Allegedly, with steroids in 1998, Clemens made 35 starts, struck out 271 batters, had a 2.65 ERA, and went 20–6, another Cy Young performance.

Clemens was traded to the Yankees in 1999. Despite a Cy Young Award and a 20-game winning streak aided by the first team in history to win 14 straight World Series games, Clemens suffered the worst years of his career. These included the 2000–2001 seasons, a period that constituted the majority of his alleged use of performance enhancing drugs. His ERA with the Yankees elevated to 4.01 compared to his career average of 3.12. He gave up 8.5 hits per nine innings with the Yankees compared with his career average of 7.7. His New York walks per nine innings increased to 3.2 compared to a career average of 2.9. And his career strikeouts—to walks ratio of 2.96 declined to 2.55.

When Clemens retired from the Yankees and unretired with the Houston Astros, his pitching performance improved in every category. He turned 41 years old on August 4, 2003, was considered to be no longer on anabolic steroids, according to Brian McNamee's story, and yet pitched better than when he was in New York and supposedly using steroids. From 2004 to 2006, playing for a weak-hitting Astros team, Clemens went 38–18 for a winning percentage of .679. His ERA was 2.40, and he gave up only 6.8 hits per nine innings, compared to 8.5 with the vaunted Yankees. His walks per nine innings declined from 3.2 with the Yankees and returned to 2.8. His strikeouts to walks ratio per nine innings also improved in Houston, rising from 2.55 to 2.97.

These numbers proved, from a timeline perspective, that if in fact Roger Clemens had ever taken any performance enhancing drugs, they had absolutely no impact on his pitching performance.

In addition, by the second half of his career, Roger Clemens was acutely aware of his place in baseball history. He understood he ranked next to the greatest pitchers ever: Cy Young, Nolan Ryan, Steve Carlton, Grover Cleveland Alexander, and Walter Johnson. As his time in baseball wound down, he pitched primarily against them, in competition with them. These were the players he cared about, the players he revered. He would never cheat in any manner, shape or form in the game of baseball, because to do so would be to admit that he did not belong with these men in the pantheon of baseball's greatest pitchers. Clemens would finish his career 9th all time in wins, 354, compared to Cy Young, 1st, 511, Walter Johnson, 2nd, 417, and Grover Cleveland Alexander, 3rd, 373. He would finish 3rd all time in strikeouts, 4,672, compared to Walter Johnson's 9th, 3,508, and Cy Young 20th, 2,803. Clemens would finish 16th all time in batting average against him, .229, but it was quite close to Walter Johnson, 12th, .227 BA against him.

When it came to baseball, Clemens was simply not a risk-taker. He left nothing to chance in his preparation. Despite having a reputation as a beanball pitcher who would hit batters to move them from crowding home plate, he was meticulously careful not to antagonize umpires, who were, after all, the judges of every pitch he threw. To risk his place in baseball history for at most six to eight shots of anabolic steroids, a handful of HGH injections, and an unfinished packet of testosterone, according to Brian McNamee, made no sense at all.

Tellingly, the players who defended Clemens upon the release of the Mitchell Report were the ones who knew the most about his pitching, his catchers: Rich Gedman of the Red Sox, Charlie O'Brien and Darrin Fletcher of the Blue Jays, Jorge Posada of the Yankees, and Brad Ausmus of the Astros. O'Brien and Fletcher testified on his behalf at the 2012 trial. Rich Gedman said, "I have no reason to believe he's guilty until it's ever proven that he is or that he lied."[67] Jorge Posada said, "We're still very good friends and hopefully everything will be all right. I'm going to support him and going to be behind him, and that's all I can say."[68] Brad Ausmus said, "He's a good person, he's a good teammate and he's a good friend. I'm pulling for him 100 percent to be completely vindicated."[69]

3

The Passive Injector

Some nights conditioning coach Brian McNamee met Roger Clemens in the Yankee Stadium parking lot and followed Clemens' car to the pitcher's apartment, he said. On other nights, when McNamee supervised the physical training of other players after the game, McNamee drove to Clemens' apartment alone. He never made the trip on nights Clemens pitched or the day before. The route to his appointments led from Yankee Stadium in the Bronx down to the Third Avenue Bridge in Manhattan, onto Second Avenue, and then over to First Avenue and 98th Street, where Roger Clemens lived during the baseball season in a 23rd-floor residence.[1]

According to McNamee, Clemens would summon him up to the apartment by calling down to Carlos, the doorman. Carlos would park McNamee's car next to a fire hydrant and watch it till McNamee completed his task and made his getaway. Upstairs, Clemens would lay out the steroids or HGH on a towel on a chair, all ready to go, usually in the kitchen or his master bedroom.[2]

The materials included a bottle of rubbing alcohol, cotton gauze, and ampules containing HGH or anabolic steroids such as Sustanon-250, Deca-Durabolin or Parabolan, and a syringe. Clemens stored the HGH in his refrigerator and the steroids in a Ziploc bag on the shelves of his walk-in closet, McNamee said.

McNamee drew the steroids into the syringe and then injected them into the upper left part of Clemens' buttocks, or the upper right part, alternating each time. It was Clemens who remembered which butt-cheek had been injected the previous time and so directed the location of the new shot. HGH injections went in to the right or left of Clemens' belly button. "We didn't really socialize," McNamee said. "We maybe took five minutes to do the injection."[3]

He was asked during his congressional deposition, "And where in the residence did the injections take place, typically?"

"They were in the kitchen and then he had a spare bedroom off—as you went in off to the left."

"Was there ever anybody else in the residence besides you and Mr. Clemens when these occurred?"

"Never."

"Do you know if he kept records about what was to be injected when?"[4]

"I don't know, but I think he did. He was methodical about doing stuff on his computer or whatever. The guy had a program from the time he woke up to the time he went to bed, a schedule.[5] So I couldn't tell you when he needed an injection, he did."

McNamee fended off the difficult, probing question of the critical decision-making about both when he injected Clemens and the lack of a paper trail by putting it all back on Clemens. Yet, in the extraordinary, subsequent investigations across the United States and Canada, through the computer files of Major League clubs and through the voluminous personal files Roger Clemens voluntarily handed over to the government, the Federal Bureau of Investigation found no such details of any illegal drug injections, or a schedule of drug injections, involving Clemens.

"Anything else?" Waxman Committee attorney Steve Castor asked.

"Testosterone—like Sustanon-250."

"So there is a total of three max?"

"Yes. No. Yes. Parabolan."

"Who drew the liquid into the syringe, you or him?"

"I did."

"And did he give you a tutorial on how to do that?"

"In the first time, back in '98, he made a reference that he knew what he was doing about drawing it, about not getting bubbles or something in it."

"Were these injections going in his upper left buttocks or upper right buttocks?"

"Both."

"And how would he make the decision where the injection was going to go."

"I alternated it. He just said this time left, this one right, this one left, this one right. I said which one was the last time, left or right. He would go left."

"So it had nothing to do with when he was pitching?"

"I'm sure it did because I wouldn't inject him on the days he'd pitch or the day after."

This was a clever answer, and literally true, because McNamee knew, as did everybody associated with the Yankees, that Clemens would not meet with or talk with anybody the day he pitched, and McNamee knew that Clemens played golf the day *after* he pitched, apparently to unwind.

Castor inquired whether Clemens had a system down where he was never injected on the day he pitched.[6]

"I don't know," McNamee replied.

McNamee's responses, either because of his own cop-like ability to anticipate the direction of the questions, or excellent preparation, provided him with maximum deniability for these crucial issues. McNamee claimed, in essence, that even though this was the information to bring down Roger

Clemens, he never wrote down important details such as the particular days that he injected Clemens. Considering that Clemens maintained a consistent routine of what days he ran when not pitching, what days he weight-lifted, what days he played golf, what days he did other workouts, how is it possible that McNamee, a man who worked with him for his conditioning, did not know the days he was injected? McNamee had testified that Clemens had a schedule and routine from the moment he got up till the moment he went to bed. That schedule included his workouts with Brian McNamee and—if McNamee was telling the truth about injecting steroids and HGH—when McNamee would have injected him. Yet, the man "who knew his body, knew how to train him, knew how to push the right buttons on him" according to Clemens,[7] who even served as his personal valet and grocery shopper when Clemens was in Houston, did not know the routine of what days he risked his professional career and his personal liberty by committing a crime, did not know when he took that risk.

McNamee said he could not remember how many times he injected Clemens in total. He agreed with an estimate, tossed out by a Congressional investigator, that he may have injected Clemens 20 times in 2000.[8] McNamee felt more confident in guessing that he injected Clemens 13 times in 2001, although his original estimate to the Mitchell investigation put that number at between eight and 14.[9]

McNamee said he disposed of the syringes and other evidence himself and thought Clemens deposited the used gauze in the trash inside his apartment. McNamee said he threw the syringes and broken ampules into a garbage can in the hallway of the 23rd floor.

Clemens was also injected, according to McNamee, near the Jacuzzi in the old Yankee Stadium clubhouse,[10] the portion of the ballpark where players dressed, showered, met, ate, and were worked on by doctors. Injections did involve some bleeding, and the clubhouse injection resulted in bleeding right through Clemens' designer dress pants, which was noticed by pitcher Mike Stanton, McNamee said. Thereafter, Clemens traveled with small Band-Aids in case of posterior bleeding. Stanton later denied seeing any such bleeding.

McNamee next rambled on, in a rather hedging manner, about how often he injected Clemens with steroids, perhaps every ten days; perhaps seven to ten days; probably no less than eight to ten, no more than maybe 14 or 15; maybe 16 to 20.[11] McNamee suggested that he injected Clemens with testosterone in 2000 more than four to six times over a six- to eight-week period; or perhaps more than six and less than ten. McNamee said Clemens received three to four weeks of HGH treatment from him in 2000. "I think he took a little less than a kit, which I think there's seven or eight or six double vials in it.... And I think he either took one or two less than a full kit.... All I know is he didn't finish the kit."[12]

Castor returned to demonstrative photos of the drug paraphernalia.

"And so tell me everything you can as quickly as you can about the four pictures here."

"The ampules, the unbroken ampules are types of testosterone. The plastic, those are twenty-two-gauge needle heads sealed in plastic. The white pills are either Anadrol-50 or Clenbuterol. *Jeff Novitzky assumed they were Clenbuterol.* I didn't know. I've never asked—this stuff I can say I got from Kirk [Radomski] in 2001 probably most likely. I've never gotten those from Kirk for Roger, so I don't know where those came from."

McNamee's response was disturbing. First, why was it that Jeff Novitzky apparently knew so much more about these materials than McNamee, who claimed to have injected Clemens and who purportedly kept the discards all those years? McNamee's answer raised the obvious question: What exactly was Jeff Novitzky's role? Second, McNamee claimed these were the materials he had saved for years as his insurance policy and salvation, to bring down Roger Clemens. McNamee's stash was the key evidence prosecutors employed to hound Clemens through two perjury trials, and McNamee did not know what these materials actually were?

How could that be? My theory is that Brian McNamee never injected Roger Clemens with performance enhancing drugs, and these materials, altered somehow, or perhaps recreated from some unidentified laboratory, were carted by McNamee from somewhere to his lawyers' offices in Rockefeller Center. In short, McNamee was not an assassin, but merely a messenger boy, to quote Marlon Brando's famous line in the movie *Apocalypse Now*, in the government's rush to judgment against Roger Clemens.

The Committee's senior investigator, Michael Gordon, asked, "So the material depicted on these photos, is it correct that you provided this to your attorney and then he took care of making photographs?"

McNamee answered, "Yes."

"If I could draw your attention to the first photo which is Exhibit 2. Can you briefly describe what is depicted in this photo?"[13]

"Leftover stuff that was in Roger Clemens' possession at his New York apartment prior to him leaving for the off season. A Miller can or Lite can[14] that was used to store hazardous material, the open wrapper to a used 22½ inch gauze [pad and] syringe [sic]. In the upper somewhat left corner, you'll see the tail end of a broken ampule, the body of a broken ampule of that stored testosterone.

"The white napkin, the length of the white napkin was toilet paper from Roger Clemens' apartment that I wrapped the syringe in that was used. The needle part of the syringe is a needle from the end of the syringe that injected Roger Clemens.

"I believe the cotton balls were used to apply alcohol to the area prior to the injection. This is gauze pad that was used because of blood on it. It was used, I believe, to clean the area after the injection. That piece of cardboard has nothing to do with anything that I can recall.

"And what is the substance that was injected?"[15]

"I *think* it is."[16]

3. The Passive Injector   45

Richard Emery, one of McNamee's attorneys, jumped in to say, "He is asking you what the substance was in the photograph."

McNamee replied, "I've got it. I was looking here because it is the same bottle I was trying to read it. *I don't recall*. But it is that bottle."[17]

Gordon queried, "So it was definitely a steroid, an anabolic steroid; is that right?"

"Sustanon-250—yes, it was definitely a steroid, a testosterone based—a testosterone-based steroid." But this answer obviously contradicted his previous answer, above, that 'I don't recall.'

"Why did you keep them?"

"I kept them—well, because throughout my time with Roger Clemens, it was—there was always somewhat in the back of my mind I distrusted him to a degree, and my gut feeling and my—the fact that I was an ex-cop, I just felt.... I just felt that if I was going down, I wasn't going down alone."

A good response, for sure, if you like truth to come right out of a movie script, but notice that McNamee did not provide an explanation of *why* he did not trust Clemens. To say it was instinct was a "cop out," particularly because McNamee continued to work with Clemens on and off for six more years.

McNamee had no way of knowing in 2001 that the government would reverse its usual prosecutorial tactics if they discovered he was dealing anabolic steroids. The normal course would have been to squeeze Clemens, the user, to get to McNamee, the dealer. As an ex-cop, McNamee surely understood it was more likely that an end-user such as Clemens would never be prosecuted, but the dealer, McNamee, would. Therefore McNamee's argument that by saving the purported injection leftovers he could bring down Clemens had no force in 2001. McNamee clearly lacked the political savvy even to imagine that the Justice Department would, more or less, try to entrap Roger Clemens as a perjurer like they had with President Clinton. As a distributor and injector in 2001—and indeed, at least up until 2002, with Pettitte and Knoblauch, if not untold others—McNamee risked bringing himself down by keeping the materials. If Clemens had been outed as a steroids user as a byproduct of a criminal investigation against McNamee, Clemens *would have been ruined*, but that ruin would not have saved McNamee, nor would it have mitigated any sentence that McNamee would have received. There was no sentencing guideline, on its face, that allowed drug dealers to receive lighter sentences if they supplied drugs to a celebrity.

Gordon asked McNamee, "Did you ever tell anyone else that you had kept this material?"[18]

"My wife knew. She kept referring to it. Not this exact stuff, maybe references to having something to cover myself if anything happened."

"You told your wife you were retaining items similar to this that had been used in connection with providing steroids to Mr. Clemens, is that right?"

"Yes, I did."

In fact, Eileen McNamee testified at trial that she happened upon material in a FedEx box by accident. She had no way of knowing, of course, whose samples of PEDS and DNA were inside, because McNamee only claimed it "was from players." McNamee, additionally, took no photographs of the stored materials as proof that he had not recently acquired other or different "evidence" along the way. Photographs were later taken by his attorneys *after* he had brought the materials to them in Manhattan.

Technically, the chain of custody for evidentiary purposes, where each moment must be accounted for, did not commence until McNamee's lawyers placed the materials into the hands of federal prosecutors. In addition, McNamee claimed that he had no experience in handling evidence, although that seemed strange testimony coming from a former policeman who had investigated drug dealing. Federal agents later photographed the locations where McNamee had said he had stored the evidence.[19] McNamee's failure to prove he had stored physical evidence at his home for seven years raised all kinds of credibility questions about his story and the integrity of the evidence—including allowing Clemens' defense team to assert the notion of evidence tampering. Curiously, the defense team *did not* raise another obvious question at the second trial: Did someone *other than McNamee* tamper with the evidence?

Gordon asked whether McNamee told anybody else besides his wife about having Clemens-related drug evidence in his house.[20]

"I don't really—not that I can really pinpoint down—you know, I don't think I would have.... I don't think I did." McNamee told a far different story at Clemens' second trial, stating that he told David Segui and others. Yet, as it turned out, neither David Segui, the former first baseman for the Orioles and Mets, nor the other witnesses at trial, said that McNamee specifically identified Roger Clemens as somebody he injected with steroids or HGH and for which he retained evidence.

Castor asked, "What do you know about Mr. Clemens' use of anabolic steroids during the 2002 season?"[21]

"I don't really know anything, you know," admitted McNamee.

"And during the '02 season, what was your overall working relationship with Mr. Clemens?"

"I could go out in public and say I was his trainer, his strength coach. I trained him—in the winter. Then, during the season, it was sporadic."

"And how would he pay you during 2002?"[22]

"Money wire."

"How much in each wire, and how many wires, to the best of your recollection?"

"Five grand per wire—I don't know if it was five wires or ten wires."
"And what services did that cover other than working out with him?"
"I got him some vitamins?"
"Do you remember any conversations with him after 2001 about what he's doing on the anabolic-steroid front?"
"No."

McNamee was rather vague about injecting Clemens with performance enhancing drugs during road games away from New York in 2000 and 2001, but he did claim that he injected Clemens once in Tampa, Florida, a state with particularly tough penalties for the use of anabolic steroids. Taking anabolic steroids was a third-degree felony that could have earned up to five years' imprisonment in Florida, and merely giving the drug to another person was considered a sale and could have led to a 15-year prison sentence. Under Florida Statute 893.13, mere possession of anabolic steroids came with a mandatory three-year jail term. Had McNamee and Clemens been prosecuted under federal law for steroid use, the most likely outcome of a successful criminal action would have been that Clemens could have been sentenced to one year in prison for possession and McNamee could have received five years in a federal penitentiary for possession with intent to distribute, a sentence that was subsequently raised to ten years.[23]

Federal sentencing for anabolic-steroid use was generally more severe than state sentencing, with Florida serving as an exception to the rule. Part of that enforcement strategy was the societal trend toward treating people for drug use instead of prosecuting them. In New York, for example, where McNamee said he performed most of the illegal injections, neither Clemens nor McNamee probably would have served jail time had they been convicted in a criminal trial. Possession of anabolic steroids and the administration of them to another person were only Class-A misdemeanors. While the penalty could have reached a year in prison, few first-time offenders ever went to jail. On the other hand, if McNamee had sold or even given away anabolic steroids to Clemens, rather than Clemens obtaining them, McNamee could have been handed a seven-year jail term if convicted.[24] In addition, on top of a prison sentence, a fine of a quarter of a million dollars could have been levied on McNamee.

According to McNamee, Clemens first asked to be injected with the anabolic steroid Winstrol in 1998 while in Toronto, Ontario, Canada. Clemens had signed with the Blue Jays the year before for the highest pitcher salary in Major League history, more than $8 million USD. The Blue Jays that he joined were four years removed from Joe Carter's dramatic, ninth-inning, seventh-game home run against the Philadelphia Phillies that brought Canada its first-ever baseball championship. The 1997 Blue Jays finished 76–86, last in the AL East, when Clemens' 21 wins in 34 starts accounted for 27.6 percent of the team's win total. They finished last in the American League in batting, .244, last in hits, 12th out of 14 teams in home runs, and last in the Major Leagues in runs. The hero of the 1993 World Series, Joe Carter, batted .234 though he did drive in 102 runs. First baseman Carlos Delgado, in his prime, hit .262 with 30 home runs. Catcher Charlie O'Brien, who would testify in defense of Clemens at the 2012 trial, hit .218. Thirty-six-year-old Juan Samuel hit .284 in 45 games and Shawn Green batted .287 with 16 home runs.[25] Essentially Clemens was a one-man staff with his 21–7 record, 2.05 earned run average and 292 strikeouts. As mentioned previously, Clemens's 1998 pitching statistics were basically identical to his 1997 pitching statistics, 20 wins, 6 losses, 2.65 ERA, and 271 strikeouts. What was different was the Blue Jays' batting average, which improved from dead last in 1997 to ninth out of 14 teams in 1998, although the team did strike out the most in the American League, 1,132 times. The Blue Jays finished second in home runs with 221. Free agent slugger Jose Canseco belted 46 home runs with a modest .237 average. Mike Stanley batted .240 and added 22 homers. Carlos Delgado had an outstanding year, 38 home runs, a team-high 115 RBI, and a .292 average. Thirty-six-year-old Tony Fernandez hit .321. Darrin Fletcher, a 31-year-old catcher, hit .283, and would also testify on Clemens's behalf in the 2012 trial. Shawn Green, in the prime of his career, batted .278 with 35 home runs. On the mound, Clemens got help from veteran Pat Hentgen, who was a workman-like 12–11, despite 5.17 ERA, as was Woody Williams, 10–9, 4.46 ERA with 151 strikeouts. Twenty-three-year-old Chris Carpenter, on the cusp of a long and successful career, mostly with other teams, was 12–7, with a 4.37 ERA and 136 strikeouts. And 21-year-old Roy Halladay, soon to become the Blue Jays' ace for years, was a promising 1–0, with a 1.93 ERA, and 13 strikeouts in 14 innings. And unlike 1997, the Blue Jays' bullpen made a major contribution when 35-year-old Randy Myers saved 28 games.[26]

Possession of anabolic steroids was not even a punishable crime in Canada. While importation into Canada of anabolic steroids could have led to an 18-month prison sentence, mere possession had no penalty. Canada was not a culture where politicians frothed at the mouth to punish those who used illegal drugs. Anabolic steroids were obtained by prescription, and sellers were licensed by the government.[27]

McNamee said he injected Clemens four times during the 1998 season with the Winstrol.[28] Clemens supplied the Winstrol. McNamee, apparently, was merely the passive injector, the steroids equivalent to the passive observer of the art world, Andy Warhol, doing as Clemens asked.

For Toronto in 1998, Clemens was nearly as masterful as he had been the year before, also with the Blue Jays. He won the Cy Young Award both years (courtesy National Baseball Hall of Fame Library, Cooperstown, New York).

Castor returned to the issue of how Clemens allegedly paid McNamee for the illegal, performance enhancing drugs.

"And then how much were you paying Kirk [Radomski] per transaction?"[29]
"The growth, the growth he had to pay for."
"No, no, just 2001."

"Gee, I have no idea."

"To the best of your recollection. I'm not asking you to—"

"It was a one-time shot: I think it was probably just—I don't think he [Kirk Radomski] charged me for the ampules because he thought they were for me. And he either charged me $800 or $1,600 for the kits."[30]

"The kits, that's in reference to growth hormone?"

"Oh yeah, I'm sorry."

"I would like to if we can just keep this discussion about 2001."

"All right. I don't think Roger paid. I don't think Roger—he didn't pay. I didn't have to pay for those, the ones that I got for Roger from Kirk. Kirk would give me like a bag of stuff or I would ask him, what's good for pitchers? And he'd just—Kirk made a reference to, like, 'hey you take care of me; we do favors for each other.'"

"What do you mean by that? Did he mean, get me other clients?"

"Probably, maybe. No, the vitamins, it was all the vitamins. And I used to give him like hundreds of dollars' worth of free vitamins. And did I get him clients? No. I would refer people to call him if I didn't want to deal with something or whatever. But he would call me to ask about training some guys, some other players, stuff like that."

"So he was getting vitamins from you?"[31]

"Yeah."

"From the Invite Health outfit?"

"Yes."

"And you were trading essentially, you were giving him the Invite Health vitamins and he was giving you anabolic steroids?"

"Yeah, but I—I got those as comp to me because I worked for the company so it wasn't costing me anything. I don't know what he was doing with them, I don't know. I didn't ask not to pay for the steroids. It wasn't very long. It was just 2000, 2001, you know. That I'm just fuzzy a little bit on."

"Fair enough. Stepping outside of 2001, looking at the total universe of anabolic-steroid use by Mr. Clemens, did he ever pay or give you money, something of value for steroids?"

"Not directly."

"Okay. Would he do it indirectly?"

"It was never like, here you go and then he would be like whip it out. He would just—I was always ahead of him. You know, he would give me some money, extra cash outside my salary. So I believe there than kits, I mean, you're only talking about $100 worth of stuff. I wasn't going to hit him up—if I needed money, I never went to him anyway. I went to one of his agent people."

"Miss Shahi?"

"Yes. And you know, if you're five grand short or something like that, she would wire the money. So I started getting the money wired into my account, my business account."

"Were there any transactions where he paid cash specifically for anabolic steroids?"

"No, that's what I was trying to articulate. No not really, but probably, probably giving me some extra money but not related to that."[32]

By positioning himself as the passive injector, McNamee accomplished two objectives in my view. First, by claiming that he only did what Clemens wanted, and by further claiming that Clemens was the supplier of at least the steroids, he guaranteed himself that he would avoid the intimidating quarter-million-dollar fine, which probably scared him more than the five to seven years of federal jail time for distribution of illegal drugs. As a first-time offender, McNamee likely realized that he probably would not face any jail time either. And as mentioned previously, taking or possessing anabolic steroids and human growth hormone in Toronto—as opposed to selling them—was not even illegal. Second, by claiming Clemens was his own supplier, McNamee cleverly reduced the number of questions he could be asked, particularly concerning the source of the drugs.

Yet only McNamee knew that there was no paper trail linking Clemens to the consumption of anabolic steroids, and only McNamee knew there was no traceable evidence of a source for the purported human growth hormone and anabolic steroids. The role of passive injector, therefore, in my opinion, helped McNamee cover up the fact that there was no supplier of steroids and human growth hormone for Roger Clemens. And the only way that Brian McNamee could be certain that no such paper trail or supplier source existed, in my view, was that he knew he never injected Roger Clemens with performance enhancing drugs in the first place.

4

Keeping Up Appearances with George Mitchell

George Mitchell did not have to highlight the role of Roger Clemens in his report when he sat down at the Plaza Hotel in New York City to address the sports media on December 13, 2007. Some of the names in the report, including Clemens, which Mitchell kept so close to his vest that he did not even inform Players' Association President Donald Fehr of its contents, had been leaked to the press the previous day. While Clemens' alleged use of performance enhancing drugs was not emphasized over that of other players in the report, Mitchell had not become the Majority Leader of the United States Senate by being naïve about what player's name would set off a bombshell and garner widespread public attention; in essence, it would sell his report to the press, baseball fans, the general public, and Congress.

As Mitchell began his remarks, a frustrated Jose Canseco tried desperately to gain entrance to the Plaza's ballroom in order to watch the press conference. But Mitchell had banned him from the gathering. Despite the fact that Canseco's book, *Juiced*, which had been read by Congressman Henry Waxman's aide Phil Barnett and had prompted not only Congressional hearings in 2005 to investigate the use of performance enhancing drugs in major league baseball, but also Mitchell's 2006 investigation, former Senator Mitchell chose to snub Canseco and instead to act like the social-climbing snob Hyacinth Bucket in the BBC television show "Keeping Up Appearances," treating Canseco as if he were the slovenly, dead-beat brother-in-law, Onslow. If Mitchell viewed Canseco as a kind of Onslow, he could be excused for his perception. Canseco had somehow blown through more than $45 million, lost his home, managed to lose a $785,344 judgment after a Miami bar fight, and filed for bankruptcy.[1] Indeed, it might have been apt if Mitchell had viewed Canseco as the down-and-out boxer portrayed by Anthony Quinn in the 1962 movie "Requiem for a Heavyweight." The former baseball star had been reduced to making attempts at wrestling and boxing, and writing books confessing to anabolic steroid use and accusing other players of taking anabolic steroids.

Yet why did Mitchell ban Canseco from the presentation? After all, they took the same position that steroids in major league baseball was pervasive. Canseco confessed to his own steroid use, outed some players, and accused others in writing without any actual knowledge of their steroid use—Mitchell doing the same in a report compiled by him and his team of lawyers at the New York law firm of DLA Piper. Indeed, the entire premise of Mitchell's work, involving a considerable number of billable hours, estimated to have added to up to approximately $20 million,[2] and rationale for his report, was based on the purported widespread use of performance enhancing drugs in Major League baseball. Canseco had alleged that almost all of the players, 85 percent, used the drugs.[3] Canseco had accused all but the Pope in Rome of taking anabolic steroids, but he did *not* accuse Roger Clemens. Actually, as Nick Cafardo observed in the *Boston Globe*, Canseco turned out to be "right on the money" in his guesses about who did and did not take anabolic steroids.[4] Furthermore, Canseco, according to Mitchell, had supplied the most damaging evidence against Clemens, third-party testimony that he and Clemens had discussed steroids in 1998 when they had played together in Toronto. That was the same year that strength-and-conditioning coach Brian McNamee said not only that he had injected Clemens with the illegal drugs, but also that Canseco had interacted with them in the team locker room as they passed steroids back and forth.[5] The purported Canseco testimony was far more damaging than Andy Pettitte's vague recollection that Clemens confessed to taking HGH, particularly because Pettitte could never recall the context or any details, and although McNamee said he was only five feet away he admitted he heard nothing of what each said.[6] Canseco should have been Mitchell's star witness and the star witness for the government at the 2012 trial. He was not.

Perhaps Mitchell, like Hyacinth, feared that Canseco, in the manner of Onslow, would simply do something embarrassing, such as show up only in an undershirt with a can of beer in his hand, or shout something outrageous at him or the reporters. No, George Mitchell must have had a far more serious reason for banning Canseco. Maybe he feared Canseco would contradict him and thereby undermine his report. Despite assurances by Mitchell that Canseco had discussed with his investigators the specifics of steroid use and dosing regimes, including the practice of "stacking" of different types, and indeed, had declared so in his written report,[7] Canseco denied it. Worse for Mitchell, Canseco denied the most important claims by McNamee, that the three of them passed anabolic steroids back and forth in the Toronto Blue Jays' locker room, thus triggering Roger Clemens' steroid and HGH use. Canseco made his denials in a sworn affidavit.[8]

The FBI questioned Canseco many times in the years between the release of the Mitchell Report in 2007 and Clemens' second trial in 2012,[9] but were unsuccessful in getting him to agree with Brian McNamee's claims. Hence, federal prosecutors never subpoenaed Canseco to testify at Clemens' trial because Canseco told the federal grand jury investigating Clemens in 2010 that none of it was true. Canseco, in fact, was so outraged by McNamee's contentions that he replied emotionally at the time of his grand jury testimony, "He is a liar and I challenge him to polygraph with me. Roger Clemens was not there. For McNamee to say that, he is a liar and I despise liars."[10]

The substance of the Mitchell Report consisted of only 92 pages of more than 409, and perhaps as much of a third of even that space were occupied by huge blowups of checks and mail receipts from offending players.[11] The Report was filled mostly with rumor and innuendo, not with facts—and what facts existed in the form of cancelled checks and mail receipts were supplied to Mitchell from two sources: The raid on Balco's San Francisco laboratory, the fruits of which implicated Barry Bonds and Jason Giambi in the use of performance enhancing drugs; and the results of Jeff Novitzky's federal investigation of former New York Mets clubhouse attendant and distributor of performance enhancing drugs, Kirk Radomski. Novitzky investigated on behalf of the Food and Drug Administration. At the time of his testimony at Clemens' trial he worked for the Drug Enforcement Agency (DEA). Little of the meat of the report stemmed from the multi-million-dollar investigation conducted by Mitchell and his New York law firm, DLA Piper. By emphasizing the number of footnotes and alleged number of times certain people had been interviewed, Mitchell was able to veil, almost like a magic trick, the fact that his 18-month-long investigation turned up little. In fact, Mitchell and his team talked to only two active Major Leaguers, Jason Giambi and Frank Thomas. And Giambi was forced by Commissioner Bud Selig to meet with Mitchell. Among all active Major Leaguers, only Frank Thomas voluntarily talked to Mitchell. Again, in that time honored tradition of baseball playing by its own rules, Thomas was rewarded for this cooperation by being elected to the Baseball Hall of Fame in 2015, however qualified Thomas was with 521 home runs and a .301 lifetime batting average. Mitchell's effective use of the old lawyer's trick of burying his case in dates led the general reader, naturally, to be beguiled into thinking that, if there were a lot of dates, particularly years, important events must have occurred on those dates and during those cited years.

Despite Mitchell's statement that he did not include three players in his report to whom Kirk Radomski said he sold performance enhancing drugs,[12] Mitchell's handling of the Report was basically like that of a bed and breakfast proprietor who runs out of fried chicken and mashed potatoes and thereafter loads up his buffet with iceberg lettuce and day-old bread. Mitchell surely understood his Report lacked substance, for he made a last-minute desperate attempt, in the early autumn of 2007, to get more information from active players. Using the Players' Association as intermediary in the form of a letter signed by union officials Donald Fehr and Michael Weiner, Mitchell begged for more player input.[13] Mitchell acknowledged that cooperating players could still be disciplined by Major League baseball, although they could appeal through the grievance procedure. And they could still be prosecuted for crimes committed.

Having thrust out the stick, Mitchell offered the carrot: "Senator Mitchell ... will honor any player request for confidentiality, in his report." Yet the carrot was qualified by the condition that while the player's name would be kept confidential regarding the Mitchell Report, the information would not. Rather, that information could be disclosed to federal or state prosecutors, to a Congressional committee, or could even be turned over in a private lawsuit. Such conditions would have been both impossible to accept and confusing for a player to understand.

Mitchell fended off criticism of his conflict-of-interest jobs, such as serving as a consultant to the Red Sox and working on the Board of Directors of the Florida Marlins, by saying he owned no stock in the teams, as if the average fan cared if he were paid in stock instead of good, old-fashioned American dollar bills.[14] He even extolled his own greatness as the broker of the Irish Good Friday peace accords under President Clinton.[15]

Mitchell was quick to say that since 1971, Major League Baseball's drug policy prohibited use of any prescription medicine without a valid prescription.[16] Yet, at this point in his introduction, Mitchell did not admit that some players did, in fact, have prescriptions from doctors for performance enhancing drugs; human growth hormone, for example. Anyone reading the Report had to hunt through literally hundreds of pages to discover this fact. For example, that pitcher Paul Byrd had been prescribed HGH for the treatment of a tumor on his pituitary gland was not revealed until page 293.[17] In the case of Rick Ankiel, who bought HGH with a doctor's prescription to speed his recovery from ligament surgery, the reader did not have to hunt quite as far. That fact was reported on page 290.[18] You had to travel to page 54 of the Report to discover that HGH was not banned by the 2002 Collective Bargaining Agreement because HGH was not a controlled substance under federal criminal law.[19]

Continuing to swat at proverbial windmills like Don Quixote, to simultaneously fight off imaginary and contradictory charges of unfairness and lack of action by his client, Major League Baseball, lest somebody claim performance enhancing drugs were good for you or a constitutional right, or that baseball had had NO POLICY, Mitchell said that no player was disciplined for steroids use before it was prohibited by collective bargaining in 2002.[20] Refuting an unidentified claim, Mitchell then declared that it was incorrect to state that "baseball's drug policy was not binding on players before it was added to the collective bargaining agreement. Many players were suspended for drug offenses before 2002." But then, a startling admission that "none of those suspensions related to the use of steroids or other performance enhancing substances." In other words, performance enhancing drugs were illegal in major league baseball, one way or the other, since 1971, and there was insufficient evidence to suspend one single player for taking anabolic steroids and HGH since 1971, casting further doubt on the thesis that there ever was a "steroids era."

The brutal truth on that cold December morning was that George Mitchell no longer possessed the sterling reputation of his Senate days, of the Clinton years when he was on the short list to be appointed to the United States Supreme Court, or of the time when his diplomatic genius was said to have brokered an impossible peace in Ireland. In fact, Mitchell's role in the Irish peace process had been as grossly over-inflated by the American press as Ronald Reagan's role in imploding the Soviet Empire. British Prime Minister John Major had brought Mitchell into early negotiations in Northern Ireland and achieved a brief ceasefire.[21] Mitchell chaired talks between the various Catholic and Protestant political parties and drew up principles of non-violence that set a broad framework for negotiations to come.[22] Yet, by the time Tony Blair and his New Labour Party swept Major and his Tory Party from office in May 1997, Mitchell felt that the peace talks could no longer bring a settlement.[23] It would take new Prime Minister Tony Blair, with hands-on intervention from President Bill Clinton—not George Mitchell—to broker a successful deal. And it would take another difficult decade of Blair's time in office to implement the process of the actual peace and a new government for Northern Ireland. Far more damaging for his reputation, in 2005, a year before Mitchell was hired by Commissioner Bud Selig to investigate performance enhancing drugs in the sport, and therefore get Congress off Selig's back, Pulitzer Prize-winning journalist James B. Stewart published an expose of the Walt Disney Company. In his book, Stewart described Mitchell's role as one of passive acquiescence when, as Chairman of Disney's Board of Directors, Mitchell stood by as CEO Michael Eisner engaged in a dictatorial attempt to retain power.[24] By 2013 Mitchell had, more or less, evolved into a PR icon-for-hire, a kind of Good Housekeeping Seal of Approval, monitoring Penn State's implementation of safeguards to make the stink of its pedophile scandal dissipate.

When it came to public relations and politics to sell his Report, however, Mitchell proved to be a master. First, calling his private probe "The Mitchell Commission" was a piece of public relations genius because the term gave the false impression that the inquiry was somehow backed by governmental authority. Second, as bland as Mitchell was by movie-star standards, his dull reading of the introduction and summary of his report, sitting at a table, his grave eyes only occasionally peering over his glasses, was highly effective as political theater. Mitchell's placid manner lent the false impression that he was acting in the role of a somber, impartial judge who had just conducted an objective investigation. Nothing could have been further from the truth. He had been paid by a private client, Major League Baseball, to serve as its advocate in order to demonstrate to Congress that baseball had finally "done something" to address the widely held belief that performance enhancing drugs had corrupted the game.

Perhaps because he had spent most of his life working in Congress, Mitchell was far more impressive during the hearings than he had been in cobbling together the Report. He was, understandably, politically brilliant: he played up to the Congresspersons' desires to be portrayed as the saviors of teenagers against the scourge of anabolic steroids. Yet Mitchell refused to make Major League baseball players the scapegoats for this alleged national problem. "This goes far beyond baseball," he declared, "way beyond baseball. Baseball players are not the only persons who are role models for young people. All professional athletes and entertainers are. Political leaders are. It is a broad societal issue that—of which baseball is only a part."[25] Mitchell refused to take the bait from law-and-order conservatives on the House Committee on Oversight and Government Reform to punish the active players by reneging on the amnesty he offered to contributors to his Report. "Let me just say that it is the policy of the United States Government, and has been for many years, not to prosecute individual users of some illegal substances, but to concentrate prosecutorial resources on manufacturers, distributors and dealers. That's the case today."[26]

Mitchell even acknowledged the players' 4th Amendment privacy rights.

Mitchell's Houdini act, or magic act, if you prefer, consisted of convincing the baseball press and public that his report was prospective, that is, his investigation and recommendations would fix baseball's performance enhancing drug problem in the *future*, while admitting in little-recognized parts of the Report that baseball had already lessened its drug problems in the *past*, with the deterrent of the 2003 random tests and the subsequent decline from more than a hundred players testing positive in 2003; to 12 in 2005; to three in 2006 to eight in the year of his report, 2007.[27] Mitchell certainly knew that the 535 persons in the United States who understood such mixed messages would be delighted that the problem was both already solved and would be solved in the future simultaneously, a kind of existential reassurance that came with a heavy dose of flattery for members of Congress in crediting them with addressing the purported epidemic of teenage use of anabolic steroids at the same time by holding hearings in 2005, that prompted Mitchell and Major League Baseball to the solution. It was all rather like a report to Congress and the public about the rubout of a foreign agent who was already dead when the CIA rubbed him out.

Fortunately for Mitchell, Commissioner Bud Selig, the man who paid an estimated $20 million for the Report, was happy with the Commission's work. After all, Representative Henry Waxman had suggested to Selig—none too subtly at the time of the 2005 Congressional hearings on anabolic steroids—that if Major League Baseball could not solve its own steroids problem, somebody else would. By contracting for the Mitchell Report in 2005, Bud Selig was able to survive until 2007 with a generous salary increase of $4 million a year.[28] More hypocritically, Selig wanted to cap player salaries and end arbitration as a means for settling salary disputes.[29] Selig served as baseball commissioner through the 2014 season, and his annual salary eventually grew to an estimated $22 million.[30] Selig stayed on as an adviser to MLB beginning in 2015, with the title of Commissioner Emeritus and an annual pension of $6 million.[31]

Mitchell claimed that "For more than a decade there has been widespread illegal use of anabolic steroids and other performance enhancing substances by players in Major League Baseball."[32] In fact, in a sport with from 750–1,200 players, depending on which 25 of a team's 40-man roster were playing at any one time, that were "active," the proven violators in 2003 were approximately 100. As noted above, that number declined to 12 in the first year of full-blown testing, fell to three in 2006, and consisted of eight violations in 2007, the year of the Mitchell Report.[33] By any fair means, 12 players or eight players or three players did not constitute "widespread use." More sophisticated testing procedures were implemented in 2012, and 1,369 blood tests for HGH showed not one single positive test. In addition, 4,022 tests conducted to find performance enhancing drugs in 2013 produced zero players who tested positive for anabolic steroids use.[34]

"We identify some of the players who were caught up in the desire to gain a competitive advantage through the illegal use of these substances," Mitchell suggested. Yet Mitchell admitted the reasons players took PEDs were varied. No evidence emerged subsequently to suggest that many players took PEDs "to gain a competitive advantage." In fact most of the acquired evidence suggested that Major League players took the illegal drugs in a last-ditch, desperate attempt to heal chronic injuries late in their careers.

"The illegal use of performance enhancing substances poses a serious threat to the integrity of the game," declared Mitchell, again providing no evidence to buttress this melodramatic conclusion. "Widespread use by players of such substances unfairly disadvantages the honest athletes who refuse to use them and raises questions about the validity of baseball records."[35] Assuming that Barry Bonds, Mark McGwire and Sammy Sosa did use anabolic steroids to achieve their home run records, the reality was that they were the leading home run hitters of their time to begin with, and no amount of lamenting by Mitchell could help "honest athletes" without power compete with these three. Likewise, while the thesis of this book is that Roger Clemens did not take performance enhancing drugs and separately that his record bears out no effect in the years he is accused of taking them, he was still the greatest pitcher of his time, and no amount of PEDS that could have theoretically been used by other pitchers would have turned them into Roger Clemens, despite what Mitchell's argument might otherwise suggest.

While press hysteria about the Mitchell Report helped to reinforce the public notion that steroid use could be causally linked in lock-step fashion to improved hitting or to sounder pitching, it was much more complicated than that. The physiological and psychological mechanics of swinging a baseball bat and throwing a little round ball at speeds between 90 and 100 miles-per-hour were not an established science taught at Harvard Medical School. Unlike track and field, where the effect of anabolic steroids have been established, for example, on a runner's speed or a shot putter's strength, the causal link between anabolic steroids use and baseball performance has only been speculated upon and surmised by professors of physics, biology, and other sciences. Tufts University Physics Professor Robert Tobin said, "Physics cannot tell us whether a particular home run was steroid-assisted, or even whether an extraordinary individual performance indicates the use of illicit means."[36] In addition, trying to measure the impact of anabolic steroids on baseball is further limited by the lack of uniform field dimensions and the force of gravity and wind conditions that mitigate the height and distance a batted ball may travel.

Contrary to the belief of many, the side-effects from abusing anabolic steroids are not uniform: they affect the user individually. While some develop signs of abuse such as acne, others do not. There is no general rule. Furthermore, research into the impact of anabolic steroids, synthetic chemical compounds similar in structure to cholesterol, remain limited and hobbled by poor methodology, according to a study by the British Government.[37] Research was also impeded because doctors usually prescribed minimal dosages to patients with legitimate medical needs, such as for men whose bodies could not produce enough testosterone, making it nearly impossible to compare such patients with "gym rats" who may have taken massive steroid doses—and thereafter anecdotally self-reported the side-effects.[38]

True, the outsized home run numbers by three individuals, Mark McGwire, Sammy Sosa, and Barry Bonds, suggested that these men did gain a competitive advantage by taking anabolic steroids. Most importantly, McGwire and Bonds admitted to their use, and Sosa reportedly failed the 2003 random test. Together, this trio collectively holds the top six one-season home run totals. In a similar fashion, Alex Rodriguez's leading home run number, 57, and third-highest number, 52, were achieved with the Texas Rangers when he said he used anabolic steroids, although his second-highest, 54, and fourth-highest, 48, were hit with the Yankees in 2007 and 2005, respectively, when he claimed not to have used steroids.[39] Major League Baseball suspended Rodriguez for the entire 2014 season after it learned that he had lied about his relationship with Miami's Biogenesis Clinic for Aging, where he had purchased testosterone.

Like Manny Ramirez, Rodriguez seemed pathologically incapable of not taking some drug or receive some procedure all the time to improve his body. In December 2011, with the permission of the Yankees, Rodriguez traveled to Germany for plasma therapy, a process in which certain components of his blood were isolated, and the isolate—a platelet-rich plasma—was re-injected into his left shoulder and right knee.[40] Although no further medical updates came from Rodriguez after the 2011 season, his hips seemed to be remarkably rejuvenated in the spring of 2015, after barely being able to turn on them at the end of 2013 season, and he clobbered 33 home runs during the regular season in an outstanding return to the game.[41] Outfielder Melky Cabrera had his best season in San Francisco, hitting .346, after taking testosterone.[42] There may have been other factors that contributed to these extraordinary numbers, but if a baseball fan wanted to conclude that these home run totals were inflated by anabolic steroids and thus were achieved by cheating, that was fair enough. Yet it was not fair to extrapolate from this that anabolic steroid use was widespread throughout Major League Baseball. Nor was it fair to conclude that Roger Clemens used anabolic steroids and HGH, as the Mitchell Report alleges, when the witnesses and purported evidence against him were so unreliable, and when Clemens, from his earliest years, copied the workout routine of his hero, Nolan Ryan, another Texas pitcher who still excelled at the game in his 40s.

Even so, the difficulty in demonstrating a "performance impact" from anabolic steroids, implied by Mitchell and his Report, was illustrated by the case of David Ortiz. Ortiz improved his batting numbers considerably in 2003, the year he failed a random drug test.[43] Yet to put those numbers in perspective, in the years that Ortiz played at least half a season in Minnesota, he hit .277,

.282, .234 and .272, quite close to his career average, as of 2012, of .285.[44] Most importantly, Ortiz was 27 years old when the Twins released him due to chronic injuries and the Red Sox signed him as a free agent; therefore he was entering his prime years as a player. It makes sense that "Big Papi's" power numbers would increase, particularly in hitter-friendly Fenway Park. The lovable Falstaff of Boston baseball, Ortiz finally addressed the PED allegations in a bizarre midnight press conference in the bowels of Yankee Stadium. Ortiz's amusing and elliptical explanation reads as if it were written either by Clemens or Casey Stengel: "I definitely was a bit careless back in those days when I was busy buying supplements and vitamins over-the-counter-legal supplements, legal vitamins over-the-counter—but I never buy steroid or use steroid.... I never thought that buying supplements and vitamins, it was going to hurt anybody's feelings."[45]

Not even the case of Barry Bonds could be totally attributed to "performance impact" from anabolic steroid use: Bonds' perjury trial was pointless and politically inspired—after he had already admitted to taking performance enhancing drugs, even if inadvertently. Witnesses testified they saw Bonds receive injections, but none of them had any earthly idea of what. Only his nine-year mistress, former Playboy model Kimberly Bell, provided compelling testimony as to side-effects of anabolic steroids, namely acne and erectile dysfunction, which she noticed on his body.[46] The other credible testimony against Bonds came from San Francisco Giants clubhouse manager Mike Murphy, who said Bonds needed a larger hat size during the 2002 season.[47] Increased head size was believed to be another side-effect of the abuse of anabolic steroids. Yet the jury probably would not have convicted Bonds of any variation of perjury had his personal trainer not gone to jail after refusing to testify. The jury's compromise verdict of obstruction of justice was overturned on appeal when the U.S. Court of Appeals for the Ninth Circuit held that Bonds' rambling answer before a grand jury in 2003 was not material to the government's investigation into steroids distribution.[48] Bonds, according to government records presented at his perjury trial, did test positive for three anabolic steroids in November 2000: metenolone, nandrolone, and clomiphene. He also tested positive for THG, testosterone, and D-amphetamines.[49] But where did one drug end and another drug begin in helping Bonds to hit more home runs (73 in 2001), take more walks, (232 in 2004), and exhibit a higher batting average (.370 in 2002) than any other year in his career? The .370 batting average in 2002 stood out more because he was only a .298 career hitter, while the 73 home runs in 2001 and 232 walks in 2004 were less dramatic if you consider that Bonds became the all-time home run leader with 762 and the all-time walk leader with 2,558.[50] An analysis of possible impacts of anabolic steroids on

Bonds' late-career performance was further complicated by the reluctance of National League umpires to stop Bonds from crowding home plate. Therefore, if a pitcher's options were limited to placing the ball on a hittable portion of the plate or walking Bonds (his 232 walks in 2004 is the major league record)—which could explain the dramatic increase in all three categories of home runs, batting average, and walks—several questions remain: How much impact was due to anabolic steroids? How much impact was due to amphetamines and other drugs? And how much impact was due to a narrow strike zone?

Worse for fanatical believers in a "steroids era" was the very real possibility that Bonds abused himself with anabolic steroids and a variety of other PEDs, and they still had little impact on his outsized statistics which have been called into question. The reason would be genetics. He was the son of Major League outfielder Bobby Bonds, who hit 332 home runs over 14 seasons.[51] He was the distant cousin of Hall of Fame outfielder Reggie Jackson, who hit 563 home runs.[52] And he was also the nephew of hurdler Rosie Bonds, who finished eighth in the 80 meter hurdles at the 1964 Olympics in Tokyo.[53] Indeed, from his earliest boyhood Barry Bonds was recognized for his superhuman eyesight. His Little League teammates claimed that Bonds could see road signs miles before they could. Bonds' extraordinary eye sight was confirmed by Dr. Bill Harrison, visual specialist for Major League Baseball, who tested the eyesight of players for more than 50 years. He said,

> In testing thousands of Major League hitters, Barry Bonds tested out with the highest vision readings of any baseball player we had ever worked with.... Barry is the only player who had achieved 100 percent in each of those categories and subsequently received a 100 percent in terms of high level binocularity.... I had never seen a baseball players as gifted visually and mentally as this guy.... This guy was really phenomenal because he visually tracked every pitch, saw it deep and squaring the ball every time.... He not only could see pitches deep, but every time he saw the ball early out of the hands of the pitchers.[54]

Ophthalmologists called Bonds' eyesight *stereoscopic vision*, the ability to identify slight changes of speed from the same pitch.[55] In fact, Barry Bonds' questioned numbers were predicted almost from the beginning of his major league career. In 1990, Pirates outfielder R. J. Reynolds said, "Barry's the only individual I've met who can turn it on and off. I think one day he will put up numbers no one can believe."[56]

No baseball player destroyed himself more than Ken Caminiti, who died after years of abusing his body with anabolic steroids, cocaine, and alcohol.[57] The former All-Star third baseman with the Houston Astros and several other teams was quoted by Mitchell as claiming that "at least half" of Major League players used anabolic steroids. Mitchell's lawyering instincts caused him to conclude that particular paragraph of his Report by admitting that the estimates were "all impossible to verify."[58] In between this note of candor, Mitchell cited other off-the-cuff guesses; one by a former light-hitting infielder with the Minnesota Twins, Toronto Blue Jays, and Oakland Athletics, Dave McKay, that 30 percent of players used anabolic steroids; and former Cincinnati Reds pitcher Jack Armstrong, that between 20 and 30 percent of the players in his era, 1988–1994, used steroids. Despite this barroom sort of wisdom, neither McKay nor Armstrong claimed to have seen or even to have known of one single player who used anabolic steroids.

If there really were a "steroids era," the number of stolen bases might have increased dramatically during this period, for running speed was the one factor shown conclusively to be enhanced by anabolic steroids. Yet that was not the case. Stolen base statistics have remained consistent throughout the game's history. There were 3,403 in the Major Leagues in 1911. The highest total of the modern era was 3,587 in 1987. There were 3,421 in 1999 and stolen-base totals remained under three-thousand for most years in the early twenty-first century. The all-time individual stolen base high was 138 by Hugh Nicol in 1887. The highest total of the modern era was 130 by Rickey Henderson in 1982. The highest stolen base totals in the purported "steroids era" belong to Vince Coleman, 77, in 1990, and to Jose Reyes, 78, in 2007.[59]

Likewise, if steroids-injected pitchers were striking out more batters, the number of whiffing batters might have shown up in the records. They didn't. Strikeout totals have gradually increased over time. There were 9,283 strikeouts in Major League Baseball in 1913. The 10,000-a-year barrier was not reached until 1952.[60] In 1969, the sport saw 22,473 strikeouts as it passed the 20,000 a year milestone, 31,898 in 1998 as it passed the 30,000-a-year barrier, and reached 36,710 strikeouts in 2013.

And there were the much talked about home runs. If the use of anabolic steroids were pervasive, as George Mitchell claimed, and there was a connection to baseball performance in the first place, the Major League totals would have been off the charts during the "steroids era," not just the numbers for Barry Bonds, Mark McGwire, and Sammy Sosa. They were not. Home run totals, like strikeout totals, showed graduated increases through the history of the game. In fact home runs *declined* through most of the "steroids era," after peaking at 5,693 in 2000.[61] Major League home run totals did not reach 2000 until 1950, 3,000 until 1969, 4,000 until 1987, and 5,000 until 1998.

The deaths of baseball player Ken Caminiti and football player Lyle Alzado, in addition to the outsized baseball numbers of Barry Bonds, suggested that a combination of drugs, not just anabolic steroids, may be required to provide dramatic increases in athletic performances. Alzado, most associated with the Oakland Raiders, took both anabolic steroids and human growth hormone in large quantities, and continued to do so after his retirement, spending an estimated $30,000 a year on the steroids alone.[62] Caminiti, the National League MVP in 1996 when he played third base for the Houston Astros, took massive quantities of steroids with large quantities of cocaine and alcohol and died of a "speedball," a combination of cocaine and heroin.

The intricacies of the "cause and effect" of anabolic-steroid use did not stop thousands of internet users—yet to meet their older selves—from drawing conclusions about Clemens, Barry Bonds and Mark McGwire by comparing "before" photographs of the ballplayers as skinny 22-year-olds to "after" photos of those same, now more generously proportioned men in their 40s. Clemens' college coach, Cliff Gustafson, who thought the steroids charges against him were "ridiculous," said, "He was the same pitcher throughout his career; and the same size, he was always a big guy."[63]

Mitchell preserved his legacy, despite the Report's flawed analysis, by calling for amnesty for past offenders who took performance enhancing drugs:

> I urge the Commissioner to forgo imposing on players for past violations of baseball's rules on performance enhancing substances, including the players named in the report, except in those cases where he determines that the conduct is so serious that discipline is necessary to maintain the integrity of the game. I make this recommendation fully aware that there are valid arguments both for and against it; but I believe that those in favor are compelling.[64]
>
> "Spending more months, or even more years, in contentious disciplinary proceedings will keep everyone mired in the past."

Of course, the baseball writers wished nothing so much as to continue such contentious proceedings because they were mired in the past. They just could not get enough drug scandals to write about. The coincidence that the three players the baseball writers hated the most—Clemens, Barry Bonds and Alex Rodriguez—were all accused of taking steroids, blew up the issue beyond all proportion. There was less enthusiasm to pursue the PED allegations against the jolly and portly David Ortiz of the Red Sox. Ortiz usually kept the Boston press at bay with his wide smile that revealed the toothiest grin since Teddy Roosevelt. Clemens would have done well to get PR advice from Ortiz, if not his dentist's phone number. The media did not have the heart to beat up on Ortiz' teammate Manny Ramirez, the free-spirited hitting-machine who looked like a bullfight clown when he struggled with the intricacies of playing left field at Fenway Park. Among Ramirez's eccentricities was casually taking a leak between innings in the ancient toilet hidden in the massive left field wall known as the Green Monster. The writers apparently believed that the more serious the impact of steroids proved on Major League baseball, the more important they were in their jobs. Ironically, having whipped baseball fans—at least obsessed male ones—into a frenzied state, baseball writers were later accused by angry internet users of covering up the use of performance enhancing drugs in baseball.

Perhaps hoping to discourage defamation suits from the players he named in the report, Mitchell said, "While the interest in names is understandable, I hope the media and the public will keep that part of the report in context and will look beyond the individuals to the central conclusions and recommendations of this report."[65] Of course, this purported "hope" was patent nonsense. George Mitchell did not become Majority Leader of the United States Senate because he was politically naïve. In addition, he remained a devoted fan of the Boston Red Sox all his life. He had a pretty good idea of which former Red Sox player would dominate the news once he was named in the report.

5
Evidence? What Evidence?

The 13 players whose histories preceded Roger Clemens' unveiling in the Mitchell Report had two things in common. First, they had all purchased performance enhancing drugs from former New York Mets clubhouse attendant Kirk Radomski. Second, physical evidence of the purchases sat on Mitchell's desk in the form of cancelled checks and billing addresses. The players were: Lenny Dykstra, later to serve prison time for extortion; David Segui, who had taken anabolic steroids the longest and therefore remained the most loyal to Radomski; Larry Bigbie, Brian Roberts, Jack Cust, Tim Laker, Josias Manzanillo, Todd Hundley, Chris Donnells, Mark Carreon, Hal Morris, Matt Franco, and Rondell White.[1] There was, at the time of Mitchell's decision to include him in the Report, no such evidence against Clemens.

The Mitchell Report, in general, was painted with such a broad brush to include not only those players who took steroids, but also those who were only *rumored* to be "juicers." Thus, Mitchell's making a case against Clemens despite lacking physical evidence was hardly unique.

Mitchell described McNamee as "one of Radomski's customers and possible sub-distributors."[2] He noted that as part of his written agreement with the U.S. Attorney's Office for the Northern District of California, McNamee "agreed to three interviews by me and my staff, one in person and two by telephone. McNamee's personal lawyer participated in the interviews. Also participating were federal prosecutors and agents from the FBI and Internal Revenue Service."[3]

In his Report, however, Mitchell did not discuss the extraordinary arrangements he had made with McNamee or the confusing legality of forcing a witness in a federal investigation to participate in a private investigation, for a private client, Major League Baseball. Indeed, in order to ward off a defamation suit by Clemens, McNamee's lawyers insisted that their client was "forced" to cooperate with Mitchell.[4] Mitchell also took, at face value, McNamee's contention that he had trained "Olympic caliber athletes" outside of baseball.[5]

"On or about June 8–10, 1998," the Report claimed, "the Toronto Blue Jays played an away series with the Florida Marlins. McNamee attended a lunch party that Canseco hosted at his house in Miami. McNamee stated that, during this luncheon, he observed Clemens, Canseco, and another person he did not know meeting inside Canseco's house, although McNamee did not personally attend that meeting."[6] Without pause, Mitchell piled on an unrelated allegation that "Canseco told members of my investigative staff that he had numerous conversations with Clemens about the benefits of Deca-Durabolin and Winstrol and how to 'cycle and stack' steroids. Canseco has made similar statements publicly."[7] In short, this portion of Mitchell's report was a little of this and a little of that, more grade school book report than valid investigation.

Mitchell did not acknowledge that McNamee had begged him to keep the purported conversation between Clemens, Canseco, and the mystery man out of his report because he did not see any drug transaction or other illegal activity.[8] The fact that McNamee begged Mitchell to exclude the story leads to the conclusion that it was probably just that, a story. In addition, according to McNamee, the federal agents did most of the talking and questioning in Mitchell's presence. These same agents, according to McNamee, claimed to have separate verification of a drug conversation.[9] No such separate verification showed up, in any manner, shape, or form, at Clemens' 2012 perjury trial.

Jose Canseco never backed up Mitchell's contention that Canseco had told Mitchell's investigators he and Clemens had had detailed discussions about how to stack steroids. Both Canseco and Clemens, in separate statements, characterized their passing comments about steroids in the most general terms. Considering that Canseco had more or less become a spokesman for steroids use, these statements make perfect sense. Without any practical foundation in steroid-dosing regimens, Clemens could have gained little understanding from Canseco's complicated instructions concerning cycling and stacking.

Mitchell repeated McNamee's claim that Clemens asked McNamee to inject steroids into his buttocks and that, later in that summer of 1998, Clemens supposedly asked McNamee to inject him with Winstrol, which Clemens possessed, according to McNamee.[10] Unfortunately, McNamee's claim that Clemens originally obtained his own steroids when Clemens was a novice, and asked McNamee to inject him, was in contradiction to the rest of McNamee's narrative to Congress that the subsequent supply of anabolic steroids and HGH in New York came from Kirk Radomski. McNamee reconciled the contradiction at trial by going back to the first explanation, claiming that Clemens always supplied all the steroids.

Yet, if Clemens had his own Canadian supplier in 1998, and therefore was experienced in receiving the injections, either by his supplier or by injecting himself, why did he need McNamee? McNamee's contention that he knew Clemens asked him to inject him with Winstrol, on the first occasion, because the bottle was so labeled, also seems quite far-fetched. It makes no sense that McNamee could remember exactly what steroids Clemens took the first time, when McNamee claimed to know nothing about performance enhancing drugs. If the latter were true, McNamee would have been unfamiliar with the particular brand-names of steroids at the time of the initial injection. Yet McNamee could not identify the brand of anabolic steroids that he claimed Clemens had used three years later, when McNamee would have been much more familiar with steroids on account of his having injected Clemens and other athletes.

Could it be that this contradiction was not addressed by George Mitchell because McNamee did not tell Mitchell about a dark secret, and Mitchell did not want to know, or failed to ask, the obvious question? Indeed, this writer guessed the dark secret when he first saw a photograph of the strapping Brian McNamee. Yet the question was not asked at McNamee's closed-door deposition with Congressman Waxman's attorneys. Nor was it asked in the melodramatic, televised cross-examination by Waxman's full Committee. Nothing relating to the unspoken question was leaked to reporters—or if it was, the press ignored it because they were looking for dirt on Clemens, not McNamee. The question appeared neither in Waxman's Committee Report nor in the Clemens' referral to the Justice Department to face possible perjury charges. Nor did the question appear in the Republican Minority Report, a report which was hypercritical of the conclusions drawn by the Democratic majority. Nor was it mentioned in Clemens' 2010 grand jury indictment. The answer to the unposed question did not become publicly known until near the end of Roger Clemens' trial in 2012, long after its omission had played a part in ruining the life and reputation of Roger Clemens. The trial evidence and testimony showed that Brian McNamee was not just a dealer in performance enhancing drugs; he was a user and abuser of anabolic steroids. Not only that, he took HGH, too.[11] Further, he kept his personal stash of anabolic steroids and human growth hormone at his residence.[12]

Addressing the steroid user's dubious cause-and-effect claim, Mitchell stated, "According to McNamee, 'from the time that McNamee injected Clemens with Winstrol through the end of the 1998 season, Clemens' performance showed remarkable improvement.'"[13] Mitchell's acceptance of the next purported quote by Clemens had the smell of the aristocratic *Washington Post's* belief in the made-up 1980 drug story by reporter Janet Cooke.[14] "During this period of improved performance, Clemens told McNamee that the steroids had a pretty good effect on him."[15] Mitchell apparently did not notice that Clemens' 1998 season, in which McNamee claimed he first took performance enhancing drugs, was almost identical in performance as the prior year, 1997, before Clemens ever laid eyes on Brian McNamee.

McNamee claimed that his injection of steroids into Clemens was responsible for the star pitcher's elevated performance after June 1998, in which Clemens went 11–0 with an ERA of 1.68 after starting slowly at 9–6 with an ERA of 3.91. First, baseball is a game of streaks, and we are interested in how a player finishes for the entire season, not cherry-picked ups and downs within the season. Second, Clemens pitching stats were a matter of public information which anyone, including McNamee, could simply look up. It was not the kind of firsthand information that "only the criminal would know," to put it in detective novel language.

Considering that McNamee's credibility was at the heart of Mitchell's case against Roger Clemens in his report, and realizing that offering up a pound of Roger Clemens' flesh would be key to pacifying Congress and to selling his Report to the public, one would think that Mitchell would have been troubled by McNamee's work history—a story of frequent firings under questionable circumstances. Yet the man who laid the groundwork for peace in Ireland seemed to regard McNamee as a kind of Martin McGuiness, the deputy to Gerry Adams, the lionized leader of the Catholic nationalist party, Sinn Fein. Only a year before Mitchell interviewed McNamee, McGuiness had allegedly been outed as a British double agent.[16] Perhaps Mitchell regarded McNamee as a kind of double agent. Unfortunately, the evidence subsequently suggested both that McGuiness was not a British double agent and that McNamee was not a reliable witness. As it turned out, Mitchell's star informant, McNamee, had quit the New York Police Department under circumstances that remained unclear. Other than Clemens and Pettitte, McNamee had trouble keeping clients for his strength-and-conditioning work. Worse, Mitchell was less than complete in his explanation of McNamee's hiring and firing by the New York Yankees. Mitchell said the Yankees hired McNamee as an assistant strength-and-conditioning coach, mainly because Clemens urged them to do so. That much was true, confirmed at trial by Yankees general manager Brian Cashman. If Mitchell had talked to Cashman for his report, he might have hesitated in placing so much confidence in McNamee's credibility because, like most of the nominal prosecution witnesses against Clemens, Cashman thoroughly disparaged both McNamee's work habits and reputation.[17] Furthermore, McNamee had forged his wife's signature on a loan application. McNamee had also placed on-line orders for hydrocodone, a powerful opioid, for himself and his wife, illegally using her name.[18]

August 2001 was the final instance when Roger Clemens asked McNamee to inject him with steroids, Mitchell said. Mitchell failed to mention that Clemens and McNamee trained together, on and off, for another six years.

> McNamee stated that Clemens did not tell him why he stopped asking him to administer performance enhancing substances, and McNamee has no knowledge about whether Clemens used performance enhancing substances after 2001.[19]
>
> McNamee assumed that Clemens used performance enhancing substances during the second half of the season so that he would not tire, but they did not discuss this directly. It was Clemens who made the decision when he would use anabolic steroids or human growth hormone.[20]

Mitchell was apparently unperturbed by an account that painted the McNamee-Clemens relationship not as a friendship, or any other kind of human relationship for that matter, but rather as a circus lion tamer, only in McNamee's account it is the lion who growls the instructions.

Nevertheless, Mitchell did concede, first directly—"Clemens never gave money to McNamee specifically to buy performance enhancing substances"[21]—and then indirectly, the lack of a paper trail that would otherwise implicate Roger Clemens in the use of performance enhancing drugs.[22] "Radomski produced four checks from McNamee that were deposited into Radomski's checking account and drawn on McNamee's checking account. All the checks were dated in 2003 and 2004, several years after McNamee said he supplied Clemens, Pettitte, and Knoblauch. McNamee said these purchases were for non-baseball clients."[23]

Since Pettitte paid McNamee for the HGH injections and travel expenses in one lump sum, that made Roger Clemens the odd-man out.[24] Furthermore, there was no connection between the 2003 and 2004 checks and Clemens. That meant, of course, that all the money McNamee was paid for injecting baseball players was accounted for, and none of it came from Clemens.

It would seem from a distance of more than nine years since the Mitchell Report that the prevalence of steroid abuse in Major League Baseball was overstated by Congress, the press, and Major League Baseball itself. As Derek Jeter suggested, "The thing that I was most frustrated with is people making this blanket statement that it was the steroid-era and everybody was doing it.... That's not true."[25] Legendary coach Cliff Gustafson, who directed Clemens' early development as a pitcher at the University of Texas, agreed that the steroids hullabaloo was overblown.[26] Yet the sports press, in a hysterical frenzy, continued its hunt for a steroids epidemic in the ranks of Major League Baseball.

The percentage of players failing baseball's random drug test, mostly minor leaguers, remained roughly the same before and after the release of the Mitchell Report in 2007. In 2005, for example, 87 minor leaguers failed random tests for performance enhancing drugs. Five years later, in 2010, the number was 86.[27] That number climbed to 105 in 2012. The Major League numbers were 12 failed tests in 2005, three failed tests in 2006, eight in 2007, one in 2008 (the year after the release of the Mitchell Report), four in 2009 (including Manny Ramirez), two in 2010, two in 2011, and five in 2012.[28] The 2012 numbers were subsequently updated to reflect 18 player-disciplines (including four for testosterone).[29] In 2013, 14 players were suspended for apparently buying various banned substances from Miami's Biogenesis Aging Clinic, although only half of them were established Major Leaguers. Unrelated to the Biogenesis scandal, one player, Miguel Tejada, tested positive for amphetamines, although he apparently had a lapsed prescription for the drug.[30]

Most important, by 2013 the positive tests reflected *none* for steroids. The results for 5,391 tests, including the off-season period of 2012–2013, showed eight positive tests for stimulants—seven for Adderall, one for methylhexanamine—and *none* for steroids. Major League Baseball allowed 122 therapeutic-use exemptions, 119 for attention-deficit disorder and four for hypogonadism.[31] In 2014, as well, there were *no* suspensions for anabolic steroids.[32] Baltimore Orioles first baseman Chris Davis and San Diego Padres first baseman Cameron Maybin were suspended 25 games each for testing positive for an amphetamine.[33]

The fact that the numbers of Major Leaguers who failed a drug test declined from 103 in 2003[34] to 12 in 2005 and no anabolic steroids in 2013 clearly showed that the Collective Bargaining Agreement negotiated between Major League Baseball and the Players Association succeeded as a deterrent to PED use. This Agreement, and not anything Mitchell and his publicity circus achieved, accounted for the decline in use of PEDs among Major Leaguers. Several players who failed the 2003 random test proved to be repeat offenders and therefore exhibited their own, chronic, particular personal problems. The list included Manny Ramirez, Mike Cameron, Jose Guillen, Ryan Franklin, Rafael Palmeiro, Alex Rodriguez, and Guillermo Mota. By 2016 the list of chronic users included Marlon Byrd, Miguel Tejada, Jenrry Mejía, Neifi Perez and Cody Stanley.[35] The self-confessed steroids king, Jose Canseco, flunked a test for performance enhancing drugs nine years after the 2003 random test, and long past his retirement, causing him to be banned from playing in the Mexican League in 2012.[36] Indeed Mitchell admitted in his report, "I have been warned by a number of former players that some players will use performance enhancing substances no matter what they are told."[37]

By the time Commissioner Bud Selig enlisted George Mitchell in 2006, therefore, the sport had already mitigated its steroids problem. Selig did not need George Mitchell. He just did not know it. The real story of performance enhancing drugs in baseball, therefore, was its use by desperate and marginal minor league prospects, and by some aged and injured veteran players who were mostly retired when Mitchell talked to them, not the corruption of home run records.[38] Since testing began, the positive tests as of June 2016, showed 771 minor leagues and only 80 for major leagues, ten of whom were repeat offenders. The Mitchell Report, therefore, served no purpose as a deterrent to the use of performance enhancing drugs in Major League baseball, or apparently any purpose beyond the purview of Congress or minor league baseball. Its only purpose, unintended of course, was that it provided a means to prosecute Roger Clemens.

Brian McNamee's legal team, in crafting its motion to dismiss Roger Clemens' defamation suit, made the somewhat novel public-policy argument that McNamee's statements to Senator Mitchell should be immune from liability. They argued that statements given under circumstances "where prosecutors arrange and attend a meeting with a witness because those prosecutors decide that inclusion of such third-parties will serve law enforcement purposes, the proper investigation of criminal activity compels protecting that witness's statements from a subsequent defamation lawsuit."[39] The argument suggested that Mitchell's role had little to do with investigating steroid use in Major League Baseball after all, rather, his work consisted mainly of performing as a vigilante—an unarmed, civilian crime-patroller in the war on drugs, sort of like New York's Guardian Angels. The thrust of McNamee's assertion was that Mitchell was acting as a newly deputized sheriff, sworn in for one particular mission: to participate in the prosecution of Roger Clemens.

During a Yankees-Red Sox broadcast on the night of May 14, 2011, Joe Buck, the Fox-TV announcer, suggested that amphetamines have had a far larger impact on baseball than the limited use of steroids. He said, "There's been obviously so much talk about performance enhancing drugs and trying to limit the use of that in this game. But I think taking amphetamines out of this game has taken a big bite out of what some of the older players have taken over the years." His colleague, Tim McCarver, replied, "I think that's a valid point."[40] While players continued to test positive for amphetamines through the 2014 season, baseball had succeeded in practically eliminating amphetamine use from the game. While no verifiable statistics exist to support this contention either, many in the baseball business believe that from the 1950s until the millennium, the majority of Major League Baseball players used amphetamines at some point in their careers, while no more than five percent of players used anabolic steroids or Human Growth Hormone.[41]

A little-discussed portion of the Mitchell Report should have given the former Senator pause to make grand conclusions about the purported widespread use of anabolic steroids. Back in 1990, when there was no hysteria about the alleged use of performance enhancing drugs and therefore a time when players could be more honest about it without foreseeable consequences, Major League Baseball had conducted a confidential survey. The confidential survey "reported that 1.5 percent of the players said they had used anabolic steroids during their lifetime and 0.5 percent said they used steroids in the preceding twelve months."[42] In 2015 and 2016 there was a dramatic increase in positive tests for anabolic steroids, 5 and 8. Yet the 8 failures in 2016 included repeat offender Jenrry Mejía (Mets), now banned for life. Marlon Byrd (Indians) was a repeat offender for HGH in 2016. Cody Stanley of the Cardinals tested positive for the second time in 2015 for testosterone. MLB suspension statistics for 2015 showed 5 for steroids, 4 for substance abuse (not identified but most likely cocaine or marijuana), 2 for HGH and 1 for diuretics. In 2016 the numbers were 8 for steroids, 4 for drug abuse, 4 for HGH, 3 for domestic abuse, 2 for testosterone, and 2 for diuretics.[43]

In a country where most people seemed to be taking drugs of one sort or another, legal or otherwise, one might ask: what was the big deal about whether a baseball player took performance enhancing drugs? Indeed the Clemens saga revealed a huge gender gap and cultural divide. Women wondered more about the positive impact of HGH in making them look younger and the benefits of steroids in healing serious medical illnesses than the negative health consequences to professional athletes who used mega-dosages. John F. Kennedy, for example, probably could not have lived long enough to become elected president had he not received steroid injections to battle various illnesses, including Addison's disease.[44] Clemens' wife, Debbie, testified at trial about receiving injections of human growth hormone: "I was totally comfortable. I didn't know there was anything bad about it."[45] She also testified, "It's not like doing heroin or something crazy. I am not ashamed of taking that shot. I am embarrassed that it went across the world incorrectly. I didn't think it was a bad thing, and I still don't."[46] Women tended either to view the case as much ado about nothing or to sense the government's case against Clemens was weak. The effect of gender was significant because the jury in Clemens' first trial was comprised of ten women and only two men.

Baseball, however, was a sport and a business of course, integrated to the American ethos of fairness and honesty. This American belief was as enshrined as in the legends of George Washington not telling a lie and Abraham Lincoln walking back miles to return a penny to a country store. That ethos was written into the commerce clause of the United States Constitution, encouraging fair trade among the states. It was written into the federal Securities Acts of the early 1930s as well as Sarbanes-Oxley in 2002—laws that demanded transparency of the finances of public corporations and of their corporate officers.

In baseball, put simply, *you did not cheat*. And taking anabolic steroids was not just cheating in the manner of a pitcher throwing a ball with spit on it or cut with a file, banned by the rules; their use and distribution was also a *crime*. Furthermore, the numerical accomplishments of baseball players mattered and were part-and-parcel of the game's appeal as a shared national experience among generations. Few football fans could name the number of touchdown passes of the leading professional quarterback or the exact number of yards of the greatest running backs. But every American child who knew baseball knew the magical number 714, Babe Ruth's home run total, and 56, Joe DiMaggio's consecutive-game hitting streak. Roger Maris's single-season homer total that stood for a generation, 61. Ruth's homer total that stood for almost two generations, 60. Baseball also had been haunted for a century by the allegation that the 1919 Chicago Black Sox including their greatest hitter, Shoeless Joe Jackson, were bought off by gamblers to throw the World Series to the Cincinnati Reds.[47] In truth, a wholesome image was integral to baseball's marketing strategy since the sports' earliest days, and it was as important to baseball to forbid cheating as an ethical concern—although, oddly enough, an overabundance of foul language, unfit for children, still permeated many ballparks in the 21st century. Major League franchises limited alcohol consumption,[48] installed extensive ballpark security, upgraded food menus from the traditional hotdogs and peanuts to offer gourmet food and even to include fancy restaurants, created family sections, and committed themselves to anti-discrimination policies regarding all minorities.

Cheating, however, cut both ways. Governments, and companies, particularly companies with a quasi-government relationship such as Major League Baseball, were not supposed to cheat the Constitutional rights of American citizens and employees, whether that cheating involved collusion or random drug testing.[49] Nor cheat baseball players from other countries, who enjoyed, as nonresident workers for a specified time, the same Constitutional protection as players who were citizens of the United States. Did federal prosecutors and agents cheat in their zeal to prove Barry Bonds and later Roger Clemens were guilty of taking performance enhancing drugs? Did George Mitchell cheat when he essentially sold his report based on the fame of Roger Clemens when he had no physical evidence against Clemens? Did Congressman Henry Waxman and his fellow Democrats cheat in their one-sided depositions and Congressional Hearing of Clemens, a Republican and a social friend of President George W. Bush? Did the sports media cheat in their subjective rush to judgment against Roger Clemens? Federal prosecutors were not expected to cheat in their trial tactics by trying to sneak into a trial inadmissible hearsay to blow up a jury, as they may have done in the first Clemens trial. Federal prosecutors were not supposed to cheat by trying to get on the record testimony that the judge had ruled inadmissible on other grounds, such as the fact that Brian

McNamee had injected Andy Pettitte with HGH, something that both the prosecutors and Brian McNamee did continually despite admonishments from Judge Walton. Clemens' attorney, Michael Attanasio, could only exclaim, "Mr. McNamee is practically part of their team, what he's doing is shameful. Certainly ask that it stop and stop right now.... The witness is intentionally dragging Pettitte's name into this. McNamee has now connected Pettitte to HGH four times."[50]

The Mitchell Report, and Mitchell's appearance before Congress to claim its success, typified the way problems were examined in the United States. Rather than investigating the demands of the game that might lead some to cheat by using performance enhancing drugs, the issue was held up to melodramatic light where it would either die or become a sensational television series about drugs. Major League Baseball successfully banned users from the game as they failed drug tests, but Congress had no stomach for addressing the purported impact of the use of PEDS by teenagers. Of course, given the impact of the cash machine known as television contracts, there was no interest in investigating the increase in injuries to baseball players at all positions. In addition, television demanded a longer playoff format, putting a premium on near-perfect pitching and inflicting excessive strain on human arms—body parts that God likely did not design to throw round objects at 95 miles-per-hour for an extended month each year just to meet the scheduling requirements of television networks and the ever-growing appetite of Major League Baseball to compete with the National Football League as an international marketing machine. What was the matter with a starter who finished losing games when the score ended 11–3 instead of emptying a team's bullpen to achieve a 7–2 loss? Those old days of the nineteenth and twentieth centuries, before endless set-up men, were truly a kinder and gentler time on the arm, if not baseball in general. Most importantly, are games that are "shortened" by endless relief pitchers really good for the aesthetic pleasure of enjoying a baseball game?

Buried at the end of his report, Mitchell admitted that there was a limit to the deterrent of education and random drug testing. "I have been warned by a number of former players that some players will use performance substances no matter what they are told."[51] That was apparently where MLB found itself by 2016: some players, aware that the tests were coming, aware of the risks, which included a lifetime ban, took PEDs anyway.

The uptick in PED violations in 2015 and 2016 suggested that professional baseball in the United States, like college football and professional football, was in for a protracted, if restricted drug problem. It just may be that the deterrent to performance enhancing drug use, of random testing, had reached its limit in effectiveness. The age old problem with all criminal deterrents was that they were most effective against people who have little proclivity for committing the crime in the first place. The vast majority of positive tests for performance enhancing drugs in professional baseball came from poor, non-citizens of the United States. They played mostly in the minor leagues, not Major League Baseball, and minor league players tested positive for these drugs at nearly ten times the rate of major leaguers. Most were struggling, often marginal prospects. Among players testing positive for PEDs in the majors, they continued to break down as desperate players trying to recover from injuries, who mostly took HGH, and players who seemed pathologically incapable of quitting PEDs even though they were clearly aware the tests were coming. Furthermore, with little fear of criminal prosecution, particularly for the non-citizens in the minor leagues, and thus little fear of immediate deportation, cheating on drug tests probably seemed worth the risk. And to a new generation of athletes, who did not face the draconian drug sentences of the 1960s, being punished for taking PEDs may seem like an unfair punishment for stealing a loaf of bread.

6

Roger Clemens' Last Brawl with the Baseball Writers

Only 13,414 Red Sox fans showed up to Fenway Park on the freezing cold night of April 29, 1986. The city's sports fans were focused on their dynastic basketball team, the Celtics, who were playing the Atlanta Hawks that night in the second round of the NBA playoffs. Only one photographer, Red Sox team photographer Jerry Buckley, was on hand to record the game for posterity. It was the 18th game of the season and Clemens was already 3–0, but it was only his fourth start since major reconstructive surgery on his throwing shoulder the previous August. A strong wind blew in from Boston Harbor, and damage could be done to a pitcher's arm on a night like that. Clemens opened the game by striking out his University of Texas shortstop, Spike Owen. Then he struck out Seattle Mariners left fielder Phil Bradley. And then he struck out first baseman Ken Phelps. Gorman Thomas, a key player for the Milwaukee Brewers team that played in the 1982 World Series, led off the top of the second by lining out to left field. Clemens struck out third baseman Jim Presley and right fielder Ivan Calderon. Six batters, five strikeouts. Danny Tartabull, son of former outfielder Jose Tartabull, who played on the 1967 Red Sox World Series team which lost to the St. Louis Cardinals in seven games, and who became a construction worker after baseball, grounded out to second base. Clemens struck out center fielder Dave Henderson and induced a fly out to center by catcher Steve Yeager, once a Dodgers star.

Spike Owen stepped up for the second time in the top of the fourth innings and singled, the first of three Mariners hits that night. Clemens proceeded to strike out Bradley, Phelps, and Thomas. In the top of the fifth, Clemens struck out Presley, Calderon, and Tartabull, all looking. Sixteen batters, 12 strikeouts. Dave Henderson led off the sixth for Seattle. Later in the year, the Mariners would trade Henderson to the Red Sox, where he would hit a Game 5, two-out home run in the top of the ninth inning against the California Angels in the ALCS that staved off elimination and sent the Series back to Fenway Park, where it was won by the Red Sox in seven games. Henderson batted .400 in the World Series against the Mets.[1] But on this April night, Henderson struck out for the second time. Clemens struck out Steve Yeager, and Spike Owen flied out to center field. In the top of the seventh, Clemens struck out Bradley and Phelps but Gorman Thomas broke a scoreless tie with a home run. Clemens had 16 strikeouts but was losing, 1–0. In the bottom of the seventh, old reliable, Red Sox right fielder Dwight Evans, came to the rescue, hitting a three-run homer off Mike Moore to put Clemens and the Sox ahead, 3–1. Ivan Calderon led off the eighth inning and struck out. Danny Tartabull singled, Dave Henderson struck out, and Al Cowens, a mainstay of the Kansas City Royals for six years, flied to center.[2]

It was a baseball superstition, and tradition, not to tell a pitcher that he was on the verge of a record in order not to jinx him. Yet Red Sox starting pitcher Al Nipper believed Clemens was "not the type of guy who would be affected by knowing"[3]; therefore Nipper informed Clemens before he took the mound for the ninth inning that he had 18 strikeouts, one short of the record for a nine-inning game, a record shared by five pitchers. Coincidentally, the first 19-strikeout, nine-inning game was pitched against the Boston Beaneaters, a forerunner of the Red Sox, by Charlie Sweeney of the Providence Grays in 1884. The most recent was by Texas native, and Clemens hero, Nolan Ryan, in 1978. The most strikeouts in a game was actually 21, but that was a 16-inning game in 1962 pitched by Tom Cheney of the Washington Senators. Appropriately for Clemens, he tied the record of 19 by striking out Spike Owen, who had once accused him of stealing sweat pants. Phil Bradley stepped up to the plate and watched a third strike go past him without the bat leaving his shoul-

A young Roger Clemens in Boston's home whites. A highly touted first-round pick in 1983, he pitched well in the minors but struggled to find consistency in his first two major league seasons (courtesy National Baseball Hall of Fame Library, Cooperstown, New York).

der. Now there was only one player in a nine-inning game since the Major Leagues began in 1871 with 20 strikeouts. His name was Roger Clemens. It was that kind of year for Clemens. He went 24–4 with a 2.34 ERA, pitched 18 complete games, seven shutouts, and struck out 256 batters in 281⅔ innings. He pitched the Red Sox into the World Series with the Mets, where he was 0–0 in two starts, with an ERA of 3.18 and 11 strikeouts in 11⅓ innings. He was named both Cy Young Award winner as the best pitcher in the American League and Most Valuable Player for the American League.[4]

That winter introduced a side of Clemens that did not endear him to baseball's writers. Red Sox management had told Clemens during the 1986 season that they would reward him for his outstanding work by giving him a raise from $340,000 to $1 million for the 1987 season. But Commissioner Peter Ueberroth, a lawyer no less, wanted to set an example to limit salary increases. Just as the team began spring training in Winter Haven, Florida, Ueberroth ordered Red Sox General Manager Lou Gorman not to give Clemens the million dollars. The order looked like and smelled like collusion. Roger Clemens thought so and blew his top. Clemens walked out of spring training and flew home to Houston. Call it a temper tantrum. Call it a matter of principle. Ueberroth eventually interceded in the contract dispute, and Clemens and the Red Sox reached an agreement for their ace to make $650,000 for 1987 and $1.5 million in 1988.[5]

The tactics invoked by Clemens were similar to those used by Sean Connery in his lawsuit against producer Albert R. Broccoli and United Artists Corporation for what he alleged were "for twenty years of unpaid royalties" from the James Bond movies.[6] And that was the problem. Baseball writers thought Clemens acted like a movie star, too, and they were outraged. Baseball players were supposed to act like grateful UPS deliverymen, not Hollywood celebrities. The Boston press saw Clemens' behavior as "a superstar's unparalleled self-centeredness." They believed that Clemens represented Henrik Ibsen's *Master Builder:* "The Titans of all fields of endeavor, it seems, are impelled by their very genius to trample over or knock down all obstacles which impede them in the fulfillment of their goals even at the cost of hurting or destroying fellow men or women."[7] Yet, Clemens asked for perks for his teammates and their families too, not just for himself. The list included upper-box seats, a security guard for the family room, parking for wives, and a telephone in the clubhouse in Fenway Park. One of his Red Sox catchers, Rich Gedman, said, "I saw the way he treated teammates—the stars, the twenty-fifth man on the team—and he treated people so well. I know this. He's taken the heat for a lot of other people."[8] Clemens' penchant for knocking down opposing hitters, although not at the rate of the knuckleball specialist Tim Wakefield or the scowling Randy Johnson, was almost identical to Nolan Ryan.[9]

Baseball writers had long suffered the delusion that the game belonged to them. They were wrong. Baseball belonged to ten-year-old children who went to major league games for the first time, fell in love with this graceful ballet on grass, and returned to the ballpark for a lifetime, where they spent their hard-earned money and perpetuated this shared American experience into another generation and beyond. This was, after all, a sport that had outlasted steam engines, railroads as the major transport of goods, streetcars, trolley cars, typewriters, clotheslines, coal-burning stoves, icehouses, horse-drawn taxis, affordable college tuition, usury laws, unions as a political and social force, deductible credit-card interest, discharge of credit card debt in bankruptcy, legal boxing in all but a few states, silent movies, subway tokens, automobile running boards, three Depressions, 22 recessions, the manned space program, vinyl records, floppy disks, clipper ships, two Madison Square Gardens, the telegraph, the teletype, the Austro-Hungarian Empire, the Soviet Union, the Turkish Empire, the British Empire, Apartheid, the Pony Express, movable type, segregation, hoop skirts, amateur Olympics, amateur tennis, reel-to-reel tape recorders, cutting and splicing audio tape, the Charleston, the can-can, gaslights, bathing suit tops for men, formal hats for men, pocket watches, dirigibles, hospital stays for minor surgery, and silver dollars. Baseball writers also suffered the delusion that life consisted of their cynicism regarding steroids writ large. The steroids in baseball phenomena, however overblown, appeared as a heaven-sent gift to make them relevant again, and they all clung to it like a life preserver. It was an illusion; but who among them wanted to face the reality of their own demise? "So what is the baseball writer to do? Adapt? Nay; ATTACK! Blast those numbers geeks! Howl against the players of the steroid era! Logic does not matter; neither does the truth. Facts are meaningless. This is life or death! So attack, attack, and go down fighting. The war is on, and the HOF [Baseball Hall of Fame] vote will be the final battle."[10]

Part of our more relaxed standards, from no longer wearing suits to church to the easy use of vulgar language in our society, was that sportswriters could now accuse players of arrogance, of being a bullies, blowhards, lazy, obsessed with money (though another million dollars one way or the other would seem hardly to matter), liars, or even criminals, without attribution in rather loose, indeed sloppy, use of language. This sloppy use of language was not well-suited to discussing legal issues, and presented difficulties for sportswriters trying to get their arms around the mystery. In some ways, this cavalier style of reporting was evidenced by the coverage of the Isiah Thomas sexual harassment case—a case that the majority of the sportswriters treated as a *criminal case*. In fact, sexual harassment is a civil wrong; Thomas and his employer, Madison Square Garden Company, owner of the Knicks, were *sued*, not *indicted*.[11]

In contrast to most countries which have one, national standard of laws, the United States operates a complicated system of conflicting and interweaving rules, laws, and court decisions that may offer opposing decisions at the local, state, and national level that somehow have to be ironed out and decided upon. A lawyer who serves as a newspaper source cannot offer a reporter a good opinion or background on a case unless he or she knows all the facts, and a reporter is unlikely to know the important facts that have legal consequences. Reporters, unfortunately, have a tendency to seek out lawyers who agree with their perspective on a case. The Clemens case was complicated, but it was not nearly as complicated as the pursuit of Penn State football coach Joe Paterno, which involved pedophilia, a district attorney who was supposed to investigate it but disappeared and was never found, the subletting of Penn State facilities by a former coach who was living on a state pension, Jerry Sandusky, and a friendly relationship between Sandusky and university officials which allowed the sex offender to watch games in executive suites after he fell out with Paterno after learning he was not a candidate to succeed him as head coach, and hence retired.

The coverage of the Clemens scandal involved a hypocritical conflict of interest for the baseball writers, who have the only votes to decide who does or does not get into the Hall of Fame until various veteran committees can evaluate their credentials many years later. The baseball writers first bought hook, line, and sinker the *unproven* allegations against Clemens in the Mitchell Report. Then they defiantly ignored the determination of an American jury that Clemens was not guilty of perjury and the underlying crime of possession of illegal, performance enhancing drugs. Finally, they not only took the law into their own hands, as it were, but history, and voted against Clemens for the Hall of Fame. He received only 34.7 percent in 2014 and 35.4 percent in 2015. A vote of 75 percent of the writers was required to become a member of the Baseball Hall of Fame.[12]

Sportswriters have historically reflected the bias of management when it comes to players' salaries—perhaps because they, themselves, made lower-middle-class money. Working under dreadful conditions, as a group, sportswriters lived life on the run, eating lousy fast-food and facing tight deadlines, screaming editors and badgering managers who scrutinized the fine details of coach-class-travel expense reports. Sportswriters were a lot like parents. They worked for low wages and all they ever heard were cries and complaints. In 2007, the year of the Mitchell Report, when utility players made millions, newspaper salaries in major league markets ranged from $87,152 at the *New York Times* and *Boston Globe*, both owned by the *Times*, to $35,100 at the *Oakland Tribune*. In 2009, the average starting newspaper-reporter salary in the United States was $26,000. Glamorous local television reporters started at $23,500.

The average website writer started at $32,000. There was also the practical problem of objectivity in that primary news sources came from the management side of the business. In summary, the sports media portrayed athletes as wayward children while characterizing ownership and management as all-knowing parents.

Well into the second decade of the twenty-first century, baseball writers continued to bloviate about exorbitant player salaries with the gleeful knowledge that such a characterization virtually guaranteed resentment of pampered players by their male readers, although attitudes were changing in the age of the entrepreneur. Major League owners had unparalleled tax advantages, including being able to deduct from their franchise tax bills the cost of players' salaries and to manipulate home and away cost-of-living differentials and state-income tax structures.

It was no wonder that middle-class parents discouraged their literary-minded children from practicing journalism and urged them, instead, to become doctors and lawyers. You had to be a special breed to be a journalist—to spend countless hours making telephone calls in order to write stories about contemporary life that mostly earned you an angry reaction from the people about whom you wrote. You had to have a pious conviction in your own beliefs and a tough hide to withstand a life of criticism. You had to be stubborn, too, and hold to your guns. The typical journalist, therefore, did not readily admit mistakes. Unfortunately, the Clemens case proved them not to be valiant seekers of the truth or champions of citizens, but rather, to be water-carriers for the political and baseball establishments as they raked Roger Clemens over the coals. In addition, in their rhetoric, sportswriters clung stubbornly to an earlier era. They invented an artificial lexicon of terms, insisting that professional sports was not a game and fun, but rather, was work that had to be endured. The joyless phrase, "We got the job done," became the mantra of all athletes after a win. "He's a blue-collar guy, a lunch-pail guy," sports announcers declared with endless repetition and admiration. George Will even wrote a baseball book entitled *Men at Work*.[13]

It was all phony. Baseball players had been entertainers since the game's earliest days following the Civil War. In almost every town in America, whether the players got paid or not, they provided entertainment. They played on Sundays after church and everyone came. Baseball was family entertainment, and the game created a community bond. After being underpaid for a century, Major Leagues players saw their salaries skyrocket as television beamed out across the nation and they were freed from one-team bondage with the advent of free agency in 1976. In the first years of the twenty-first century, it was interesting to notice that the highest paid athletes—Alex Rodriguez, Tom Brady of the New England Patriots, and Spice-Girl hubby and soccer star David Beckham, made approximately the same amount of money per year as the famous opera tenor Luciano Pavarotti, $30 million. The hardest-working players turned out to be lavish-living superstars such as Roger Clemens and Alex Rodriguez. Rodriguez, for example, lived in a $30,000-a-month, two-bedroom, Central Park West apartment during the baseball season. The ultimate blue collar guy, of course, was the legendary diplomat and biracial heart-throb of the twenty-first century's single woman, who was also a great baseball player, Derek Jeter. Jeter was the son of a sociologist, although that fact was always pushed under the proverbial rug to discuss his grandfather the janitor. Nobody ever mentioned that Clemens' mother, a generation closer to him than a grandparent, also worked as a janitor. Alas, Jeter spent his social hours dating supermodels, dancing in famous nightclubs, and resting between making television commercials in his $15 million New York penthouse.

Rather than give the expected platitudes about competition and hard work, as if he were a ditch-digger like Dan Rather's father, Clemens delivered long lectures on the mechanics of his pitching—speeches that always came off to reporters as excuses instead of answers. Or as one writer put it, "Clemens has his own personal vocabulary that has often made him the butt of sportswriters' acerbic columns, as if to prove he is less than a brain surgeon. He uses words like 'fillier' and 'recorrect,' and once said of himself, 'I'm the goodest guy you can find.'"[14]

Yet by the second decade of the twenty-first century, unbeknownst to baseball writers, rage against the rich, particularly among non-sports fans, was fading in America as the new heroes were billion-dollar tech moguls and investment gurus such as Microsoft's Bill Gates, Apple's Steve Jobs, Donald Trump, and Warren Buffett, and couples regularly watched television programs such as *House Hunters International*. In this age of the entrepreneur, Donald Trump was elected president of the United States in November 2016. What was a populist baseball writer to do when the purportedly liberal PBS televised such fare as *Downton Abbey* and *Mr. Selfridge*, in which lords of the manor and business tycoons were portrayed as humanitarians and concerned caretakers of their employees? Even Lester Munson, who by far had the best grasp of the 2012 Clemens trial, wrote that Debbie Clemens

> gave the jury of eight women and four men a glimpse into her life with Roger and their four sons that could alienate some jurors…. Two maids. One nanny. Six bedrooms in their mansion with another in the pool house. Ten bathrooms, with two more in the pool house and the separate gym building…. As Debbie described an HGH episode with McNamee, the family's lawyer, Rusty Hardin, displayed photos of the master bedroom and master bathroom, two mammoth spaces that featured elaborate moldings, custom carpets. An enormous circular

bathtub and marble everywhere.... With a smile on her face, she described her family as a "corporation with six schedules," and told the jury she worried about the family's "brand".... A final look at the world of Debbie and Roger came later Friday when another Clemens attorney, Michael Attanasio, asked an FBI agent whether he was aware that elite athletes such as Clemens were accustomed to withdrawing $8,000 or $9,000 in cash from their bank accounts.[15]

As it turned out, Clemens' wealth made no difference to the jury whatsoever.

The predominance of Munson's reporting and his analysis of the Clemens trial revealed two important aspects of American sports journalism in the twenty-first century. First, ESPN had replaced newspapers as the most important conveyer of sports news. Second, it took a lawyer to understand a complex criminal case. No one could question Munson's academic, legal, and journalism credentials. An editor on the undergraduate paper at Princeton, he had also graduated from the one of the nation's elite law schools, the University of Chicago. Munson had practiced civil law for 13 years, had worked as an investigative reporter since 1990, beginning with *Sports Illustrated*, and taught at the prestigious Medill School of Journalism at Northwestern University.[16] Munson proved unfailingly fair in covering the 2012 trial, giving due credit to the prosecution in the early stages as they seemed to score points with testimony and physical evidence, but chronicling their every failure as the case against Clemens rapidly collapsed. Munson's coverage of the trial demonstrated an understanding of the criminal legal rules and procedures, as did the reporting of his ESPN colleague, TJ Quinn, a non-lawyer.[17] Quinn's coverage was excellent, informative, and insightful, and is incorporated into this book's final chapters. Although Quinn had once worked for New York's *Daily News*, this did not skew his coverage of the trial.

Nevertheless, there were editors and headline writers at ESPN.com who suffered little sympathy for Clemens. Their headlines were often incongruous with major points in stories that were often favorable to Clemens from a legal standpoint, thus creating, in this book, a dichotomy between legal analysis and endnote headlines. The incongruity was common in the coverage of the anabolic steroids narrative. In a 2014 story with a headline that read, "Report: Alex Rodriguez Admitted Steroid Use to DEA," Matt Snyder of cbssports.com stated that Rodriguez told drug enforcement agents that he received testosterone and HGH from the notorious Biogenesis Clinic in Coral Gables, Florida. Nowhere in his story was there anything about anabolic steroids.[18]

A major part of this story, therefore, was the exceedingly contentious relationship between baseball writers and Roger Clemens that extended to his early years in Boston. Of course, going back at least far as Ted Williams, Red

Sox superstars have experienced bad relationships with the Boston press. Los Angeles Dodgers left fielder Carl Crawford, who was injured much of his time with the Red Sox and underachieved, talked about what it was like to play in Boston: "That smile turned upside down quick. I think they want to see that in Boston. They love it when you're miserable.... Burying people in the media, they think that makes a person play better. That media was the worst thing I've ever experienced in my life.... I took so much of a beating in Boston.... Look how they treated [John] Lackey. Adrian Gonzalez hit thirty home runs."[19] While Red Sox icon David Ortiz was defending himself by invoking the distinction between performance enhancing drugs, for which he tested positive in the 2003 random test, and anabolic steroids, which were not identified as the substances producing his positive test, *Boston Globe* writer Dan Shaughnessy did not hesitate to paint Ortiz as a steroids user by stating, "A number of players from the Dominican Republic have tested positive for steroids."[20] A lifelong Red Sox fan may have put it best, "The Boston writers sure like to eat their own."

Yet it was even more hostile and more personal with Clemens. Focused and obsessed with pitching, Clemens, like Bill Parcells and Bill Belichick, possessed little patience for the inanities of most sports questions. When he could not discuss the mechanics of pitching—which to Clemens was pretty much everything he had to say—he answered questions in a confusing, elliptical, indirect manner, flying off on tangents, eventually returning to that day's pitching mechanics. Most of Clemens' ramblings were incomprehensible to beat reporters who just needed a quick quote to meet a tight deadline. Indeed, Yankees announcer Michael Kay saw how Clemens generously shared his pitching knowledge with any hurler who would listen and suggested Clemens "could be an evangelist for pitching." Clemens' conversion of Curt Schilling from a sloppy, out of shape, mid-career pitcher into a disciplined, prepared disciple of the art of pitching was part of baseball lore. Clemens approached Schilling when he was working out at the Astrodome in Houston and Schilling was pitching for the Astros. Schilling said, "He felt at the time that I was someone who was not taking advantage of the gifts God had given me ... I walked away saying to myself, you know, no. 1 why would he care as much as I did. I began to turn a corner at that point in my career, both on and off the field."

Clemens had his own sense of meting out justice. According to *Sports Illustrated* writer Jeff Pearlman, Clemens once threw a hamburger bun in the Boston clubhouse at *Boston Herald* reporter George Kimball, after Kimball falsely accused Clemens of refusing to sign an autograph for a 70-year-old grandmother whose grandson had Down Syndrome. Like hockey superstar Wayne Gretzky, Clemens was a faithful autograph signer for fans.

Given that Bostonians believe they live in the "Athens of America," with its many universities, sportswriters treated Clemens with the contempt they believed he deserved, especially since they thought of him as a boastful and ignorant Texan.[21] *Boston Globe* writer Jack Craig declared that it was "nature's revenge in giving Clemens a weak mind to go with a strong arm." The *Globe's* Mike Barnicle stated that if Clemens had not made it to the Major Leagues, "he would be wearing bib overalls and sitting on a milk crate at the open door of a trailer somewhere, brushing his tooth while shooing flies away from his head." Another sportswriter declared, "The man is a complete dope. You would not for a single second—even with his guaranteed contract—want your child to grow up to be like Roger Clemens: selfishly spoiled and seriously deficient in character." In short, to baseball writers, Clemens was "trailer park trash." Sean McAdam, who covered Clemens for the *Providence Journal*, took exception to exaggerations Clemens made about being recruited to play college football and stated, "He was a liar, plain and simple." Author Jeff Pearlman said, more benignly, Clemens "often stared at reporters with the vacant gaze of a seven-year-old boy in an adult spelling bee." Another reporter suggested that "Clemens' egotism was more childlike and innocent. He doesn't realize that he sees himself as the center of his small universe, at the center of every story he tells."

Clemens did demonstrate an odd detachment from other people, a result perhaps of being the center of attention his entire adult life. When a high school classmate wrote a book about him, Clemens did not exhibit the slightest interest in even meeting the author, referring offhand to the fact that his former classmate had collected notes about him as a youngster and incorporated them into a story of Clemens' major League career. Apparently that's what people did as a matter of course: take a personal interest in Roger Clemens. When Clemens hired Gene Grabowski and the public-relations firm, Levick Strategic Communications,[22] to rehabilitate his reputation in 2009, he appeared on the ESPN radio program "Mike and Mike in the Morning" and spoke of himself in the royal "we," as if he were a corporation or a politician. Clemens said that "the message was being put out there," as if there were no connection between himself and his PR campaign designed to show he was clean of any drug charges. Clemens suggested that he was headed out the door on vacation with his beloved wife, Debbie, and was living a normal, happy life, contrary to the press stories that claimed he was hiding in shame at his 13,000-square-foot Houston mansion. During his deposition before Congressional lawyers, Clemens urged the committee to seek out his former chiropractor to attest that his body had not changed in ways that would evidence steroids use. "But go ask the girl that's worked on me two or three time a week, that's seen my body, every inch of my body except my private area, and she would know if my body changed or if I had a problem."[23] Clemens obviously did not know her name.

Lou Gorman, caught in the middle between his 1986 promise to raise Clemens' salary to a $1 million a year and Commissioner Ueberroth's counter-order, later said, "I think a lot of what Roger did was misunderstood by the media. But not all of it. He wasn't *that* likeable of a guy."

Clemens was quiet by nature, unless he lost his temper—not unlike Bob Knight, the mad genius of American basketball. Clemens must have felt a loss of control and goaded as the Boston press called him "extremely arrogant" and "insufferable." Clemens, like Knight, was a control freak, refusing to be sidetracked from his pre-game focus by chatting with other *homo sapiens*. Clemens once explained his side of the battle. "My answers to the media are always blasé, not very informing because they don't ask me the right questions. They ask me, 'How'd you feel tonight?' Well, I say, I struck out fifteen batters: how do you think I felt?'"[24]

Athletes, politicians, and entertainers often suffer critical press. Most who survive in the professions develop a thick skin. Clemens never did. In an unguarded moment, he once admitted, "I have a big heart. I'm sensitive."[25] Of course, as Jeff Pearlman revealed in his book, not every major league baseball star or politician has been subjected to a regular, derogatory column such as the one employed by the *Boston Herald*, "The World According to Roger," riddled with unedited comments intended to ridicule him, including "stutters, stammers, and pauses."

And Clemens *did* lose his temper, that's for sure, although George Vecsey of the *New York Times* put it in proper perspective when he observed that a "couple of times he has appeared to snap on the field."[26] Clemens once delivered a forearm shiver to a photographer who was resting against the Fenway Park batting cage. In a memorable playoff tirade, Clemens swore at umpire Terry Cooney and threatened to come after him in the off-season.[27]

According to Pearlman, in the early part of Clemens' career, the corporate world already perceived him as exhibiting a negative image—Clemens was unappealing to advertisers and reputed to be difficult.

By 1990, according to Pearlman, Clemens had taken to calling reporters "rats" and got the media banned on the Red Sox bus to and from Logan Airport. A year later, Pearlman described Clemens as "an ornery, arrogant, deceitful country boy." Clemens "was challenged when it came to telling the truth," Pearlman declared, citing tall tales by Clemens about playing college basketball at Texas and garnering the interest of the Boston Celtics and Seattle Supersonics. Clemens had become a "marked man" by the Boston press, Pearlman said. "Finally fed up," Pearlman wrote, "the city's press corps declared an unofficial war on Clemens. If he wanted to treat Boston's writing establishment like shoe bottom crud, the favor would be returned." Clemens was then only 28 years old. His major league career would extend for another 16 years.

Clemens' wife Debbie said, "I loved Boston. But it was hard for me, the thirteen years, the media could be very miserable. It's hard living a hero and a villain every other day."[28]

Clemens enjoyed two relatively peaceful years with the press, at least the uncritical local reporters in Toronto, during his Cy Young Award-winning years in 1997 and 1998. After the 1998 season, Clemens was traded to the Yankees for David Wells, Australian left-hander Graeme Lloyd, and Homer Bush. Yankees principal owner George Steinbrenner had more grooming rules than the Philadelphia Kennel Club. You would have thought that the straight arrow Clemens, sporting an old-fashioned, 1940s crew cut, would have fit in nicely. Clemens was so old-fashioned and antiquated that he induced howls of laughter at the Waxman Committee televised hearings after the following exchange:

Congressman Bruce Braley: "Have you ever been a vegan?"
Roger Clemens: "I don't know what that is. I'm sorry."[29]

And he told congressional lawyers that "I have never smoked dope,"[30] a phrase for using marijuana that had probably not been in common usage since radical Jerry Rubin marched in the siege of Chicago in 1968.

But, in fact, all bets with the New York press were off. New York sportswriters did not suffer fools gladly and were eager to examine the bad reputation Clemens brought to town. As *New York Times* sports columnist George Vecsey once told an NFL commissioner, a New York sportswriter's job was like that of a street urchin who tosses snowballs at important people in top hats.[31] Most New York writers and reporters believed that they possessed the street savvy of a pickpocket.

The release of the Mitchell Report on December 13, 2007, turned the New York press loose on Clemens without restraint. It was "Eyes Wide Shut." Nobody with a notebook wanted to see anything that undermined the conclusion that Clemens took performance enhancing drugs, hopefully to include the menacing word *steroids*. Clemens' attorney, Rusty Hardin, said, "The New York media has from the beginning been the most hostile toward him.... I don't know why it is. They are just vicious. It's like they want to get back at him for not confessing to what they think he did." Eleven months after Clemens' Congressional testimony, the *Daily News* wrote, "When it comes to creeps, Roger Clemens stands above and beyond every other Anti-Sportsman of the Year Nominee. This loser is a winner! It's gotten so bad with this guy that just writing his name makes us shudder and want to shower immediately." Usually restrained in the use of hyperbole, Vecsey declared of the pitcher's testimony before Congressman Waxman's House Committee, "Clemens came off an incoherent bully.... He believes himself so much, he could probably pass a lie detector test ... he sounded pathologically unbelievable."[32] New York's highest-rated sports-talk-show host, WFAN's Mike Francesa, in between swigs from enormous plastic bottles of Pepsi Cola, intoned almost daily in his New York nasal voice, "Roger Clemens is going to jail." In an example of just how far the press coverage went down, Mike Lupica, the star columnist of the *Daily News*, watched Clemens' January 2008 appearance on *60 Minutes* with McNamee's lawyers.

Most disturbing about the New York press was its disinterest in checking out Brian McNamee's story. New York was, after all, what we call in law the *situs*, or location, of the alleged crimes of the illegal distribution of anabolic steroids and the possession of anabolic steroids. Suburban Long Island and Flushing, Queens, home of the Mets, were the territory of PED distributor Kirk Radomski. The Upper East Side of Manhattan was the location of Roger Clemens' New York apartment. Apparently no New York reporter attempted to verify McNamee's allegations by visiting these locations, talking to possible witnesses there. No attempt was apparently made to talk to non-baseball clients of McNamee's PEDs, such as the "Wall Street gym rats" or "Olympic caliber" athletes he supposedly trained. Neither did the New York reporters make the slightest attempt to delve into McNamee's work history—a history that turned out to be quite a mess when the facts of it were revealed at trial in 2012. One can only say, facetiously, that the New York press sat passively by their telephones waiting for their sources at the FBI and Justice Department to serve up on a silver platter more circumstantial evidence against Clemens.

Part of the problem of Clemens' relationship with the press was cultural. He possessed a sense of his own righteousness that was deeply Southern and Texan, even though he lived in Ohio until high school. He had his own moral code. He believed in good manners, not always a plus in cities such as New York where people often forgot their manners, and where a northeastern press corps could be gruff. One of Clemens' more outspoken adversaries was a pockmarked Irishman named Will McDonough of the *Boston Globe*, a newspaper worth $1.1 billion when it was purchased by the *New York Times* in 1993.[33] Collaborator of the autobiography of Bill Parcells, McDonough, in a locker-room melee, once decked a tight end of the New England Patriots.

Texas was a state where natives didn't just welcome you with open arms. Texas was also a state where people believed in their own legends. That three of the last eight American Presidents came from Texas did not hurt in furthering their legends. Clemens' psyche was deeply infused with the legend of the Alamo, the battle in San Antonio where Texans fought to the last man despite being overwhelmingly outmanned by Mexican fighters. Well into adult life, Clemens could not resist a good brawl. When Red Sox teammate Oil Can Boyd was robbed at gunpoint trying to hail a cab outside a nightclub in a Baltimore ghetto, Clemens tried to convince Boyd and other teammates to go after the perpetrators and beat them up. According to Jeff Pearlman, Clemens even got into a brawl at a high school basketball game coached by his brother.

The rest of America's deep resentment of Texans lies just under the surface, bubbling up in times of stress. Then out-pours a deep-seated belief that the state is an "outpost of braggadocio and prejudice." After the assassination of President Kennedy, aide Ted Reardon blurted, "I'd like to take a fucking bomb and blow the fucking state of Texas off the fucking map.... I wish to hell the goddamned state of Texas ... had never been invented."[34] Bill Bugli, a former newspaper reporter in Yonkers, New York, and who grew up in the suburbs of New York City, fought in the Marine Corps in World War II and told the author in 1989 that such anti-Texas remarks were routine in the Marines. Clemens' pro-prosecution trial judge, caught in the middle by Justice Department lawyers who pushed him to the limits of legal rules, and defense attorney Rusty Hardin, who ferociously stood by his client on the government's home turf in Washington, D.C., glared across the courtroom at Hardin and said, "I don't know how you do things down in Texas, Mr. Hardin, but that's not how we do them here."[35]

"Same as anywhere else," Hardin declared in defense of Texas.

"Just as you can get mad, I can get mad too," Walton thundered, losing his temper. "Don't look at me like you're going to intimidate me."[36]

To his credit, Judge Walton apologized for his inappropriate outburst as both sides prepared to leave the courtroom, "Mr. Hardin, I do apologize for what happened."[37]

To which Hardin responded graciously, "As do I, Your Honor."[38]

The fallout from the Mitchell Report was a horror for Clemens. Subsequent Congressional hearings involving Roger Clemens and his conditioning coach Brian McNamee, with its absurdly one-sided press coverage *against* Clemens, ruined forever the reputation of the pitcher who, up until then, was considered by many to be the greatest ever. A federal grand jury in Washington, D.C., investigated whether Clemens committed perjury when he insisted to a Congressional committee that he did not take anabolic steroids or HGH. The grand jury handed down an indictment. Furthermore, with his character at issue in a potential defamation trial, Clemens was accused in four books of statutory rape, emotional abuse of his mistress, bribery of baseball umpires (for obtaining good tee-times on the best golf courses in return for a wider strike zone),[39] and the illegal importation of steroids into Canada (in addition to the illegal use of anabolic steroids and HGH in the United States). It was amazing that more was not made by the baseball writers of the allegation that Clemens in essence bribed umpires by helping them get favorable golf times, the implication made by Jose Canseco in *Juiced* that Clemens expected a more favorable strike zone in return. But then again, sportswriters were absolutely *consumed* by their obsession with anabolic steroids. Thanks to the one-sided reporting and commentary, Clemens lost at least $3 million a year in endorsement income.[40]

Caught in the middle, Brian McNamee suffered marital difficulties, faced a defamation suit from Clemens, and ended up in the hospital for treatment of depression.[41]

The sale of Roger Clemens' guilt to an eager press and public was the last great moment for supply-side economics, as it trickled down from George Mitchell's inflated masterpiece, before American financial institutions ripped apart the world's monetary system in October 2008 like an angry Samson.

Within 24 hours after the release of the Mitchell Report, there were more than three million internet hits for the phrase "Clemens Liar."

Indeed, the vast majority of articles declared Clemens guilty, and a typical title was invoked by Sean Cunningham in *Esquire* two years later on August 19, 2010: "The Roger Clemens Web-of-Lies Timeline." It was easy to be amused by the later lawsuit McNamee filed against Clemens for defamation, claiming that Clemens "smeared" him. If Clemens and his public relations advisor Joe Householder set out to "smear" McNamee, it was truly the most unsuccessful "smear" campaign in American history because it ended up convincing the public that Clemens was lying and McNamee was telling the truth.[42]

When baseball writers immediately concluded that Clemens was guilty of taking steroids upon the release of the Mitchell Report in 2007, Clemens complained to Mike Wallace on *60 Minutes*, "I'm angry that what I've done for the game of baseball and the personal, in my private life, what I've done, that I don't get the benefit of the doubt." If Clemens really thought that he was going to get the benefit of any doubts from baseball writers, he had ignored his own press clippings for a quarter of a century.

The Roger Clemens portrayed in the press in the aftermath of the Mitchell Report was a kind of Jack the Ripper: a diabolical monster, conniving to use illegal, performance enhancing drugs; controlling all around him and what they said; destroying or hiding the evidence in the manner of the Ripper; paying off witnesses who might implicate him; engaging in pathological denial; and then suddenly stopping his injections in 2001, just as the Ripper suddenly stopped his murders in 1888. Clemens even carried around a large, black bag with his computer and other items, according to McNamee, just as Jack the Ripper is said to have carried a large, black doctor's bag. In fact, *Sports Illustrated* reporter Jeff Pearlman wrote, "Yet much like the serial killer who cheerfully shows up for work each day at the post office, Clemens had (and still has) an uncanny ability to compartmentalize these parts of his life."

An overarching and clever theme of the baseball writers was for them to insist on comparing the 45-year-old Clemens to a petulant child who stubbornly refused to acknowledge his wrongdoing. Clemens' obvious emotional outrage would ordinarily have been judged as truthfulness from an adult.

A favorite theme of the baseball writers during the Clemens controversy and trial was the silly notion that the wealthy Clemens was able to bully McNamee with a public relations campaign to question his story and to beat up on the poor media and federal government with its purported limited resources. George Vecsey made their case when he contended that the Justice Department was "like a small-market team trying to compete with a large-market team of defense counsels." Exuding his not inconsiderable talents at overstatement, the finest sportswriter ever posited that "with the federal government about to run out of money because of the budget crisis in the divided town, if another jury selection begins in early September, will there by money for bailiffs and stenographers and clerks, to say nothing of judges and prosecutors?" Yet the truth was that the resources brought to bear against Clemens by the United States Government were not small, $120 million by one estimate cited in our introduction. And the wealth of the media resources brought against Clemens, including Vecsey's *New York Times*, were considerable.[43]

The *Times* did have the grace to remind readers that Brian McNamee had written an article for them several years before the Mitchell Report came out saying he had not injected Clemens. The *Times* also published the best profile of Clemens in their Sunday Magazine by Pat Jordan. The profile revealed that it took Clemens a long time to warm up as a pitcher, and since the use of anabolic steroids is often associated with an energy boost, this is another argument to suggest Clemens did not take steroids. Furthermore, the interview with Jordan was conducted when Brian McNamee was working out Clemens at his Houston home in 2001.

William C. Rhoden, an African American sports columnist for the *Times*, suggested that Clemens should be compared to a white apartheid leader in pre–Nelson Mandela South Africa. Fearing that Clemens would not be put on trial when Barry Bonds had already been indicted for perjury, Rhoden told Tony Cox of *National Public Radio*,

"I think if Barry Bonds remains the face it's because people in our industry want him to be the face. They want to protect sacred cows like Roger Clemens, like Andy Pettitte."[44] The profile revealed, perhaps most importantly, that it took Clemens a long time to warm up as a pitcher, and since the use of anabolic steroids is often associated with an immediate energy boost, this is another argument to suggest Clemens did not take steroids. Furthermore, the interview by Jordan was conducted when Brian McNamee was working Clemens out at his Houston home in 2001, a year that McNamee alleged Clemens used steroids.[45]

> Cox: Clemens is not ever going to be subpoenaed.
> RHODEN: Yeah, because he's white and a star, and they want Barry Bonds.... I would like to see a hearing with subpoena power. I'd like this to be sort of like the truth and reconciliation hearings they have in South Africa.[46]

However, unlike the claims of weapons of mass destruction in Iraq by President Bush, published by the *Times* only after a vigorous internal debate about truthfulness,[47] the great newspaper never questioned the allegations against Clemens and remained devoted to his guilt.

Part of the problem in the *Times'* coverage seemed to stem from the affection their sportswriters held for New York Mets icon Mike Piazza, the great-hitting catcher who was hit on the head by a Clemens pitch in 2000.[48] Quick to crucify Clemens, and separately not bashful in piling on with respect to Mark McGwire's use of the diet supplement androstenedione as the most heinous of violations, the *Times'* sports page took 27 long paragraphs to address Piazza's admission of androstenedione use in a 2013 feature interview discussing Piazza's memoirs.[49] Piazza, by his own account, also took amphetamines, creatine, ephedra, and asthma medicine to perk himself up. Only the first two were mentioned by the New York paper.[50]

The controversy had erupted in 2000 after Clemens hit Piazza in the head after he went seven-for-twelve, with three homeruns, against Clemens during the regular season. The situation was aggravated in the World Series by an unusual overreaction from Fox Sports commentator Tim McCarver, who suggested that Clemens actually tried to hit Piazza with a splintered bat.[51] Clemens presented his version of the events a year later.

> So here I am pitching against this guy in the World Series I'd hit in the head, and he and his manager had grandstanded about it. Nobody mentioned that the ball hit his wrist first and then his head. Nobody wrote the story. That after the inning I went to the clubhouse and asked my trainer to call the Mets clubhouse to see if he was all right. When he called over there, Piazza told him to tell me to go to hell. To me, then, it's over.
> Now, the next time I pitch against this guy, I'm fired up, ready to get it on, what everyone in the country wants to see, me versus this guy. So I throw him a fastball, and he shatters his bat and pieces of it come at me. I fielded what I thought was the ball, and when I realized it was a piece of his bat, I threw it in disgust toward my dugout. I didn't want his bat in my life anymore. And he's half way to first base, and the bat flies by him. Usually a guy shatters his bat and he goes to the dugout for another. Why was he running toward first base?

Clemens raised a good point. Piazza was quite far down the first base line for a right-handed batter who was a slow runner and who had first base in his sight line as he watched the foul ball travel toward right field.

Most likely the incident developed so quickly that both players were in shock and didn't realize what was happening. This is supported by George Vecsey's account of the incident which indicated that Piazza was still unsure after the game what had happened, and that Mets Manager Bobby Valentine said there was no consensus from his players on what had occurred.

The *Times* writer who did most of the reporting on the Clemens investigation, Michael S. Schmidt, was clearly in way over his head in covering such a complex, legal story. For example, in July 2009, writing about an interview with Clemens' lawyer Rusty Hardin, who had noted that he had provided Congress with the pitcher's test result from the 2003 random test by Major League Baseball, Schmidt insisted, "The disclosure of Clemens' test results from 2003, however, has no direct bearing on assertions about drug use that have put Clemens, the forty-six-year old pitcher, in legal jeopardy."[52] In fact, the disclosure had everything to do with the assertions because Brian McNamee claimed that he had warned Jim Murray, Clemens' agent at the Hendricks Agency, that Clemens could fail the 2003 random test, that he had injected him in late 2001, and that he had seen an article suggesting steroids could stay in the body up to 18 months. Indeed, McNamee's biographers at the *Daily News* went to extraordinary lengths in their book, *American Icon*, to discredit Murray's Congressional deposition wherein Murray did not recall McNamee's warning allegedly given during their meeting at a New York Starbucks in 2003.[53] Schmidt seemed to buy the spin—or perhaps he was the one perpetuating it—that Clemens was not entitled to defend himself and that any attempt by Clemens to do so was a "public attack on McNamee's credibility."[54] What credibility? McNamee had been bounced out of the New York City Police Department, had struggled to keep a job for most of his working life, and as a dealer in illegal drugs certainly had no quantum of public reputation, in my opinion, which could be damaged.

Ironically, the *Boston Globe*, a publication that had given Clemens so much grief over the years, was restrained in its coverage of the allegations against Clemens. Nick Cafardo, who followed Clemens longer than any other writer for the paper, 13 years, was even-handed in his reporting, noting both allegations that would be harmful to Clemens and factors that would be helpful, including quoting players such as Red Gedman, who supported Clemens. Former *Globe* writer Peter Gammons, who wrote Clemens' 1987 book, *The Rocket*, initially called Brian McNamee a "sewer rat" on ESPN, but later said he believed McNamee after his Congressional testimony.

Thomas Boswell, the highly respected baseball columnist for *The Washington Post*, a $3.5 billion media empire[55] of enormous impact and reach, acted as both puritanical scold and preacher in the manner of Cotton Mather, when he declared, "Baseball has lived a lie since the late '80s, then stonewalled throughout the '90s, as a "corrupting code of silence.... The Mitchell Report called it, dragged the game to the bottom rung of the moral authority ladder in American sports."[56]

Houston Chronicle baseball writer Richard Justice, whose rush to judgment against Clemens so enraged the pitcher that Clemens stormed out of his Houston press conference in January 2008 after playing a recording of a telephone conversation between himself and Brian McNamee, declared: "Mitchell exposed big stars like Clemens and Andy Pettitte.... That's the dirty little secret of steroids. They've made players and owners rich beyond their wildest dreams."

In invoking a sportswriters' favorite, if absurd, smear that young boys somehow knew who among their heroes used steroids and so copied them, Justice propounded, "Worse, maybe some of the cheats sent the wrong message to high school kids. Thousands and thousands of them are using steroids, and they may be doing it because big leaguers sent the message that it was okay."

In a sentence that must have made Clemens crazy, considering that the *Chronicle*, the largest newspaper of the Hearst chain, with the third-largest Sunday circulation in the United States of 526,317 customers,[57] was, after all, his home town paper, Justice insisted, "If you had one view of Bonds you ought to have the same view of Clemens because they're accused of doing the same thing."[58] So much for evidence and proof. And so much for the fact that Bonds had acknowledged using anabolic steroids inadvertently, while Clemens had not. The *Chronicle* did provide thorough daily coverage of Clemens' trial in the spring of 2012, including an online blog. But the paper did Clemens no favors, as the reporting was blandly objective. The *Chronicle* covered the local hero from a careful distance, as if his possible conviction would infect greater Houston with some kind of contagion.

New York's *Daily News*, whose dominant coverage of the Clemens-McNamee dispute shaped the nation's opinion on those issues, worked closely with McNamee's legal team. Within four months of the release of the Mitchell Report, Clemens' attorney, Rusty Hardin, complained accurately, "The *Daily News* throughout this entire episode has been the house mouthpiece for McNamee's lawyers." Indeed, with the fanatical zeal of William Randolph Hearst during his papers' support of the Spanish-American War, the *Daily News* continued to champion McNamee's side of the story even after Clemens' exoneration in the criminal case, as McNamee's defamation case against Clemens remained on the federal docket in Brooklyn in 2014. In the U.S., where it is a time-honored tradition to reinvent yourself, there is a great urge for small actors to want to play the hero in large events. You see it among low-level staffers in political campaigns. You saw it among athletes all the time when they tried to do too much instead of "just doing their job."

McNamee told Congressional lawyers that Clemens' wife, Debbie, and Jose Canseco's wife, Jessica, had shown each other their boob jobs, as if he had been a witness. The *Daily News* reported that the story had originated from Roger Clemens himself. Clemens was said to have told this tale to others in the Yankees' clubhouse, with the paper citing its source as an anonymous player.[59] Thus, Brian McNamee could not have been the source of the information. The *Daily News*, therefore, obviously intended to vouch for McNamee, but ended up contradicting him. The context of the Congressional lawyer's question was the infamous Miami pool party and whether McNamee saw a discussion concerning drugs between Clemens, Canseco, and a mystery third man. Just to be sure, the lawyer followed up and asked McNamee, "And this was during the same party?"[60] McNamee ignored the question and rambled on about Clemens' nannie of the time, Lilly, who left his employment on bad terms and was sure to dish some dirt on the great pitcher.[61] Lily Strain did not recall the Blue Jays party at Jose Canseco's house but did remember that Clemens played golf that morning.[62] In any case, *The Daily News*, feeding 644,879 readers with the nation's second-largest Sunday circulation after the vaunted *Times*, reported valuable information.[63] It revealed that McNamee's success in convincing the American people of his side of the story, and of portraying himself as a contemporary David, against Clemens as Goliath, benefitted from the input of Fred Schwartz, a renowned New York public-relations man. New York's *Daily News* covered the Clemens steroids mystery like no other American newspaper had dominated a story since *The Washington Post* reported on Watergate. To be fair, the newspaper had been out in front on the allegations of performance enhancing drugs in baseball long before the accusations against Clemens came down. It was the only newspaper found which reported the results of an analysis made by the Chairman of the Baylor College of Medicine's Department of Molecular and Cellular Biology, which found no signs of PED use in Clemens' medical tests going back a decade and a half.

Ironically, one of the few journalists who kept an open mind was former *Daily News* sports reporter Michael Kay. Kay, having moved on to a nationally syndicated daily radio program on *ESPN* and become the main announcer for the New York Yankees on the *YES* cable television network, reminded his listeners of the complications of criminal evidence and refused to take wild guesses concerning Clemens' legal fate. In short, Kay covered the Clemens controversy like he did the Yankees games, as an objective and detached Walter Cronkite, the late network television icon, reporting the news and raising his voice only when the Yankees achieved something extraordinary.[64] Kay was the first former beat reporter for a daily newspaper to become a team's play-by-play announcer.

Taking its lead from the *Daily News,* upon the release of the Mitchell Report, America's sportswriters single-mindedly handed down a swift, severe, and often venomous judgment against Roger Clemens. He was guilty as charged. Moreover, he was a despicable human being.

The relentlessly negative view of Clemens continued in periodicals up until his first trial in 2011. Typical of the bias was a title used by Sean Cunningham in *Esquire* on August 19, 2010: "The Roger Clemens Web-of-Lies Timeline."

Typical was the emotional outburst by Gregg Doyel of CBSSports.com that passed for sport commentary:

> Clemens won't admit it. So we can't move on. Because he's playing all of us for fools. Congress, fans, me, you. He thinks we're stupid.
> We can tolerate a lot. But we can't tolerate it when someone as dumb as Roger Clemens thinks *we're* stupid.
> Go to trial, Roger. Then go to jail.
> Then go to hell.[65]

The conclusion of Clemens' trial was bound to be unsatisfactory to both sides in this brawl, no matter the verdict.

If Clemens were convicted of perjury, he was not going to the Baseball Hall of Fame. If exonerated, he was not going to the Baseball Hall of Fame, either—at least not while these baseball writers were alive.

A finding of "Not Guilty" would leave baseball writers furious.

A finding of "Guilty" of perjury alone would leave the baseball writers angry, too, because the worst punishment he could receive would be a jail term and fine, and not his body stacked upside-down like kindling wood and burned for two days in the Alamo's shadows in San Antonio, thousands of vultures circling his corpse, like his Texas forefathers killed by Santa Anna's Mexican Army.[66]

7

An Investigation of the Investigation

The success of Roger Clemens' enemies, who pursued him with the fanaticism of Henry VIII trying to convict Anne Boleyn in order to marry Jane Seymour, resulted partly because baseball executives did not contest, at least publicly, the Mitchell Report for the hurriedly-assembled, flimsy substance of which it was contrived.

Clemens' lawyers, understandably, were disgusted by the slipshod manner with which the Mitchell Report was assembled. Rusty Hardin said,

> As we have investigated this case, we have been shocked at things the Mitchell people haven't looked into.... The Mitchell people did not go to Canseco to check and vouch for things they say he said in there.... We did several things. We go down to talk to Canseco to find out when he read that portion of the report, he goes, "That's a lie." We think, well, how do you know? He said, "Roger wasn't at that party." We said, "How do you know he wasn't at that party?" "Because that's the only party I ever gave at my home for the team. Roger was supposed to come and he didn't come. And I heard later he was out playing golf."[1]

Lanny Breuer, one of Clemens' lawyers during his Congressional deposition and hearing, stated, "We have been deeply concerned about the nexus between Mr. Novitzky and the prosecutors, the Mitchell Report, and really how our client was the major subject."[2]

Regarding Mitchell's questioning of McNamee, Breuer declared,

> We have no reason to believe whatsoever—maybe we are wrong—that Senator Mitchell's people asked questions, that they asked questions in a setting that was really conducive for him to lay out what really happened, as opposed to the prosecutors themselves asking it. That was the first thing.
> We understand Senator Mitchell then got up and hugged the witness. That's what we understand.[3]

The players themselves, obviously, did not want to challenge the report for reasons of legal protection and career advancement. After all, St. Louis Cardinals star Curt Flood, winner of seven consecutive Gold Glove Awards as a National League outfielder in the 1960s, was essentially blackballed from baseball after he challenged the game's reserve clause. A challenge to the Mitchell Report could certainly diminish the chances of a player ever to become a manager, coach, or even general manager. Yet, during Roger Clemens' deposition before the House Committee on Oversight and Government Reform, his lawyer Rusty Hardin said, "There are many players who believe that the Mitchell Report is completely inaccurate and inaccurate about them. But they are not willing to go forward."[4] "And why are they not willing to come forward? Because they are worried if they come forward then they will become the focus of criminal investigations."[5]

The players were wise in their reluctance since two players who challenged the report, Roger Clemens and Miguel Tejada, were, in fact, prosecuted.

Mitchell apparently led those he talked with into thinking he would not name names in his report concerning what players used—or were accused of using—performance enhancing drugs. This conjecture was partly based on the testimony of drug distributor Kirk Radomski at Clemens' trial, when he said Mitchell first promised him that player names would not be included in the report, but the Report did contain names.[6] The conclusion was also based on the following exchange at the trial between Brian McNamee and Rusty Hardin: "You didn't know Mitchell would name names. Until December 5, [2007] you thought you'd be able to stay under the radar." McNamee: "True. I thought I could keep that in house."[7]

In addition, the September 6, 2007, letter to active players from Mitchell, mentioned previously, did offer confidentiality for players supplying information for the Mitchell Report. Furthermore, Jason Giambi, one of the only two active players Mitchell interviewed, took the Fifth Amendment regarding questions about his use of anabolic steroids as a player with the Oakland Athletics, essentially refusing to address the allegations made against him by Jose Canseco in the book, *Juiced*. Giambi, thereby, testified only "post–Clemens," meaning he was only asked about anabolic steroids use when he and Clemens played for the Yankees. By acting most pleasing for Mitchell and his investigators in discussing only his use of illegal PEDs during his time with Clemens, Giambi was left alone to collect another $55,357,142 in salary from 2007 to 2013.[8] Yet, there was nothing in the Mitchell Report to suggest that Jason Giambi had fingered Clemens for taking HGH or anabolic steroids or that Giambi had corroborated anything McNamee alleged.

Two days before the Report's release, and less than a day before investigators working for Clemens visited McNamee in his Long Island house to set his story in stone, ESPN.com's Howard Bryant reported on his investigation into Mitchell's investigation.⁹ Bryant's article was not particularly flattering toward the former senator. Bryant's credibility in this investigation was certainly enhanced by his subsequent judgment that Clemens was guilty of taking performance enhancing drugs. But the writer's story had apparently been quickly forgotten. Mitchell called up Bryant at his previous employer, the *Washington Post*, and asked to meet with him. Bryant declined. Mitchell's investigators were interested in authors who had written extensively about anabolic steroids over a period of time.

What we do know is that many inside Major League Baseball were unhappy with the Mitchell investigation. Managers, team trainers, and strength coaches told Bryant that Mitchell's investigative team pressured them to *guess* who was using steroids, insinuating that Mitchell was producing a report heavy on high-profile names but low on solutions to the alleged problem of widespread use of PEDs. They complained that the investigators were clueless about baseball's day-to-day operations, culture, locker room atmosphere and ways, and, moreover, had no idea what questions to ask.

ESPN.com's investigation included talking to clubhouse assistants, team presidents, former trainers, strength coaches, and members of Congress. ESPN interviewed dozens of players, unlike Mitchell's investigators, who talked to only two active players out of 750 (Jason Giambi and Frank Thomas) and did so only as the result of Commissioner Selig's edict.[10]

Trainers and strength coaches (Brian McNamee was a strength and conditioning coach, *not* a trainer) told Bryant that they were forced to cooperate with Mitchell's query on pain of a $100,000 fine or termination if they refused.[11] According to Bryant, one employee was read a list of players on his team and asked to speculate about which players could have used steroids.[12] One coach said he was asked merely *to guess* about who might be taking steroids, Bryant reported. A team trainer agreed that mere speculation was the primary weapon of investigation, and said that when he refused to speculate because he said he did not know, Mitchell's investigators harangued him, insinuating that he must have known because he worked on the players' bodies every day.[13] Bryant quotes a team executive as saying, "They were upset with me because I didn't know that players might be having drugs sent through the mail. But guess what? It's illegal to open up someone else's mail."[14] General managers felt pressured by Mitchell's investigators' questions which insinuated that they had condoned performance enhancing drugs and believed they were unfairly taking the heat for the owners, Bryant wrote.[15]

According to Bryant, a lot of baseball executives did not trust Mitchell because of his paid relationship with the Boston Red Sox and his various conflicts of interest. Mitchell, in fact, served simultaneously on the board of directors of the Red Sox and of the Walt Disney Company, the corporation that owned the Los Angeles Angels. Mitchell originally tried to extricate himself from this embarrassment by writing a letter to the *New York Times* claiming that there was no conflict of interest because he owned no Red Sox stock—as if Boston banks deposited only wages and not dividends. Mitchell's plea, however, was ineffective in wiping away his name under team owner and vice chairman on the Red Sox's corporate chart. Frustrated that his bit of sophistic reasoning did not convince anyone of his argument that there was no conflict of interest, Mitchell stated that his Red Sox pay had been suspended. But he did not claim his Red Sox position had been suspended.

Yet hardly an eyebrow was raised at Mitchell's contention that it was okay for him to remain a Boston Red Sox Director while conducting the investigation. When his buddy Bud Selig introduced him at a 2006 press conference, Bryant reminded us, Mitchell declared, "I do not intend to resign from the Red Sox. I don't believe there is any reason for me to do so."[16]

Assertions by Mitchell to the contrary, team officials across baseball remained convinced, Bryant wrote, that Mitchell's investigation favored the Red Sox, the team that had failed to re-sign Roger Clemens because he was allegedly "in the twilight" of his career.[17]

Anyone who had lived in Washington, D.C., for more than 45 minutes would not have been shocked that Mitchell used his own New York law firm, DLA Piper, to do the investigation and thus collect the fees, or that he turned to the former law firm of MLB president Bob DuPuy to share the field work and billing. Yet most executives represented teams not in Washington, D.C., Boston, and New York, and were not as familiar with the Northeast Old Boys Network, and consequently objected to Mitchell's methods of sharing the wealth.

Baseball executives were uncomfortable with Mitchell's relationship with the former members of Congress over whom he had once presided as Senate Majority Leader, according to Bryant.[18] He also reported that team lawyers were concerned that any information given to Mitchell could be used in criminal cases, and of course, we now know that in the persons of Clemens and Miguel Tejada, it was. Worse for the lawyers, individual clubs would have to foot the bill for any lawsuits that might arise from the Report's finding, Bryant revealed.[19] Therefore, if someone, let's just pick a name out of a hat, Roger Clemens, sued, the Astros, Yankees, Blue Jays or Red Sox would be expected to pay, not Bud Selig and the New York offices of the Commissioner of Baseball—making it harder, of course, to sue Selig or George Mitchell. Who said it was a bad idea to hire your friend as your lawyer?

Some teams honored Mitchell's request for team records from computer drives, Bryant reported, but many teams did not, obviously indicating the opposition to Mitchell's query at the highest levels of team management, even though Selig sent letters to all 30 teams in 2006 telling them that they had to cooperate with Mitchell.[20]

Union officials, understandably, were not happy about the Mitchell investigation, although they said they never ordered or inferred that players not cooperate. But of course those American citizens who earned millions of dollars, which by then included baseball players, had lawyers—and no lawyer in his right mind would have allowed a baseball player to appear before Mitchell in his New York office with no guarantees against criminal prosecution, no matter how benignly Mitchell characterized the experience.

Donald Fehr and Gene Orza, heads of the Players Association, felt double-crossed by the Mitchell investigation because they had already compromised the Constitutional rights of the players against unreasonable searches and seizures under the Fourth Amendment to an unprecedented degree, when they had permitted drug testing in 2004 and 2005, as part of the collective bargaining agreement. They had in fact "waived" the rights of the players when they allowed random drug testing, and here was George Mitchell looking to dig up information on steroids against the spirit of that agreement. The exception carved out by the Supreme Court against random drug testing involved industries where public safety was of concern.[21] Major League Baseball was certainly not contemplated by the Court to be part of that group.

Worse, Mitchell kept his actions away from the knowledge of the Players Association, an abject disregard for the manner in which baseball had operated in the free-agency era. The annoyed union leaders told Bryant they were kept in the dark by Mitchell's investigators. "It was a unilateral decision. They said that this was what they were going to do and they did it."[22]

Furthermore, the Players Association became angry, Bryant wrote, when Mitchell asked for the results of the confidential 2003 random drug survey, showing that roughly 100 players out of 750 tested "positive" for steroids.[23] Major League Baseball and the Players Association had agreed in collective bargaining, Bryant reported, that the results were to be kept confidential. Once in the hands of Mitchell, however, some results were eventually leaked to the press, and stars such as Alex Rodriguez and Manny Ramirez were outed as anabolic steroids users. The release of Roger Clemens' results to Congressman Henry Waxman's House Committee on Oversight and Government Reform, however, did not lead to the outing of Clemens as a non-steroids user, even though he tested negative.

The cagey Mitchell even wanted to interview former players who were coaches and managers, according to Bryant, apparently because they were no longer protected by the Players Association and its lawyers. Mitchell, according to Bryant's report, originally agreed to tell the union who would be interviewed in advance, but then reneged on the promise and did not tell the union.[24]

The Players Association, Bryant reported, retaliated by sending out a mass e-mail alert to former players who were entitled to have a union lawyer sit in on any interviews they had with Mitchell inquisitors.[25] Mitchell retaliated in kind by releasing his Report on December 13, 2007, without notifying the Players Association.

When Baseball Commissioner Bud Selig announced the Mitchell investigation on March 30, 2006, he declared that the investigation "will take as long as it needs to." It did not. At the time of the publication of the Report, George Mitchell lacked both sufficient information and facts about performance enhancing drugs in baseball to release any kind of credible report.

Professor Rich Hawley suggested the "Sports media ... will have much to say about this, but fans have long since shrugged their shoulders and moved on."

Robert Jarvis, law professor at NOVA Southeastern University, concluded,

> I don't think the report will have any consequences. The CBA [Collective Bargaining Agreement between players and management] is locked down hard on this issue; most of the players who will be named have either admitted their use, retired or both, and the only people who Mitchell talked to had already gone public before he saw them. In addition, Mitchell and his investigation were suspect from the beginning due to their conflicts of interest, so anything he came up with is tainted from the get-go.[26]

8

Clemens Gets Clobbered in Congress

When Roger Clemens arrived on Capitol Hill in the first week of February 2008, a few days before undergoing a deposition by staff attorneys of the House Committee on Oversight and Government Reform, he must have believed naively that meeting the Congresspersons who would question him in a televised hearing, after his closed-door testimony, was merely courtesy, good manners. Yes sir, thank you, ma'am. He shook hands. Like most people, Clemens could be charming when nobody was stepping on his neck. He gave out autographs to admiring Congressional staffers, the little people as they were; they seemed to adore him. Three and a half years later, Clemens befriended the security guards at the federal court house in Washington where his first perjury trial took place. Clemens' lawyers later sent the guards autographed baseballs even though Clemens had not received any kind of preferential treatment.[1] The guards obviously liked Roger Clemens. But they didn't count any more than low-level Congressional staffers did. One of Roger Clemens' liabilities throughout his life continued to be an inability to connect with important people while obviously feeling comfortable with everyday people. He was a guy who preferred dining in what McNamee's biographers referred to as "regular guy" restaurants.[2]

No doubt, in the mind of this tall Texan, he was simply exhibiting the politeness of the cowboy gentleman in *The Horse Whisperer*, played by Robert Redford, a man as "stoutly independent" as Clemens.[3]

The cynical press and even more cynical political class saw Clemens' meet and greet campaign as abject bribery, trying to befriend the very Committee investigating him. Clemens' Houston lawyer, Rusty Hardin, making the rounds with him, looked like a fish out of water in Washington as well. Where were those astute Texas politicians such as Sam Rayburn and Lyndon Johnson and Jim Wright, to steer Clemens through the Washington gauntlet? His other attorney, Lanny Breuer, who did noble work in the defense of President Clinton in the impeachment proceedings, acted as if he were a young, inexperienced rube from Nebraska who had just arrived in the nation's capital. Clemens really needed the help of another political fixer from Nebraska, Ted Sorenson, JFK's bosom buddy, lawyer and speechwriter. Breuer, unfortunately, was equally incompetent in the public relations war between his client, Clemens, and the pitcher's former strength coach, Brian McNamee.

Clemens' legal team was no match for McNamee's lawyers and PR legend Fred Schwartz, a friend of the McNamee family. They were all New Yorkers, and there was a reason that Madison Avenue was in New York City. The best practitioners of the art resided in New York, hired guns for the highest bidders in corporate America. From the moment the Mitchell Report was released, the New York press rushed to support their hometown guy from Queens, Brian Jerome McNamee, graduate of St. John's University and a second-generation New York City cop. Working mostly through the *Daily News*, McNamee's lawyers were often successful in getting three or four separate stories, or "hits," in PR parlance,[4] out of a negative or allegedly negative development regarding Clemens. Indeed the McNamee team, showing how personal all this was, subjected Clemens to a steady beat of revelations about his alleged criminal actions through the pages of the *Daily News*, daily drips on Clemens that were the equivalent of Chinese water-torture.

Analyzing Clemens' incompetent PR campaign, Jonathan Mahler noted in *The New York Times*, "Clemens, meanwhile, was violating every rule in the celebrity crisis management handbook, which calls for humility and composure, not petulance and obstructionism."[5] The PR problem for Clemens was that he couldn't be anything other than himself. As Pat Jordan put it, "There is no subterfuge about Clemens, no desire to be P.C., no desire to say anything other than what's on his mind.... He's just what he claims to be, a 'country boy' who has spent most of his life playing a child's game."[6]

Worse, Clemens challenged the Mitchell Report, funded by Major League Baseball.

In his introductory remarks to the House Committee on Oversight and Government Reform, Clemens explained why he agreed to testify.

"I know that a lot of people want me to say that I have taken steroids and be done with it. But I cannot in good conscience admit to doing something that I did not do; even if it would be easier to do. That is not the type of person I am. Instead, I will try to set the record straight, and I will do so directly to Congress under oath. I have been told that by doing this, I am subjecting myself to possible criminal prosecution. I know that some people will still think I am lying no matter what I say or do."

The Grand Inquisitor of Waxman's legal staff, Phil Barnett, provided the highlight of the Clemens deposition, a series of tricky questions designed to confuse Clemens about who he knew had taken HGH. Clemens had been answering questions about his own lack of use of anabolic steroids. He was like a hitter primed to hit nothing but fastballs in regards to his own use. Barnett threw him one fastball Clemens was prepared to answer in order to set him up for a sequence of curveballs that Clemens was not prepared to answer, about the use of HGH *by others*.

First Barnett's fastball right down the middle: "Have *you ever possessed*," and then in the same question a curveball cleverly thrown in the same question: "*or seen* human growth hormone."[7]

Clemens whiffed, "I have not." Or did Clemens whiff? Clemens clearly remembered, as he would testify in melodramatic detail later, that McNamee had injected his wife Debbie Clemens with HGH, but he said he had not been there so maybe he had not *seen* HGH after all.[8]

Barnett threw another sharp curve: "Did you ever discuss *taking* human growth hormone with *any person outside of baseball* during your career?"

The question was, again, intended to confuse Clemens about talking about HGH for his own use with somebody else's use. He certainly whiffed this time if you take the interpretation that he was being asked about somebody else's use: "I have not."

Before throwing the third curveball to strike out Clemens, so to speak, Barnett wasted one with an easy question. "Do you have personal knowledge of players taking human growth hormone, and I will make this before the release of the Mitchell Report, did you have personal knowledge of players taking human growth hormone?"

Clemens handled this question easily, "Personal knowledge, I do not."

Knowing how eager the high-strung Clemens was to assert his innocence of steroids use, the experienced Barnett loaded up five questions in one, the third curveball as it were, and finished him off when Clemens eagerly swung early with a blanket denial. "And did you have personal knowledge of other persons, acquaintances, people you worked with, family members *who were taking* [Emphasis added] human growth hormone?"

"I did not."[9]

The question *sounded* as if Barnett had asked Clemens whether he knew of anybody taking HGH on a regular basis, but in fact was intended to trick Clemens into denying he had personal knowledge of a family member who *had taken HGH once*, his wife Debbie. And it worked. Barnett knew that Brian McNamee had injected Debbie Clemens in their Houston home.

A good lawyer, Barnett showed no sign that he had just taken down

Clemens with his suave questioning. He moved calmly on. "And have you ever taken amphetamines or other performance-enhancing drugs during your career?"

Clemens provided a surprise answer. He did not issue a blanket denial. "I don't know, a list of items that I have taken, I have an ephedra product, but I don't believe it was banned.... I don't think that Hydroxycut or Thermacore..."

"Amphetamines?" asked Barnett, quickly moving the subject back to a substance that was actually banned.

> "No."
>
> "You said you have taken some things that may have had ephedra in them?"
>
> "Hydroxycut and Thermacore I have taken. And from what I have learned it has ephedra in it ... and it was banned in 2004. The FDA banned it, not Major League Baseball. So I stopped.... I took Hydroxycut and/or Thermacore, I can't remember which one.[10]
>
> "I am not a coffee drinker. I did drink a cup of coffee, maybe two cups of coffee before I pitched. And of course that ruined my stomach, so I had to take Tums or something after I did that.[11]
>
> "When McNamee stayed at my Houston house he would ... the daily routine of the five, six days, he would make a protein shake for me.... He would bring the powder in and mix the powder.... It was ready for me to drink.... The vitamins he would have open in a little like butter dish or something like that where I would come in and take it."[12]

Perhaps Clemens, and certainly his lawyers understood, that he had just lied under oath, or more accurately, did not understand that he had denied knowing his wife had taken HGH. Fortunately, he got another bite at the apple when Republican lawyer Jennifer Safavian later returned to the curveball question. "And you were also asked earlier," Safavian began, "whether or not any of your family—to your knowledge, whether any family member has ever used HGH."

Clemens, entranced in the tunnel vision focus he exhibited on pitching days, patiently waited for the words to break, and then he hit the question into history. "Sure. Yeah. I thought we were asked about employees or something like that. I think it was asked to me in three or four—but I didn't catch family."

"There was a grouping," Safavian admitted, "I think, in the way it was asked. So let me ask you specifically with regard to family members, do you have any knowledge of any family members using HGH?"

"I do," Clemens answered eagerly. "My wife received a shot of HGH from Brian McNamee at my house. I think it was in our master bedroom."[13] This testimony added credibility to Clemens' claims because his wife, Debbie, testified at trial that the shot was administered in the master *bathroom*, not the master *bedroom*, suggesting that he was not present and that he had learned of the injection second-hand.

The year I'm going to say 2003 *possibly* [emphasis added]. I believe there was an article from what I understand, about HGH in the *USA TODAY* that came out a couple days earlier that week. I don't know if it was the only article my wife had read. And he gave her a shot of HGH. She tells me that it happened extremely quick [sic]. He was gone after it happened, literally gone. He went to the airport, I found out. I was not present at the time.[14] I found out later that evening. And the reason I found out, because she was telling me that something was going on with her circulation, and this concerned me. The very next day it wasn't as bad, but I don't know if it was her feeling bad about it, you know, I'm not discussing too deep of detail about it with her other than that at this point she's embarrassed, she feels part of a trap that McNamee has set.[15]

The other highlight of the day was Barnett's insistence that Congressman Waxman's Committee was not out to get Clemens. He declared, "And there may have been a suggestion that the signal coming from the Committee or the Chairman if someone challenged the Mitchell Report that would be a basis for a criminal referral. There has been no such *statement* [Emphasis added] by the Chairman nor by the ranking member."[16]

Of course, it was necessary for Barnett to make that statement—for the record—for history. Clemens' attorney, Rusty Hardin, used to deference toward judges—and Barnett was essentially the judge here—and wanting to appear agreeable, backed down. "I take it back," Hardin stated. "Because I have no evidence that the Chairman has said any such thing. I really was talking about a perception rather than actual quotes or positions of the Committee."[17]

While it was literally correct that Waxman and Davis had not officially made such a statement, sources on their Committee did tell Hardin that Clemens would face a referral for prosecution if he denied taking performance enhancing drugs. Davis would admit subsequently and publicly, in an interview with the *New York Times*, that indeed it was Clemens' challenge to the Mitchell Report, wherein "Congress had an investment," which led to the narrow focus of the Congressional query to just one player: Roger Clemens.

"There was also a statement that the hearing is because there was an attack on the Mitchell Report," Barnett said defensively. "And might have been a suggestion or implication that because the report was being attacked there was a hearing. The committee is trying to investigate steroids in baseball. The Mitchell Report is important, and an assessment of where it is accurate and where it is not accurate is important. And that was the motivation for the hearing."[18]

Barnett's declaration was utter nonsense and double-talk. The Waxman Committee could hardly investigate the use and impact of performance enhancing drugs in Major League Baseball, and a report about them, by calling only a witness who said he knew nothing about the drugs! That would be like limiting an investigation into organized crime to one mob member who took the

Fifth Amendment—the logic was ludicrous. Assuming for argument's sake that Clemens had taken the anabolic steroids and HGH, he certainly was not going to give any details since he asserted he had not. Therefore, what was the point of spending the taxpayers' money on depositions and a public hearing not about illegal drugs in baseball but the alleged use of illegal drugs by one man? Why wasn't the House Committee on Oversight and Government Reform focused on present and former players who had admitted to Senator Mitchell that they had used anabolic steroids and/or HGH? *They*, unlike Clemens, could have and would have provided Congress with details of their own use, why they used it, the impact of their use, and their estimate as to how widespread the use was. *They*, unlike Clemens, could have provided Congress with an assessment or at least their own opinions as to the accuracy of the Mitchell Report. Furthermore, if the Waxman Committee hearing were anything other than a political show trial, it would have provided *somebody*, a scientist, a leading researcher, to vouch for *any* connection between performance enhancing drugs and baseball performance. It did not.

For argument's sake, let's give Barnett the benefit of the doubt and agree that verifying the accuracy of the Mitchell Report was the purpose of the depositions and subsequent hearing. But to accept that argument, you would have to suspend reality and agree that the only question of interest to Congress was whether Roger Clemens took performance enhancing drugs. The accuracy of drug use reports by other players simply did not matter.

The truth, of course, was that without the allegations against Roger Clemens, nobody would have paid any attention to the Mitchell Report. George Mitchell must have understood this. Nobody cared that Mo Vaughn, Gregg Zaun, Kevin Brown, or Kent Mercker, all of them outstanding players at one time, and well known to fans, were named in the Mitchell Report. Indeed, since the release of the report in 2007 none of these former major league stars prompted articles in the press, or probably discussion among baseball fans, either. In addition, ESPN would not likely have televised a Congressional hearing that grilled Denny Neagle or Ryan Franklin or Mike Bell about their use of performance enhancing drugs while playing Major League Baseball.

Congressional hearings, particularly televised ones where Committee members get to preen and show off for the cameras, are known for their partisan, unfair, low standards of conduct. After all, Congressional hearings made Joseph McCarthy and Richard Nixon famous. The hearings into the purported use of performance enhancing drugs in Major League Baseball outdid the usual partisan bickering. Its transparent rationale for the circus, to determine the accuracy of the Mitchell Report—because of the contention by one player, Roger Clemens, that he had been falsely accused—was contradicted at

Clemens' first trial in 2011 when Waxman Committee attorney Philip Barnett testified that the purpose of the hearing was to investigate steroid use nationally, not just in Major League Baseball. This was untrue. The House Committee on Oversight and Government Reforms' 2008 televised hearing, as opposed to the 2005 hearings with its broader mandate, was limited to allegations against one player, Roger Clemens, and was based only on performance enhancing drugs in Major League Baseball, with a tangential reference to such drugs in minor league baseball (over which Major League clubs had authority). The 2008 spectacle began with dramatic references from the 2005 hearings about two young boys who had committed suicide after taking steroids. One of them was the son of former Los Angeles Dodgers pitcher Burt Hooton, who, like Clemens, had pitched for the University of Texas. The previous day's witnesses, George Mitchell, Baseball Commissioner Bud Selig, and Players Association chief Donald Fehr, were subjected to questions and emotional speeches about the impact of baseball players using performance enhancing drugs on impressionable teenagers. The examples implied that these youngsters somehow knew which Major League players took steroids, looked up to them, and thus the players were somehow responsible for the death of the boys. It was a disgusting innuendo, indeed a smear, and committee members who participated in this cheap implication should have been ashamed of themselves. The baseball media who repeated the story to heap more abuse on Clemens did themselves no honor either.

Waxman, who had received a $2,000 political contribution from MLB's political action committee for his most recent campaign in 2006,[19] began his four-and-a-half-hour show trial[20] with prepared remarks that repeated the Mitchell Report's dubious claim that "The illegal use of steroids and performance-enhancing drugs was *pervasive* [emphasis added] for more than a decade."[21] As was established earlier in this book, there was no evidence to suggest that the use of performance enhancing drugs in Major League Baseball ever exceeded the five to seven percent, as revealed by the 2003 random tests. If anything, the subsequent tests, conducted with the cooperation of the Players Association, confirmed that the 2003 test acted as a successful deterrent. By the time of the 2008 hearings, as previously mentioned, the number of offenders had declined from more than a hundred in 2003 to two—an extraordinary drop in use. There were 750 major league players in 2008 and the two failures constituted a usage rate of .0026 percent, light years from the 30 to 50 percent claimed by the Mitchell Report and implied by Congressman Waxman.

Waxman, like Mitchell, succeeded with the false impression that he was somehow an impartial judge instead of a partisan advocate against Roger Clemens. Referring to Clemens, Waxman declared, "During his deposition he made statements we know are untrue.... In other areas his statements are contradicted by other credible witnesses or simply implausible."[22]

On the other hand, Waxman insisted, "Mr. McNamee's credibility will be bolstered by the testimony the Committee received from Mr. Knoblauch and Mr. Pettitte in their depositions."[23] Waxman did note the fact that this credibility of Pettitte and Knoblauch rested mostly on what they admitted about their own HGH use, not what they said about Clemens' use. The distinction, however, was missed by most viewers eager to hear the nitty-gritty detail of the drug possession claims against Clemens. Waxman proceeded to make misleading statements throughout his introductory remarks. He said, "Mr. Pettitte also told the committee that he talked about both of these conversations with his wife.[24] In fact, Pettitte said he did not remember telling his wife and said only that he "must have" because he told her everything. No matter, Waxman plunged on, supposedly paraphrasing Pettitte's testimony, "I had a conversation with Roger Clemens in which Roger told me he had taken human growth hormone. He did not tell me when he got the HGH or from whom, but he did tell me that it helped the body recover."[25] In fact, Pettitte did not say in his deposition testimony that Clemens told him that HGH helped the body recover. Waxman confused what *McNamee told Pettitte*—that HGH would help the body recover—with what Pettitte actually recalled Clemens saying—absolutely nothing of substance and giving only the general impression that Clemens had alluded to having taken HGH.

Waxman next addressed, all in his introduction mind you, what he and his Committee and Clemens haters everywhere thought was the full proof positive that Clemens was lying about his use performing enhancing drugs. They believed they had Clemens trapped. Andy Pettitte had recounted a conversation he had had with Clemens back in 1999—or maybe it was in 2000 or 2001. You see, Pettitte wasn't exactly sure. The upshot of the story was that it was Clemens' wife Debbie who took HGH, not Clemens himself.[26] Waxman intoned, as did others, that Clemens could not have said his wife took HGH in 1999 or 2000, or 2001, if McNamee had injected Debbie Clemens in 2003. But none of these dates were set in stone, including 2003 as the date of Debbie Clemens injection by Brian McNamee. And although Pettitte had referenced what he believed had been their conversation *before* 2003, he gave no testimony that he indicated to *what specific year* he was referring when he and Clemens spoke in Florida (in Pettitte's recollection) or Atlanta (in Clemens' recollection). As usual, Clemens had a better memory than Pettitte. The conversation *did* take place in Atlanta.

Then Waxman made the claim that turned Clemens' legal team furious. "I was particularly influenced," Waxman insisted, "by the view of Mr. Clemens' attorneys, who thought it would be unfair if the Committee issued a report without giving Mr. Clemens the opportunity to testify in public."[27] This was, in the view of Clemens' attorneys, patently false, and they vehemently disagreed that Clemens volunteered to testify in front of the cameras. Indeed they felt they had been railroaded into putting Clemens, not particularly adept at words, on television. They were particularly angry at Congressman Tom Davis, a recipient of a $1,000 contribution from Major League Baseball for his 2006 campaign,[28] who said he told Clemens' legal team that the star pitcher did not have to speak at the televised hearing. The usually circumspect Hardin said heatedly, "That Tom Davis comes down to us, calls us aside and urges us to have Roger testify. And now that son of a bitch is on TV saying that Roger insisted upon it."[29] Since Hardin delivered the final advice on whether his client would or would not testify on television, it makes no sense not to accept his version.

"At the beginning of his sworn deposition," Waxman stated, "Mr. Clemens repeatedly told the Committee that he never talked with Brian McNamee about human growth hormone. We know from his later testimony that these statements were false."[30] Waxman's claim was more outright wrong than misleading because the Congressman purposefully made it out of context. In the same manner as he had done with Clemens' deposition testimony, Waxman had conflated Clemens' statements about Debbie Clemens' use of HGH as referring to the pitcher's use of the hormone.

Ironically, Maryland Democratic Congressman Elijah Cummings whose filmed endorsement of the guilt of Roger Clemens would lead to a mistrial as hearsay evidence,[31] began the grilling of Clemens: "Mr. Clemens, do you think Mr. Pettitte was lying when he told the Committee that you admitted using human growth hormone?"[32]

"Mr. Congressman," answered Clemens, who worked hard to bite his tongue and not lose his temper during the proceedings,[33]

> Andy Pettitte is my friend. He was my friend before this. He will be my friend after this. I think Andy has misheard.
>
> And I say that for the fact that we also used a product called Hydroxycut and Thermacore. It had ephedra in it, from what I understood to be a natural tree root. I believe ephedra was banned in 2004, something of that nature. A player in Baltimore passed away because of it.
>
> Andy and I talked openly about this product. And so there is no question in my mind that we would have talked, if he knew that I had tried or done HGH, which I did not, he would have come to me to ask me those questions.[34]

Cummings refused to believe a word of Clemens' answer. "Would he tell the Congress that one of his close friends was taking an illegal, performance-enhancing drug if there were any doubt in his mind about the truth of what he was saying?"[35]

Clemens struggled to get a word in edgewise,

"Mr. Congressman, once again, I believe…"
"Please."
"I am sorry."
"No, I just want you to go ahead and answer that. Do you think he would do that?"
"I think he misremembers…"

"Very well," declared Cummings sarcastically.
Clemens pressed on,

And let me add, in 2006, he and I had a conversation in Atlanta's locker room when this *LA Times* report became public about a Grimsley report, and they said that Andy's and my name were listed in that.[36] And I remember him coming into that room, the coach's room, the main office, there of the clubhouse attendant, and sitting down in front of me, wringing his hands and looking at me like he saw a ghost.

And he looked right at me and said, "what are you going to tell them?" And I told him that I am going out there and I am going to tell them the truth, I did none of this.

Seething with disbelief, Cummings asked derisively, "What possible motive would Mr. Pettitte have to fabricate a story about you, his friend?"[37]

Baseball's third-ranking strikeout pitcher attempted to answer the rhetorical question. "Andy would have no reason to."

"Mr. Clemens, once again I remind you. You are under oath," declared Cummings heatedly.[38] "You have said your conversation with Mr. Pettitte never happened.[39] If that was true, why would Laura Pettitte remember Andy telling her about the conversation?"

"Once again, Mr. Congressman, I think he misremembers the conversation that we had."

Yet not for nothing was politics a partisan game. Massachusetts Democrat John F. Tierney plunged on like a bull in a china shop.

"Mr. Clemens, according to your account, Mr. McNamee injected your wife in your bedroom without your knowledge."[40]
"That is correct, sir, yes."
"Mr. Clemens, your own statements now show that you had two specific and memorable conversations with him about HGH. So when you were asked on three specific occasions why didn't you tell the Committee about those conversations when you were asked?"[41]
"Prior to injecting my wife, Mr. Congressman, we had no conversations about HGH in any substance or any detail whatsoever."
"How do you reconcile three times saying you didn't and then later when somebody specifically finally asks you about your wife you have a recollection of two very distinct and memorable conversations?"[42]
"During my testimony with the Committee…. And I believe the Committee ran down when they were asking me the question about front-office people, other employees, and that's when they said family in the question."
"You testified that your wife didn't feel well and started to have circulation problems."
"She felt that she was having circulation problems, yes."

"But you never called a doctor. Certainly, it seems, with most reasonable people I think if that were the case.... That you would have called a doctor to find out what the consequences were. You never did that?"[43]

"We did not, and I did talk to Deb about it, if we should call our doctor."

"What steps did you take to learn about the effects of HGH after you learned that your wife had taken the injection?"

"I didn't take a lot of steps."

"But despite all that, you never made inquiry of a doctor and you never even looked up to see what the effects might be, is that right?"

"Mr. Congressman, I don't believe I ever said serious effects. She said she was having itching and she had some type of circulation problem that she was feeling."

Republican Congressman John Mica of Florida asked,

"Mr. Clemens, you claim that you were injected with vitamin B-12, and also you admitted to Lidocaine. Okay, what color is the vitamin B-12 shot? You told us you had quite a few shots."

"Brian McNamee gave me shots on four to six occasions of B-12." "It is red or pink in color. Lidocaine, I do not know the color of Lidocaine. He gave me one shot of Lidocaine in my lower back, and that happened in Toronto. I have no idea—"[44]

"Now, he could have gauze with your blood sample on it, is that correct?"

"Absolutely."

"You say he would have gauze with possibly your blood DNA sample on it. That would be correct?"[45]

"He sure could have."

Chairman Waxman declared,

This is what I think we've learned: Chuck Knoblauch and Andy Pettitte confirm what Brian McNamee told Senator Mitchell. We learned of the conversation that Andy Pettitte believed he had with Roger Clemens about HGH. And even though Mr. Clemens says his relationship with Mr. Pettitte was so close that they would know and share information with each other, evidently Mr. Pettitte didn't believe what Mr. Clemens said in that 2005 conversation.[46]

Clemens objected strenuously to that characterization of the facts. "Doesn't mean he was not mistaken, sir. It does not mean that he was not mistaken, sir."

An angry Waxman cut Clemens off. "Excuse me. But this is not your time to argue with me. Evidently he didn't believe it in your second conversation because he went ahead and issued a statement to us, as did his wife."

North Carolina Democrat Bruce Braley invoked sarcasm, to the delight of Clemens' enemies, in asking the pitcher whether he suffered from a catalog of improbable diseases associated with taking B-12. It was yet another strange attempt to suggest somehow that B-12, one of the most used over-the-counter supplements in the United States [indeed a bottle of it rested on my kitchen table as I wrote this] was an exotic medication that was indicated only for the most unusual of medical conditions. The attempt at sarcasm, however, was lost in the humor of the straight-laced, conventional Clemens, who never smoked and seldom drank alcohol.

> BRALEY: Have you ever been diagnosed with anemia?[47]
> CLEMENS: I have not.
> BRALEY: Have you ever been a vegetarian?
> CLEMENS: I am not a vegetarian.
> BRALEY: Have you ever been a vegan?
> CLEMENS: A what? I'm sorry.
> BRALEY: A vegan.
> CLEMENS: I don't know what that is, sorry.

It was not a politician who summed up the days' show trial, but Clemens, the inarticulate athlete with courage the size of Texas. "Somebody's tried to break my spirit in this room," Clemens said. "They are not going to break my spirit. I am going to continue to go out and do the things that I love to do and try and be honest and genuine to every person I can be. It is the way I was brought up. It is what I know. But you can tell your boys that I did it the right way, and I worked my butt off to do it."[48]

Clemens, of course, did not get the last word on the government's home turf. Congressman Waxman, quite put out that some members of his committee had given McNamee as tough a time as he had given Clemens, came to the defense of his star witness. "Mr. McNamee, you've taken a lot of hits today. In my view, some were fair and some really unwarranted. There will be some members who will focus on your inconsistencies. That may not be unusual in these types of situations. I want you to know though, as Chair of this Committee, I appreciate all your cooperation with our investigation. And I want to apologize to you for some of the comments that were made."[49]

So came to an end the televised hearing about the purported widespread use of performance enhancing drugs in Major League Baseball, and their possible impact on American teenagers. Yet, in large part, the hearing had not been about baseball players or teenagers, it had been about the use of HGH by a well-to-do woman from the Houston suburbs, Debbie Clemens—and whether Clemens had lied in discussing his wife's use of that hormone. The Committee's ranking Republican member, Tom Davis, would say more formally about the investigation of Clemens and the majority report issued by Waxman, "We believe the Democratic memorandum does not fully represent the investigative work of the Committee or the evidentiary record. Instead of concentrating on the ultimate question—whether Clemens was untruthful about his use of anabolic steroids and human growth hormone—the memorandum goes far afield into Clemens's recollection about inconsequential matters."[50]

9

The Desperados

Yes, Virginia, there actually were Major League baseball players who used performance enhancing drugs in those days, either anabolic steroids or human growth hormones, and they did it mostly out of desperation at the tail end of their careers, as their bodies betrayed them and broke down. They sought quick solutions as the sand in the hour glass of their Major League fame rapidly ran out.

Some retired players confirmed to George Mitchell that their cancelled checks to Kirk Radomski were indeed in their own handwriting. Perhaps Mitchell derived the idea of amnesty for all past transgressors after these players essentially supplied the real substance of his report. Because the retired players were no longer in the Players Association, Major League Baseball could not discipline them; they were not necessarily free from prosecution by law enforcement, although the statute of limitations had probably expired in most cases.

You would have thought, if logic ruled the nation instead of Hollywood-contrived fantasies, that Jose Canseco, Jason Giambi, Kevin Brown, Mo Vaughn, and the other players would have had their day in the sun when the Mitchell Report was released on December 13, 2007. Instead, everybody shunted them aside like slowpokes at the running of the bulls in Pamplona, and the baseball writers salivated over the allegations that Roger Clemens used anabolic steroids and HGH. Unlike Clemens, who faced no purported physical evidence at the time, these former players enjoyed the status of cheaters, violators, and criminals, if charged. As Norman Mailer once said, the only man sexier than an athlete is a criminal. If justice ruled, these former players could have testified before Congress, revealed their use of performance enhancing drugs, discussed why they did it, shed light on this perceived "steroids era," and let sports fans in on what had really gone down for perhaps two decades and had perhaps compromised important baseball statistics such as home runs in a season and a career. Or at least Jose Canseco could. Canseco had confessed endlessly and in books about his steroids use. Indeed it was his book, *Juiced*, that set everything in motion, prompting Congressman Waxman to hold his first hearing into anabolic steroids in baseball in 2005. No rational subsequent Congressional hearing, especially one televised by ESPN, could happen without Jose Canseco speaking into the bright lights and telling his story.

If Henry Waxman's House Committee on Oversight and Government Reform were seriously interested in using its power to investigate increased anabolic steroids use in the nation in the wake of a report by the Center for Disease Control, as it claimed three years later at Roger Clemens' trial, these former players would have appeared and discussed their role in this reported increased use of steroids. Waxman, however, understood that after decades of directing important and successful hearings about the tobacco industry and other domestic problems, he was still a national nobody. All that changed with a televised grilling of baseball's pitching rock star, Roger Clemens. The Clemens hearing made Waxman famous and gave him the national adulation from ordinary people for which every politician lived. In fact, after four years back in relative obscurity again in 2012, Waxman agitated for a Congressional hearing into the use of HGH in professional football. Apparently, after he had bathed, coast to coast, in those television lights, it was hard for Waxman to return to C-Span and an audience of fourteen late-night insomniacs.

The press-driven hysteria over anabolic steroids and the exciting possibility that the enemy of the baseball writers, Roger Clemens, might have taken them, was yet another example of baseball existing in a bubble above the law. A district court judge, Kennesaw Landis, made the bizarre ruling in 1919 that baseball was exempt from anti-trust laws. He was thereupon rewarded with the job of Commissioner of Baseball, only to be defined by a compliant press as a paragon of virtue and integrity for decades. Justice Oliver Wendell Holmes, of all people, a follower of George Mitchell's team, the Boston Red Sox, wrote for the United States Supreme Court in 1922 that baseball was indeed above the law, or exempt, from anti-trust regulation. Worse, Holmes claimed that the sport was not a business because it did not cross interstate lines, patent nonsense because there were then teams in many states between Boston Harbor and the western side of the Mississippi River at St. Louis that charged admission and paid salaries to players on the Red Sox, Cardinals, and Browns. The so-called "Reserve Clause," holding baseball players to one team for their entire careers, and held illegal by lower courts since shortly after the Civil War ended in 1865, was upheld, not only by Holmes and his cronies in 1922, but was also again in 1972 by a different band of careless chauvinists on the high court. Never mind that the Reserve Clause violated a basic principle of contract law, probably extending back several thousand years into antiquity, that is, a contract of a human being cannot extend to perpetuity. Admittedly, lawyers were no less complicit in placing baseball above the law, when we mostly went along with the Jim Crow laws banning most persons of color from playing in the Majors until 1946—although it was a lawyer, Branch Rickey, who integrated baseball with the signing by the Brooklyn Dodgers of Jackie Robinson. The last team to employ a black player? The favorite team of Justice Holmes and Senator Mitchell—the Boston Red Sox. Although Major League Baseball technically did not admit to guilt in settling with several former players over allegations it colluded to keep player salaries down in the 1980s, no one seriously believed that Major League Baseball did not engage in that practice. Baseball was also a sport where logic was not always in play. For example, almost everybody associated with the sport firmly believed that Shoeless Joe Jackson threw the 1919 World Series for the Chicago Black Sox by hitting a home run, swatting three doubles, driving in six runs, and batting .375.[1]

Given all this, Congressman Henry Waxman's making the societal issue of the consumption of illegal, anabolic steroids secondary to a hearing of a dispute between a player and his occasional strength and conditioning Coach Brian McNamee, was not so unusual for baseball. Besides, at the actual televised hearing, Waxman acted as if he wanted to adopt McNamee as his own. Waxman apparently had no interest in adopting Jose Canseco, Jason Giambi, David Segui, Kevin Brown, or even Mo Vaughn.

Ordered to go the principal's office, as it were, by Commissioner Selig, Jason Giambi told Mitchell he used Deca-Durabolin in 2001, the year he was voted the Most Valuable Player in the American League; he injected it into himself at home. By 2002, Giambi was taking it weekly.[2] In late 2002 or early 2003, Giambi met Barry Bonds' strength and conditioning coach, Greg Anderson. Giambi bought injectable testosterone, the "cream," "clear," and other unidentified pills.[3] Giambi later added human growth hormone (HGH) to his regimen and wrote Anderson a check for $7,000 and a money order for $10,000, apparently all of it for a kit of HGH.[4] Anderson explained that the "cream" and the "clear" were alternatives to steroids that would boost testosterone.[5] For a brief period, Giambi injected himself with HGH three days each week and testosterone once each week. He took the unidentified pills three times per week and the cream and clear twice each week, all in accordance with a calendar Anderson provided him. (A similar calendar was ruled inadmissible hearsay in Barry Bonds' perjury trial).[6] Giambi followed the routine until the 2003 All-Star break, after he injured his knee sliding into a base.[7]

George Mitchell asked Giambi about taking performance enhancing drugs *before* 2001. On the advice of counsel, Giambi refused to answer the question, asserting his Fifth Amendment right against self-incrimination.

If Jason Giambi was not the champion of performance enhancing drug consumption, David Segui might have been. By his own account, Segui took steroids he purchased from Kirk Radomski throughout the 1990s and apparently up until his retirement in 2004.[8] Segui suffered from joint pain. The last check Segui wrote Radomski was dated July 27, 2004, appeared on page 151 of the Mitchell Report, and was for $1,800. Oddly, Segui apparently received his HGH from a Florida doctor instead of Radomski.

Eric Gagne, most famous during his years with the Los Angeles Dodgers, illustrated, like Barry Bonds and David Ortiz, the difficulty of calibrating the influence and impact of performance enhancing drugs in baseball. If the timeline of Gagne's use in the Mitchell Report was accurate, he saved 55 games, won both the Cy Young Award as best pitcher in the National League and the Rolaids Relief Pitcher of the Year Award as best relief pitcher in the National League without performance enhancing drugs in 2003. In 2004, Gagne received two kits of HGH that his Dodgers catcher, Paul Lo Duca, had purchased. That year Gagne saved 45 games and once again won the award for best relief pitcher in the National League.[9] What was the difference in performance? *With* HGH, Gagne arguably had a worse year, at least in terms of having ten fewer saves. Indeed, Gagne's Major League record of 84 consecutive saves over three seasons involved two seasons without HGH and one with HGH.[10] How do you determine where, what, and how this insidious drug affected Gagne? Or was it a coincidence that he took HGH in the second half of this streak and it had no effect?[11]

By June of 2001, Kevin Brown was no longer the dominating pitcher who had led the 1998 San Diego Padres to the World Series. He was with the Yankees, the team that had rolled over him in that World Series, and Brown was nearing the end of his productive career. The Yankees placed him on the Disabled List in June with a neck injury and then again in July with an elbow injury. Perhaps in exasperation and desperation that his body was breaking down, Brown called Kirk Radomski for HGH. Radomski delivered the goods and Brown paid Radomski $8,000 in cash.[12] The next year, 2002, Brown was placed on the Disabled List again, and again for an injured elbow. Radomski said he sold Brown the anabolic steroid Deca-Durabolin this time. Through 2003 and perhaps into 2004, Radomski sold Brown performance enhancing drugs on an estimated five or six occasions, most often multiple kits of HGH, paying perhaps as much as $10,000 in cash.

Chuck Knoblauch was called to Washington to testify before Waxman Committee attorneys and to discuss his use of performance enhancing drugs, apparently in the hope that he would implicate Roger Clemens. Press reports and misleading comments by George Mitchell, Congressman Waxman, and others to the contrary, Knoblauch did not implicate Clemens. Worse for the

Clemens haters, Knoblauch seriously undermined McNamee's carefully cultivated image as a passive injector who sheepishly acquiesced to the demands of Roger Clemens. Attorney Phil Schiliro began the Knoblauch examination with the blanket question that began all the depositions, "Is the information relating to you yourself accurate?"[13]

Knoblauch replied,

> "I would say generally accurate.... When it says that he acquired human growth hormone from Radomski for myself, I just want to note that I did never know and still to this day don't know Radomski. If he were here I wouldn't be able to point him out."
>
> "You were giving the money, essentially to Jason Grimsley, you didn't know where it was going to end up?"
>
> "And I had no idea where it was going. I didn't know where Grimsley and I didn't know where McNamee was getting this from."

Knoblauch acknowledged receiving a letter from Mitchell and said, "I got a request from Senator Mitchell, but I didn't know the specifics of what he was going to ask me." Unlike Clemens and Pettitte, however, Knoblauch was retired in 2008 and Mitchell did not have to go through the Players Association or their lawyers to send him such a notice. On the other hand, since he was retired, he could not be punished by Major League Baseball for taking performance enhancing drugs, should MLB have attempted to do so retroactively.

Schiliro read from the Mitchell Report: "McNamee injected Knoblauch seven to nine times beginning in spring training and continuing through the early part of the 2000 season." Knoblauch agreed.[14] Knoblauch added that McNamee had trained him personally, but was not sure whether that was in McNamee's capacity as assistant Yankees trainer or just for him personally, and he could not recall paying him at all.[15] Knoblauch said he had no personal relationship with McNamee outside of his role as the team's assistant strength coach. "I didn't know him that well personally."[16]

Knoblauch was asked,

> "In the context of what he has said in the Mitchell Report, do you think he's a credible person?"
>
> "I can only comment about the report in regards to me."[17]
>
> "And in that regard?"
>
> "Yes, somewhat."
>
> "Was the first time you used growth hormone with Brian McNamee or had you done that previously?"
>
> "I had never done growth hormone previously. Still to this day, I have never taken a steroid.
>
> "First time with McNamee. I had a throwing problem towards the end of my career. I went to spring training a month early to deal with it. The problem actually started at the end of 1999, not 2000, as Yankee fans will say it started when I first got there. I got to my wits' end with that.[18]
>
> "So when spring training started, I felt myself weak, vulnerable, you know, grabbing for— trying to get something—you know, just weak and vulnerable. *And McNamee happened to*

approach me in spring training. And that's the first time I ever heard the three letters HGH or human growth hormone. [emphasis added]"

"What do you remember about the conversation?"[19]

"Okay. He approached me and talked about human growth hormone and said it was a natural substance occurring in your body, and that this could be of some help to you, could make you feel better, could replenish—I mean, he described to me that you lose growth hormone in your body as you get older."

"And how long did you end up using it?"

"I would say, to the best of my knowledge, spring training and then I stopped sometime during the year."

"Any reason why you stopped?"

"I don't know exactly why. It wasn't working for me."

"When you had the conversation with Mr. McNamee, did you think—with your throwing problem, was that a physical problem, or do you think it was a psychological problem?"[20]

"I still do not know to this day, if it was physical or—I mean, my arm physically I think was okay. There was no injury, you know. But it hurt all the time."

"From our investigation, we know that players often discussed the benefits and risks of steroids, human growth hormone, other performance-enhancing substances, with each other.[21] In your experience in baseball, did you see that happen? Were you part of that?"

"I don't remember ever being a part of a conversation or anything of that nature."

"Were people by their lockers saying, 'Hey, I tried this; I am getting good results'?"

"I never had any conversations like that, never heard anybody talking about it."

"I will start with Roger Clemens. Did you ever have conversations with him about performance-enhancing substances?"

"Never had conversations with Roger Clemens about anything like that."

"And did you have any knowledge of anything he might have been doing?"

"I had no knowledge, none."[22]

"Any suspicions when you were playing."

"No."

"So there's nothing you would have that's relevant to Mr. Clemens?"

"There is nothing I could tell you at all about Roger Clemens in regards to any of this."

"Why do players take B-12 injections?"

"Because with the game of baseball, you get sick because you get run down, because you play three nights in a row, especially with the Yankees because you play prime-time games. So instead of a smaller-market team playing a day game on a getaway day to go to the next city, the Yankees always played at night. So you are finding yourself getting up or getting to the next town at four or five o'clock in the morning. So guys get sick. And that was a little bit of a boost, I think, just like taking vitamins would be." [This could explain why Clemens had his worst years, statistically, with the Yankees.]

"On any team you were with, do you remember it being a normal thing, people would go in and get B-12 shots?"

"I don't think it was any more normal or less normal than trying to go get medicine if you were sick, you know."[23]

Schiliro asked Knoblauch if he had knowledge about what McNamee did with his other clients with any substances. "I had no knowledge of anything about that."

Knoblauch's lawyer, Diana Marshall, of Liskow & Lewis in Houston, suggested, "Something about the context of, would have had the opportunity to actually see or know what these other people were doing in the way of B-12 injections or penicillin injections."[24]

"Yeah," replied Knoblauch.

> "That was something that everybody would see.
> "The Yankee trainer room is big, but there is a back room where the orthopedic doctor would come in and look at the X-rays or whatever. And if you were sick or had to be checked, you went back in this room, you know, not hiding anything, but just for the players' privacy with doctors. So there wasn't, you know, nothing was done like amongst everybody, in the middle of the locker room or anything."
> "Were there other places in the locker room where there was privacy?"[25]
> "The bathroom, if you are in the bathroom stall or shower. It is not very private you know. And I am talking about the Yankees because there is so much media attention. There are people looking at you getting dressed every day. So the privacy thing, it doesn't exist. There are very few spots where you can be by yourself in a locker room."[26]
> "Has anyone from the Hendricks firm been in touch with you?"[27]
> "I haven't spoken to Randy or Alan Hendricks. It is not a regular practice of mine. I have been out of the game for five years."
> "Do you remember paying McNamee?"[28]
> "I don't recall paying McNamee."
> "Can you recall for us some of the details of how you got shots from McNamee?"[29]
> "In spring training I would go to his apartment. There was a vial in a box, a powdery substance, and then a vial of something. I am assuming it was sterile water. And you mix the two. And then he would inject me in my stomach area.[30]
> "In '02 when I did get it from Grimsley, I injected myself. It was not a fun thing, and I didn't know what I was doing. I was waiting for something to work, I still had the problem.
> "And then I had another devastating thing happen in spring training '02. My father passed away. I was in bad shape. So unfortunately I made the mistake of still trying to do the stuff, and having no knowledge about it."

Ironically, baseball writers made Andy Pettitte into a hero for saying he heard Roger Clemens admit to taking HGH, although Pettitte remembered absolutely nothing specific about their conversation. Pettitte's real value was actually providing the most detailed account of any player as to *why* he took a performance enhancing drug. The following discussion before Congressional lawyers began when Michael Gordon of the Committee on Oversight and Government Reform said to Pettitte,

> "As I'm sure you know, the Mitchell Report contains some allegations by Brian McNamee regarding your use of human growth hormone, HGH. McNamee told Senator Mitchell that he obtained HGH on your behalf and that he injected you with it multiple times in 2002. Is the information in the Mitchell Report generally accurate?"[31]
> "Yes."
> "Do you remember how it came up or who raised the idea?"
> "Well, I flew Mac down to Tampa when I went on the DL. He wasn't working with the Yankees anymore and I asked him to come down and train me. And I know that I either brought it up to him or he brought it up to me from the standpoint, 'I'm like, dude, I am hurt, you

know my elbow is hurt. What can I do? Is there anything I can do?' So that is where the initial, you know—it had to come up to me getting it and him injecting me with the HGH."[32]

"Do you remember whether you knew about it first or whether he planted the idea of HGH?"

"I think that he had to have told me that, you know, 'I hear this stuff's good man. I hear this stuff can repair your tissue, you know.' All I know is that I know for sure that he told me that it could help repair my tissue in my elbow. I know that my ligament was either fraying or something else was going on as far as the tissue in my elbow. And you know, since 1996 [Pettitte's rookie year], the Yankee doctor, Dr. Andrew, has been telling me that my ligament was fraying. I've had elbow problems my entire career. From '96 until this season, my arm's just hurt. I've had a lot of stuff done, and a lot of medication."[33]

"You initially talked to him and he discouraged you from using it and later he ultimately agreed to give it to you. Is that generally correct?"

"Yeah."

"What did he tell you?"

"He knows I'm a Christian man. And he told me that he did not think that I would feel comfortable doing it once I did it. "I felt like it was the right thing to do. I was making an awful lot of money. I wanted to give back to the team. I had been on the DL before. But I knew I had hurt my elbow pretty bad this time. I was on there for an extended period of time, where before with my elbow I'd only missed a couple of weeks. And I just felt like it was the honorable thing to do, if I could do whatever I could to try to get back on the field and try to earn my money. I just told him I think that I ought to do it. And so that's why he agreed to do it."[34]

"Do you remember whether at the time you knew that other players were taking it and it was helping them; was that in your mind?"

"No, it wasn't talked about a lot. I can't really ever really remember talking about it in the clubhouse with guys."

"I guess the second paragraph it says, 'McNamee recalled that he'd injected Pettitte with human growth hormone that McNamee obtained from Radomski on two to four occasions.' Is that right?"[35]

"Yeah. I believe he injected me for two days, which would have been four occasions. It would be morning and night. And you know it wasn't anything that he brought to my room and so, you know, I went up to his room to get it."

"And why did you stop after the four injections?"

"I did feel uncomfortable with it. I can't explain any better than that, just knowing if you've ever been somewhere and you didn't feel right about it, so you just leave. Before, any injections I'd ever had had been administered to me by a team doctor or a trainer."[36]

"Where did you receive the injections?"

"In my stomach."

"And what part of the stomach?"

"I would say right close to the belly button."

Pettitte's attorney, Robert Ferrell, interrupted at this point to say, "I think you should explain that it's under the skin instead of a deep one."

Pettitte agreed. "Right. Yeah. It was a smaller needle. He would kind of pull away a little bit of fat on my belly button area and just put the needle right there."

"Do you have any idea where he got the HGH?"

"I could have sworn I thought he'd told me that he got it from his family doctor. I know he didn't tell me he got it from a Mets clubhouse trainer."

"Oh, right."

"Because I know if he had told me that, I would have never done it."

"Did you say you were under the impression he had a prescription for it or that he had gotten it from a doctor?"[37]

"I'm not real sure. Just being as honest as I can, I probably didn't think he had a prescription for it."

"Do you remember what it looked like?"[38]

"I don't. It was in a syringe."

"You didn't see him prepare the syringe?"

"No."

"Did it help? Was it effective for your elbow?"

"I don't think so because I think you have to take the stuff for an extended period of time. And you know, I didn't believe it did."

"Other than the HGH that McNamee provided you in 2002, was there ever any other time that you used HGH?"[39]

"Yes."

"Can you tell me about that?"

"In 2004. I was on the DL. My dad had been using it. I had found out I believe *through McNamee* [emphasis added]. My dad's had a world of health problems. I know my mother came to me also and was extremely concerned and asked me to get him to stop. So I had a conversation with my dad. When my mom came to me and was showing so much concern, I didn't know much about it. All I knew was what McNamee told me that it could repair tissue. I went to the Astros strength trainer, asked him about it. He didn't know a whole lot about it. He had just heard that it could accelerate the process for some kind of disease, cancer or something. So I went back to my dad and told him that I didn't think he should do it.

"Again, I was on the DL. First start of the season with the Houston Astros in '04.[40] I check swung, very first at-bat, and I popped a tendon in my elbow.[41] My flexor tendon. The next day I had an MRI, found out I needed to have surgery and decided not to have surgery. But I just signed a $30 million contract with the Astros. My first start with the hometown team and I was like, there's no way I'm going out like this. So I got a few cortisone injections into my elbow that year through the team doctor to try to help me get back.[42] I came back off the DL after trying to rehab it. Went back on the DL again.[43] Had to miss a start here and there. Through all this I was getting Toradol injections, which was a painkiller, administered by the Astros team doctors and trainers. I ended up going back to my dad and asked if he had any of the HGH that he had before. He ended up bringing me two syringes over to my house. I injected myself once in the morning and once at night. I did it for that day. And to this day, I don't know why, it doesn't make a heck of a lot of sense. *I was desperate and you know I really knew that it wasn't going to help me* [emphasis added]. My flexor tendon was already torn. I knew I needed surgery."

Pettitte's lawyer, Thomas Farrell, asked for the record, "And you did have surgery later that year to repair it?"

"Yeah. I had surgery about a month and a half later."

"What type of supplements have you used—creatine?"[44]

"Yeah."

"How about androstenediol? It's not an anabolic steroid. You know, it's the thing that Mark McGwire said he was taking."[45]

"Yes."

"Have you ever used Andro?"

"No."

"I thought you said a trainer for the Yankees may have given you B-12 shots?"[46]

"Yeah. The B-12 shots that I got with the Yankees were administered to me by our trainer, not by our team doctor."

"Any GNC products?"[47]

"All I can tell you is that I take a protein drink that I get from our trainers with the Yankees. I don't know what the stuff has in it. I don't ask a whole lot of questions about stuff. I just kind of trust people to give me what's good for me."

10

The Mysterious Mister McNamee

"Well, he hasn't told you many lies. It's really a creditably clear and consistent account of what happened, with everything of importance left out."—G.K. Chesterton

A man seldom gets an opportunity in this life to confess to a crime he did not commit in order to be exonerated from crimes he did commit. Yet that was apparently the wonderful opportunity granted Brian Jerome McNamee as he sat down before the Waxman Committee lawyers to give his Congressional deposition on March 9, 2008. It was the third time McNamee told his tale of injecting Roger Clemens with performance enhancing drugs, and his basic outline was polished by that day. Such a confession offered McNamee the freedom of the essayist or novelist such as the apparent confessions of Zeno, Voltaire, Montaigne, and the Marquis de Sade. Who knew if these literary confessions were true, but they were certainly entertaining. Of course criminals make such "confessions" and/or accusations all the time in exchange for reduced jail time, but those informants do so privately, in deals worked out with prosecutors, and they are not made public. McNamee made the confession for no jail time at all, a far better deal than most informants get.

More than eight years after McNamee's congressional deposition, it is interesting to reflect upon the acceptance and support his appearance engendered at the time. With his supporters at New York's *Daily News* dominating the daily reports of wrongdoing by Clemens, McNamee had his purported interrogators in the palm of his hand even before they asked a question: "Can you guys refer to me as Brian or Mac? I would feel more comfortable instead of Mr. McNamee."[1]

"I will try to do that," Majority senior investigative counsel Michael Gordon answered obediently. Imagine if Clemens, several days before, had asked to be called the Rocket or Roger? The sports media would have gone berserk when they heard about it.

Brian McNamee remained a shadowy, unknown character, mainly defined over the years as *not Roger Clemens*. By all accounts, and particularly his own, his relationship with Clemens was complicated. McNamee portrayed himself as an overused house boy who not only injected Clemens with illegal, performance enhancing drugs without being paid either for the drugs or his service,[2] but also serving as Clemens' dietician, baby-sitter in taking care of the Clemens boys when he was in Houston, buying groceries for Clemens[3]—and even packing up Clemens' clothes into travel bags—all these other tasks apparently without compensation. In short, McNamee believed that life with Roger Clemens was a one-way street and, like a lot of famous people used to being catered to, McNamee believed Roger Clemens was a user. "I couldn't count on him for things,[4] "McNamee said. "I did a ton of things for his family, a ton of things for his kids."[5] Clemens apparently made a lot of promises to McNamee in order to keep him around. McNamee became frustrated with the way Clemens was always "telling me things that never came through. Time and time again I cancelled family plans, I cancelled this, I cancelled that. And then he would just go, sorry, man, I got to do something else."[6]

In fact, when asked in his congressional deposition whether he had ever gone to Clemens' house and not injected anabolic steroids or HGH into him, McNamee replied somewhat pathetically, "I was at his house during Christmastime because he asked me to buy groceries for him."[7]

Later, he was asked whether he had ever been alone in the house with Debbie Clemens. He responded,

"A lot of times."[8]
"Did you socialize at all with Roger and Debbie?"
"A couple of lunches."
"You'd work out Roger during the day, but you wouldn't necessarily hang out with them in the evenings?"
"Hang out in a social sense, no. Hang out in a kids' practice, baseball practice; basketball games, yes. Work the kids out, you know, stuff like that. Watch TV after we got done working maybe, in the kitchen, but not social."
"So is it fair to say that you were an employee of his?"
"I was an employee of his."
"As opposed to a colleague or a buddy?"
"I was an employee—we were buddies at an arm's distance."
"You were asked also before when you first met Mr. Clemens in Toronto and what your view of him was.... I think you said, well, he was another pitcher, and you didn't admire him yet; is that about right?"[9]
"I treated him as another pitcher on the staff that I had to train, yes."
"Did there come a time during your relationship where you really started to admire him?"
"I admired him for his work ethic and the way he was with his kids, with his family."
"As a person?"
"As a father and as a Major League Baseball player."

"Anything more than that?"

"No."

"Did you have any resentment to him?"

"None whatsoever."

"No reason to?"

"I could have been, but I wasn't though—you know the only issues I had with Roger were between scheduling conflicts and, you know, telling me things that never came through and me—he would do a schedule. Time and time again I cancelled family plans, I cancelled this, I cancelled that. And then he would go, sorry, man, I got to do something else. He made everyone else upset, but I didn't get upset about it."

"You didn't say you admired him for his personal qualities."

"Well, your evaluation of my words are correct. But I'll say it again, I didn't believe the things that he'd tell me to be true most of the time. And most of the time, the things that he would tell me weren't true. And it wasn't like I ever confronted him on those things. I just wrote it off as him just liking to hear himself speak."

"Do you want to provide any specific examples?"[10]

"Yeah, he would just say things out of nowhere ... he'd show me an ad and he'd say he was getting ten of those, I'm going to give you like five watches. Okay great. If I won the Cy Young this year, I'm going to take care of you and your family the rest of their lives. I think he still goes—was his wife ever a Dallas Cowgirl cheerleader? He goes with that one all the time. But it was to the point where I didn't listen to what he was saying any more about stuff like that."

"So there is a contradiction between how you felt he treated you and not being honest. But also as you said in the phone call, he treated you very well in other ways?"

"Yeah, brought me into his house, fed me. There was a fine line. There was a very fine line between employer/employee, loyalty, and trust and then you have the friendship thing. You know, I don't think I could count on him for things.... I did a ton of things for his family, a ton of things for his kids. We did things for each other."[11]

Obviously, McNamee either remained in denial about his clear resentment of Clemens both in the civil suits for defamation against each other and in the criminal trial that everyone assumed from the beginning would be arranged for Roger Clemens.

The Brian McNamee who emerged from this national controversy seemed to be man who was desperately torn between his desire to be accepted by Clemens—a man he understood had many acquaintances but few real friends—as a close confidant and buddy, and his angry motivation to act as Clemens' assassin—because of the deep humiliation he felt by being treated as Clemens' cabana boy rather than his friend. Roger Clemens, according to Brian McNamee, could have done a lot more for Brian McNamee. Therefore McNamee implied that Clemens, like a lot of successful people, saved his valuable chits to cash in himself and never gave McNamee anything in return—say, for instance, a recommendation for a high-paying job or supplying McNamee with important contacts that could either make McNamee real money or a real career. Indeed, according to McNamee, Clemens seldom even recommended McNamee to others as a conditioning coach even though

Clemens liked and praised McNamee's work. Clemens admitted as much. "I don't think I recommended him to—any other players."[12] These conflicts may have remained sublimated until federal prosecutors squeezed McNamee.

The famous 17-minute telephone conversation between Clemens and McNamee that Clemens taped and played to the press after the release of the Mitchell Report betrayed an affection and even tenderness. The circumstances were extraordinary. Only a few weeks before the release of the report, knowing by then that Clemens would be implicated as a criminal by the trainer's words, McNamee telephoned Clemens to borrow a fishing rod for his son. It was as if Lee Harvey Oswald had called up JFK the week before he assassinated him and asked to borrow his yacht, the "Honey Fitz." McNamee had just destroyed Clemens' legacy and certain path to the Baseball Hall of Fame. Both men knew their conversation was taped. Both men attempted to exonerate themselves in front of the world. Clemens stuck to his script, stated for the record that he was not guilty of the steroids and HGH allegations, but his voice wavered when McNamee brought up his son's illness and pleaded, "Roger, what do you want me to do? What do you want me to do?" McNamee's voice was desperate despite his insistence later that he was in command and merely holding back from implicating Clemens.[13] It was either the voice of a man who was scared to death of Roger Clemens or a man who missed Roger Clemens. Indeed, two months after Clemens had infuriated McNamee by playing the tape about his son's illness, which McNamee claimed prompted him to retrieve the vial and syringe from his basement; after Clemens had said on *60 Minutes* that McNamee injected him with B-12 and Lidocaine and not steroids and HGH; after Clemens had initiated a lawsuit for defamation—and after they dueled daily through their lawyers and PR spokesmen—McNamee still lamented, "I would rather everything go back to the way it was before the Mitchell Report was released."[14]

It seemed that Clemens did talk Texas-big about what he would do for people, perhaps really meaning it at the time he said it, perhaps just talking instinctively when he felt good about something. Grateful for being brought to the Yankees, where he was able to earn two World Series rings, he claimed the only way to repay the Yankees was to "make money for the coaches and the grounds crew and the clubhouse attendants by getting into the playoffs and World Series. There's a bond there and it's meaningful. It's important to me to do well in the Series so they get a check that maybe helps them put an addition on their house."[15] Clemens did not give McNamee the kind of money to put an addition on his house.

"If I needed money, I never went to him anyway," McNamee said. "I went to one of his agent people."[16] Clemens promised McNamee an interest in and a salary from a fitness center that never materialized. "I thought I could fall back on that," McNamee said.[17]

McNamee also thought he could fall back on a start-up vitamin company.[18] "This company was a ground-floor company that was just up and coming and they had two great doctors behind their product.... You can't get better than that as far as nutrition," McNamee said. "And I was going to get an opportunity to help design a sports line. And Roger was going to ruin it."[19] Indeed Roger Clemens did ruin that opportunity for Brian McNamee. McNamee tried to use a photograph of Clemens, McNamee, and Andy Pettitte on exercise bikes to advertise the company. He did not have permission to use the photograph, Clemens' lawyers got involved, Debbie Clemens insisted upon a $300,000 fee for her husband,[20] and in the end the start-up company went belly-up. The failure of McNamee's vitamin startup undermined the strongest logic that he was telling the truth about injecting Clemens—that he told Andy Pettitte and others that he was giving HGH to Clemens, and told only Pettitte that Clemens was taking steroids—because the claim to Pettitte about the steroids came *after* his blowup with Clemens over the company. Perhaps intimidated by Clemens, McNamee complained about this and other issues to Andy Pettitte. "Mac would tell me all kinds of stuff," Pettitte recalled. "And I just kind of was an ear for him to chew on. And I just listened to him ... acknowledging him and kind of pacify him and just listened to him gripe."[21]

Money dominated McNamee's priorities, not any loyalty or sentimentality about Roger Clemens. He admitted at trial to selling even some of the memorabilia and gifts Clemens had given him.[22] When U.S. Magistrate Judge Cheryl Pollack urged Clemens to settle McNamee's defamation suit in April 2014, McNamee, no doubt, would have accepted in a New York minute any reasonable financial offer from Clemens.[23] Clemens and attorney Rusty Hardin, as a matter of principle, had no interest in giving McNamee even 50 cents.

When McNamee landed in trouble with the law, when he faced a defamation suit from Roger Clemens, he expected to be financially supported. A Brooklyn attorney McNamee queried about representing him said that McNamee wanted free representation and had no intention of paying for a lawyer. Fortunately for him, he found two attorneys, Earl Ward and Richard Emery, who agreed to lead a team of experienced lawyers to work *pro se* (along with some interns, who likely wanted to work on such a high-profile case to pad their resumes). The only way for McNamee to pay Ward and Emery was to win his defamation suit against Clemens. While McNamee did not win the defamation case, he did manage to settle with Clemens' insurance company in 2015.[24] Clemens paid nothing personally and retained the future right to sue McNamee.[25] Indeed, Clemens told the *Houston Chronicle*, "I was not present,

10. The Mysterious Mister McNamee

nor would I have participated in paying one dime." McNamee's attorney Richard Emery called the agreement fair.[26] Emery also said, "At this point it's water over the dam. It's high time. This is old news these days."[27] Of course, the details of such settlements, including the amount of money involved, is negotiated between the lawyers and is privileged and confidential as a matter of law.

Houston Attorney Chip Babcock, who handled the settlement negotiations for Clemens, told the author in 2016, "I stood up in district court and said, 'I want it to be clear that Mr. Clemens does not want to settle. He wants to go to trial.'" Babcock added, "We were prepared to call Dr. James R. Andrews (the legendary shoulder and arm specialist who has performed most of the Tommy John surgeries on pitchers for many years), who gave Roger a complete physical every year from 1986 onward, and he would have testified that there was no way Roger had been doing steroids. We would have called Chuck Knoblauch who would have contradicted everything McNamee said about the pool incident in Florida. We had a baseball stat guy who would have explained Roger's pitching patterns. We would even have called Jeff Novitzky to testify about McNamee's truthfulness. But the Magistrate Judge wanted a settlement and pushed Roger's insurance company to do so. We wanted a public settlement so everybody could get an accurate read on how much Roger's homeowner's policy paid. The other side would not agree to that.

McNamee, described as a "sour, taciturn man with a long jaw and narrow eyes,"[28] a man with a bit of a resemblance to Woody Allen, only with the nose of Karl Malden, was mistrusted by Roger Clemens' agents at Hendricks Sports Management. Agent Jim Murray, testifying before Congress, called him "shaky," meaning strange, not really knowing him and wondering where he was coming from.[29] Murray, who represented more than a hundred Major League players in marketing and equipment deals, said: "He did from time-to-time send some e-mails that I couldn't really figure out."[30] Murray testified that McNamee always wanted something, whether it was free merchandise and equipment from Clemens' marketing deals, such as with Louisville Slugger, a job as an agent with a percentage of the action, Clemens' help in promoting the vitamin company, or to sue somebody. For reasons that Murray could not recall, McNamee even threatened to sue the Hendricks Agency.[31] Murray also referred to McNamee as "suspicious."[32] Moreover, Randy Hendricks, a principal of the agency, referred to McNamee as "a nut" and "crazy."[33]

Murray, and therefore the Hendricks Agency, also did not trust McNamee because he believed the strength coach leaked information about their clients to the press, specifically inside information about player injuries or impending signings.[34]

In a transcribed interview of McNamee, conducted by John "Billy" Belk and John Yarbrough, investigators for Clemens' legal team,[35] 42 lines of the transcript are redacted—hinting at some sort of sexual allegation. McNamee makes reference to the government prosecutors asking a question about Andy Pettitte and states, "they did ask something about Andy that was messed up."[36] Did government agents conjecture that Andy Pettitte, who had a young, smooth face, had sexual relations with McNamee or was gay? Or did prosecutors ask McNamee whether he and Clemens were lovers? There was no evidence of that, but Eleanor Holmes Norton[37] remarked during the hearing—after learning that Clemens had obtained Bruce Springsteen concert tickets for McNamee—"I call that love."[38]

Who was Brian McNamee? The man who claimed to have conspired to inject Roger Clemens with illegal, performance enhancing drugs and also to engage in an unlawful side business (or was it his main business?) with Wall Street bankers, was dropped like last year's mistress by the press when his questionable past undermined his credibility and the possibility that he could bring down the hated Clemens. In its zeal to convict Clemens, Brian McNamee remained a fragmentary person in the press accounts. Even his biographers at New York's *Daily News* stated that his exit from the New York Police Department remained a mystery.[39] This much was certain: he grew up in Breezy Point, New York, a small sandy island in Queens that borders the Atlantic Ocean, not far from JFK International Airport. Breezy Point was eminently affordable and its rows of homes were populated by New York City police officers. The town was devastated by Super-Storm Sandy in October 2012, fire and floods destroying more than a hundred homes. McNamee's father was a cop and obviously a good one, for he became an FBI agent. A brother also served the NYPD. Young Brian played catcher on a good baseball team at St. John's University and graduated with a degree in finance.

But McNamee's story became sketchy in a hurry. Why didn't he try to get a job in finance? Instead he became a cop like his father and brother, serving in the NYPD for three and a half years, according to his own account. Nothing wrong with becoming one of New York's finest, of course, but why did he become a cop? Was law enforcement simply in his blood and he determined he had to follow in his Dad's footsteps? Or did he take the easy way out and join the police force instead of climbing the greasy pole of the financial world? Was there a recession that made it difficult to find employment on Wall Street or with some business? Did he lack ambition? Was he really a jock who would forever miss being around his beloved sport of baseball? Was he just a confused young person like a lot of young people and didn't know what he really wanted to do yet? Was he just a "wannabee" who liked to hang out with famous athletes?

More to the point, why did he give up his secure job as a cop? New York

City policemen were not rich but they had good benefits. His wife was a school teacher. Once McNamee quit the police force and worked as a personal trainer/conditioning coach, the couple depended entirely on his wife's employment for important benefits such as medical insurance. And McNamee's son, Brian, Jr., had diabetes. The trial did reveal that McNamee was once suspended from the NYPD for 30 days for losing his gun,[40] however that happened. He also got in trouble while on the force for tampering with a dead body.[41]

McNamee's *Daily News* biographers described him as "a sardonic wise guy from working-class Queens."[42] The description was 180 degrees from that given by his part-time employer, Roger Clemens: "Not much of a personality, but that's all right."[43] But then in the kind of maddening discrepancy that made it difficult to get a handle on McNamee, the same book written by the *Daily News* reporters provided this description of the former cop at a party: "McNamee was sitting on a chair against the wall, removed from the din of the guests, his typical behavior in social situations."[44]

That book portrayed Jerome Brian McNamee in the light of his namesake Saint Jerome, the fourth-century monk known for his biblical commentaries, along with a little martyrdom of Saint Paul thrown in. Saint Jerome created controversy, too, when his late translations of the Old Testament from Hebrew to Latin adhered to a more fundamental vision of the Old Testament out of fashion at the time.[45] The gospel, according to *The Daily News*, began with the heart-breaking story of Brian McNamee, Jr.'s diabetes, the official explanation for McNamee's skill with a syringe. Roger Clemens then turned him into a drug dealer. How Roger Clemens forced McNamee into his side business of selling anabolic steroids and HGH to Wall Street gym rats was not explained by the *Daily News*, or any other media organization for that matter.

McNamee worked as a bullpen catcher for the Yankees for two years. His stint ended in 1995 when the team cleaned house upon the firing of manager Buck Showalter and the arrival of a new administration under manager Joe Torre. McNamee found a job in Toronto three years later as a conditioning coach for the Blue Jays, through connections with a St. John's classmate who was working as an executive with the Jays. What exactly did McNamee do from 1995 to 1998? No one seemed to know whether McNamee was involved with illegal performance enhancing drugs during those years.

McNamee met Roger Clemens in spring training in 1998, the season after Clemens won the Cy Young Award with the American League's Blue Jays. Clemens was so out of shape he looked like the Pillsbury Dough Boy, according to McNamee—apparently for the first time in Clemens' storied career. McNamee did disclaim the idea that the steroids injections alone led to Clemens' 1998 success. He stated for the record that his workout regimen plus the performance enhancing drugs spurred on Clemens. The subsequent claim by McNamee that it was his workout regime, however, made Clemens even more furious than the steroids allegations. He fumed, "Brian McNamee did not make me an athlete, despite his ongoing claims by he and his lawyer that they continue to throw stuff out there that he made me. I had a great workout ethic before I met him. I have never smoked a cigarette, I have never smoked dope, I have never done cocaine. I would not put anything—allow anybody to put anything in my body that's going to be harmful to me. That's who I am as a person."[46]

Upon completion of his spectacular 1998 season, Clemens apparently decided his outsized accomplishments in the game were not enough. He wanted to be on a championship team. The news that Dave Stewart, his old playoff pitching adversary for the Oakland Athletics, would be coming to Toronto to assume the duties of pitching coach no doubt hastened his departure from the Jays. Stewart had complained publicly that some of the Cy Young Awards won by Clemens should have been given to him.

McNamee remained in Toronto for another season and, apparently at the suggestion of Blue Jays' management, pursued an online degree in nutrition and conditioning to enhance his credentials. Several books, based on newspaper stories, have suggested that Roger Clemens was desperate to have McNamee with him in New York and pulled strings to make it happen. Clemens admitted he did put in a good word for McNamee with Yankees General Manager Brian Cashman, and Cashman testified at the trial that Clemens asked him to hire McNamee because "he knew Clemens' body."[47] But McNamee's biographers at the *Daily News* reported that McNamee also made a direct application to Cashman himself. It seems unlikely that the Yankees would have hired McNamee without at least a courtesy call to one of their video technicians, Charlie Wonsowicz, Brian McNamee's college roommate at St. Johns.[48] Wonsowicz also did duty as a batting practice pitcher.

Over the next two years, 2000–2001, Brian Jerome McNamee said he served William Roger Clemens as private injector of performance enhancing drugs, personal trainer, off-season workout instructor, and house servant. Coincidentally, 2001 marked the last year of McNamee's employment with the Yankees, the year Roger Clemens stopped taking illegal drugs (presuming that he ever used them in the first place) for some unexplained reason, and the last year that McNamee could be prosecuted for drug distribution based on his 2007 admission to federal prosecutors, due to the six-year statute of limitations. It was also, perhaps not coincidentally for McNamee's narrative, Clemens's best year pitching for the Yankees.

As the Yankees made a dramatic run through the playoffs in the aftermath of 9/11, losing the World Series in seven extraordinary games to the Arizona Diamondbacks, McNamee sedated himself with alcohol, various medications, and perhaps other drugs. He collapsed and passed out in the bar of a Seattle hotel.[49] During a heated cross examination by Rusty Hardin during the 2012 trial, McNamee denied that he was an alcoholic.

The Yankees of 2001 were a lot like Clemens himself, in the latter throes of a dynasty that had begun in 1996 and would stumble on, somewhat like the tottering Ottoman Empire in its final centuries, until a final World Series title in 2009, when only Derek Jeter, Jorge Posada and Andy Pettitte remained from the original nucleus of players. Clemens' astonishing statistics of 20–3, a 3.51 ERA and 213 strikeouts in 2001 were somewhat humanized by the run support the Yankees provided him: 5.74 runs a game.[50] Yet this Yankees' dynasty was not based on the power-hitting "Five O'Clock Lightning" of the 1950s and early 1960s dynasty, but rather on outstanding pitching, smart baseball, and clutch hitting. These years witnessed perfect games by pitchers David Wells and David Cone and a no-hitter by aging Dwight Gooden. The team was fourth in the American League in home runs in 2001 with 203, and fifth in runs, 804, but it was also second in stolen bases, 161. Indeed, 38-year-old Paul O'Neill stole 22 bases, Alfonso Soriano 43, Derek Jeter 27, and Chuck Knoblauch 38. Center fielder Bernie Williams batted .307 and Derek Jeter .311. First baseman Tino Martinez swatted 34 homers, Bernie Williams 26, and Jorge Posada 22. Mike Mussina went 17–11, with a 3.15 ERA and 214 strikeouts. Andy Pettitte went 15–10 with a 3.99 ERA and 164 strikeouts. The bullpen, of course, was anchored by the greatest relief pitcher of all time, Mariano Rivera, who had 50 saves, but his season would be marred by losing the seventh game of the World Series on plunk singles.

The manager of the Yankees, Joe Torre, had a similar record to that of Casey Stengel, when Stengel arrived in Yankee Stadium in 1949 to take over the team. Stengel, the clown prince of baseball since his earliest playing days, came to the Yankees with a winning percentage of only .453 (208–251) in three years running the Brooklyn Dodgers and only .432 (373–491) in six years managing the Boston Bees, later the Braves.[51] Torre had suffered through five seasons as manager of the New York Mets with a .405 winning percentage (286–420), achieved a much better .529 winning percentage with the Atlanta Braves (257–229), and returned to St. Louis, where he had been a star catcher and third baseman, to win 351 games and lose 354 games (.498) in six years.[52] Both hires were somewhat of a surprise. Stengel had not managed in the majors for six years when he was selected, and Torre had done nothing to revive the Cardinals. Both men brought their own styles. Stengel, a pioneer of player platooning, found a team that could actually hit. Torre, having spent his entire playing and managing career in the National League, brought a disciplined, tight defense, good pitching, opportunistic, base stealing approach to the American League.

Stengel was a flamboyant figure with huge elephant ears and flapping jaws that were large even by the standards of his massive head. In his final years he resembled Pope John XXIII. He was the only human being who ever lived who achieved the rhetorical feat of being satiric and sarcastic simultaneously. Stengel presided over ten Yankees pennants in 12 years and seven World Series titles, winning 1149 games and losing only 696, for a gaudy winning percentage of .623. He sort of traded places with Torre by managing the Mets at the end of his career instead of the beginning. According to a reporter who covered him at the time, Stengel concluded every game with a virtuoso performance in the clubhouse, walking around naked, his ancient, wrinkled body exposed to all in the days before women were allowed in to cover these events, gesturing to make a point, pounding his chest to complain that his general manager George "fucking Weiss" had stuck him with this bad player or that bad player, and he'd just as soon trade the bum at the first opportunity.

Torre was a patient, principled, wise father figure who came to New York as a good manager. He turned into a genius in the Bronx by taking a slow, plodding walk to the mound, where he made the sign of the right hand for Mariano Rivera to come in from the bullpen. Rivera saved 652 games in 19 seasons, the most in baseball history, achieved a stingy ERA of 2.21, and struck out 1173 batters in 1283 ⅔ innings.[53] Considering that Torre had to manage through an extended playoff calendar instead of just one post-season event, as Stengel had with the World Series, their numbers are similar. Torre won 1173 games and lost 767, a winning percentage of .605. He managed the Yankees to 12 playoff appearances in 12 years, which included six American League pennants and four World Series titles. The Steinbrenner family, which owned the Yankees eventually rewarded Torre for 12 straight years of making the playoffs in 2007— by offering him a pay cut. He politely declined the honor and went West old man to manage the Los Angeles Dodgers for three years.[54] The Dodgers, of course, originated in Brooklyn, where Joe Torre grew up.

The Yankees finished first in the American League East in 2001, with a 95–65 record, beat back the Oakland A's in a tough Divisional Series, three games to two, and then put away the Seattle Mariners, four games to one. Typical for Clemens, he was awful in the first round against the Athletics, lasting less than five innings in each of two starts, losing Game 1 and leaving with no decision in Game 5, with an ERA of 5.40. Naturally he was much better in the League Championship Series against the Seattle Mariners, allowing only one hit and no runs in a no-decision, striking out seven in a 3–1, Game 4 win. Yet once again, his age was showing. He ran out of gas after five dominant innings.[55]

10. The Mysterious Mister McNamee

Throughout the playoffs, New York Mayor Rudolph Giuliani, who had stood in the soot of the burning Tower 1 of the World Trade Center, and then ran for his life as the building collapsed in front of him, covering him with smoke and dust and debris,[56] sat in a luxury box behind the Yankees dugout, where he seemed to will the Yankees to victories.

In one of the best World Series ever played, particularly from a pitching standpoint, the Diamondbacks' dynamic duo of Randy Johnson and Curt Schilling conquered the Yankees in seven exciting, tense games, 4–3. Randy Johnson won three games, striking out 19 batters in 17⅓ innings with a spectacular 1.07 ERA. Sharing the Series MVP Award with Johnson, Curt Schilling struck out 26 batters in 21⅓ innings, was 1–0, and achieved a scintillating 1.69 ERA. Lost in the brilliance of the Arizona aces was the dominating pitching of the 38-year-old Clemens. With the Yankees behind two games to zero beginning Game 3, Clemens threw a three-hitter, allowing only one run, in a tight, 2–1 New York victory, to get them back into the Series. The ones who never quit did fight back. For the first time in World Series history, in back-to-back Games 4 and 5, first Tino Martinez, and then Scott Brosius, hit dramatic, two-out, two-run homers in the bottom of the ninth inning to set up extra-inning Yankees wins, and sent them back to Arizona, leading three games to two. Clemens did his part. In the seventh and deciding game, he scattered seven hits and one run and left in the seventh inning with a 1–1 tie, giving the ball over to the most reliable relief pitcher in the game's history.

In October 2001, Brian McNamee became ensnared in a pool incident in St. Petersburg, Florida, allegedly involving rape and the date rape drug GHB. McNamee was found by a hotel security guard, who said he saw McNamee naked in a hotel pool having sex with a woman, while his St. John's roommate Wonsowicz looked on, also naked. A police report said the woman was basically unconscious.[57]

McNamee's *Daily News* biographers put the best face possible on the incident, reporting that the woman lied to the police about her reason for being in the hotel and refused a rape kit, suggesting that Chuck Knoblauch mixed the GHB, and asserting that McNamee was not having sex with her but merely skinny-dipping, and that he was looking for a chain necklace that she had lost in the pool. It is possible that the woman did not press charges because she was having an affair with a married man and did not want the publicity. The *Daily News* alleged that Wonsowicz confirmed McNamee's story until "pressured" to change it by the New York City Police Department.[58] Wonsowicz then admitted that McNamee may have had sex with the woman. Police records revealed that McNamee denied even knowing his former roommate, Wonsowicz. When the season ended, McNamee was terminated by the Yankees. They

In 2001, the Yankees provided strong offensive support for Clemens, scoring 5.74 runs per start for their ace, who posted a 20–3 record and won his sixth Cy Young Award (courtesy National Baseball Hall of Fame Library, Cooperstown, New York).

said he had ignored his duties of training other players at the expense of working with Clemens and Pettitte. His boss with the Yankees, general manager Brian Cashman, provided this job evaluation during the Clemens trial: "This particular individual, Mr. McNamee, did not get along with people." The *Daily News*, of course, disagreed with the Yankees' explanation. "The incident," according to their book, "also revealed another side of McNamee: how far the trainer was willing to go to cover for ballplayers."[59]

The problem with the *Daily News* interpretation was that their own details contradicted their conclusion. Far from falling on his own sword, so to speak, to protect Chuck Knoblauch, McNamee accused Knoblauch of giving the woman GHB in order to save his own skin. However, Knoblauch was not caught naked in the swimming pool. Neither were the other Yankees who partied earlier in the evening with McNamee in a hotel room, Todd Greene and Clay Bellinger.

Despite the efforts of the *Daily News* to paint a benign picture of this incident, it hung over the Clemens trial like a dark cloud. Federal prosecutors successfully kept specific details of the alleged rape story out of the Clemens trial, but allusions to rape permeated the proceedings and jurors certainly got the drift that McNamee was alleged to have committed some unstated, awful act in Florida.

Another popular defense for McNamee was that his ambiguous statements not identifying Clemens as the recipient of his performance enhancing drugs, except to Andy Pettitte when he was angry at Clemens, should be construed as meaning he intended to implicate Clemens because he talked in "police code." Unfortunately, that rationale failed because none of the parties with whom McNamee discussed injecting players or keeping evidence and who testified at trial, including his estranged wife Eileen McNamee, baseball player David Segui, and baseball drug dealer Kirk Radomski, were cops, and therefore were not qualified to interpret this "code."

To summarize their relationship, Clemens believed he did a favor by giving McNamee work—literally true because McNamee did turn to Clemens when he was hard-up. McNamee, on the other hand, clearly believed that his work for Clemens would lead to more lucrative business possibilities and explained in part his loyalty to Clemens. McNamee felt Clemens did not give him much of *value* beyond being paid for his conditioning chores. McNamee no doubt thought he was ingratiating himself with Clemens by taking care of and exercising his children, and in performing menial tasks.

11
Squeezing McNamee

The single most important issue in the prosecution of Roger Clemens was whether Brian McNamee changed his story from insisting that Clemens did not take performance enhancing drugs, to claim not only that Clemens *did take performance enhancing drugs*, but also that McNamee, himself, injected Clemens.[1]

McNamee was quoted as saying, "I'm not supposed to say the government put a gun to my head." That emotional confession was made in the Belk Deposition to two former Houston cops whom McNamee spoke with at his Long Island home just prior to the release of the Mitchell Report. One could say, of course—and the government has—that McNamee was merely lying to the investigators to make it seem like he did not betray Clemens but was later forced to give him up, so to speak, or face a criminal indictment. First, McNamee's words sounded real; the words of an agitated man under intense pressure, squeezed by the Feds, without money to defend himself, estranged from his wife who sought a divorce, a man severely down on his luck. Second, the phrase "not supposed to say" sounds like what it means: he was not supposed to say he was under government pressure to change his story, an obvious defense for Clemens that the government had clearly anticipated. Circumstantial evidence suggested that federal prosecutors anticipated indicting Roger Clemens at the outset—at least a full year before any purported "medical waste" emerged. The conclusion was, therefore, inescapable: from the moment Kirk Radomski's records indicated that a strength coach of Roger Clemens distributed anabolic steroids, Clemens' fate was sealed. The Feds would pursue Clemens and send him to jail as a shiny prize to mask their failed crusade against the use of performance enhancing drugs in professional sports.

Federal prosecutors were aware that McNamee was on public record in newspapers stating that Clemens had not taken steroids or any other performance enhancing drugs.[2] To say otherwise was a change in his story, which, of course, would be hammered home relentlessly by Clemens' lawyers, as indeed it was in his second trial. Therefore, the Feds had to set up McNamee's con-

11. Squeezing McNamee

version in advance to be able to claim they never pressured him. They did this initially by leaking their case against Clemens in the press. Because of all the leaking, the government offered few surprises at trial some five years later. While the prosecutors eventually were unable to convict Clemens before a jury, they did succeed in convicting him before the audience of male sports fans. Unfortunately, both the federal prosecutors and defense attorneys weeded male sports fans from the second jury. Eight females sat on the final jury after several of the original jurors were dismissed for sleeping.

Brian McNamee, however, told an unbelievable story before the Waxman Committee attorneys. He claimed that he was never nervous about being squeezed by the Feds; gee whiz, the federal prosecutors, in fact, were such upstanding guys who really did a great job, gee whiz, you know, and wow they were so professional he wanted to kiss their feet. That was actually a contradiction to the testimony of the government's star crusader against PEDs, Jeff Novitzky, who said McNamee was "a nervous witness" who always complained about one health problem after another.[3] So the logic here was that the resentful McNamee, who seethed at Clemens for being treated like a manservant, was not angry or frightened one tiny bit at the federal attorneys who must surely have given him a good grilling. Could this be the same former cop who professed to be against steroids and other performance enhancing drugs when he simultaneously could never say no to a possible opportunity to inject a client? He even injected Andy Pettitte, who he knew would feel regret about taking such a drug.

During McNamee's Congressional deposition, House committee lawyer Michael Gordon asked him to provide a "logical background discussion in your interactions with the Federal agents that presumably was a precursor to your communications with the Mitchell folks."[4]

McNamee's "background" information made the context of a federal proffer agreement guaranteeing his freedom sound like a Sunday picnic in the park.

"I got a phone call from Jeff Novitzky on my cell phone. He then followed it up with an e-mail identifying himself. I think that was in May."

"What year?"

"Of '07. A day went by. I think I had my attorney call Jeff Novitzky, and they said they wanted to meet with me. So I think it was like June 18th, I met with Jeff Novitzky, Matt Parrella [federal prosecutor] and two other federal agents from the IRS in an office in midtown Manhattan. They came in, I was sitting there; they introduced themselves. And then Matt Parrella had gone over the scope of the proffer agreement and also why we were being asked questions about Kirk Radomski, distribution and baseball players and drug use.

"They asked, I answered. They were professional, they were courteous, they were respectful, they were to the point, and there were times where they pushed to get—and, I mean, I was never uneasy at any time throughout the whole first meeting."[5]

"You didn't feel threatened?"

"I did not feel threatened."

"You didn't feel that you would be hauled off to jail if you didn't answer questions a certain way or spoke about a certain professional player?"

"I didn't feel pressured to talk about a certain baseball player, and I didn't feel threatened by them. I was angry to be there and that I put myself in that situation. I was kind of uptight not knowing—like I didn't know what was going on as far as, you know, how much trouble I was going to be in.

"So the first meeting was tough. It was tough really for me, not on them, because their mannerisms and their professionalism transpired and just transcended into the next meeting.[6] Then we finished that meeting, you know, shaking hands. I didn't know where this was going. All I know is they were going to ask me a series of questions the following day and I was not to lie to them."

It is the author's opinion, and thereby the theory of this book, that McNamee went home that night and created his story of injecting Roger Clemens with performance enhancing drugs. The initial questioning the next day did betray an uneasiness, perhaps guilt, on McNamee's part, as he changed his long-standing story that he had never injected Clemens. But he came in to see the prosecutors the next morning with the story intact that he would tell for the next five years. And probably forever. Since there were no statutes of limitation for perjury, prosecutors decided to charge Clemens with that offense because the six-year window for indicting him for possession of illegal anabolic steroids was about to close. McNamee's creation that night had to stand the rest of his life. If he ever changed his story back to his original version, that he never injected Clemens, the federal prosecutors could indict him at any point until his dying day. One can only speculate whether McNamee felt assured, based upon the fact that his father was an FBI agent, that the Feds would protect him so long as he implicated Clemens. IRS agent Jeff Novitzky, for example, did testify for the Government in the second trial, and Novitzky also showed up to lend his moral support to the former New York City cop when McNamee testified before Congressman Waxman's committee.

His biggest challenge was to create a story that was vague on the crime that did not happen, since he had no corroborating witnesses to what did not happen, and to be specific as possible about general, every day incidents of working for Clemens, which were true, to enhance his general credibility. It would take sophisticated lawyers at trial to find him out.

McNamee met again with the federal prosecutors in the morning after what must have been a dramatic night of thought and creation. "So the next day," he began, "I don't think they were too happy with me not being honest, like holding back. They kind of knew that I was holding back. They definitely explained the proffer agreement again and said 'just tell us everything as if you were taking a lie detector test,'" a precipitous come-on because lie detector tests were not considered reliable outside the context of television dramas. Indeed most states considered them basically worthless.

The unreliability of lie detectors did not prevent McNamee from telling his tale to Congress.

"I was honest, and everything is true, but I was still probably a little withholding, and I couldn't help it.[7] But they were happy, and at the end of the meeting, they said, you're not a target,[8] and we would like you to talk to Senator Mitchell. And I said, well, I would really like not to do that, you know, because I felt terrible about that. I just did. And they said, well, really you should talk to Senator Mitchell. The fashion that it was going to happen was they wanted to control the information that Senator Mitchell got. And the information was based on facts that I had told them.

"When I met with Senator Mitchell and his panel, with also the federal people that were there during the first two meetings, and Senator Mitchell sat across the table, and Jeff Novitzky sat on my right. And it was basically here are the facts, and I would okay it. And if they had an additional question or, like if they wanted me to elaborate on that fact, that's how we proceeded. I think it was two hours."

"And do you remember roughly when that was?"

"It was always a month later, July 18th, maybe that's when it was."

"And when you met with the Mitchell staff, did they interview you like we are here today, or was the information presented to them first?"[9]

"It was both."

"Could you walk us through?"

"It was just like a list of—it was a time-line list of facts that Jeff would start it off. And then I would say, yes, I said that. And then if they had a question about that first, they would say, 'Brian, what do you mean by that, can you elaborate a little bit on that?'"

"I guess on December 2nd, investigators came to your residence."

"Yes."

"And you supplied them with a two-hour-and-a-half interview, as we now know, was recorded?"

"Yes."

"Did you have any idea when you met with those folks that they were recording you?"

"I asked them two or three times. They said no, but I had an idea in the back of my head, but didn't really care if they were."

"During the course of that interview, you articulated to those two gentlemen, I believe their names were Jimmy Yarbrough and Billy Belk—"[10]

"Yep."

"Some concerns that you had with your interactions with the federal agents. What's your best recollection about concerns you raised?"

"I was a person and a man that was for, the first time speaking to somebody else besides my attorney and the federal government and the Mitchell panel about what was going on. I couldn't talk to anybody. And being as upset with myself to have to tell on my two clients, I was enraged. I was not happy that I had to speak to Mitchell. I was not happy I had to talk to Federal investigators so, if anything, I exaggerated every part of the truth. But I never, ever veered from the truth in that conversation other than exaggerating and making up[11]—you know, trying to plead my case."

"And did you exaggerate the manner and the technique used by the Federal agents?"

"Everything was exaggerated."

"So did the federal agents ever threaten that they were going to haul you off to jail?"

"No. They just used it as a tactic for me to be forthcoming as far as taking two-steps to the proffer agreement, that's all."

"So was the discussion of being incarcerated, was that only related to truth-telling, or was that also related to your handling of anabolic steroids and growth hormone?"

"I think both. I'm not sure what you're saying."

"Well, you said at the end of the second meeting you met with the Mitchell folks—"

"Yes."

"They told you that you were not a target."

"Yes."

"Up until that point did you have some question whether you were a suspect in a criminal investigation?"[12]

"I mean, not really, but I think I could have been."

"So to the extent anybody says that you were pressured to provide information, there were a number of other individuals other than yourself and a federal agent that were there to help corroborate that?"

"That I wasn't pressured?"[13] [emphasis added]

"Right."

"Yes, yes, there is. I wasn't pressured to give information. I put pressure on myself not to; they made me aware that it would be in my best interest to talk to Senator Mitchell so I talked to him."

"Was that part of your agreement that you had with the federal agents at the outset?"

"It was an agreement after I was done with the second meeting with them that I would talk to Senator Mitchell."

"Was that conditioned on you not being a target of a criminal investigation? Like—how did that—how did that come to be that you sort of had to go talk to Senator Mitchell?"[14]

"I'm pretty sure that if I didn't talk to Senator Mitchell, I would become a target again. That was my understanding."

"And so it was your understanding that you pretty much had to talk to Senator Mitchell or go back to being a suspect in a criminal matter?"

"Yes."

"So in your own mind, you really had no option; you had to sit down with the Mitchell staff?"

"No option."

"Sorry?"

"I talked to my attorney, and he did tell me that—I didn't have to go in front of Mitchell ... but advised me that it would be in my own best interest to do that ... but as far as me personally, I sat there, and I thought that if I didn't, I would be in trouble."

"And then how many interactions did you have with Senator Mitchell's staff?"

"The one in person and two by phone."

"And the second phone interview or conversation, is that the one where they read the content of what became the Mitchell Report relating to you?"[15]

"Yes, no, well, we talked, what three times on the phone?"

Apparently at this point McNamee's lawyers cut him off and they huddled in conference with him. After conferring with the lawyers he continued, "The first time over the phone was—I believe it was to read back what I said and then to see if I could add anything. Every time I talked to them on the phone was just to recheck and for me to reaffirm that's what I believe to be true or know to be true."

Congressional attorney Castor asked him, "And did at some conversation you had with the Mitchell people, they read the report to you, correct?"

"The last time. I didn't know that's what they were doing, though, until I asked."

"Did you ever have an opportunity to make suggestions that others take certain things out?"
"Oh absolutely."
"And did they?"
"Yes."
"Did they take out everything you asked them to take out?"
"I believe so. I'm pretty sure they did, yeah."[16]

The most obvious starting point to questioning McNamee's "official version" that he was not pressured by the U.S. government to cut a deal and implicate Roger Clemens was his proffer agreement to cooperate with the federal prosecutors in order to prosecute Roger Clemens for perjury in allegedly lying to Congress about the use of the illegal drugs. The proffer agreement with the United States Attorney's Office for the Northern District of California stated that McNamee could not be prosecuted for cooperating with "future" investigations, meaning the pursuit of Clemens. Since they had no interest in prosecuting McNamee, probably because he would not help them get Clemens if they did, he was absolved of all of his criminal actions in the distribution and conspiracy to distribute anabolic steroids, and fraudulently dispensing HGH without a prescription.

The Belk Deposition reinforced the one admission that McNamee made concerning his treatment by the Feds: he absolutely did not want to testify before Senator Mitchell, and they made him do it. And what McNamee quoted federal prosecutors as saying in the Belk Deposition made the most sense: "We want to make sure you're a reliable witness."[17]

To believe that McNamee was not pressured seriously by the federal prosecutors, you would have to accept a parody by the late *Saturday Night Live* actor John Belushi that would go something like this: "You don't want to accept an immunity agreement? That's cool. You want an immunity agreement? That's okay. You want to testify against Roger Clemens? That's good. You don't want to testify against Roger Clemens? We're fine with that too. Say, while you're making your decision, you want to relax with a couple of joints?"

The guess here is that the federal prosecutors did not make their arrangement for Brian Jerome McNamee to testify against William Roger Clemens in this manner.

More likely, the federal prosecutors did suggest they could prosecute McNamee for conspiracy to distribute anabolic steroids if he did not cooperate, even as they said at the same time, "We don't see you as a target."[18]

McNamee, in fact, suggested that the government pressured him by pretending they had information, such as details about Jose Canseco's Miami pool party. McNamee believed that "as far as the government and Mitchell, they know that he got the Winstrol at Canseco's house at a party; and that's when he did Winstrol."[19] "I think he got it at Canseco's house. I didn't know that until the government led me to believe that's where he got it from, that somebody—someone else that the government talked to was—I guess those were the facts that they were checking on with me.

"And some guy walked into a room with him and Canseco and that's how they got the drugs; the Winstrol. They led me to believe that they knew I injected him, but wanted to hear it from me after they said they had video of me injecting Roger once in a clubhouse in Tampa."[20]

Understandably, McNamee later denied during his televised confrontation with Clemens before Waxman's committee that the federal prosecutors claimed to have information that he had injected Clemens, when they did not. Congressman Lynn Westmoreland, Georgia Republican, asked him, "When you first spoke with the government about this case, did they tell you that they already knew that Roger Clemens used steroids or human growth hormone?"[21]

"No, sir," claimed McNamee.

"When you first spoke to the government about this case," Westmoreland asked, "did they pressure you into saying that Roger Clemens used steroids or human growth hormone?"

"Not so ever," insisted McNamee.

Yet McNamee did admit that the federal prosecutors pressured him. "They kept hounding me to find out if Roger had any medical problems due to injections.[22] What took a lot of time was when I was investigated in Florida for sexual assault. They asked me a lot about that, players involved.[23] I said, 'Listen, Roger and Andy—you know what? You have to talk to them. I don't know anything about that.'[24] So the next day I have a new attorney, Earl Ward. Assistant United States Attorney Peralta says, 'you have three strikes to go to jail.' And then right away, 'So what about Clemens?' They kept pressuring me, 'what else?'"[25]

When asked whether there was any kind of paper trail to prove that he injected Clemens, McNamee admitted, "Not that I know of."[26]

At one point, McNamee reflected, "You know what, in hindsight, I don't think they knew anything."[27] Reinforcing the fact, of course, that the case against Clemens was almost entirely the testimony and the purported evidence of McNamee, with a tiny pinch of Andy Pettitte's bad memory.

> "So by holding the arrest, the federal arrest on both ends, 'lying and distributing,' over my head to give them more information than what they needed, which is what in turn they wanted because they wanted me to talk to Mitchell.[28]
>
> "So then, when I told them I was not going to talk to Mitchell, thank you, have a nice day, they said, 'Well, then, all bets are off and then you'll become a target again.'
>
> "There were phone calls from Peralta and Novitzky to me and my attorney, yelling at me, telling me if I don't show up to the Mitchell interview, that I'm going to jail.... Then providing

Mitchell with my bank records, providing Mitchell with everything private that's private about me and then sitting me in front of Mitchell.

"Novitzky read down a list of stuff that I said yes or no, a list of things that I agreed to, that I knew that happened; and all I had to do was sit there and say yeah.

"And then all this coercion.[29]

"I went on record twice, 'I don't want to talk to Mitchell,' right to Peralta. 'Well then, you're going to be considered a target again and we're going to consider charging you.' 'So wait a second—and my lawyer is sitting right there—so what you're telling me, is if I don't talk to Mitchell with you, that I'm going to get locked up? That's what you're telling me?' He said, 'yeah, that's what we're telling you.'"[30]

Perhaps to enhance McNamee's credibility, Senator Mitchell's lawyers took out his embarrassing alleged sexual assault incident from their report, just as federal prosecutors were able to keep the incident out of Roger Clemens' perjury trial, because it may have led to his firing by the Yankees at the end of the 2001 season. McNamee explained, "I had them take that out because I didn't want them to bring that shit up again. So, then, they took that out. They just said McNamee wasn't retained after the 2001 season." Clemens' attorney, Rusty Hardin, questioned the legal ethics of that at Clemens' deposition before Congress, but his concern fell on deaf ears.

What spoke most loudly against McNamee's calm tale of no government pressure to implicate Roger Clemens, was, once again, the actual facts. McNamee was so upset by his situation that he was hospitalized for depression.[31]

12

The Trial That Wasn't

The first perjury trial of Roger Clemens ended abruptly on Bastille Day, July 14, 2011, in a dramatic and shocking manner that made spectators seem like the stunned prisoners who were awarded their freedom that day in 1789 when the famous and notorious Paris prison was stormed and unlocked.

Trial Judge Reggie Walton, a former high-ranking official in the war on drugs and appointed to hear the case by the likewise pro-government Chief Judge Norma Holloway Johnson,[1] was forced to declare a mistrial when federal prosecutors attempted to sneak in hearsay evidence that had already been ruled inadmissible. Hearsay evidence consists of out-of-court conversations between two or more parties. The Sixth Amendment to the United States Constitution says that a citizen has the right to be confronted with the witnesses against him. Under the hearsay rule that extends from that basic Constitutional principle, witnesses are not allowed to discuss what somebody else said to them, with the exception of situations that are specifically enumerated in the Federal Rules of Evidence.

Judge Walton had made a routine ruling at the beginning of the trial that excluded what Clemens' former teammate Andy Pettitte had said or not said to his wife about thinking he had heard Clemens admit to using Human Growth Hormone.

Less than 24 hours before, the same prosecutors had tried to sneak in information that Judge Walton had likewise ruled inadmissible, the fact that baseball players Pettitte, Chuck Knoblauch and Mike Stanton were injected with HGH by Brian McNamee. Such evidence is almost always held to be inadmissible by trial judges, and therefore this ruling was routine as well.

It unfolded like this. Prosecutor Steven Durham, who had known Judge Walton for a long time, rose. "All right. Why don't we take a look here at Government's Exhibit 3-B2, *which has been admitted into evidence* [emphasis added]."[2] Onto the screen, for the benefit of the jury of ten black women and two white males, appeared a video wherein Maryland Congressman Elijah

Cummings, an African American, discussed an affidavit by Laura Pettitte that stated her husband told her he thought Roger Clemens told him he used human growth hormone, a performance enhancing drug that had not been banned by baseball until 2005. The tape essentially showed Cummings endorsing the prosecution of Roger Clemens.

Judge Walton, an African American himself, seemed stunned. Two experienced federal prosecutors, the best and the brightest so to speak, had just violated one of the cardinal principles of fairness and due process. Worse, if Judge Walton, an experienced judge at age 62, allowed that evidence to be admitted, it would raise all kinds of questions about his competence and threaten his job security. Walton, in fact, came into this high-profile trial with a reputation well-known to these prosecutors, that of being fair, handing down long and tough sentences to convicted felons, but demanding strict adherence to hearsay rules.

"Approach for a moment," barked Walton.

After a heated discussion out of hearing of the jury, the lawyers returned to their tables in the court room and Walton admonished both sides. "I hate to raise with experienced counsel, testimony that's coming in without objection, but we have talked about this and there's some issues. But if you're not objecting, I just want to get on the record that you've made a tactical decision." This statement, while technically accurate on the law, was misleading and unfair to Hardin. Rules 801(a), (b) and (c) of the Federal Rules of Evidence preclude a party from complaining about hearsay that was sneaked into a trial, so to say, "who does not make a timely objection."[3] Hardin had objected to the tape the week before, and Walton had ruled it inadmissible, and here was Durham trying to sneak it back into the trial. Hardin had not objected before Walton himself had noticed the outrageous attempt to flaunt his own ruling. Essentially, Judge Walton had made the objection himself, quickly, immediately, probably before Hardin could get the words out of his own mouth.

Hardin responded, "No, here's my problem, Judge. I've got a visual to the jury of a document that we did not object to being in evidence, which was the hearing. I don't know quite what to do in front of the jury. I object to all of this. It does violate the motion *in limine*.[4]

Essentially, Hardin had objected to Laura Pettitte's hearsay but not to the clips of the televised Congressional hearings. Therefore, the prosecution tried to sneak in what Hardin had failed to object to, questioning by Congressman Cummings, and thereby admit Laura Pettitte's comments through the proverbial backdoor. Hardin said, "And my dilemma is, standing up in front of the jury objecting to something that we agreed to allow into evidence."[5]

Durham responded, "Well, but these exhibits, these admissions have been turned, this video clip and this transcript was turned over in early May," pretending that they had not been ruled inadmissible by Judge Walton. Rationalizing the tape that had been ruled inadmissible, Durham bravely talked on, "This is part of the Congressman's question to Mr. Clemens. If this has been raised before, then we could…"

Gently, Walton said to Durham, "It has been raised, maybe not specifically in reference to this clip, but it had been raised as to whether … information coming from the wife, Laura Pettitte, would come in."[6]

One of Clemens' attorneys, Michael Attanasio, said, "It's incumbent on the prosecutor to them redacting or altering his exhibits."[7]

Rusty Hardin, Clemens' lead attorney, declared, "I think we had every right to assume that after the Court rules a certain way in motion *in limine*, that the government rather will adjust their exhibits to comply with the motion *in limine*. But it is perfectly proper for the defense to assume that that they have altered exhibits to comply with the motion *in limine*.[8] That was the assumption I made." The prosecution made that same assumption—the defense would assume they obeyed the judge and never imagined they would try to sneak the forbidden evidence past the judge.

Judge Walton was torn. Although Hardin had objected to the hearsay evidence on the first go-around, and had succeeded in his routine request to have it banned, he was required to do so again when the prosecutors attempted what seemed like a devious trick. He had not, although one could argue that the sequence of apparent perfidy had unfolded so fast that Walton had not given Hardin time to object. All this must have been on Walton's mind and he tried to play the middle. First he admonished the Clemens defense: "But there wasn't an objection." Secondly, he addressed the offending prosecution team: "And I'm perplexed, having made that ruling, as to why these exhibits were not altered to ensure that there was not a violation of my order. I don't particularly like making rulings and lawyers not abiding by those rulings."[9]

Later apologists for the prosecution would claim that the prosecution's Trojan Horse was simply an innocent mistake and that the two experienced litigators trying to send Clemens to jail were themselves stupefied and in shock and beside themselves with wonder about how it all unfolded. The next several words out of prosecutor Stephen Durham's mouth suggested otherwise. Trying to sneak hearsay already ruled inadmissible into a trial was an automatic dismissal of the case, Durham understood, but a second bite at the apple, a retrial, could not be denied unless the Judge could be completely convinced, a practically impossible task for defense lawyers, that the prosecution had *intentionally* blown up the trial, to use the modern football phrase for stopping an offensive play.

12. The Trial That Wasn't

The next words Durham uttered were, "There was no *intention* [emphasis added] to run afoul of any Court ruling, Your Honor."

Ignoring the allusion to the test for a retrial, Walton played out the proverbial string and acted as if the present trial could be continued despite the grievous error. "Well, how would this come in?"

Durham played on, "Well, these items were delivered to the defense table months ago, these clips. This is part----?"[10] No doubt, Durham had also put his trousers on that morning.

Rusty Hardin, obviously cognizant of where this was all heading, said dryly, "[The] problem we have here is, is this is the second, so there must be a total misunderstanding of the government's part as to their obligations, because this happened during opening statement, too. I had to object during opening statement to a mention of other players. The Court ruled and reminded them that was a violation of the motion *in limine*."[11]

Perhaps still in shock, perhaps trying to be a good government soldier and reach back into his knowledge of the law and desperately find some way for the prosecution to continue, Judge Walton suggested, "Well, you know, as I said, maybe there was some misunderstanding of what my ruling was."[12] On its face, of course, the statement was incredible and absurd. No admitted attorney, much less the best and brightest at the Justice Department, could possibly misunderstand the most basic exclusion of hearsay evidence.

Durham gamely played out his part. "We didn't run afoul of the Court's ruling within the context of the opening statement."[13]

Almost on cue, Hardin made his request for a mistrial official. "But I think, reluctantly, we're going to have to move for a mistrial because of the prejudicial nature of what's happened in front of the jury."[14]

Right on cue as well, Durham fulfilled his obligation to object to the motion. If he failed to do this he would have given up the government's right to demand a retrial. "We object, Your Honor. This exhibit, these exhibits were admitted into trial without objection," he said in a last, desperate attempt to confuse the Court and jury regarding what was admitted and what was not admitted. "They had been previously…"[15]

Walton embarked on a final admonition of the parties, and his reasoning, before he had to do his duty and grant the mistrial.

> There should have been a request by the defense for copies of these new exhibits which counsel as I understand had at least the prior documents, prior to my observation *in limine* ruling. Once I made those rulings, I agree, counsel should have made a request for that information to make sure that whatever the government was going to use was in compliance with my ruling. But in the first instance, the obligation of doctoring those exhibits to make sure that my ruling was not violated rests with the government.[16]

Clemens' veteran add-on to the defense team, Michael Attanasio, declared, "We did not get the exhibits until July 11, 3:11 p.m. And then they moved them rapidly this morning, and then suddenly we see it on the screen."[17]

Judge Walton responded to Attanasio. "The other thing that bothers me is that, there was no objection, there should have been an objection. Now, again, whether the defense had the opportunity to review this in light of the hours in which it was produced and review the transcript, is another issue."[18]

Walton summed up by addressing the offending hearsay.

> Not only do we have Mr. Pettitte's wife saying that Mr. Pettitte told her something consistent with what she says Mr. Clemens said, but we also have Congressman Cummings *opining on his credibility that he places on Andy Pettitte* [emphasis added]. [We] have before this jury two items that inappropriately bolster his credibility. I think Mr. Pettitte's testimony is going to be critical as to whether this man goes to prison.... I think it's going to be very difficult to undermine his credibility. And when you add his testimony with all of the other evidence, I think, it becomes very difficult for Mr. Clemens."[19]

Clearly, Clemens was lucky that his fate was in the hands of a jury and not Judge Walton's.

It was not unheard-of for prosecutors to use demonstrative videos as a Trojan Horse in an attempt to sneak inadmissible evidence into a trial, but trying to crawl hearsay evidence through the camera lens onto the screen on the same day Walton admonished the prosecutors for trying to sneak in another piece of excluded evidence, the HGH use of Pettitte and other Clemens teammates, Chuck Knoblauch and Mike Stanton, and in a trial of considerable public interest, was a brazen piece of lawyering.

At first glance, it seemed as if prosecutors Stephen Durham and David Butler had either purposely tried to sneak elementary hearsay evidence, already ruled inadmissible, into the trial, or they had simply forgotten to take the offending hearsay of Laura Pettitte out of their opening statement video—a seeming blunder that was derided by other lawyers because the error suggested that two veteran lawyers of 25 years did not understand the rule against hearsay. Alan Dershowitz, legendary professor at Harvard Law School from 1964 until 2013, said, "There is no innocent explanation for why prosecutors put in inadmissible evidence in front of the jury."[20] The prosecutor's insistence that they forgot to take out the hearsay begged the question of what was it doing there in the first place. Professor Dershowitz added, "The government constantly does this because they think they can get away with it."[21]

Race was certainly a concern for the prosecutors. Nine black female jurors sat in judgment of the government. Who better than black Baltimore Congressman Elijah Cummings to vouch for the prosecution of Clemens by reading the affidavit of Andy Pettitte's wife, wife of the baseball player who thought he once heard Clemens admit to using Human Growth Hormone? Laura Pettitte's affidavit, however, was not entirely accurate. Her husband testified before Congress that he *thought* he heard Roger Clemens say he took HGH, and that he *might have* told his wife, and became more positive only after continuous prompting by Waxman lawyers. The prosecutors certainly knew that O.J. Simpson had been exonerated for murder with a jury of nine African Americans while held liable for wrongful death with the same set of facts by an all-white jury. In fact, for the prosecution, the first Clemens jury composition was uncomfortably close to the Simpson jury—ten women and nine blacks. Coincidentally, both juries were composed of two whites, the only racial distinction being that the Simpson trial had one Hispanic juror.

Indeed, gender was also a deep concern for the federal prosecutors in their case against Roger Clemens. The recent Barry Bonds trial had concluded with the government's failure to convict Bonds of perjury with a jury of eight women, two of whom were African American.

To understand the prosecution's problem with the jury composition, and therefore its desire to make it go away, we can take a glance at the differing desires of the government and the defense in jury selection. A week before the Clemens trial imploded, the law firm of Davis & Hoss, PC, offered an excellent tutorial concerning what the opposing sides were seeking in a jury.[22] The lawyers noted that the prosecutors would be looking for baseball fans not impressed with fame, parents, business owners and home owners. Basically, prosecutors always want solid, middle-class citizens with middle-class values, citizens in favor of strong law-and-order to insure the safety of themselves, their families, and their property. Prosecutors do not like independently wealthy people who are likely to be liberal, opened-minded and perhaps sympathetic to defendants. Prosecutors also do not like extremists of any kind because they are likely to bear a grudge against the government and, by implication, government prosecutors. And prosecutors do not relish unemployed people who might not be scared as much by crime because they do not have as much of an economic stake in society.

Conversely, the attorneys suggested that Rusty Hardin wanted jurors who had no knowledge whatsoever of baseball or of Roger Clemens, because Clemens was disliked by many baseball fans who were convinced that he had unfairly hit their favorite batters at one time or another. Such fans wanted to see Clemens punished whether he had had committed perjury or not. The Davis & Hoss firm suggested that, in general, good jurors for Clemens would be drug users or those who thought most drug laws were stupid, liberal Democrats, who might be in favor of a fair trial, school teachers, who were known for patience, understanding, and sympathy gained from their difficult and demanding profession, NASCAR fans, who apparently possessed a healthy skepticism of government in general, and people pissed-off at law enforcement. Clemens' attorney would not want engineers and scientists who might know a lot about chemical compounds, relatives of law enforcement officials who would favor the prosecutors, and again, anyone who was a serious sports fan and thus inclined to believe the relentlessly negative press that Clemens had received for a quarter of a century.

The federal prosecutors had to be concerned with the opinions that many jurors had toward the government because residents of the District of Columbia, particularly African Americans who have not been particularly favored by the U.S. government historically, did not generally stand in as much awe of federal institutions as some Americans. Many of them worked for the government or had family members who did, and knew that the emperors of government often wore no clothes. Furthermore, they or their families may have had bad relations with the police or other law enforcement institutions.

The Clemens defense team understood this independent streak in D.C. juries. As the defendant, Clemens had the right to ask that the trial be removed to a different locale, or venue, where he might get a fairer or more favorable jury. After briefly considering this option, the Clemens team decided they liked their chances with the citizens of D.C.

The District of Columbia presented unique demographic problems in jury selection, according to trial experts.[23] Consequently, the process was slow and Judge Walton complained to the lawyers that their questions took up too much time.[24] To begin with, the District of Columbia had a low number of registered voters. Jury pools were universally taken from voter registration lists, although overly aggressive venues such as New York City also used driver's license records.

Washington was, therefore, atypical of the United States in its population and thus in its jury pools. Although a selected jury did not have to mirror the proportionate ethnic composition of a population, the jury pool from which it is chosen must comport with the Sixth Amendment requirements for a fair trial.[25] The African American population of the District of Columbia—including many descendants of the slaves who constructed the city—comprised 50.7 percent compared to the national average black population of 12.6 percent.[26] Middle-class home ownership, a criterion of the ideal prosecution juror, was considerably lower than the national average, 45 percent in D.C. as compared to 66.9 percent in the nation. Conversely, citizens in D.C. living below the poverty level, people considered sympathetic to defendants, was higher than the national average, 17.6 percent to 14.3 percent. In fact, multiunit-housing structures, often housing the poor, are more than twice as prevalent in the District of Columbia as nationally—60.4 percent to 25.9 percent. The District had nominally as many high school graduates as the national average, approximately 50 percent, but those figures are skewed by the fact that so many highly educated people moved into Washington for government work. The education dynamic impacted the trial when Judge Walton dismissed 15 persons from the original jury pool, most of them because they did not even understand the basic presumption of innocence for the defendant and did not understand that the burden of proof was with the prosecution under United States law.[27]

Given these demographics in Washington, what kind of jury, after all, did the federal prosecutors face? A jury that could not and would not, in a million years, convict Roger Clemens of perjury. Or as CBSsports.com put it, "An overwhelmingly female jury with little interest in baseball will decide whether pitching star Roger Clemens lied to Congress."[28] Ten women and two men were selected, with the four alternates split equally by gender. One of the women, a yoga instructor, had declared that U.S. drug laws were "heavy handed."[29] Another woman, a part-time health aide, was the cousin of former Baltimore Orioles star Al Bumbry. A young mother who worked two jobs believed that football player Michael Vick had been "done wrong" when he was convicted for running a dog-fighting operation. A retired mail-carrier sat on the jury along with a male FCC lawyer. With this socio-economic dynamic, perhaps the prosecution could count on the FCC lawyer for a vote for conviction. Unfortunately, criminal juries with 12 members require unanimity, that is to say, a 12–0 decision. With this lineup, it may have been heading toward an 11–1 vote, and either the 11 would have to convince the one to acquit Clemens, or the jury would deadlock and a mistrial would result. In short, conviction of Roger Clemens with this jury was impossible, and the federal prosecutors probably understood that.[30]

Why not just throw in the towel and walk away? First, the prosecutors, the Obama Justice Department, the sports media, and the American male were heavily invested, either career-wise or emotionally, in the conviction of Roger Clemens. Second, the prosecutors must have noticed, as did Richmond Law School Professor Carl Tobias,[31] that the high percentage of female jurors selected, 83.3 percent, was far above the female population of the District of Columbia, 52.8 percent.[32] Tobias said of the jury of mostly women, "It's high. It should be closer to 50–50. This strikes me as rather atypical."[33]

Atypical indeed. The prosecutors, who had begun chasing Roger Clemens more than a year before any evidence against him surfaced, certainly understood that these unusual demographics in Washington could cause them problems at trial. Even with an atypical proportion of women on the jury, these were demographics heaven-sent for the defense. The only chance for conviction was to win over male jurors, most likely black male jurors, perhaps on the subject of sports and away from the socio-economic factors that would lead them normally to sympathize with defendants on trial. With only two male jurors, the government's strategy of "chauvinism's last stand" was impossible. The female jurors had to go. The government's only chance to convict Roger Clemens existed with another, as yet to be determined, jury.

Maybe in another trial the prosecution could get a jury that was closer to 50–50, say six women and six men, or maybe they could get really lucky and end up with a jury of eight men and four women, or in their wildest fantasies, a jury of 12 men!

Durham and Butler understood their judge. They knew he was a team player. He had been a good government soldier in the war on drugs in both the Office of the President and as a judge handing out long sentences. They knew Walton was not individualistic enough to call their bluff on blowing up his trial and deny a retrial. Therefore it was reasonable to suggest that they loaded up Congressman Cummings's speech endorsing the guilt of Roger Clemens into their opening video and had no intention of ever removing it. Either they would sneak it past Rusty Hardin before he could object—and try to make an impression on the ten black female jurors—or Hardin would object in timely fashion and demand a mistrial. Judge Walton would have little choice but to end the trial and dismiss the troublesome jury. They probably did not count on Judge Walton noticing the infraction before Hardin. The prosecutors, in this scenario, employed excellent psychology against Hardin and his defense team. The prosecutors knew the defense lawyers were psychologically more likely to spot an omission of evidence in the video that was supposed to be there than the opposite, evidence they had seen that was supposed to be taken out. After all, as a matter of professional ethics and lawyerly courtesy, Clemens' attorneys expected the prosecutors to obey Judge Walton's order to remove the offending hearsay. That the prosecutors were actually sneaking in Congressman Cummings's speech added to the brilliance of their strategy.

When Judge Walton made the only call possible under the circumstances, declare a mistrial, prosecutor Steven Durham, apparent author of both violations, looked like a man who had just passed a note to a teller requesting all of a bank's money, only to turn around and face 25 rookie cops waiting to cash their first paychecks.

In the end, Walton, despite his personal feelings about the war on drugs, lived up to his reputation for fairness. The conniving prosecutors had only themselves to blame for being handed a mistrial when violating the known concerns for hearsay evidence Walton had built his entire legal career on. Prosecutors Steven Durham and Daniel Butler, this theory contends, had pulled one over on the judge and were confident they would get another trial and a more sympathetic jury.

Baseball writers could not contain their anger at the mistrial. After all, it was they who had forced Clemens into coming out of seclusion, luring him to Washington to tell his side of the story, because they held over his head what they believed he desperately wanted, admission to the Baseball Hall of Fame. Their poison pens were buttressed by the nation's weak libel laws against public personalities where only malicious errors of fact were actionable,[34] and free speech rules that provided their corporate masters an equal say with an ordinary citizen.[35]

ESPN's Howard Bryant was right about one thing when he wrote of Clemens, "He achieved nothing even close to the vindication that set him down this path after the publication of the Mitchell Report."

The press had damned Clemens as an ignorant redneck from his earliest playing days, as they had once damned Harry Truman. It was the small people, the regular people, the Congressional clerks, the cops, the secretaries on Capitol Hill, court personnel such as the janitors who had ignored the incendiary charges against him on his several visits to Washington, and now on this final day as he walked out of the mistrial, shaking their hands, they asked for his autograph.

How alone Clemens looked as he walked from his well-wishers, casually strolling away from the courthouse with only his lawyer, Rusty Hardin, no entourage as usual for this famous athlete, true to himself till the end: Roger Clemens against the world.

Clemens walked away from Washington with his reputation for meanness intact, but he still had not been given an opportunity to tell his side of the story. Perhaps partly because of that, and partly because he felt he was on the verge of clearing his name forever, he wore the disappointed expression of a man who had expected to feast on Brian McNamee for Thanksgiving, only to learn that he would have to settle for a cold TV dinner instead.

13

A Prosecutor's Dream Jury

As the second Clemens trial for two counts of perjury, three counts of giving false statements, and one count of obstruction of justice of Congress approached in the spring of 2012, sports writers grew nervous that the case against Roger Clemens was draining away like the days of their own lives. In fact, the nation's paper of record, the *New York Times*, professed not to care any longer about the outcome, even as it presumed Clemens' guilt. Before the first trial, in 2011, Jonathan Mahler had written, "Roger Clemens ... just another guy who disappointed us. The sports world, like the real world, is full of them. Do we really need to devote scarce government resources to proving they let us down?"[1] And in presuming Clemens guilty, Mahler laid the main blame on Major League Baseball. "It's still hard not to see Clemens as a kind of victim, the unlucky scapegoat for a conspiracy of willful blindness across baseball during the game's steroid-fueled renaissance."

Yahoo's Les Carpenter, who suffered from a basic lack of understanding of how trials worked, nonetheless seemed to get the big picture of the pursuit of Clemens that his colleagues lacked, an understanding that Andy Pettitte was not the divine answer to the prayers of the prosecution that everybody thought he was, and that a second jury in Washington, D.C., might not be favorable to the prosecution either. As we saw in the previous chapter, none other than Judge Walton himself had pontificated on the credibility and importance of Pettitte to the government's case. "I think Mr. Pettitte's testimony is going to be critical as to whether this man goes to prison.... I think it's going to be very difficult to undermine his credibility. And when you add his testimony with all of the other evidence, I think it becomes very difficult for Mr. Clemens."[2] Carpenter sagely observed in the wake of the prosecution's destruction of the first jury:

> But whether the episode was intentional or not, the government still has an Andy Pettitte problem. Pettitte isn't the golden witness here he might be somewhere else.... There remains a good chance the government doesn't have enough to convince a DC jury that Clemens lied to Congress even in a second trial.

Maybe the prosecutors will get lucky and find a few true baseball fans, but the greater probability is that the next jurors won't like baseball and will be mistrustful of government. That's a condition of the locale.[3]

The second Clemens trial began in the context of, and not long after, the questionable prosecutions of Senators John Edwards of North Carolina and Ted Stevens of Alaska. Two federal prosecutors were suspended for "reckless conduct" for failing to disclose information that might have helped to acquit Senator Stevens. Disclosing such information is a routine function for any prosecutor. Stevens was convicted of failing to report on an ethics form that an oil services company firm remodeled a house he owned.[4] An embarrassed Attorney General Eric Holder asked the trial judge to throw out the conviction. A third prosecutor in the case committed suicide.

Former Senator and Democratic Vice-Presidential Candidate John Edwards won a mistrial when a jury acquitted him of one charge and failed to reach a verdict on five other charges for violating a campaign finance law.[5] The Justice Department, in fact, was riven with inside politics and ideological warfare. When to prosecute and when not to prosecute a federal case had not been free of politics for some time.[6] The Department's ideological divide compromised its work. During the Clinton Administration, for example, a rump group of departmental lawyers attempted to shut down the department due to ideological differences with the President, organizing a national call-in to the department to overtax its telephone lines on the false charge that the Administration supported child pornography. A source who answered the phones at the Justice Department said she talked to some "concerned citizens" dozens of times.

That the Feds took the prosecution of Clemens seriously was evidenced by the talent it threw into the battle. Lester Munson wrote, "The team representing the U.S. government includes five prosecutors, at least three federal agents and a couple of techies. Its leader is Steven Durham, a seasoned and talented lawyer."[7] The government also benefitted from the fact that the same federal prosecutors who conducted the grand jury questioning wrote the indictment and tried the case.

The Justice Department was armed with the largest crime-fighting budget in the history of the world, with its "cavernous office" of the Attorney General that counter-terrorism czar Richard A. Clarke once suggested "could have accommodated a few of the Saudi King's throne rooms."[8] The forces brought to bear against Roger Clemens by the Department of Justice and its $30 billion 2011 budget included a six-percent *increase* for court litigation costs.[9] It was unclear how much of that was prompted by the pursuit of Clemens, if any, whose conviction was a high priority for both the Justice Department and the White House.

In the period between the mistrial of 2011 and the retrial of 2012, the prosecutors proved to be busy little beavers. Three additional prosecutors joined their ranks, including David B. Goodhand, an expert in appeals. Fifty new interviews involving hundreds of hours of "meticulous preparation"[10] were conducted over nine months. Every key prosecution witness was interviewed and re-interviewed. Agents from the FBI, IRS, and Drug Enforcement Agency examined 15,732 pages of Clemens family bank records from J. P. Morgan Chase, 1,139 pages of records from American Express credit cards, in excess of 300 pages of medical records from the Major League teams for whom Clemens played, and hundreds of pages of phone records from nine companies. Ninety-three government agents interviewed 171 people in 68 locations and created 235 reports. The FBI conducted 72 interviews between Houston and New York City. The government's trial team of Steven Durham and Daniel Butler conducted many of the interviews.[11]

"Although these lawyers have all been involved in other big cases," Munson observed, "there is little doubt that both sides are viewing this trial as a career event. Both are carefully attending to every detail. Both are working overtime, filing papers late in the evening and in the early morning hours."[12]

Munson, whose opinion of the case would be changed by Brian McNamee's unconvincing and contradictory testimony, started out with the press' universal belief that Clemens was guilty when he wrote, "But Clemens' defiance makes a settlement almost inconceivable."[13] The word "settlement" implied Clemens' guilt.

In fact, early developments in the trial *did* favor the prosecution. In contrast to the mistrial jury of 2011 with its majority of unemployed, out-of-work minorities most prone to favor the defense, the 2012 jury consisted of professionals and middle-class homeowners, a shockingly unusual composition for a Washington jury, and one most likely to favor the prosecution. The government's detonation of the 2011 case with its attempt to sneak in inadmissible hearsay, probably in the vague hopes of getting a more favorable jury the second time around, worked beyond their wildest dreams. Unfortunately for the prosecutors, the old adage, "Be careful of what you wish for," came back to haunt them.

CBSSports.com baseball writer Gregg Doyel wished for such a pro-prosecution jury but was so confident that Clemens was guilty that any jury would do. Doyel claimed of Clemens,

> He's so guilty, the federal government could get a conviction with creepy former trainer Brian McNamee tied behind its back.[14]
>
> This assumes the government can find a jury of twelve people who didn't grow up collecting Clemens' baseball card. But if the government can find such a jury, it's over. Reasonable doubt that Clemens took steroids? There is no reasonable doubt. And it has nothing to do with Brian McNamee.[15]

Doyel got his wish, at least in the composition of the jury.

The Clemens jury consisted of 12 main jurors and four alternates, with ten women and six men. Most said they did not follow baseball or know much about Clemens. Seven jurors said they had never even heard of Roger Clemens. The jury consisted of a single female supermarket cashier, a retired female elementary school teacher, a female program analyst with the federal government who had taken pre-law classes, a female occupational therapist, a male who studied engineering and biology at the University of Pennsylvania, a female curatorial researcher at the Smithsonian, a male expert in cyber legislation in the financial sector, who worked for the Treasury Department and had studied at Yale Management School, a female teacher of the deaf, a black male administrative assistant at the Canadian Embassy who had majored in pre-med at Howard University, a female librarian at the American Council on Education, an unemployed male, a retired male who had taught political science at Smith College and the University of Massachusetts for 25 years, a retired female who had worked for the U.S. Department of Transportation and Bureau of Public Debt, a female environmental lawyer, a male senior program analyst for the Nuclear Regulatory Commission, and a second female environmental lawyer. It may not have been an exaggeration to suggest this was the most educated jury in the history of trials in Washington, D.C. Even better for the prosecution was the fact that Judge Reggie Walton allowed his jurors to write down questions that he could ask trial witnesses on their behalf.[16] That way any slick lawyering by Clemens' team could be blunted by the natural curiosity of these insightful and well-educated jurors. In addition, with so many jurors educated in the sciences, the more learned ones could help the less educated ones to understand the chemistry of anabolic steroids, the illegal substances that were at the heart of the prosecution's perjury case. The prosecutors must have celebrated somewhere on the night of the jury selection.

The prosecution benefitted from several decisions by Judge Walton on the issue of admissible testimony.

Walton ruled that Brian McNamee could name former Yankees leadoff hitter Chuck Knoblauch, former relief pitcher Mike Stanton, and pitcher Andy Pettitte as receiving human growth hormone from him in 2001. Walton instructed the jury that they could use this information to help establish McNamee's credibility as a witness, but could not use it to infer Clemens' guilt. Prosecutor Daniel Butler, understandably, took advantage of Walton's helpful ruling to utter the names of the three players at every opportunity. The jury gained the impression that these players had been up to no good, and despite the judge's instruction, could have inferred that Clemens was up to no good as well.

The Clemens defense desperately wanted to be able to impeach Brian McNamee, the government's main witness, by showing that he had lied to police during an investigation into an alleged rape incident in Florida. Under Rule 608(b)(2) of the Federal Rules of Evidence, a witness may be impeached to examine his truthfulness by inquiring about specific instances of conduct, even if not leading to a conviction for a crime; indeed, even rumors that might even turn out to be untrue, "reputation in his community," are often permitted to test a witness' truthfulness.[17] Charges were not filed in the case because the woman was unwilling to submit to an exam and had no memory of the incident because she was given the "date rape drug" GHB. However, if there is a danger that such impeachment would create unfair prejudice in the eyes of the jury or incite them to make an emotional decision that outweighed the value of the information, the Court may do a "balancing test" pitting Rule 608(b)(2) against the "fairness doctrine" of Rule 403.[18] Walton ruled that the defense could not mention the nature of the criminal investigation because McNamee was not charged, but could ask, "Weren't you investigated for a serious crime? Didn't you lie to investigators and try to have evidence destroyed?"[19]

Judge Walton also ruled that Clemens' baseball contracts were inadmissible, no doubt to prevent any prejudice the jurors might feel about player salaries, because he observed, "Some people think the salaries that pro athletes make are obscene."[20] The prosecutors wanted to include the contract amounts to allege that Clemens had a financial incentive to take performance enhancing drugs to prolong his career.

Thousands of baseball fans were convinced that the expanded, middle-aged body of Clemens, like the middle-aged bodies of Mark McGwire, Jason Giambi, and Barry Bonds, proved he had used steroids. In fact, the government had argued in the Bonds prosecution for perjury that changes in Bonds' body proved he used steroids. Therefore Clemens' lead attorney, Rusty Hardin, was happy to prove that Clemens' body had not changed much since early in his career. This presented a dilemma for the Government because Clemens' body *had not* changed much.

The Roger Clemens who showed up every day for his trial in the spring of 2012 was apparently "thin-skinned about his beefy-looking body, his jowly face, his double chin, his thick neck," once described as "the body of a body builder who has gone off his diet."[21] He usually wore dark blue, almost black, suits, presumably to make himself look thinner. Unfortunately, the dark suits, often accompanied by equally dark ties, gave him the look of an old movie gangster, not the image to portray in the courtroom. A crew-cut adorned Clemens' head. He possessed an unusually dark beard for a man with light brown hair, and therefore probably should have worn the light, creme-colored suit Rusty Hardin wore to emphasize that he, Clemens, was the good guy. In any case, Clemens was a large man at age 21 and he was a large man at 49 when the trial was held. No problem for the prosecution. Having argued that it should be allowed to present evidence in the Bonds trial to argue that steroids impacted changes in the body, the federal prosecutors apparently felt no hypocrisy in arguing in the Clemens trial that steroids did not always impact body change, therefore the defense should not be allowed to present evidence of the *lack* of body changes to show Clemens *did not* use steroids. The accommodating Judge Walton sided with the prosecution. Hardin could only mutter, "I respectfully disagree,"[22] perhaps to preserve that issue as a grounds for appeal if needed. Throughout the trial, federal prosecutors "pushed the envelope" in their trial tactics, each questionable motion or move deemed "an honest mistake" by Walton. There were a lot of "honest mistakes" for such an experienced prosecutorial team.

Perhaps most damaging for the defense, Judge Walton ruled that it could not bring in McNamee's indebtedness to argue that his relative destitution prompted him to blackmail Clemens. It was a devastating blow to the defense because their theory of the case was that McNamee made up the story of injecting steroids to blackmail Clemens. Blackmail was McNamee's motive, Hardin wanted to argue. "Where's the proof?" retorted a skeptical Judge Walton as he ruled against the defense.[23]

However, ten days later, Walton changed his mind about the Clemens theory of the case, allowing the defense to argue that McNamee was preparing to blackmail Clemens when he collected physical evidence.[24]

Judge Walton ruled out questioning by United States Attorney Steven Durham of Pettitte regarding injections of HGH by McNamee—with the caveat that if Hardin slipped up by inferring that Pettitte somehow got HGH from McNamee, it would "open the door" to allow the prosecution to ask Pettitte about it.[25] However, Walton ruled that Pettitte could testify that he took HGH, just not that some of it was injected by McNamee.[26] Judge Walton and many reporters remained confused about whether these other players took steroids or HGH from McNamee. If this decision sounded confusedly similar but with a different result from Walton's decision to disallow questioning of Andy Pettitte on the same issue, that's because it was. In any case, Munson suggested accurately, that "If Pettitte went to McNamee for HGH, it would have made it more probable that Clemens also went to McNamee for the drug, and it would have supported McNamee's account of what he did for Clemens."[27] Munson continued, "But Walton would not permit Durham to ask Pettitte where he obtained the HGH or allow Pettitte to describe who helped him with its injection."[28] Certainly the jury could have concluded that since McNamee injected Pettitte with HGH, he probably injected Clemens, too. And if Judge Walton permitted Pettitte to testify to that, he would have been compelled to allow the Government to put Knoblauch and Stanton on the stand to testify that they, too, had been injected with HGH by McNamee.

Munson's point about the conclusions the jury might have made based on the knowledge of others McNamee injected was well taken but debatable. In a trial that became a double-edged sword for the prosecution with witness after witness, such testimony could have come back to bite the prosecution as well. In fact, Rusty Hardin suggested as much. He admitted, "There is a side of me that wants to say have at it. The government's case has always been flimsy."[29] First, McNamee's mode of operation with the three men, according to his own testimony, differed, and that inconsistency might have bothered the jury. McNamee testified before Congress that Clemens and Pettitte had approached him for PEDS, but Chuck Knoblauch testified that McNamee had approached him about using HGH, and other players testified at trial that McNamee approached them about using B-12, even though McNamee claimed he never injected Clemens with it. Second, Pettitte and Knoblauch testified in their Congressional depositions that they had no knowledge of Clemens taking performance enhancing drugs, only of their own use. Third, Clemens' defense could have then distanced him from the other players because their payments to McNamee for performance enhancing drugs were accounted for, while no direct evidence of payments by Clemens for performance enhancing drugs existed.

In any case, although Judge Walton's ruling displeased Munson, it was probably the right decision. Under Rule 403 of the Federal Rules of Evidence, relevant evidence may be excluded to prevent bias and confusion of the issues which might lead the jury to "overvalue" the information.[30] Since Judge Walton himself seemed confused about who was injected with what, it certainly could have confused men and women less schooled in evaluating evidence.

Walton also denied the defense team's motion for details of McNamee's divorce record, calling it "a fishing expedition." Hardin wanted the evidence to argue that McNamee's divorce was part of his dire financial situation and why he blackmailed Clemens. Judge Walton said again that Clemens had provided no evidence that McNamee blackmailed him.[31] Eileen McNamee's attorney argued a point of law that in New York she could waive her privacy right to testify about it but had not done so. Richard Emery, one of McNamee's civil lawyers, argued essentially the same legal point: the McNamees would have to waive their privacy right covering marital privilege in a civil case and they had not done so.[32]

Due to the lack of proof presented by the government, Judge Walton dismissed two of the 15 acts of the Obstruction of Congress count: Clemens' statement that he had no idea that George Mitchell wanted to talk to him for his investigation; and Clemens' statement that, "I couldn't tell you the first thing about HGH." That left standing 13 alleged misleading statements from the grand jury indictment—only one was needed for a conviction.[33]

To Lester Munson's surprise, the prosecution decided to put one of its star witnesses, Clemens' purported "best friend" and teammate on the Yankees and Houston Astros, Andy Pettitte, on the witness stand early in the trial. Munson noted that many prosecutors would have held Pettitte's testimony until late in the trial when it would have been fresh in the minds of the jury as they were about to deliberate.[34] The prosecutors apparently put Pettitte on the witness stand early to accommodate his return to pitch for the New York Yankees after one of his several retirements from baseball.

Munson positively gushed about the impact of Pettitte's first day of testimony for the prosecution when he said that Clemens told him he used Human Growth Hormone. "It's a critical piece of evidence for the prosecutors," wrote Munson, "and it's a serious problem for the Clemens' legal team—clear and convincing testimony from a Clemens friend and protégé that contradicts everything that Clemens told the U.S. Congress.... Pettitte may have been reluctant, but his answers were quiet, categorical and persuasive."[35]

Another surprise early witness providing compelling testimony against Clemens was super-sleuth Jeff Novitzky, the former IRS investigator who worked for the Food and Drug Administration at the time of the trial. Although Novitzky had testified last in the Barry Bonds trial and proved to be an effective witness, prosecutors thought it necessary for Novitzky to testify *prior* to Brian McNamee taking the stand, to lay the groundwork and vouch for McNamee's credibility because they knew the former cop would face a furious and perhaps devastating cross-examination. Novitzky testified that checks written by Brian McNamee to drug dealer Kirk Radomski "connected" Clemens to Radomski.[36]

On cross-examination, Rusty Hardin asked Novitzky, "Would you agree that it is incredibly unusual for law enforcement to make a deal with a drug dealer that he won't be charged if he goes to a private organization and helps them with their investigation?" The prosecution objection was sustained by Judge Walton and Novitzky was spared attempting to explain McNamee's strange journey as star witness in the Mitchell Report and the Clemens trial under circumstances where the Government claimed he was never a target for prosecution. Nevertheless Novitzky stated, "We thought it was a good idea for Brian McNamee to cooperate with Mitchell," and that none of them knew what was going to be in the report, "including whether Mitchell would name names." Trying to put distance between the defense contentions that McNamee had been forced to change his story in return for immunity and that the government was "out to get Clemens," Novitzky insisted that Clemens was never a target for prosecution by the Government. "No, he was never.... We never targeted the end-user of these drugs."[37] Novitzky insisted that he had asked McNamee "about a dozen professional athletes using performance-enhancing drugs."[38] Nominally this contention by Novitzsky was corroborated in McNamee's interview with Rusty Hardin's investigators in the Belk Deposition. "They asked me a lot about that, players involved."[39] Yet the context in which Novitzky and the federal prosecutors asked McNamee questions clearly showed their obsession with Clemens. "So the next day, I have a new attorney, Earl Ward. Peralta says, 'You have three strikes to go to jail.... And then right away, 'So what about Clemens?'"[40] "They kept hounding me to find out if Roger had any medical problems due to injections."[41]

Lester Munson praised Novitzky's testimony. "The prosecution ended the day on a positive note with the testimony from Jeff Novitzky, the FDA agent. Novitzky is a formidable witness who can capture and maintain the attention of the jury."[42]

Another important government witness was former New York Mets clubhouse attendant Kirk Radomski, who was at the center of the PED-distribution network in the New York area that implicated McNamee and Clemens. Radomski and McNamee were close friends. Radomski had called McNamee in a panic after his home had been raided in a six- to seven-hour search by Novitzky. Radomski told McNamee that he would be in trouble because the investigators "probably" had his checks.[43] During the raid, Novitzky told Radomski he could even lose his house. Radomski's subsequent conviction for distribution of illegal drugs and his jail term clearly frightened McNamee and must have played a major role in his decision to cooperate with federal prosecutors and the Mitchell investigation.[44] Radomski received a $500,000 advance to write a tell-all book that was billed as a confession and would prove Radomski's role in giving illegal performance enhancing drugs to Brian McNamee that were used by Roger Clemens.[45] The finished product did not meet the description of the advertising. Apparently few buyers actually read Radomski's book—it was actually a passionate argument *for* the use of human growth and steroids, not a first-person regret over using and distributing them. Most importantly, Radomski admitted in the book that he did not know that Roger Clemens used steroids or human growth hormones that he sold McNamee.[46] That did not discourage Radomski, however, from declaring at trial, that "steroids and HGH can be used for endurance and recuperation, two things that are critical to starting pitchers such as Clemens."[47] Radomski's broad attempt to imply that steroids he supplied helped Roger Clemens regain his dominance late in his career was, unfortunately, undermined by his buddy, Brian McNamee, who insisted at the trial that Clemens always supplied the steroids. McNamee injected, not Kirk Radomski. Furthermore, Radomski did not venture an opinion as to why Clemens would need human growth hormone or anabolic steroids to recuperate from his 1985 shoulder surgery between 13 and 16 years later. Radomski did confirm McNamee's testimony that George Mitchell originally promised not to disclose publicly the names of baseball players who used performance enhancing drugs.[48]

The prosecution obtained helpful testimony from former trainers Charlie Moss and Jim Rowe of the Boston Red Sox, and Tommy Craig of the Toronto blue Jays, who testified that they had no authority to administer injections of Lidocaine and vitamin B-12, two drugs that Clemens said he was injected with.[49] Munson wrote that Assistant U.S. Attorney Gilbert Guerrero highlighted that Craig observed that Clemens "did whatever it took" to maintain proper conditioning. Gene Monahan, trainer for the Yankees, testified that he had never seen needles lined up after a game for B-12 shots, in a further effort by the prosecutors to mislead the jury into thinking that Clemens had claimed to have received such injections from all the teams he played for, when in fact Clemens said it had occurred only in Toronto.[50]

It's a phrase we are likely to hear again and again from prosecutors. They will argue that Clemens "did whatever it took" to prolong his career, including the use of steroids and HGH.[51]

Such testimony by baseball trainers, inside the action of the clubhouse, prompted Munson to wax eloquent about the progress of the government's case.

> The government's evidence against Roger Clemens is beginning to form a foundation that could be a problem for the former New York Yankees pitcher.[52]
> The pieces of evidence began to fall into place in ways that may produce an unexpectedly coherent package of guilt.[53]
> In total disagreement with what Clemens told Congress, the trainers said that only team doctors could give injections, and that any injections would be given to the doctor's treatment area ... two of the three ... said they had never seen needles "lined up and ready to go," during the years when Clemens played for their teams.[54]
> When the jury deliberates, the jurors will be asked to answer specifically whether Clemens is guilty of the fifteen statements, and it will be difficult for the Clemens legal team to explain that Clemens was truthful when he described the needles "lined up and ready to go."[55]

The other witnesses were, of course, minor characters in the prosecution's presentation, for as Lester Munson so aptly summarized it, "McNamee's testimony is the basis for the government's assertion that Clemens lied in ten specific sworn statements to the committee. McNamee even has a role in the remaining five specific statements described in the indictment."[56] As the government's star witness, McNamee was well prepared with catch phrases to drop on the ears of the jury, a common practice for both prosecution and defense lawyers, so that jurors might remember key points. Therefore McNamee's testimony was littered with "booty shot," "Don't ask, don't tell," "I was enabling," "I wish I wouldn't have done it. I was young."

McNamee began his testimony with the heartwarming, if questionable, story, that he learned how to inject liquids by giving his son insulin shots for juvenile diabetes. The real point of this story centered on the small size of the insulin needle and the government's hope that jurors would make the connection that human growth hormone could be injected with a small needle as well.[57] Near the trial's end, McNamee conceded in melodramatic fashion that he, too, had diabetes, and it remained unclear if his diabetes preceded that of his son. In addition, McNamee said that he was hypoglycemic, explaining why he had had to excuse himself numerous times during his testimony to elevate his low blood sugar.[58] To take the sting out of what surely would be painful cross-examination by Clemens' lawyers when McNamee first confessed that he himself used human growth hormones and anabolic steroids, the government put it on the table first in order to minimize the damage. McNamee's spin, because no other word would suffice, was that he started taking HGH after "almost decapitating" his pinky with a chop saw.[59] Furthermore, McNamee claimed that he started using steroids after right shoulder surgery in 2004 or 2005, injecting himself. That was some three to four years after he claimed to have stopped injecting Clemens, or maybe slightly shorter if he injected Clemens after 2001—a notion he advanced for the first time at trial. McNamee told his story of Roger Clemens' use of performance enhancing drugs, for at least the 12th time, in Lester Munson's estimation.[60] "The story that McNamee tells is long and can be compelling," Munson wrote.[61] "Assistant U.S. Attorney Daniel Butler is leading McNamee through the story in painstaking detail, repeating important aspects of the tale to build the case against Clemens."[62]

When Butler asked McNamee why he helped inject Clemens the first time in Toronto in 1998, the strength and conditioning coach said Clemens was "already on his own program," already had needles and drugs.[63] McNamee said he knew steroids were wrong but that he was "trying to do what my client wanted." Although Clemens himself had readily admitted that he wanted McNamee in New York to be available to train him after he joined the Yankees, McNamee testified that it was not until sometime into the regular 2000 season that Clemens came out of the training room and said "he was ready to get back on the stuff again."[64] In other words, although the prosecution's theory was that Clemens asked the Yankees to hire McNamee in order to give him performance enhancing drugs, neither man so much as discussed or hinted at doing so when they met again in spring training that year. Nevertheless, McNamee testified that Clemens asked him, "You have a guy, right?" McNamee said he went to Kirk Radomski to see if he could get PEDS to inject Clemens. After being assured Radomski could be his supplier, he told Clemens, and Clemens said, "Sure, get it."[65] McNamee said he told Radomski he needed "stuff for pitchers" but did not mention Clemens' name.[66] McNamee testified that Clemens kept performance enhancing drugs in his locker in the clubhouse[67] at Yankee Stadium.[68] McNamee said that the next year, 2001, Clemens came to him again and wanted more steroids, but not HGH. Clemens "didn't like the belly button shot" for human growth hormones, McNamee stated.[69] Apparently Clemens had not minded the "belly button" shot in Toronto in 1998 or in New York in 2000, but by 2001 could not tolerate it. McNamee's claim here that Clemens asked for anabolic steroids and not HGH, of course, contradicted McNamee's claim that Clemens always supplied the steroids. Keeping track of McNamee's at-odds claims was an exhausting task. Although McNamee had previously stated he had not discussed performance enhancing drugs with Clemens after 2001, and implied that is why he saved materials from injecting Clemens from that year as "protection," he now testified he was "not sure" he did or did not inject Clemens with PEDS after 2001.[70] To explain the bloody gauze that he had saved, McNamee said he sometimes bled from handling the broken drug ampules.[71]

McNamee said he saved medical waste after injecting Roger Clemens with steroids because McNamee's wife complained that her husband was going to be the fall guy.[72] With his estranged wife, Eileen McNamee, ruled out of the trial by Judge Walton and therefore not able to contradict him, McNamee said she was giving him a "hard time every single day," so he took a swab and cotton ball from a Clemens steroid injection in 2001, put it in a beer can from Clemens' apartment in Manhattan, and brought it to his Long Island home. When he showed it to her, she said, "All right." McNamee said he stored the material in a FedEx box, first in a closet in his basement, then in a closet in his master bedroom. He said, for the first time, and in contrast to his previous public statements, that he did not have any plans to use the material in any way.[73]

McNamee's version of why he injected Debbie Clemens with human growth hormone, at least on the day of his direct testimony in court, was that Clemens told him Debbie wanted HGH and to get some.[74] McNamee was aware that Radomski's trial testimony varied from what he had stated in his book—Radomski's book claimed that McNamee mailed the human growth hormone to Clemens. At trial, Radomski now stated that McNamee approached him and asked him to mail the HGH to "'William Roger Clemens in care of Brian McNamee." For his part, McNamee suggested that Clemens picked up the shipment of human growth hormone at his door—in fact, no one signed for the package. McNamee then gave a melodramatic account of being summoned from Clemens' pool to his bedroom. However, according to McNamee, even though he was the injector extraordinaire, Debbie Clemens asked her husband, not him, to give the injection. When Clemens asked McNamee to give her the shot, she protested. Not enough, in McNamee's account, however, to convince her husband to do it, and therefore McNamee took up the task of preparing the shot, teaching her how to inject herself as he did so, and then injecting her with HGH in her belly button.[75] He claimed he would have not injected Debbie Clemens had Clemens not been there.[76] Under cross-examination, McNamee, describing Debbie Clemens as a "fitness enthusiast," admitted that she had asked him about HGH outside of any conversation about it with her husband.[77]

Despite disowning the Belk deposition in which he had acknowledged government pressure to name Clemens as a user of HGH and anabolic steroids, McNamee's trial testimony was consistent with the Belk deposition on the issue of cooperating with George Mitchell. McNamee stated that he did not want to talk to George Mitchell[78] and cooperated with Mitchell and federal prosecutors because "My concern was if I lied to them I'd go to jail. They were going to prosecute me."[79] McNamee said he was not offered immunity from prosecution but could not be charged with anything that "came from his help." McNamee maintained that he did not expect Mitchell to name names in his report, that he wanted to maintain a relationship with Clemens, that he did not foresee a public outcry about steroids in baseball, and that when he learned to his surprise that Mitchell had indeed named names in his report, he called agent Jim Murray, instead of Clemens, to tell him Clemens was in the report.[80] McNamee proceeded to contradict that benign view of the consequences of cooperating with Mitchell and the Feds regarding Clemens and Pettitte when he admitted, "It was going to ruin my working relationship and friendship with them, which in turn would wreak havoc on my livelihood." He said he did not tell federal prosecutors he had vials and needles because "I wasn't giving it up. It was the last thing I had to hold onto."

Lester Munson was impressed by McNamee's testimony.

> It is the kind of evidence that, when stitched together in a final argument, could lead a jury to convict Clemens of Obstruction of Congress and perjury. And, as the result of Butler's questions to McNamee, the jury knows Pettitte used HGH. A "discerning juror" would notice McNamee testified before the committee and the grand jury, and that both panels appeared to believe and to conclude that Clemens was lying.... In a decision by the trial jury that could be a close call, the decision by these previous panels could tip the balance in favor of the prosecution.[81]

ESPN's TJ Quinn was more skeptical of McNamee's direct testimony than Lester Munson. "He's being very specific about times, places, circumstances. So does it show the jury a command of facts or does it seem contrived?"[82]

Many Clemens haters had been excited when news leaked before the trial that an 11-year-old boy had taken a photograph that allegedly proved that Clemens had attended Jose Canseco's 1998 Miami pool party. At trial, the prosecution showed a photograph of Alexander Lowrey, 25 in 2012, standing on the deck of the pool with a smiling Roger Clemens standing in the shallow end of the water. Clemens' hair was bleached blond from the summer sun. Normally it could be described as light brown.[83] Lowrey testified that he did not see Clemens at the party for at least two, and perhaps as long as three hours, after he arrived, although he did not have a watch and could not put an exact time on when he first saw Clemens. Nevertheless, putting an estimate of two to three hours after Lowrey got there before Clemens arrived—accounting for the time Clemens and Debbie spent having lunch after their golf outing—would place Clemens' arrival time at the party, according to a guess by ESPN's TJ Quinn, at 3 or 3:30 p.m., i.e., after McNamee had left.[84] "Did you see Clemens talking to Canseco?" Lowrey was asked. "No," Lowrey replied. Lowrey also testified that he did not see the buses that took players, coaches, and trainers, such as McNamee, to the ball park in Miami for the game that night.[85] At least from Lowrey's statements, Clemens and McNamee were probably not at the party at the same time. Actually, Lowrey was not even sure that the day he was at Canseco's pool was the day of the Blue Jays party. When asked, "Do you remember the date of these pictures?" he replied "No, sir." When asked the month, he could only answer, "No, sir." Lowery did believe the photographs were taken sometime in 1998.[86]

The Government obtained more helpful testimony than Lowrey's from one of McNamee's former Wall Street clients for human growth hormone, Anthony Corso, who paid McNamee an estimated $5,000 a month for strength and conditioning coaching and the HGH.[87] Corso, with lower back problems, testified that he received one HGH injection from McNamee, apparently in 2002, and injected himself thereafter. Corso testified, "Mr. McNamee had mentioned that Mr. Clemens was one of the athletes that was getting positive results from HGH."[88] Corso testified that McNamee told him that he had saved syringes, thrown them in a beer can, and put them in a FedEx box.[89] However, Corso did not directly link Clemens to that statement and the government resorted to reading Corso's grand jury testimony, quoting McNamee as saying, "I saved two syringes that I used on Roger."[90] Corso admitted he could not recall whether McNamee used Clemens' name in connection with the syringes or not. When a juror asked Corso whether McNamee mentioned Clemens' name in connection with the needles he kept, Corso replied, "No." Corso testified that McNamee initially mentioned Clemens as one of his human growth hormone clients,[91] apparently to make the sale for his services. Only later did

McNamee tell Corso that he injected Andy Pettitte with HGH to help Pettitte recover from elbow surgery.

Perhaps most importantly, Corso also testified that McNamee told him that he injected Roger Clemens with HGH for "recovery," but did not state what the recovery was supposed to be from. Once again, Clemens' 1985 surgery was at least 17 years in the past when McNamee recruited Corso as a client. In addition, Corso made it clear that McNamee had never suggested that he injected Clemens with anabolic steroids, and said that when the Mitchell Report was released he was surprised that McNamee claimed to have given Clemens steroids.[92] Corso's testimony, therefore, backed up Andy Pettitte's testimony that suggested McNamee did not start claiming Clemens used steroids until after their falling-out over the startup vitamin company.

Corso's account of hearing Brian McNamee discuss saved items used in injecting players was supported by former major league first baseman David Segui, perhaps the player who used steroids the longest. Segui recalled a telephone conversation with McNamee 11 years in the past—in 2001—when McNamee told him he had "kept darts" to get his wife off his back. Segui said McNamee claimed his work with Clemens had put a strain on his married life, supposedly because Clemens "called him at a drop of a hat" to come train him.[93] Unfortunately, McNamee did not tell Segui what "darts" meant. Also unfortunately, Segui gave testimony suggesting that McNamee's wife was on his back not because she was afraid he would become a fall guy, as McNamee had said endlessly, but as the primary breadwinner in the family she was angry that Clemens did not pay McNamee what he promised.[94]

Nevertheless, Lester Munson thought the testimony of Corso and Segui helped the government.

> The prosecutors, in a clear and resourceful move, want to turn Hardin's "evolving story" theme against Hardin and Clemens by showing that McNamee was telling the same story before he had any reason to fabricate anything. They want to show that what Hardin portrayed as a "recent fabrication," the final step in the evolving story, are not recent but instead are things that McNamee has said earlier when things were going well for Clemens.[95]
>
> Segui and Anthony Corso ... testified that McNamee told them as early as 2001 that he saved the physical evidence to placate his wife. Both assertions ... predate McNamee's first visit with federal agents and would predate any incentives he had to bring down Clemens or tell government agents what they wanted to hear.[96]

Although the vials of steroids, brand unidentified by Brian McNamee, and the needles alleged to have been used to inject Roger Clemens, had gathered the press and public attention throughout the years leading up to the trial, it was a used Miller Lite beer can and cotton swabs that played the starring roles in the trial. An irony that must not have been lost on Roger Clemens, who seldom drank alcohol of any kind. McNamee added to the irony when he admitted at trial that he never saw Roger Clemens drink Miller Lite.

FBI forensic examiner Pamela Reynolds and chemist Jeremy Price testified that the beer can evidence contained traces of steroids.[97] Price conducted the laboratory work that evidenced steroids on two needles and a swab.[98] California forensics expert Alan Keel testified that the DNA identified in the beer can was Clemens'. Keel could not be so sure DNA was on one of the two needles linked to Clemens.[99]

Assistant U.S. Attorney Courtney Saleski, former law clerk to Chief Justice William H. Rehnquist on the United States Supreme Court, a graduate of George Washington University Law School, and an expert in health care fraud, asked the feisty Keel whether the evidence could "have been faked" by Brian McNamee.

"The sample is too small to fake," Keel insisted.[100] Keel declared that if the beer can had been contaminated, he should have found McNamee's DNA, but he found Clemens' instead.[101] Keel said that traces of Clemens DNA on cotton balls "had a random match possibility of one in 15.4 trillion and 1 in 173 trillion for Clemens' DNA. He said the DNA on the needle was a one in 449 match for Clemens."[102] To Clemens' defense attorney Michael Attanasio's leading question that Keel could not know how somebody's DNA got into a needle because he "wasn't there," Keel responded, "I wasn't there but ... best, most probably the DNA got there because someone with that DNA was injected with that needle."[103] Keel went on to say that if anything had contaminated the needle, then McNamee's DNA would have been on it. He said it was not plausible that Clemens' DNA got into the needle from saliva residue in the beer can. Keel said that if there was liquid, blood would have dissolved into the liquid and DNA would have shown up on the other cotton ball, a cotton ball that contained no DNA amount.[104] Keel concluded, "In my opinion, it would be virtually impossible for someone to have left only the trace amount of material by design."[105]

Anthony Manuele, a Miller Coors manager, after looking at the markings on the bottom of the Miller Lite can, testified that it would have been on supermarket shelves between August 2001 and November 15, 2001—within McNamee's timeframe.[106] He added that the can was processed in North Carolina and cans for the New York area were processed there. He testified that the can line from its production indicated that it had been filled with beer on July 19, 2001, between 4:15 a.m. and 4:29 a.m.[107] Manuele admitted on cross-examination that he could not say whether the can of Miller had been bought in September or October, which would have put its sale past the time frame of McNamee said he employed it to collect injection waste. Manuele also admitted that the beer could have been delivered, and purchased, on Long Island, where McNamee lived, instead of Manhattan, where Clemens lived, thereby making it unlikely that McNamee could have picked up the beer can from Clemens' apartment.[108]

FBI fingerprint expert Eric Pokorak testified that Roger Clemens' fingerprints were not found on the waste collected and stored in the beer can,[109] while five of Brian McNamee's fingerprints were identified on the materials.[110] FBI toxicologist Cynthia Morris-Kukoski testified about types of Vitamin B-12 that were not found in the materials. Clemens had stated publicly that McNamee had injected him with B-12, not anabolic steroids or human growth hormone. On cross-examination, Hardin asked Morris-Kukoski, "Are you sure there aren't other B-12 strains?" insinuating that she had not tested completely for signs of B-12. In reply, she admitted, "There is another one—B-12 A."[111]

McNamee said at the trial, for the first time under oath, that he had injection materials to placate his angry wife.[112] Previously, during his Congressional deposition, and separately before the televised hearings as mentioned several times in this book, McNamee had said publicly that he collected evidence against Clemens because he did not trust him, and he wanted to protect himself and his family, and not be the fall guy. Now at trial for the first time, McNamee claimed he had no intention to use the saved materials to get back at anybody.[113] When a juror wanted to know, therefore, why McNamee kept the FedEx box in his house, he replied simply, "I just kept it to keep it. Nowhere else to keep it."[114]

Lester Munson provided an excellent analysis of the courtroom battle over the saved materials and whether they proved Brian McNamee injected Roger Clemens with anabolic steroids.

> These formidable litigation teams spent nearly six hours on Thursday and Friday battling over two cotton balls and a used syringe.[115] In a garden-variety trial of a criminal case involving DNA on these objects, the questioning of the DNA witness might have consumed no more than 90 minutes, or at the long end, two hours.
>
> But with the extensive preparations that both teams have made for this trial, both sides have asked every possible question, have raised every possible legal issue, and have sought every advantage in every answer from every witness.
>
> In the battle over the DNA evidence, for example, assistant U.S. attorney Courtney Saleski took DNA expert Alan Keel through every detail of the laboratory processing of eleven needles, gauze pads, tissues and vials that former Clemens' trainer Brian McNamee claims he collected while he was injecting Clemens with steroids and HGH. Again and again, Saleski asked for each step of the procedure, never once suggesting that the procedure for one item was exactly the same as the procedure for the previous item.... Saleski demonstrated impressive mastery of DNA arcana, and she was trying to anticipate what the Clemens team would ask the expert in cross-examination.[116]
>
> When it was time for Michael Attanasio to cross-examine the expert, he returned the favor. He raised the possibilities of commingling and contamination of evidence, confronted the witness with tests he did not do, asked whether the witness was being paid by the hour,

13. A Prosecutor's Dream Jury   175

inquired about the possible transfer of evidence from one item to another while confined in a beer can where McNamee stashed them, focused on the expert's college major of zoology, and raised the possibility of saliva on the beer can.

The defense lawyer's finest moment came when he confronted Keel with the fact that Keel's calculations show that there was a one in 450 chance that someone else had the same DNA that Keel found on the needle and attributed to Clemens. It was a marked contrast to the numbers for one of the cotton balls that showed a one in 1.8 quintillion chance that DNA from someone other than Clemens was on the cotton ball.

Although neither Keel nor Attanasio made the calculations, it means that there are as many as 708,666 people in the U.S. whose DNA would match the DNA that Keel found on the needle.

Saleski's finest moment came in her rebuttal questions responding to Attanasio's cross-examination, when she said to the expert: "I want to ask you some questions about pus." She then did exactly what she said she would do, asking him a series of six questions about the pus that he found on one of the cotton balls that he attributed to Clemens."[117]

As it turned out, Courtney Saleski emerged as the star lawyer of the trial, the one most praised for her techniques in direct and re-direct questioning, the one whose reputation was advanced the most. After all, Rusty Hardin was *supposed to win* his cases. Saleski, therefore, made a deep impression on legal professionals, the press, and baseball fans who hated Roger Clemens. Unfortunately, none of these people were on the jury.

14

Rusty Hardin's Comfort Zone

The early optimism of the prosecution in the Clemens trial was a little like the early optimism of the presidential campaign of Senator John Kerry on Election Day 2004. Preliminary exit polls showed Kerry winning. But a Floridian knew those projections were wrong. His name was Jeb Bush, the state's governor. He was proved right and his brother George won re-election. Another Floridian, Joel Denaro, earned immediate success and public attention as a young Miami public defender when he won an extraordinary string of appeals overturning death sentences.[1] By the time of Clemens' second trial in the spring of 2012, Denaro ran his own practice and was the go-to guy for those accused of trafficking in illegal drugs between Colombia and Miami. Coincidentally, Denaro, although a Miami native who was in fact the son of one of the city's pre-eminent criminal defense attorneys, "Black Jack" Denaro, was a lifelong Red Sox fan. When the Clemens jury was sworn in, Denaro did not hesitate a second as he read about the composition of the Clemens jury, such as the fact that it contained no baseball fans whose favorite player might have been decked by Clemens. He texted immediately, on April 23, 2012, "HUNG JURY." Clemens' legal team would do even better than a hung jury, a complete "Not Guilty" exoneration, but Denaro's foresight of victory was still apt, and pointed out the larger truth that the prosecution had the case won until the jury was sworn in.

Lester Munson introduced the Clemens defense. "The Clemens defense team includes another five lawyers, three top-of-the line investigators, a pair of techies and a group of paralegals and interns. Its leader is Rusty Hardin, one of America's great trial lawyers."[2]

Hardin had followed an untraditional path to the law. Perhaps explaining his later success before juries, he had "lived a little," as they used to say back in the twentieth century. After graduating from Wesleyan University in 1965, Hardin taught high school history for five years and then worked for a year as a Congressional staffer in Washington. Hardin joined the U.S. Army, served in

Vietnam, and retired with a rank of captain. He was 32 by the time he received a law degree from Southern Methodist University, and he served a rather long apprenticeship, 15 years, as an assistant district attorney in Houston. As a prosecutor, he never lost a felony case—a felony is characterized as a serious crime defined by the Modern Penal Code and many state statutes as involving a jail term of more than one year. On his website, Hardin expressed his comfort level with juries. "I have found that juries almost always do the right thing. Even when I disagree, I can see how they got there."[3] Hardin served as chief trial counsel in the Whitewater scandal for the Independent Counsel's Office for both Robert Fiske and Kenneth Starr.

He opened up his law firm, Rusty Hardin & Associates, in 1996. He was 53 years old. He no longer spent the majority of his time working on criminal cases. Indeed 85 percent of his firm's work involved civil litigation. Yet Hardin, with one son teaching school and another serving as a Houston cop, remained grounded in the everyday life of Houston even as he prospered with celebrity clients such as Clemens and Hall of Fame athletes Calvin Murphy (basketball), Warren Moon and Adrian Peterson (football) and Wade Boggs (baseball), and corporate clients such as Arthur Andersen, Las Vegas Sands, Burlington Resources, and Samsung.

Because civil litigation took up most of the work at Rusty Hardin & Associates, only three of the ten attorneys in the small firm could handle criminal cases: Rusty Hardin, Andy Drumheller, and Derek S. Hollingsworth. Drumheller was a graduate of Texas Tech Law School, and Hollingsworth graduated from Baylor Law School. This was not the kind of pedigree represented by the federal prosecutors, although Hollingsworth had been graduated first in his class from Baylor in 1997 and clerked on the Texas Supreme Court. Undermanned, Hardin did what all law firms and corporations do in such circumstances—he brought in outside counsel.[4] The outside counsel included San Diego lawyer Michael Attanasio, a former federal prosecutor who was the son of a baseball agent.

Hardin was a short man with wide shoulders, a square head, and large, piercing eyes that missed few details. He resembled *Wheel of Fortune* television game show host Pat Sajack in stature and the shape of his head, but his profile was dominated by reddish, sun-weathered, wrinkled cheeks. He wore a light, cream-colored suit to court on most days of the Clemens trial, with a blue shirt. On the day the jury handed down its verdict of Clemens, however, Hardin dressed more traditionally, wearing a dark blue suit. Clemens, wearing darker suits more often, dressed appropriately as "the good guy" on the day of his exoneration, wearing a light tan suit. Hardin was comfortable with regular people. After 30 years of practicing law, he was probably most comfortable in a courtroom, in front of a jury. He trusted jurors.

To be sure, Hardin had his work cut out for him. The Mitchell Report, the Congressional depositions, and the Waxman televised hearings were all, in their own way, constructed to head off any defenses that Roger Clemens might raise to the charges that he had lied under oath to Congress about taking performance enhancing drugs. On the same score, Brian McNamee's civil lawyers, and federal prosecutors, prepared him to head off allegations against him that he continued to change his story as he testified about Clemens. As a former police officer, McNamee understood the importance of motive in proving perjury—a crime that requires intent as an element. Therefore, McNamee would spend his time on the witness stand trying to run around defense contentions that he doctored evidence to blackmail Clemens because he needed money. Hardin understood this and addressed the issue of McNamee's motive in his opening statement. The lawyer showed the jury a copy of McNamee's unpublished manuscript, entitled *Death, Taxes and Mac*, which showed the X in taxes being formed by two crossed syringes, asking, "Is there any market for this book if he hadn't made these allegations about Roger Clemens?"[5] Major League Baseball also put a road block in Hardin's way by not allowing him to depose any of its employees, placing him in a precarious position of having no idea what they would say, and therefore making it almost impossible for him to prepare to cross examine the MLB witnesses.[6]

Hardin understood the emotional investment, the anger, the desperation that was behind the political trial of Roger Clemens on the part of Congress, the federal government, the baseball press, angry baseball fans, and Brian McNamee. He understood, therefore, that the opposing lawyers would stretch the rules to the limit, push the envelope in the courtroom, to try and convict Clemens. Of course, he had already experienced the prosecution's successful effort to blow up a jury it didn't like and get a new bite at the apple with a more favorable jury.

Hardin also understood that the feisty McNamee, the government's major witness, would try to fight back on the witness stand. He understood that government expert witnesses would foolishly try to play the hero to win the case. In the larger sense, McNamee was about to bestow on Hardin the greatest gift a star prosecution witness can present to a defense attorney: an ever-changing story. Rusty Hardin, therefore, decided to give the prosecution enough rope to hang itself. And it did.

For starters, the prosecutors ignored normal courtroom courtesy. Lead prosecutor Steven Durham refused even to tell the defense what witnesses he planned to call each day, a violation of common courtroom procedure and courtesy. As Lester Munson put it,

14. Rusty Hardin's Comfort Zone

With no apparent advantage to be gained, the only explanation for Durham's intransigence is that he is attempting to aggravate the defense lawyers. The prosecutors even object when the subject of Hardin's cross-examination is well within the scope of their direct examination.[7]

The situation becomes worse when Judge Reggie Walton then allows the prosecutors to argue the objection in a "sidebar" discussion held at his bench out of hearing of the jury, Munson said. These discussions of what appear to be simple issues frequently go on for five or ten minutes or more. A reading of the transcripts of these discussions show that much of the argument and conversation comes from Walton as he wonders aloud about his rulings.[8]

Hardin complained to Walton that he had "been trying cases for thirty-seven years and had never had anyone treat him the way the prosecutors were treating him. They want an order not to do this and not to do that. This is silly stuff."[9]

Nevertheless, despite the stacked deck against him and his client, the high-handed government and the judge were not deciding the case. The jury was. The jury was now in front of him, in his sight, he in their sights, and that's the way Rusty Hardin liked it. And despite the challenges of representing Clemens before Walton, Hardin admitted several years later, "You know, I grew fond of the Judge."[10]

Despite contentions that Rusty Hardin was merely Roger Clemens' hired gun, he in fact believed deeply in Clemens' innocence. As he began his defense of Clemens before Congress, he said, "I don't have enough malpractice insurance to handle the number of lawyers in this country that think I'm insane to let a man be coming in here when he's already been warned publicly there's going to be a public referral—a criminal referral. And yet we're willing to do so."[11]

Later, after the criminal trial was over, when the suggestion was made that Clemens pay a settlement to McNamee as a "Christian gesture" to give the hard-up strength and conditioning coach some financial stability, Hardin exploded in anger, according to a source within the Clemens defense. McNamee had brought it all on, Hardin said, and he would never allow the innocent Clemens to pay McNamee one penny of his own money, a highly unusual position for any attorney, who is taught to make the best deal for his client with the least amount of cost and personal aggravation.

Lester Munson raised the bar for the defense before Hardin began his cross-examination of McNamee. He declared, "The Clemens legal team will be looking for nothing less than a walk-off home run when lead attorney Rusty Hardin cross-examines the government's star witness."[12] Munson's colleague, TJ Quinn, had no doubts that Hardin would meet these high expectations when he joked, "Wondering whether they'll need dental records to ID Mac after Hardin is through with him."[13]

For his cross-examination of McNamee, Hardin wore a light-blue suit with a pink tie. Clemens, usually attired in darker colors, wore a light grey suit, white shirt, with a dark brown or orange tie. McNamee wore glasses, a tan suit, yellow patterned tie, and white shirt.

As expected, much of the cross-examination exchange between Hardin and McNamee was contentious.

> HARDIN: If you told investigators you didn't discuss PEDS after '01, and now you say you did, were earlier mistakes, faulty memory or lie? Mr. McNamee, do you sometimes just make stuff up?
> PROSECUTION: Objection!
> JUDGE WALTON: Rephrase.
> MCNAMEE: No, I didn't make it up.[14]
> HARDIN: You didn't tell Mitchell or Novitzky about your later PED conversations?
> MCNAMEE: No. File it under bad memory.
> HARDIN: Did you tell Mitchell and others about Debbie Clemens?
> MCNAMEE: I'm not sure what I told the Mitchell committee.
> HARDIN: You also testified you never discussed steroids after August '01.
> MCNAMEE: No, we talked about getting stuff for his wife after '01.
> HARDIN: You agree that you're telling the world that in a twenty-four-year career Clemens used PEDS in '98, 2000, 2001?
> MCNAMEE: Yes.
> HARDIN: Would you agree with me from the time you made these accusations about Clemens your memory has sort of evolved?
> MCNAMEE: Yes.
> HARDIN: Haven't you said your memory improved as this has gone on?
> MCNAMEE: Yes, sir.
> HARDIN: You knew Clemens played golf the day of the party but never told Mitchell or Congress?
> MCNAMEE: Why would I?
> HARDIN: Hadn't you said Clemens was at the party the whole time?
> MCNAMEE: Yes.
> HARDIN: Didn't you learn he played golf that day?
> MCNAMEE: I knew he did.
> HARDIN: You were valuable for all this, which has nothing to do with steroids and HGH?
> MCNAMEE: Yeah, I'll agree with that.
> HARDIN: You deliberately withheld information?
> MCNAMEE: Yes.[15]
> HARDIN: You remembered more and more things as you made more statements?
> MCNAMEE: Yes.
> HARDIN: You were mistaken sometimes?
> MCNAMEE: Yes.
> HARDIN: You forgot some things and remembered them later?
> MCNAMEE: Yes.
> HARDIN: You lied intentionally?
> MCNAMEE: Yes.
> HARDIN: Did you do everything you could to keep information about the Feds away from Clemens?

McNamee: No.[16]
Hardin: Why didn't you tell Clemens the Feds were talking to you?
McNamee: He didn't ask.
Hardin: How could he ask if he didn't know?
McNamee: If he doesn't ask, how can I answer?
Hardin: Here is an e-mail you sent to Novitzky. It reads, "I am happy to help and would appreciate total confidentiality." How were you not reluctant?
McNamee: The prior e-mail from Novitzky was stern so my lawyer said to respond and be friendly.
Hardin: Is it true that when you were talking to the government and Mitchell and saying Clemens used steroids, you were still working for Clemens and asking for favors?
McNamee: Possibly.
Hardin: Would you agree that between meetings you had "an evolution" in the number of shots you remembered?
McNamee: About everything.
Hardin: They were going to lock you up if you didn't tell them what they said was the truth, weren't they? The government gave you what they believed the truth was. Yes?
McNamee: Not accurate.
Hardin: Did you lie to mislead and make it sound not so bad?
McNamee: I wanted to make it look like he wasn't as big a steroid user as he was.
Hardin: You lied about the number of shots?
McNamee: I minimized, yes.
Hardin: The government says they were going after people like you, but they told you from the start they were not going after you. They were going after athletes.
McNamee: No, they were going after suppliers.
Hardin: Was anybody prosecuted?
McNamee: Yes, Radomski.
Hardin: But Radomski had already pleaded guilty.... You could have been charged with federal felonies for distributing performance enhancing drugs. Two months were left on the statute of limitations in which they could have charged you. You said you saw Clemens talk to Canseco and some other guy at Jose's party and you speculated that they discussed steroids?[17]
McNamee: It was a pretty safe assumption. We knew Canseco was an "avid" steroids user.
Hardin: We all know that, he wrote two books about it.... You assumed that without any personal knowledge, didn't you?
McNamee: Yes, sir.
Hardin: You contend that days after the party Clemens asked you for a steroids shot.
McNamee: Yes, sir.
Hardin: You told Novitzky originally that you gave Clemens a shot in Tampa Bay in June. But it turns out they weren't in Tampa Bay then. You changed the date, didn't you?
McNamee: I didn't have the luxury of a calendar like other people do.
Hardin: You didn't say to the Feds you "believed" your shot caused the abscess. You said you did? Yes?
McNamee: I believed it did. I felt bad. I thought I caused the abscess. I believe I thought that.
Hardin: Did you ever take steroids to Clemens' home?
McNamee: I never bought steroids. One thousand percent sure.
Hardin: So when was the shot you think gave him the abscess?
McNamee: I'm not sure now. I almost always shot him in the SkyDome, once in Tampa Bay.

HARDIN: Were you certain you never had them?
MCNAMEE: Mmmm.... I'd say one hundred percent.
HARDIN: Did Clemens always bring steroids to the scene?
MCNAMEE: Yes, sir. Clemens always had them.
HARDIN: You intentionally lied to government investigators and the Mitchell investigators?
MCNAMEE: That's accurate about the government. I'm having trouble with the lie thing.
HARDIN: After '01, you never asked Clemens why he stopped juicing?
MCNAMEE: Never.
HARDIN: You lied repeatedly to the Feds but not one blankety-blank thing has happened to you?
MCNAMEE: That's fair.
HARDIN: Explain why you gave evidence to the Feds?
MCNAMEE: Full story?
HARDIN: God help us. How long is it?
MCNAMEE: I wanted to protect my wife, so I kept her out of it. I told Congress I was worried Clemens would take me down.
HARDIN: Then you told Novitzky you meant to throw materials away.
MCNAMEE: I was just trying to keep my wife, the mother of my children, out of this. I forgot I had it sometimes.
HARDIN: Did you think that was a good solution to your problem?
MCNAMEE: It was a very good solution.
HARDIN: She's worried you're going to be caught for a crime, and your solution was to bring evidence of that crime to your home?

McNamee said that he brought the evidence home to get his wife off his back.

HARDIN: Isn't it true you knew Clemens was denying your accusations?
MCNAMEE: Yes, he knew.
HARDIN: So now your credibility was in jeopardy and you needed something to save yourself, yes? You felt like a rape victim?
MCNAMEE: I wouldn't say it that way.
HARDIN: You lied to my investigators.
MCNAMEE: I embellished.
HARDIN: You lied, didn't you? What in the world—in your world, the world of Brian McNamee—is the difference between exaggeration and lie? This is the needle you say you used to give Clemens steroids in the booty. Yes?
MCNAMEE: Yes.
HARDIN: Is this the evidence you created?
GOVERNMENT: Objection to [the] word "created."
JUDGE WALTON: Overruled.
HARDIN: Are we to understand that you put certain items in the beer can and then you said you gathered the gauze, *et cetera*, and put it in a bag?
MCNAMEE: Yes.
HARDIN: That's gauze you wiped the back of his lap with?
MCNAMEE: I was trying to clean up.
HARDIN: Was the blood Clemens'?
MCNAMEE: It was probably Clemens' but could be mine from breaking an ampule.
HARDIN: You didn't mention your own blood until later until the DNA test, until the DNA test showed blood was his.

GOVERNMENT: Objection.
JUDGE WALTON: I know. Sustained.
HARDIN: You've never seen Clemens drink a light beer, yes?
MCNAMEE: Yes.
HARDIN: You put needles and cotton balls in the can?
MCNAMEE: Not sure where I put cotton balls.
HARDIN: You put steroids needle, HGH needle, ampule, cotton balls into can. And you took other stuff and put it in the bag. The other needle there in the photo—why did you not also put that in the can?
MCNAMEE: I probably didn't realize it was there. It was probably wrapped up.
HARDIN: Before today, have you EVER testified, told anyone, that you saved items in a can, items from other players?[18]
MCNAMEE: Yes, many times.
HARDIN: Who did you tell; when did you tell them?
MCNAMEE: I told Novitzky, assistant U.S. attorneys, FBI agent Longmire.
HARDIN: You haven't told them at all, have you? Isn't this an example of you making it up on the fly?
MCNAMEE: No.
HARDIN: When exactly did you tell people that non Clemens materials were in the can?
MCNAMEE: I'm not sure of dates.
HARDIN: So where is the growth hormone coming from? Which player? Is that Knobby [Chuck Knoblauch], or don't you know?
MCNAMEE: I think it is Knoblauch, yes.
HARDIN: Did you tell anyone you put other players' materials into the beer can the same night you took Clemens' stuff?
MCNAMEE: No one ever asked me that way before. I told them it was in there.
HARDIN: After DNA evidence came back from the lab showing your blood on the materials, and the government asked you how your blood got on the materials, what did you tell them?
MCNAMEE: I said I cut my hand many times opening ampules.
HARDIN: Are you an alcoholic?
MCNAMEE: No sir.
HARDIN: Did your drinking increase when you were fired by the Yankees?
MCNAMEE: No.
HARDIN: You had two DWI's in a six-week period.
MCNAMEE: DUI, not DWI. Neither was legitimate. In one case I was spitting into an open can. In the second I got into an argument with a cop after I'd had a couple of beers. I was on foot. A cop told me to move my car from a hydrant. I tried to park, couldn't find a lot.
HARDIN: While a police officer, did you get called to the scene of a deceased woman?
MCNAMEE: Yes.
HARDIN: While there, did you alter the crime scene?
MCNAMEE: Not the crime scene, but yes.
HARDIN: When confronted by superiors, did you lie about it?
MCNAMEE: Yes.
HARDIN: Did you keep getting PEDs from Radomski?
MCNAMEE: Yes, but I didn't profit from it.
HARDIN: Did you order "diet pills" online from an "internet fraud?"
MCNAMEE: I ordered for myself and my wife.

HARDIN: Are you bringing your wife into this?
MCNAMEE: Yeah, she took 'em.
HARDIN: What did your wife weigh?
MCNAMEE: That's scary talking about a girl's weight.
HARDIN: You are accusing her of illegally obtaining but you're afraid to guess her weight? Did you order hydrocodone from an online site under your wife's name?
MCNAMEE: Yes.
HARDIN: Did you ever tell Mitchell or investigators about Debbie's use of HGH?
MCNAMEE: She didn't play in the major leagues.[19]
HARDIN: Didn't you always say Debbie got the HGH shot *before* the swimsuit shot in '01?
MCNAMEE: It was around that time. I didn't say I knew that was why.
HARDIN: In your own manuscript you write, "To get her prepped for the *Sports Illustrated* shoot with her hubby." Did you say that?
MCNAMEE: No, sir, I don't talk like that.
HARDIN: If the *Sports Illustrated* was in in February '03, wouldn't the HGH have nothing to do with the shoot? Because you said the HGH shot was late '03 or '04.
MCNAMEE: I misspoke. It could have been '02, '03, '04.
HARDIN: You can't narrow it down more than that!
MCNAMEE: I'm getting hammered with a lot of dates.
HARDIN: It doesn't have a blank-blank thing to do with it.
MCNAMEE: What does blank-blank mean?
HARDIN: Even if the shot came in '03 instead of '04, there would be no connection between the HGH shot and the *Sports Illustrated* shoot.
MCNAMEE: Uh, sure.
HARDIN: Reports about that article [newspaper stories regarding the alleged sexual assault case in October 2001 in Florida] and your conduct have always made you upset?
MCNAMEE: Yes.
JUDGE WALTON: Why is it relevant whether Mr. McNamee asked Mitchell not to go into the facts of the incident?[20]
HARDIN: Number one, the Mitchell people agreed not to ask about the incident.
JUDGE WALTON: What does that have to do with the government's decision to pursue this case?
HARDIN: Mitchell should've looked into McNamee's background.
JUDGE WALTON: That has nothing to do with the government's decision to pursue the case against Mr. Clemens. If your purpose is to show bias by the government, I'll allow it. If he denies knowledge of an agreement that ends the matter.
HARDIN: You left Canseco's party at 2 p.m. on a team bus?
MCNAMEE: Yes.

Lester Munson's analysis of McNamee's testimony was devastating.

Hardin extracted admissions from McNamee that he had lied to Clemens and other clients, to federal agents and prosecutors, to investigators for MLB attorney George Mitchell, to the media, to the ghostwriter of his unpublished autobiography, and to the grand jury that charged Clemens with Obstruction of Congress and perjury.[21]

Confronted with powerful evidence from the thoroughly prepared Hardin, McNamee was forced to admit to lie after lie.[22]

McNamee lied in an e-mail to Clemens, claiming that he had talked directly to Jeff Novitzky and Novitzky told him he "felt sorry" for him and what he was going through with in

McNamee's role in a sexual assault incident in St. Petersburg, Florida in 2001 ... It is, Hardin proved, pure fiction. The McNamee-Novitzky telephone conversation never happened. McNamee would not meet Novitzky until the following year.[23]

Hardin also forced McNamee to admit that his claim of gathering needles, syringes, gauze, cotton balls from Clemens' New York City apartment was "an evolving narrative" that changed as the years passed. When Hardin used the phrase "moving target" McNamee quickly agreed.[24]

Hardin asked McNamee when he decided to add his wife to his story of gathering and keeping the physical evidence. "I did it for the trial," McNamee admitted. "I was trying to keep my wife out of it and protect my family."[25]

McNamee testified that he injected Debbie Clemens to prepare for a *Sports Illustrated* swimsuit issue but Hardin showed the HGH injection came long after the photo shoot of 2002.[26]

There is little doubt to me that Hardin has proved that McNamee is a serial liar.[27]

The jury agreed with Munson. As one of them put it after the trial, "The case came down to 'Who was the liar?' We decided it was McNamee."[28]

Hardin's demolition of Brian McNamee's credibility was a lot like the demolition of Los Angeles Police Department detective Mark Fuhrman in the O.J. Simpson trial. When Fuhrman stepped off the witness stand after F. Lee Bailey's veritable karate chopping, the "Not Guilty" verdict in Simpson's favor was a foregone conclusion to the discerning observer. When Hardin finished cross-examining Brian McNamee, as the jury made clear in post-trial interviews, the conclusion that Roger Clemens did not lie about taking performance enhancing drugs was inescapable.

15

The Government's Double-Edged Swords

Nothing suggested that the prosecution of Roger Clemens was politically inspired more than the fact that most of its major witnesses were double-edged swords, people whose testimony nominally advanced the prosecution's allegations, but also raised serious questions about it. In the end, the presumed pro-prosecution jury turned out to be a double-edged sword as well. A starting point was two witnesses the government choose not to put on the witness stand: Jose Canseco, the confessed steroids user, and Mindy McCready, Clemens' alleged mistress. McNamee's story, and therefore the government's theory of their case, was that Roger Clemens learned about steroids from conversing with Canseco and saw and received his first samples of steroids from Canseco in the Toronto Blue Jays' clubhouse. If Clemens' criminal activities started there, why did the prosecutors not begin their case in court by calling Canseco as their first witness? He would have provided compelling testimony of Clemens' use of anabolic steroids from the beginning and would have confirmed McNamee's story. A slam dunk for sure, and Clemens would probably have been on his way to prison. The problem was that Jose Canseco said none of it was true.

> I have never had a conversation with Clemens in which he expressed any interest in using steroids or growth hormone. Clemens has never asked me to give him steroids or human growth hormone, and I have never seen Clemens use, possess, or ask for steroids or human growth hormone. I have played on three teams with Roger Clemens and I have no reason to believe that he has ever used steroids, human growth hormone, or any other performance enhancing drugs.[1]

According to New York's *Daily News*, the FBI interviewed Mindy McCready in May 2008 about whether Clemens had erectile dysfunction issues and how often they occurred.[2] Erectile dysfunction was reputed to be a side-effect of steroids usage. Richard Emery, one of McNamee's lawyers in a defama-

15. The Government's Double-Edged Swords

tion suit against Clemens, put great hope in McCready's testimony at the time. "She could lead to a lot of probative information," he suggested.[3] McCready later made a combination porn film/interview, entitled *Baseball Mistress*, wherein she talked about sex with country singer Alan Jackson, actor Dean Cain, who played Superman on the television series *Lois & Clark*, and Clemens.[4] She said Clemens was good in bed "when he could get it up." The misleading title did not include any taped sex with Clemens or any of the entertainers.[5] Why then did the government not call McCready to testify? Perhaps Clemens' enemies at the New York tabloid provided a hint when they reported that a source within the Yankees told them that Clemens and other players used Viagra not to help their sex lives but instead to serve as an energy boost, sort of a substitute for the amphetamines that were so popular among baseball players in the late twentieth century.[6] Or perhaps the government did not care for the idea of the jury hearing McCready's opinion of Clemens: "Roger Clemens is one of the most wonderful men I've ever known."[7] In fact, the real reason the Government did not call McCready to testify was that she had told the FBI that she never saw any indications that Clemens took performance enhancing drugs and that on the one occasion they had seen something about PEDs on television, Clemens had condemned the user.[8]

Even Judge Walton, during the final moments of the 2011 mistrial, had vouched for the credibility of Andy Pettitte as an important government witness. The failure of Pettitte, therefore, to drive a stake in Clemens' heart was all the more disappointing to the prosecutors. Essentially, Andy Pettitte's honesty undid the prosecution. Pettitte was always unsure and ambiguous about what Roger Clemens said to him about taking human growth hormone. Only a day after testifying at the trial that "Roger had mentioned to me that he had taken HGH," Pettitte essentially took it all back. First he admitted that it was a passing comment by Clemens during a workout and not a real conversation or dialogue.[9] Then Clemens' defense attorney Michael Attanasio delivered the blow during cross-examination that knocked Pettitte out of the trial, so to speak.

> ATTANASIO: Is it fair to say it was 50–50 that you misunderstood the conversation?
> PETTITTE: I'd say that's fair.

No one who had read Pettitte's Congressional deposition should have been surprised by Pettitte's 50–50 doubt about whether Clemens, in fact, told him he had used HGH, because his recollection of what Roger Clemens said about HGH was so vague that he could remember absolutely nothing about its substance, absolutely nothing about its context. Nowhere in this statement was there anything about Clemens telling him about the benefits of HGH or any benefits it might have in aiding recovery from injury. That was pure invention later at the second trial and may have been based on a false paraphrase by Congressman Henry Waxman in his introduction to his televised hearings, discussed in Chapter 8, when he claimed that Pettitte had been told by Clemens that HGH helped in recovery. As for that recovery issue, to be later repeatedly cited at Clemens' second trial by his enemies in the press, let us read Andy Pettitte's actual response instead of the one falsely attributed to him:

"Did he tell you about the pros and cons of HGH?"
"No. *I want to think that he had just said that, you know, like that he had just heard that it helped, like helped your body recover and stuff like that. But again, you know, I hate to try to—you know, I'm sorry as far as trying to—I don't want to be inaccurate*" [emphasis added].

To summarize, Pettitte heard Clemens say something in a passing conversation about HGH, thought he heard Clemens admit to taking it, could not remember the substance or context, wished that he could say he remembered something substantive such as Clemens told him that it "helped your body recover and stuff like that," but could not because quite frankly and bluntly, he did not remember anything about the conversation. Furthermore, he had no memory of telling his wife. This makes his wife's later affidavit, which the Waxman committee paraded around like a writ from Moses and the first trial blew up over, rather suspicious. Pettitte clearly had an opportunity to speak to his wife about what he told her before he came to Washington to testify, knew that he was being brought in to testify about what he thought he heard about Clemens talking about using HGH, yet admitted he had no recollection of telling his wife. Reasonable minds must conclude that she had an opportunity to remind him before he went to Washington that he told her he thought he heard Clemens admit to HGH usage and did not do so. Only later did she claim that he did tell her of his suspicions about Clemens.

Let's use some of that common sense, along with a little exaggeration, to make the point that those who do not like to face up to facts always advise us to use. "I'd have to say that I told my wife. I'd have to say that I told her that the butler murdered Holmes because I tell her everything." Imagine how far that argument would go in court. Indeed the court did not hear Pettitte explain in Clemens' second trial that he really did not remember telling his wife, any more than it heard about Brian McNamee's intended financial salvation with a vitamin company, because the government wisely chose to not expose those facts to the jury.

Given Pettitte's poor memory, it seemed likely, in hindsight, that what Pettitte remembered was not what Clemens told him about HGH at all, but what Brian McNamee said Clemens told Pettitte over the years in reminding him of the incident, but with McNamee's own spin.

15. The Government's Double-Edged Swords

In that February 2008 deposition, Pettitte was asked, "Was there anything from your memory that helps you place it in time?"

"*I just felt like* that it was early when I met Roger and Mac. *I believe* [emphasis added] it was off season in '99." In other words, Andy Pettitte could not remember when Clemens uttered this purported admission.

"Did you ever tell Clemens later on that you had used HGH?" he was asked.[10]

"No."

Pettitte also hurt the prosecution by characterizing the incident as "the conversation that I *thought* [emphasis added] I had in 1999 or 2000."[11] And that was not all the damage Pettitte unintentionally inflicted on the prosecution. The government's theory was that Clemens cared so much about getting into baseball's Hall of Fame that he would do anything to get there, use any "edge," cheat by using any substance to help his performance. This exchange with Assistant U.S. Attorney Steven Durham did not help that theory:

DURHAM: "Was it important to Clemens to be elected to the Hall of Fame?"
PETTITTE: "I can't say. I never heard him talk about that."[12]

What was instructive about the Roger Clemens/Andy Pettitte relationship was that at no time during the five-year ordeal for Clemens did Clemens ever turn on Pettitte, criticize Pettitte, or question Pettitte's honesty. Ironically, Roger Clemens believed in Andy Pettitte to the end—even though Pettitte's testimony threatened to send him to prison.

Far tougher and determined government witnesses than Andy Pettitte were marginalized by the defense's attention to detail. Former IRS special Agent Jeff Novitzky had practically served as the government's face in the war on illegal drugs in sports. His testimony in the Barry Bonds trial proved highly effective and was credited with the compromise verdict the jury rendered of guilty of obstruction of justice. Novitzky did not fare as well with this highly educated Washington jury that possessed an unusually sophisticated knowledge of science. Novitzky was supposed to act like the track anchorman who would run first, instead of his usual position of last, in this race to provide a big lead for the weak number-two runner, Brian McNamee. Novitzky was supposed to lay a clear and powerful validation of the collection and examination of the 40 government exhibits, such as syringes, cotton balls and gauze materials McNamee claimed to have saved from injecting Clemens. But on cross-examination, Novitzky admitted that he had no first-hand knowledge of the chain of custody of the beer can and other pieces of evidence received by federal investigators from McNamee.[13] It was pretty much downhill from there for Novitzky as a government witness because he did not connect with the jury.

ESPN's Lester Munson and TJ Quinn analyzed Novitzky's problems with the men and women sitting in judgment:

> "The questions that the jurors in the Roger Clemens perjury trial asked after the testimony of lead investigating agent Jeff Novitzky on Monday must have been a disappointment, even a shock, to the federal prosecutors trying to convince the jurors that Clemens lied to the U.S. Congress about his use of performance enhancing drugs."[14]
>
> "In the questions that Walton viewed as impermissible, jurors expressed significant skepticism about two basic elements of the government's case. In the first such question, a juror wanted to ask Novitzky whether he overstepped his authority with threats of jail if McNamee did not answer certain questions from Mitchell."[15]
>
> "The question was a direct challenge to Novitzky, a creative and forceful investigator who is a remarkably articulate and persuasive presence in a court room. Such a question would be the last thing prosecutors wanted to hear from a juror."[16]
>
> "The question not only showed some disbelief in a witness who should be a bulwark of the prosecutor's case, but also showed the juror's doubt about the procedures that Mitchell followed in his investigation of steroids in Major League Baseball. With a federal agent like Novitzky present in the room as Mitchell questioned McNamee and Novitzky ready to threaten McNamee if he gave improper answers to Mitchell questions, it raises the possibility that McNamee was telling them what they wanted to hear and not the truth."[17]

In fact, as early as the Belk Deposition, McNamee had given hints that indeed he had told the government what they had wanted to hear. When asked about Clemens' purported original containers of steroids that he pulled out in the Toronto Blue Jays clubhouse, about which McNamee had never really given a straight answer, he said,

> I think he got it at Canseco's house. I didn't know that until the government led me to believe that's where he got it from, that somebody—someone else that the government talked to was—I guess those were the facts that they were checking on me.[18]
>
> And somehow, whoever else the government is talking to, said that he got them there in Florida, and some guy walked into a room with him and Canseco and that's how they got the drugs; the Winstrol.[19]

In their continued analysis, Munson and Quinn noted that

> A second juror question is even more disconcerting for the prosecution team. A juror wanted to ask Novitzky about the integrity of the physical evidence (syringes, gauze pads, cotton balls, vials and ampules) that McNamee claims he kept after injecting Clemens with steroids and HGH. The trove of evidence if it is what McNamee claims it is, would corroborate McNamee's story and is critical to the government's case.[20]
>
> "Could this be planted evidence?" the juror asked. "Did anyone find it suspicious that this evidence surfaced this way, and in the way it was housed, in a beer can?"[21]
>
> The question represents the exact type of thinking the Clemens legal team was hoping to hear from a juror.[22]

Prosecutors called Brian Cashman to the stand to say that Clemens pushed him to hire Brian McNamee after a poor playoff outing in 1999. The Yankees' General Manager confirmed that much. He said Clemens asked him for the man "who could push his buttons." Cashman said Clemens talked about how he "clicked" with McNamee, how McNamee "knew his body."[23] However, despite Clemens' recommendation of McNamee, Cashman testified that he would not have hired McNamee, leaving the implication that it was owner George Steinbrenner who made the decision to hire McNamee, not Cashman.[24] Cashman, however, did make the decision to fire McNamee in 2001, after the strength and conditioning coach became entangled in the pool investigation in Florida. Cashman, however, as we saw previously, suggested he terminated McNamee's employment with the team because "this particular individual, Mr. McNamee, did not get along with people.... I was certainly having to react and deal with the toes he was stepping on."[25] Although McNamee claimed in his own testimony that he "would only cautiously suggest ideas" to players about aspects that did not pertain to his work as a strength and conditioning coach,[26] Cashman made clear that that was not the case, and cited pitching coach Mel Stottlemyre as a prime example of someone who was angry at McNamee for making suggestions to his pitchers about "adjusting their pitching mechanics."[27] Cashman also testified that he learned that McNamee, who was not a licensed chiropractor, made chiropractic adjustments to other players and not just Clemens.[28] Brian McNamee's explanation of why he got fired by Cashman was understandably different from the man who fired him. McNamee claimed he no longer worked with Yankees after the 2001 season because "I didn't want to be with the Yankees. I had already done it. I just wanted to be Roger Clemens' personal trainer." When asked if Clemens tried to bring McNamee back to the Yankees after he was fired in 2001, Cashman answered, "No."[29] Rusty Hardin felt Cashman's testimony was the turning point of the trial.[30]

Worse, Cashman destroyed the government façade that baseball players were not given injections of B-12—akin to claiming peanut butter and jelly was not a lunch food. Cashman testified that he had in fact discovered that trainers gave B-12 shots at the instruction of doctors.[31] As we saw earlier, this was confirmed by Andy Pettitte. Cashman said he learned that if trainers gave shots, that information did not go into trainer reports.[32] The government, one would hazard a guess, was betting that team doctors, concerned with losing their licenses, would not admit to clubhouse injections without prescriptions. But a reasonable guess, based on the trial testimony, suggests that it did indeed happen, yet another gamble in the prosecution of Roger Clemens that failed.

Cynthia Morris-Kukowski, a toxicologist brought into the trial by the government to rebut claims that McNamee faked and contaminated the evidence, claimed that such evidence can be co-mingled, *but not contaminated*.[33] However, Morris-Kukowski conceded the larger point, on cross-examination, that drugs on the needles and cotton balls could be "co-mingled or contaminated."[34]

Perhaps because the defense bashed Brian McNamee's testimony so thoroughly and perhaps because the jury was skeptical even of the government's chief investigator, Jeff Novitzky, the federal prosecutors decided to work out an immunity deal with Eileen McNamee,[35] the estranged wife of the chief accuser, in exchange for her expected testimony that she would vouch for her husband's story. Rusty Hardin, who suspected McNamee had ascribed all kind of things to her out of thin air when she was originally barred from testifying, was delighted to go along. As usual, Hardin's suspicions were proven correct.

For starters, Eileen McNamee, a first grade teacher, contradicted her husband's story that working for Clemens eight days a year away from the family in Houston strained their marriage. In fact, she testified under oath that their marriage began to deteriorate after her husband was investigated in the often alluded-to, alleged rape incident in Florida in 2001, and "not because of her husband's relationship with Clemens."[36]

She testified that she was unaware of her husband's FedEx box in her house until she stumbled onto it in her husband's bedroom, sitting in his closet, in 2003 or 2004.[37] She said that when she looked inside the box there was a "gallon-sized," Ziploc bag that contained unused needles, brown vials and "some paper." She said she saw a Bud Lite can, not the Miller Lite can that the prosecution presented with materials in it at trial. She said when she shook the Bud Lite can, it produced the "familiar sound" of syringes clinking against its metal sides. She testified that that she knew the sound because the family often threw their diabetic needles out in beer cans to protect others from being hurt. She testified that Brian did not tell her that he injected players with performance enhancing drugs until "right before the Mitchell Report came out," contradicting his story that he had told her years earlier.[38]

She did admit she was furious with both her husband and Clemens when the pitcher played a tape of their telephone conversation wherein her husband told the incredible lie that his son Brian, Jr., was dying, and confirmed that she told him to go after Clemens. Dressed in a blue-and-white patterned sleeveless dress, pulling at a navy blue sweater, her auburn hair cascading over her shoulders, she spoke softly, leaning into the microphone,[39] and she testified that she was alarmed by findings in a blood test her son had and wanted to inform her husband, although they were not fatal. She testified, "I asked him to call me about our son's condition, and he did not call, he called Roger."[40] Still emotionally distraught about the incident, she broke down on the witness stand, and Judge Walton gave her a break to regain her composure. Afterwards, she continued. "Brian knew nothing about the situation, but he told Roger in the recorded conversation that our son was dying. He was not dying but heard that he was dying when he listened to the press conference and the recorded conversation."[41]

15. The Government's Double-Edged Swords

The prosecution's star, Assistant U.S. Attorney Courtney Saleski, asked her,

> "Was it horrible?"
> "Yes, it was."
> "Were you mad, mad at Brian and Mr. Clemens?"
> "Yes. I never thought my child would be in the middle of this."
> "Did you tell Brian that you wanted him to go after Mr. Clemens?"
> "Yes, I did. I didn't want Roger to get away with this."[42]

When Eileen McNamee testified that her husband did not mention Clemens or any other players in connection with the saved materials, Saleski asked her about a 2009 FBI interview wherein she had said her husband told her the contents of the box were "from players."[43]

She replied, "I don't recall. I was very nervous. I had two FBI agents approach me after school." She said she only remembered "bits and pieces" of that interview because she was "shaken up."[44] Ironically, at the time the FBI "staked out" Eileen McNamee at her elementary school, the press hounded Clemens every morning as he drove his youngest son to school.

As it turned out, however, it had not been Roger Clemens' idea to play the taped telephone conversation that included Brian McNamee's breathless claim that his son was dying.

On re-direct, Rusty Hardin asked her,

> "Do you know whose decision it was?"
> "Yes, I was told—by you. You told me that it was your decision to play the tape, and you apologized to me."
> "And yet, you are testifying."
> "Yes, because I didn't have a choice."
> "Are you capable of testifying truthfully no matter how upset you are?"
> "Yes."
> "Have you testified truthfully even though you are helping a man you are upset with?"
> "Yes, I have."[45]

Lester Munson, in perhaps his most insightful commentary of the entire trial, discussed Eileen McNamee's persuasive and compelling testimony.

> On three occasions during his cross-examination of star prosecution witness Brian McNamee last month, defense attorney Rusty Hardin scoffed, "You just made that up, didn't you?"[46]
>
> On Wednesday afternoon, Hardin moved his courtroom flourish a significant step toward evidentiary reality when he offered Eileen McNamee, Brian's estranged wife, as a witness. Listening to this demure, 42-year old first-grade teacher and mother of three testify, it was difficult to avoid the conclusion that Hardin was right—Brian did make things up.[47]
>
> It's possible that federal prosecutor Courtney Saleski will be able to shake Eileen's testimony on cross-examination on Thursday, but it is not likely. It had the unmistakable ring of truth.[48]
>
> Lo and behold, there was Eileen in court on Wednesday denying and contradicting every step of Brian's story of collection and preservation of the evidence.[49]

She never complained about Brian's work with Clemens, she told the jury. She was happy with the situation because Brian was "being paid" and she was "at home with my children."[50]

Brian never showed her the materials he collected, she said, adding that she discovered them when water was leaking into the basement closet during a hurricane and she noticed the FedEx box on a shelf and discovered needles and vials.[51]

A few days later, she asked Brian about the box. "He told me it was none of my concern and refused to discuss it," she said.[52]

Brian has insisted that he preserved some of the materials by shoving them into a crumpled Miller lite can. Eileen, however, testified that she found a Bud Light can that was not crumpled, shook it, and heard the unmistakable sounds of needles rattling.[53]

Hardin asked her how she could be sure it was the sound of needles, and Eileen responded that she and Brian placed used needles in cans after they had injected their diabetic son with insulin.[54]

Is the crumpled Miller Lite can a piece of fabricated evidence that Brian added to the trove after Eileen discovered it? Are there two cans of needles? Either way, Brian's story does not work.[55]

If the jury concludes that Eileen is as truthful as she appears to be, the Clemens legal team has moved beyond the realm of reasonable doubt and has raised the serious possibility that the government has presented false testimony in an effort to win a perjury case.[56]

The trial may not conclude for another week or two. But when the jury begins its deliberations, it may well be that the trial actually concluded with the testimony of Eileen McNamee. Listening to her, you start to think that Brian McNamee "just made that up."[57]

16

When the Evidence Told Roger Clemens' Side of the Story

For 52 months, the Executive Branch of the United States government, Congress, former Senator George Mitchell, Brian McNamee, Major League Baseball Incorporated, angry baseball fans on the internet, and the aggregate voice of the American sports writing establishment had entered every nook and cranny of the public psyche in a relentless drumbeat of declarations claiming that Roger Clemens had cheated in the business of baseball and enhanced the second half of his 24-year career by using anabolic steroids, human growth hormone, and testosterone. Finally, in June 2012, Clemens presented his side of the story.

Clemens' defense team, led by Texan Rusty Hardin, introduced 22 witnesses who thoroughly destroyed the government's politically inspired prosecution.

Dr. Bruce Goldberger, a forensic toxicologist at the University of Florida, testified that it was impossible to rule out cross-contamination of the medical waste kept in a beer can, that in his professional opinion he would not rely on the medical waste to determine a source, and that "I have never seen such evidence like this being used by the prosecution." He said the prosecution's evidence "was unusual" because the medical waste could have been contaminated from the liquid in the beer can that would have transferred molecules among the items, or the releases of drugs from the needles in the can.[1] "If there's liquid in the syringes as it's placed in the beer can, there's a release of the drug onto the evidence in the beer can. Almost as if it's misted," Goldberger testified.

Goldberger said there was no conclusive test to determine whether or not cross-contamination resulted from the mechanical processes within the can, but stated that the prosecution could not conclusively determine that it did not happen. Goldberger explained that in forensics "you need absolute certainty." He added, "You learn in Forensics 101 that there are no maybes. You have to be certain that your findings are correct. If not, you send not guilty people to jail."[2]

"I think the government's conclusions are overreaching in regard to the interpretation of this evidence," Goldberger said.[3] "If you submit garbage to the laboratory, more often than not you're going to have garbage at the end," he said.[4]

Lester Munson observed,

> Speaking calmly and persuasively in what was the most powerful testimony in the entire trial, Goldberger told the jury that "the possibility of contamination leads to unreliable laboratory conclusions and there must be a certainty, beyond a reasonable doubt, before we can make the scientific connection between the material and an individual."[5]
>
> In the course of Goldberger's testimony, the language of the trial was transformed with words like "manipulation," "fabrication," "garbage," suddenly being used in connection with materials the prosecutors had described as "medical waste."
>
> Goldberger told the jury that the material was doubly suspicious because it had been "collected and preserved by the accuser." Hardin was soon referring to McNamee as the "accuser-collector."[6]

In conclusion, Goldberger testified that the physical evidence was the "worst" he had "seen in thirty years of working with trial evidence."[7]

Marc Taylor, a DNA specialist at Technical Associates Incorporated, testified that DNA from Roger Clemens found on a syringe needle could have been placed there intentionally. Taylor testified that he could not rule out the possibility that Brian McNamee's DNA had been on the needle. He disagreed with the claim by government witness Alan Keel, who insisted that the biological material on the syringe was too small to "fake."[8] Taylor testified that Roger Clemens' DNA could have appeared on the cotton balls for any number of reasons, including dabbing a cut Clemens suffered, dabbing a blister he developed, or dabbing a drop of blood on a floor. Furthermore, Taylor insisted that no scientific testing could determine *when* Clemens' DNA got on the cotton balls, *how* it got there, or *whether* "his DNA could have been placed on the medical waste at separate times." Taylor testified that it was impossible to link Clemens' DNA on the cotton balls with any other substance—including steroids.[9]

Dr. Larry Likover, a Houston orthopedic surgeon and Clemens' running partner, testified that he prescribed B-12 and Vioxx for his friend, injecting B-12 in his arm. "B-12 makes you feel good. I'm in favor of it. Anything that makes elite athletes feel better that's legal, I'm in favor," he said.[10]

Prosecutor Steven Durham asked Likover if Clemens ever asked him for illegal drugs. The doctor replied, "Mr. Clemens had plenty of opportunity to ask me for illegal drugs in private and he never did."[11]

A juror asked Dr. Likover whether he could legally prescribe steroids and HGH. "Yes," he replied, "but I never have."[12]

Massage therapist Cheryl Redfern, who worked on Clemens' body for eight years, including the two years he pitched for the Toronto Blue Jays, testified that she had never seen acne on his body, a sign of anabolic steroids use in some recipients. When asked during direct examination by Hardin whether she saw changes in his upper body, including his skull, she replied, "No."[13]

Another massage therapist, Rohan Baichu, who gave Clemens deep tissue massages four or five times a week over seven years from 1999 to 2006, when he pitched for the Yankees and Astros, also testified that he never saw significant changes in Clemens' body size (an idea that Clemens' college coach, Cliff Gustafson, dismissed out of hand so vigorously)[14] and said that Clemens' excellent body at "an advanced age resulted from a superb work ethic."[15] Baichu served Clemens in a strength and conditioning capacity as well, although his workouts, including pool work, cardio and strength training, differed from McNamee's "military style" workouts. Baichu testified that when he trained Clemens in Houston there was more emphasis on running because Clemens had to bat in the National League.[16] One such workout involved running from first to third base. Baichu also said of Clemens, "He was a great teammate to everyone. The lowest man on the totem pole. The guy that cleaned shoes in the locker room."[17]

Jerry Laveroni, Director of Team Security when Clemens pitched for the Yankees, testified that he was familiar with Brian McNamee. Laveroni said he "was not impressed with [McNamee's] reliability." Laveroni continued, "I don't believe he should be believed under oath. His credibility is zero." Laveroni said the Yankees training room was open and unregulated and that players could easily possess and use drugs in that environment.[18] After a brief cross-examination of Laveroni by the government, Clemens' attorney, Michael Attanasio, read a stipulation of fact[19] to the jury stating that Clemens had been tested frequently for performance enhancing drugs, other than human growth hormone, for which there was no test during his career, and that he passed all the tests.[20]

Charlie O'Brien, one of Clemens' catchers on the Toronto Blue Jays in 1997, helped to dispel the government's illusion that baseball players were afraid to discuss the widespread use of B-12 in clubhouses and to criticize team doctors and trainers. O'Brien verified Clemens' contention that in Toronto, vitamin B-12 shots were lined up and "ready to go."[21] O'Brien testified that Clemens owed his pitching longevity to his split-finger fastball. He told the story of arriving at 7 a.m. one morning in spring training only to discover that Clemens was already there, working on his fielding.[22] O'Brien testified that a scuffed baseball moved six to 12 inches after delivery, while a normal baseball moved only four to six inches, an obvious advantage to the pitcher, an advantage Clemens refused outright to even consider.

The following exchanges between O'Brien, another Blue Jays catcher who worked with Clemens, Darrin Fletcher, and Rusty Hardin during direct examination, and Assistant U.S. Attorneys Steven Durham and Gil Guerrero, performing cross-examination, produced some of the most informative answers in the entire trial:

> DURHAM: Clemens would do anything to win?
> O'BRIEN: He wouldn't use a scuffed ball to win.[23]

O'Brien confessed that he regularly and illegally scuffed balls by using a metal clip on his shin guard, but testified that Clemens refused to cheat by using scuffed balls.[24]

> HARDIN: Why do you think Clemens didn't want scuffed balls?
> O'BRIEN: I don't think he would cheat. At all. Ever.
> DURHAM: Is B-12 red?
> O'BRIEN: I'm not sure. I was turned around usually and bent over.
> DURHAM: Major League teams have the best medical staff available?
> O'BRIEN: No, very poor.
> DURHAM: I don't want to express any personal opinions, because it's not appropriate, but ...
> O'BRIEN: I don't think Tommy did a very good job of it. Craig was a nice guy, but one of the worst trainers I've been around.
> DURHAM: Forgive me, this topic I find interesting.... Did you complain to anybody about poor medical services?
> O'BRIEN: No.
> DURHAM: How is it that an experienced Major League player like you allowed a poor medical staff to keep giving you shots?
> O'BRIEN: I needed treatment.
> DURHAM: But you kept going back to the same quack medical staff?
> O'BRIEN: Yes.
> DURHAM: You know Clemens took Vioxx like skittles?
> O'BRIEN: I took naproxen like skittles. Wait, not skittles, M&Ms. I don't like skittles.
> DURHAM: Clemens took ephedra.... You got shots?
> O'BRIEN: Yeah, steroid injections, corticosteroids, not anabolic.
> DURHAM: Before you came to court, did you speak to anybody about seeing needles lined up?
> O'BRIEN: Nobody.
> DURHAM: None of the lawyers?
> O'BRIEN: No, sir.
> HARDIN: Would you say anything not true to help Roger Clemens?
> O'BRIEN: No, sir.
> HARDIN: Do you understand the significance of B-12 questions?
> O'BRIEN: No, sir.

O'Brien stepped down from the witness stand and was replaced by Darrin Fletcher, who caught Clemens in 1998, the year Clemens met Brian McNamee.

> HARDIN: Would Clemens cut corners?
> FLETCHER: No. He was a hard worker. He earned it honest.

16. When the Evidence Told Roger Clemens' Side of the Story 199

HARDIN: Did you notice a velocity increase on Clemens' pitches during the '98 season?
FLETCHER: No.

Fletcher testified that he attended the infamous Miami pool party at Jose Canseco's house and said that while McNamee was at the party at the same time as he was, Roger Clemens was not, suggesting once again that Clemens and McNamee were not there at the same time.[25] Fletcher did, confirm, however, that he and others "checked out" Canseco's house, providing the first testimony that guests at the party actually went into the house. Fletcher said, "To be honest with you, I don't particularly remember Roger being there."[26]

HARDIN: Do you recall discussing B-12 with Brian McNamee?
FLETCHER: Yes. We discussed it while I was injured. McNamee said where he could get it. I was uncomfortable about where.
HARDIN: Did you have a conversation with McNamee about B-12?
FLETCHER: Yes. Either in '98 or '99 in the weight room. I was on the disabled list.
HARDIN: What was said?
FLETCHER: It would come up now and again. I was hurt, wanting to come back. I was uncomfortable with the idea of a shot from a strength coach. It should come from a trainer or doctor. McNamee was passionate, but I felt that he at times could be reckless.[27]

Assistant U.S. Attorney Gilberto Guerrero asked Fletcher, "Are you sure about B-12 conversations with Brian McNamee?"

FLETCHER: "I'm sketchy on the details but I remember the topic coming up."

The defense called Phil Garner to the witness stand. Garner, a popular infielder for the World Champion Pittsburgh Pirates in 1979, nicknamed "Scrap-Iron" for his gritty, tenacious style of play, managed the weak-hitting Houston Astros into the 2005 World Series. As Garner said at trial of an Astros team that finished 13th out of 16 national league teams in batting: "You don't get to the World Series without Roger Clemens."[28]

Garner gave compelling testimony about the players' use of painkillers and, to some extent, use of anabolic steroids. He also explained why Roger Clemens pitched so well into his 40s. He said Clemens showed some physical decline with age, such as a wider gut. Garner said he personally observed players, he did not say how many, who said they used steroids and that it helped them run faster and hit harder to the opposite field.[29] He said, "I tried to talk two players in Detroit out of doing them in '00 and '01." Garner further testified that all his teams used B-12 shots. "It gives an energy boost," he said. Garner testified that the first player who told him about his use of performance enhancing drugs occurred in 1987. When Steven Durham asked him about the general use of steroids in Major League Baseball, Garner, with no attribution, suggested it was "less than fifty percent." When Durham stated that the 2005 congressional hearings suggested a need to protect kids from the influence of Major Leaguers who used steroids, Garner disagreed. He implied it was a "bottom-up" problem, because he said performance enhancing drugs came into baseball from younger players, who "influenced older players" regarding the benefits of PEDs.[30] Garner said both he and his wife took B-12 and that he still injected her with it.

The following are some of the important questions raised by the contesting attorneys with Garner.

>   HARDIN: Ever see Clemens cut corners?
>   GARNER: Never did.
>   HARDIN: Ever see him cheat?
>   GARNER: Never did.
>   HARDIN: Were you surprised Roger Clemens was in the Mitchell Report?
>   GARNER: Yes. I had seen no evidence he had used performance enhancing drugs.
>   DURHAM: Did Clemens get pain injections?
>   GARNER: Yes.
>   DURHAM: From team physicians?
>   GARNER: Yes.
>   DURHAM: Were Clemens and Pettitte close friends on the Astros?
>   GARNER: I don't think they spent a lot of time together socially. They had different lifestyles.
>   DURHAM: Did you get B-12 injections from an athletic trainer or doctor in the training room? Not weight room, right?
>   GARNER: Right.
>   DURHAM: Do you remember the color of B-12?
>   GARNER: Nope.
>   DURHAM: Did you take Vioxx?
>   GARNER: Yes.
>   DURHAM: Why do ballplayers need an anti-inflammatory?
>   GARNER: They need help with joint pain.

Yet much of Garner's testimony was dedicated to explaining how Roger Clemens pitched. Lester Munson's analysis noted the major baseball points of Garner's testimony.[31]

> Many of Garner's stories and details were enlightening even to a serious baseball fan. He used a vast knowledge of scouting reports to describe to the jury the pattern of Clemens' pitch selection. Relying on a study of 3,100 Clemens pitches, Garner said 77 percent of Clemens' first pitches were fastballs and suggested that no hitter should have ever swung on a Clemens pitch when the count was 1 and 1. The sliders that Clemens threw on 1 and 1 were "unhittable," with opposing hitters averaging only .100.[32]
>
> He attributed Clemens' success early in his career to "overpowering the hitters" and his success late in his career to "outsmarting the hitter." Throughout his career, Garner said, Clemens' fastball had "great movement" and a "good finish." A good finish, Garner explained to the jurors, meant that a Clemens fastball appeared to be moving faster as it crossed the plate than it was when it left Clemens' hand.
>
> Even though it may have been 94mph on the radar gun, it appeared to be going 100mph to the hitter.[33]

Mike Boddicker, who won 134 games and struck out 1,330 batters in 14 big league seasons, testified that he saw Clemens in the Boston Red Sox training room with his pants down and being injected in the buttocks with B-12, apparently by a team trainer. When asked how he knew it was B-12, he said he could see the label "B-12" on the vial on the training table.[34] Boddicker further testified that B-12 injections were common during his career in Major League Baseball.[35] Massive doses of B-12, such as 1,000 micrograms a day, are not uncommon among athletes, according to a decades long study by a hematologist from New York University. Because athletes often follow a low fat diet, free of cholesterol, they may not eat meat or fish or milk or cheese or eggs, the only reliable natural dietary sources of B-12. Indeed at a time in which doctors are telling all of us to keep our cholesterol low, it is not surprising that one study suggested that insufficient absorption of B-12 from foods may be common in adults as young as 26, which would put the problem right into the prime years of baseball players.[36]

On cross-examination, federal prosecutor Steven Durham asked Boddicker about secrets players kept among themselves in the clubhouse. This allowed, or "opened the door," as we say in the law, for Rusty Hardin to ask this "softball" question: "Did Clemens do anything that was kept secret from the public?"

"Yes," Boddicker answered, "Clemens would often leave the ballpark in uniform and see kids in the hospital."[37]

Because Brian McNamee claimed that the saved materials presented at trial, including the Miller Lite can, were collected from Roger Clemens' Upper East Side apartment in New York City, the defense called Clemens' cleaning lady, Fanny Gabilanez, to answer questions about seeing any such materials in the apartment.

> RUSTY HARDIN: "Ever see little bottles or vials anywhere, including fridge?"
> GABILANEZ: "No."
> HARDIN: "Ever see beer there?"[38]
> GABILANEZ: "No."

Showing Gabilanez photographs of the ampules, bottles, and needles, Hardin queried, "Ever see anything like that?"

Gabilanez answered, "No."

Hardin showed Gabilanez containers that McNamee stored the steroids in. "I never saw one," she said.

Brian McNamee had testified that Clemens asked him to inject his wife Debbie with HGH to prepare for a *Sports Illustrated* photo shoot and that Clemens had watched McNamee inject her, with the incident taking place in the Clemens' master bedroom.[39]

The Clemens defense team put Debbie Clemens on the witness stand to set the record straight. She testified that her use of HGH was inspired by a front page feature in *USA Today* that appeared on November 11, 2000. She said that her husband was away when she asked McNamee to give her the injection. She testified that she pulled up her skirt in the master bathroom, where Brian McNamee pinched her skin in order to inject her in the belly. She said she did not tell her husband what had transpired.[40]

"I didn't think that was a bad thing," she testified. "It's not like taking heroin. I am not ashamed of taking that shot. I am embarrassed that it went across the world incorrectly."[41]

She also testified that "We did not attend a party at Jose Canseco's house" even though she and her family stayed at the house that week and they played golf that day.[42] Debbie Clemens said that she, her husband, her brother, Craig Godfrey, and a fourth golfer spent six hours at the Westin Country Club, buying $265 worth of apparel at the pro shop, driving balls at the driving range, playing a round of golf, and having lunch. They did not return to Canseco's house until approximately 2:30 p.m., after the party was over.[43] When she finished her testimony, she stepped down from the witness stand, sat down briefly in the courtroom for the first time during the trial, was motioned by her husband to come talk to him, walked over to him, where they held hands briefly, dabbed at her eyes with a tissue, did a fist pump with a member of the defense team, and afterwards was hugged by Rusty Hardin.[44]

Florida Marlins broadcaster Joe Angel testified seeing the Clemens party at the golf course on the day of the Canseco party.[45]

The defense called former Boston Red Sox Assistant General Manager Steve August to discuss the issue of whether Roger Clemens was "washed up" and in the "twilight of his career" in 1996, and therefore might have turned to anabolic steroids and human growth hormone to enhance his sagging baseball performance. August had been assigned the task of evaluating whether the Red Sox should re-sign Clemens when the star pitcher became a free agent at the end of the 1996 season.[46]

Rusty Hardin asked August if Clemens was "fat or anything" and "sloppy or out of shape" at the end of the 1996 season.

August replied, "No. He was in top physical condition for a thirty-four year old."[47]

A juror wanted to know what August's recommendation to his Red Sox bosses was as far as re-signing Clemens after the 1996 season.

August replied, "To re-sign him. He was at the top of the game."[48]

With the acquittal of Roger Clemens and therefore the vaporization of the political prosecution against him a foregone conclusion, the opposing sides underwent the formality of making closing arguments, as required by courtroom procedure. Government prosecutors faced an impossible task as they prepared to address the jury. Their primary witness, Brian McNamee, had contradicted his own story on the witness stand; his own wife had contradicted his testimony; and star witness Andy Pettitte had admitted that there was a 50–50 chance that he had not heard Roger Clemens confess to taking human growth hormone after all. Defense expert witnesses had raised serious doubts about the legitimacy of Roger Clemens' DNA in a hopelessly mixed stew of saved materials with the waste of other players and that of McNamee as well, who had essentially bled all over the evidence. In addition, there was something too *pro forma*, too conventional, about the way the Government summarized its case. There were the cute phrases, such as Clemens told lies "so as not to tarnish his name," and Clemens was out to "deny, discredit, and distance himself from accusations,"[49] but they seemed somehow artificial and contrived. For example, Gil Guerrero intoned, "Now it's your turn to hold him accountable on every single count. You are the final umpires here."[50] A nice phrase to be sure, but it was said to a jury who had no interest in or knowledge of baseball whatsoever.

For his part, Rusty Hardin and his team had merely to provide a recap of the proceedings and address the jurors' sense of fairness. In summary, the case by the government was based on an unbelievable story undermined by unreliable evidence. The jury later confirmed that in their brief, ten-hour deliberation and acquittal. One juror revealed that no one had to be persuaded to vote for acquittal because every single juror was unanimous in their belief that Clemens was *not guilty* from the "beginning."[51] Another juror said the testimony of Andy Pettitte "was quite important to all of us, because he recanted."[52] One stated the obvious, "McNamee wasn't credible for the jury because of a lack of truthfulness."[53] Another juror said, "The witnesses for the prosecution were, uh, how does one put it? ... kind of wanting, if you will .... It was quite lacking. If that's what they were going to go with, then they should probably not have pursued the case in the first place if that's all they had."[54]

Perhaps most telling from such an experienced trial lawyer as Rusty Hardin, he seemed confident and relaxed on the eve of his closing argument. Federal Prosecutor Gil Guerrero gamely tried to mitigate the myriad of fabrications and contradictions in Brian McNamee's testimony by calling him a "flawed man."[55] When a prosecutor essentially has to divorce himself from his own major witness, it is never a good thing for the government, as this case, and the prosecution's disowning of star investigator Mark Fuhrman in the prosecution of O. J. Simpson, demonstrated.[56]

In what it clearly thought was a cute turnabout of phrase, the government used Debbie Clemens' statement that she wanted to "protect the Clemens brand," meaning the fame and name of her husband in their investments, to argue that he denied use of steroids before the House Committee to "protect his livelihood."[57] The problem with this contention was that by the 2012 trial, Clemens had been retired from baseball for five years, therefore his ability either to make money by taking steroids or get endorsements from playing had ended. It was a lot to ask of a jury with no interest in baseball and no knowledge of Clemens, to see that far back in a prospective judgment. Furthermore, for a player of his accomplishments and fame, Clemens had never garnered that many endorsements anyway. He was simply too hot-tempered, too controversial for the corporate advertising world.

What were Guerrero and Courtney Saleski thinking in professing shock that Debbie Clemens, the wife of a multi-millionaire, would allow a man into her bathroom to inject her and, moreover, do so without her husband's permission? Eleanor Norton Holmes had raised the same '50s, puritanical point at the Waxman hearings in 2008. Guerrero contended that "it stretched credibility to believe that Debbie Clemens allowed McNamee into their master bathroom without her husband knowing about it."[58] No, it stretched credibility that Guerrero and Saleski believed that in the twenty-first century, rich women would not do anything they felt like doing to aid their efforts to look younger. Where did these prosecutors think Park Avenue wives received their massages? In the public view of a downstairs lobby of their penthouses?

Saleski insisted, "No one saw Clemens getting B-12 or Lidocaine shots, that's remarkable."[59] What's remarkable was that Saleski thought she could get away with saying that to the jurors when former Red Sox pitcher Mike Boddicker had testified that he saw Clemens being injected with B-12 in the clubhouse in Boston, and he said it late in the trial when the jury would still have it on their minds. Other defense witnesses, also late in the trial, including Clemens' neighbor and doctor, Larry Likover, said that either they had injected Clemens with B-12, or that team records showed that Lidocaine had been injected into players, specifically the Yankees, making Clemens' contention of Lidocaine injections all that more believable.[60] Blue Jays catcher Charlie O'Brien confirmed Clemens' contention that B-12 shots were "lined up and ready to go" in the Toronto clubhouse. The jurors heard Dr. Likover testify that he legally could have written Clemens a prescription for either anabolic steroids or human growth hormone, but was never asked to by Clemens. If Clemens did not ask a friendly doctor for a prescription for anabolic steroids and human growth hormone, it stands to reason he did not ask McNamee to inject him either.

The first law of making both political and legal arguments is at least to

16. When the Evidence Told Roger Clemens' Side of the Story   205

plead the obvious. Yet when the prosecutors argued that "We submit that Andy Pettitte heard it correct—100 percent right from Day One,"[61] they were going against the obvious. In one of the most dramatic and memorable moments of the trial, Andy Pettitte, whose credibility had been deemed so obviously convincing that Judge Walton had practically paid him homage at the conclusion of the mistrial, had admitted that there was a 50–50 chance he had not heard Clemens admit to taking human growth hormone at all. In trying to turn a cute phrase and to throw the percentages back in the face of the defense, the government foolishly reminded the jurors that Andy Pettitte could not vouch for hearing the HGH confession 100 percent. And what you hear or did not hear is not "a reasonable doubt" proposition like the standard for proof. Either you heard something or you did not hear it. The scale is not 20 to 90 to 100. It is either 100 or nothing. The prosecutors therefore also violated another axiom of the court room: if the fact does not help your case, either explain it away or do not mention it at all. But never just keep it hanging out there as a reminder to the jury of one of your weakest moments of the trial.

Guerrero urged the jurors to use their common sense, look at the evidence and recognize that what they heard from Clemens was a "cover story" to hide his use of steroids and HGH. It was a case of reality versus fiction when it came to Clemens.[62] Now common sense may have a hallowed place in the American ethos, like George Washington's honesty, but in law it leads to the suspicion that the side invoking it has nothing more to offer, and thus is hiding behind a weak case.

Saleski clearly misunderstood her audience when she insisted on invoking Congress as the standard of truth by which to judge Clemens. "He did that at the expense of Congress. He threw sand in their eyes. He stole the truth from them."[63] Claiming that the government set the standard for truthfulness was like telling high school students they should admire an unpopular principal.

On the other hand, given an untenable case from the start, one that was impossible to win and therefore should never have been brought in the first place, the prosecutors must be excused some of these unorthodox and questionable arguments and approaches. They needed something dramatic, shocking, against the grain, a "Hail Mary pass," in football parlance, somehow to pull out a miracle. The truth was that Saleski and Guerrero and the other federal prosecutors had worked their guts off representing the government. Their legal careers were enhanced, not diminished, by their hard work.

Rusty Hardin buttressed his closing remarks with a chart entitled "Brian McNamee's testimony is admittedly not credible."[64] Boldly listed on the chart were more than two dozen incidents when McNamee had lied "outright" or had admitted to a "mistake" or "bad memory." Hardin declared, "Saying that

Brian McNamee lies zero times is kind of like calling the Grand Canyon a ditch."[65]

"When the government talks about lies and deceit, they have demonstrated in this case an absolute inexhaustible tolerance for McNamee's lies," Hardin declared, the wide dark circles under his eyes the evidence of a lot of long, late nights working on Clemens' behalf.

"The lies, the lies, the lies," intoned Hardin as he pounded the lectern.[66]

Hardin pounded the lectern again and shouted, "This is outrageous!"[67]

> "What happened in this case is a horrible, horrible overreach of the government and everyone involved. They haven't been in a search of the truth. They've been in search of a conviction."[68]
>
> "One of the great travesties of the trial is that Roger Clemens' reputation has been ruined."[69]
>
> "We should be rewarding Roger Clemens. Not prosecuting him. Please don't let them trick you."[70]

What will be more lasting than these final words to the jury by Hardin were his closing thoughts of this case involving the pantheon of American history and free speech, for in the greater sense this was not a trial about one man, but about one country and whether that country will long endure if free speech is chilled or curtailed.

"God help us," Hardin said, "if we've reached the point in this country when a citizen stands up after being accused publicly and says, 'I didn't do it,' it becomes a federal matter to grind him into the dust."[71]

17

A Theory of the Case

When Roger Clemens took the mound on the night of September 18, 1996, in Detroit's ancient Tiger Stadium, with its iconic tall columns and second decks which extended over the outfield, he was already in the habit of throwing sliders instead of high fastballs when he needed outs. Indeed his manager in Houston, Phil Garner, would testify 16 years later that when Clemens threw a slider in a 1–1 count, opposing hitters averaged a measly .100.[1] That night was evidence Clemens was already in the process of becoming the pitcher of the second half of his career, a pitcher who had lost something off his fastball, and threw sliders, and off speed pitches, but would still occasionally reach back and throw in the high 90s as he did with several Tigers batters.[2] He was pitching around good hitters to face easier ones. He was one year away from developing his split-finger fastball. In a sense, Clemens was returning to the gritty pitcher with control he had been before the miracle discovery of his fastball at San Jacinto Junior College. Despite a won-lost record of 10–13 (the Red Sox finished third in the AL East), Clemens had returned to form in 1996 after several years of chronic injuries. He was first in strikeouts in the American League with 257, first in strikeouts per nine innings, 9.5, and had a solid Earned Run Average of 3.63,[3] seventh among AL pitchers. He was fifth in innings pitched and had the third lowest home run rate. While the Boston offense was sixth in the league in homers, fourth in runs, and sixth in batting average, scoring 5.7 runs per game, it provided Clemens only 4.4 runs of support per game. In fact, 1996 was the third time in four years that the usually potent Red Sox bats gave him substandard run support.[4] Only 8,779 spectators were on hand that night to witness the fact that Roger Clemens was back as one of baseball's most dominant pitchers.[5] Bill Haselman was his catcher that night and hitting star, doubling twice and driving in two runs in a 3-for-4 night. Rookie shortstop Nomar Garciaparra, recently brought up from the minors, went hitless but walked twice and stole a base. Clemens struck out 15 batters in the first six innings, putting away hitters with sliders diving down into the dirt. Fifteen out of 20 batters faced fanned. This time around nobody told him that he had 19 strikeouts as he went out to pitch the bottom of the ninth. The Tigers' great shortstop, Alan Trammell, popped up. Ruben Sierra singled. Tony Clark flied out. Two outs and still 19 strikeouts for the night. Then Clemens struck out Travis Fryman to become the only man in baseball history to strike out 20 batters twice in a nine-inning game. Kerry Wood of the Cubs had struck out 20 since Clemens' first 20-strikeout game in 1986. Clemens scattered five hits and did not walk a single batter. The 4–0 win tied the Red Sox record for most career shutouts, 38, with Cy Young. It was also Clemens' win No. 192, tying the Red Sox record also held by Cy Young. Clemens' contract ran out at the end of the season, and the competition for his services was intense. Yankees owner George Steinbrenner even flew down to Texas to lift weights with Clemens in his efforts to woo him to Yankee Stadium.

The exile of Roger Clemens from the Athens of America was actually much more complicated than the question of whether General Manager Dan Duquette really believed Clemens was finished or whether he was too cheap to pay Clemens what he was worth. The team's own evaluation suggested Clemens "was at the top of his game" and should be re-signed. On his part, Clemens was comfortable in Boston, his wife Debbie was comfortable there with the exception of the media coverage, and Clemens said he would only pitch in the future for the Red Sox or teams in his home state of Texas.[6] Yet the divorce between Clemens and Duquette and the Red Sox' dysfunctional management had been brewing all season. Duquette had fired Clemens's buddy, Al Nipper, as pitching coach—the teammate who had told him a decade earlier he was on the cusp of pitching immortality with 18 strikeouts—when the Red Sox got off to a poor start. Clemens was also angry at Duquette for firing manager Kevin Kennedy and did not like Duquette's "robotic" style of running the team. It was not an issue of the whims of Roger Clemens, spoiled super star. The "turmoil" inside the Red Sox management was considered so bad around baseball that the team's efforts to sign highly respected managers White Herzog and Jim Leyland were rejected. As the hours in Clemens' contract ran out and free agency approached, Duquette, knowing that Clemens was seeking a four-year deal at $7 million a year, had offered $20 million for four years, or $5 million a year. The offer came with Duquette's public bombast that while he would like to re-sign Clemens, he would do so "only on the team's terms," a dig surely intended to inflame the already tense relationship between the two men. Worse, the offer came with an unheard-of poison pill for a superstar in a business where contracts were normally guaranteed—only $10 million of it was guaranteed.[7]

Understandably, Clemens was in a sour mood in the clubhouse on the last day of the season. "I don't know what the future holds," Clemens said. "It's more of a business situation now. It's kind of cold, but that is just another stage that has come through here now. I still feel the tradition. But now it's pretty much business, and you find out about it pretty quickly."[8] If all this was not enough to push Clemens out of Boston, Dan Duquette's foolish, probably offhand comment that Clemens was in the "twilight of his career" after such an exceptional season, surely was. A careful reader might have noticed that Duquette's offer, if providing a poison pill, would, ironically, extend past Clemens's 38th birthday.

Meanwhile in the Bronx, New York, the Yankees were certainly interested in the latest Babe Ruth to be shown the exit tunnel in Fenway Park. After Clemens filed for free agency, Duquette went through

Roger Clemens in his final year with the Red Sox, 1996 (courtesy National Baseball Hall of Fame Library, Cooperstown, New York).

the motions of an offer, probably to pacify Red Sox fans, of $5.1 million a year, but shortened the guaranteed years from four to three, with an option for the final year, an offer that clearly was not serious under the circumstances. Yankees owner George Steinbrenner knew you didn't become a dynasty by being cheap. And he loved the gutty, tough, determined, All-American straight arrow, Roger Clemens. Although the Yankees had just won their first World Series since 1978 (when they beat the Red Sox in a dramatic one-game playoff to win the AL East), their starting pitching staff had endured injuries and Jimmy Key had left to sign with the Baltimore Orioles in free agency.[9] The Yankees did have their own budgetary concerns and had decided not to re-sign closer John Wetteland, who wanted $6 million a year, but manager Joe Torre believed young set-up man Mariano Rivera "has the ability to close." Clemens was the Yankees' primary target, and they held off signing an alternative, David Wells, whose agent, Gregg Clifton, said he could sense a shift towards Clemens and away from Wells in their interest. The Yankees, however, were not the only team anxious to acquire Clemens. The Cleveland Indians, Toronto Blue Jays, and Chicago White Sox all were in the hunt by the first week of December 1996. Although Torre professed neutrality on whether the Yankees should sign Wells or Clemens, he said of "The Rocket," "He takes the ball and it's his game. He's not looking for someone to bail him out in the fifth inning."[10]

On the afternoon of December 11, the Yankees remained confident that they would sign Clemens soon. However, they were a little disappointed that they could not show him off the following day, December 12, when they introduced new signees Mike Stanton, an invaluable left-handed set-up man, and veteran catcher Joe Girardi, whose clutch hitting would supply pleasant surprises in the following seasons. Two days later, Clemens did not sign with the Yankees after all. In what his agent, Randy Hendricks, described as "exceptionally close decision,"[11] Clemens signed with the Toronto Blue Jays for $24.75 million over 3 years. It was the highest contract ever given a Major League pitcher, topping John Smoltz's $31 million, four-year deal with the Atlanta Braves in November. It was the same number of years guaranteed by the Red Sox but was for a lot more money a year, $8.25 as opposed to $5.1 million. While Clemens was the Yankees' loss that December, David Wells was their gain, as he signed as their second choice but produced extraordinary results. In four Yankees seasons, the popular pitcher with the beer gut won 68 games and lost only 28, for a gaudy winning percentage of .708, had an ERA of 3.90, walked only 139 batters in 851⅔ innings, and pitched a perfect game. These Yankees statistics were a good deal better than his career numbers, such as his career ERA of 4.13.[12] While baseball free agents were frequently overpaid, depending on the market in a particular year, no one thought Clemens got overpaid that winter. The fierce and intense competition to sign Roger Clemens as a free agent in December 1996 showed that nobody in baseball seriously thought he was at the end of his career. How then did Brian McNamee convince everybody of the opposite conclusion, that Clemens was washed up in 1996 and needed his injections of anabolic steroids and human growth hormone to reinvigorate his baseball career?

My theory of the prosecution of Roger Clemens is that Brian McNamee made up the story of injecting anabolic steroids and HGH into Roger Clemens to save his own neck, for as former White House press secretary Scott McClellan once observed, "Self-deceit is a human quality, and we all engage in it at times."[13] We certainly engage in it when our own survival and life's goals are at stake. President Kennedy lied about having Addison's Disease to win the Democratic Presidential nomination in 1960, a fact dug up by his opponent, Senator Lyndon Johnson of Texas. Lyndon Johnson lied about his business relationship with Bobby Baker, whose financial deals were under investigation at the time of President Kennedy's assassination. Had Kennedy lived, the investigation into Johnson's dealings with Baker may well have ended up with a criminal indictment.[14] For Bill Clinton, it was the initial denial that he had enjoyed the erotic delights of the extraordinarily beautiful Gennifer Flowers that allowed him to remain politically viable through the 1992 New Hampshire primary. Perhaps most importantly, for our purposes of the free speech right of Roger Clemens, Chief Justice William H. Rehnquist denied during his 1971 Supreme Court hearings that while a clerk to the dying Justice Robert Jackson, he had written a memo to his boss arguing against *Brown v. Board of Education*.[15] Once on the Court, Rehnquist spent his career dismantling the impact of the historic decision for racial equality. Rehnquist also beat back free speech claims before his Court as if he possessed the powerful backhand of tennis star Bjorn Borg.[16] We will probably never know the complete story of the McNamee-Clemens mystery or McNamee's motives. Yet it is my belief and contention, employing logical analysis and literary analysis, that given the opportunity to accuse Roger Clemens of taking performance enhancing drugs in exchange for his freedom, he did what many people would do in the same circumstances: he told the Feds what they wanted to hear.

The seeds for my theory are contained in the Belk Deposition. The government practically gave McNamee a license to claim that Clemens obtained steroids from Jose Canseco at his home in Miami and to claim he injected Clemens during a Yankees series against the then Tampa Bay Devil Rays by telling him they had corroborating evidence.[17] McNamee later concluded the government was bluffing and had no such information. "You know what, in hindsight, I don't think they knew anything."[18] While such bluffing or deceptive interrogation tactics by law enforcement was upheld by the United States Supreme Court in 1969 in *Frazier v. Cupp*,[19] the Feds did provide McNamee a means to agree with their suggestions and make them part of his own story. This idea is supported by the fact that Brian McNamee made quite clear during his discussion with Clemens investigators that the Feds had already poured through Clemens' medical records and other team records *before* they talked to him because they asked him about his medical conditions and injuries. That helped plant the seeds in McNamee's mind, allowing him to suggest that the various injuries, such as a contusion on his buttocks, resulted from an anabolic steroids injection. Clemens' lead attorney, Rusty Hardin, made the same contention in cross-examining McNamee when he asked, "They were going to lock you up if you didn't tell them what they said was the truth, weren't they? The government gave you what they believed the truth was. Yes?"[20]

Brian McNamee was the perfect vessel for the government to prosecute Roger Clemens. A former New York City policeman, McNamee possessed a cop's innate sense on the witness stand of where the narrative was going and no inhibition about either challenging a defense attorney's questions or improving the weaker points of his story with "an improved draft." Literally minutes after Judge Reggie Walton accused Clemens' lawyers of a "fishing expedition" in the second trial and refused to allow them to see information regarding McNamee's pending divorce proceedings with his estranged wife, Eileen McNamee, the former strength coach began for the first time to ascribe all sorts of weak explanations in his story to his wife's doing. Most dramatically, McNamee changed his previous versions of keeping the purported drug evidence from bringing down Clemens and protecting his family to never intending to do anything with the evidence but deciding to keep it to get his wife off his back—she who *insisted* he do it. Only to have his wife, whose testimony was originally barred from the trial for privilege under their divorce proceedings, brought back to testify by Judge Walton, whereupon she contradicted her husband's story about *when* he first told her about the saved syringes, vials and other materials and *whose* they were.[21]

McNamee might have called the government's bluff and stuck to his original story that he had told for years that he never gave Roger Clemens performance enhancing drugs. One problem for McNamee was that he knew that Andy Pettitte, with whom he was a much closer friend than Pettitte was with Clemens, was almost certain to confess to his own HGH use,[22] thus making it harder for McNamee to resist the government's deal to stay out of prison. If Pettitte confessed, and McNamee said he injected only Pettitte and not Clemens, he probably realized it was less likely he would be believed, and more likely *he* would be prosecuted as the dealer. After all, he faced this tough decision at a time when his friend Kirk Radomski had already cut a deal and was going to prison. Radomski's prison term must have been in the forefront of his thoughts when he decided to save himself by telling the government what they wanted to hear—that he injected Roger Clemens. They certainly were not going to cut him a deal if he said he *did not inject* Roger Clemens.

Besides, the Feds expressed absolutely no interest in prosecuting Pettitte, whom McNamee had indeed injected, or Chuck Knoblauch or Mike Stanton, or the former players who had confessed to taking PEDS. None of that mattered. There was then no evidence against Clemens when they confronted McNamee, but they apparently did not care and were undeterred. The only fair conclusion, therefore, was that they wanted Clemens, they wanted Clemens only, they wanted Clemens to be guilty, and the fact that no evidence then existed was beside the point. At Clemens' second trial, star investigator Jeff Novitzky went through the motions of insisting that Clemens "was not a target" for prosecution, and the government claimed falsely that only players who lied

17. A Theory of the Case

about their use were prosecuted. In fact, Mike Stanton, Greg Zaun, Jack Cust, Brandon Donnelly, David Justice, and Miguel Tejada all publicly denied they had used performance enhancing drugs, even though the government possessed their cancelled checks to Kirk Radomski. Only Miguel Tejada was prosecuted, and that was a personal issue with the government. Tejada had provided pills to Rafael Palmeiro, who tested positive for banned substances shortly after he denied using them on television in front of Congressman Waxman.

This whole controversy was more about Brian McNamee than Roger Clemens because it was McNamee's tale that was at issue. Faced with a prosecution with evidence having to do with other clients and none at all against Roger Clemens, because federal prosecutors desperately wanted a high-profile player to convict in order to justify a two-decade crusade against performance enhancing drugs, and bumping up against an ugly divorce and desperate economic circumstances, McNamee constructed a masterful story of sex, drugs, and country music, starring singer Mindy McCready, Roger Clemens, and himself. Not even the most believable part of McNamee's story, that Clemens had a decade-long sexual affair with McCready, may have been true. Clemens continued to deny a sexual relationship and McCready committed suicide on February 7, 2013. Before shooting herself, McCready shot and killed her late boyfriend's dog.[23] Clemens released a statement to reporters, minimizing their relationship, upon news of her death. It read, "Yes, that is sad news. I had heard over time that she was trying to get peace and direction in her life. The few times that I had met her, and her manager/agent, they were extremely nice."[24] McCready's best friend at the time, Jennifer Ryan Sirbaugh, who was with McCready when she met Clemens, told the *Fort Myers News* in 2008 that McCready told her she never had sex with Clemens. "She was all about the attention," Sirbaugh said.[25] Therefore, the problem here about the adultery claim is credibility. Both McCready and McNamee made the claim of an adulterous affair by the Rocket. Clemens' lawyer Rusty Hardin said McCready demanded $14 million not to go public with the claim that she and Clemens were lovers.[26] Receiving no payoff from an outraged Clemens and his lawyer Rusty Hardin, McCready decided to make a sex tape mistitled "A Baseball Mistress," which only discussed, but did not show, sexual escapades with Clemens. And that was only in part, as most of the DVD discussed other lovers. It is unknown how much money the sex tape made but it was pulled from distribution by Vivid Entertainment after her suicide.[27] Likewise, Brian McNamee claimed Clemens and McCready had an affair in the context of suing him for defamation. Furthermore, even if McNamee had seen Clemens with McCready, it is highly unlikely that he actually saw them have sex.

McNamee may have morphed onto his narrative any incident he could conjure up where Clemens was in the presence of self-declared steroids advocate Jose Canseco. His allegation that Clemens had pulled out a white bottle of the anabolic steroid Anadrol-50 in the clubhouse in broad view of the entire Toronto Blue Jays team, and discussed the contents with McNamee and Jose Canseco, and that McNamee gave the steroids to Canseco for safekeeping, brought this response from Canseco: "McNamee's allegation is completely false."[28] Furthermore, McNamee claimed that Canseco was so brazen about his use of performance enhancing drugs, he kept them in the clubhouse fridge in Toronto.[29] To be sure, McNamee overreached with the improbable claim that Clemens pulled out a container of steroids that he handed to Canseco in a crowded locker room, but to be fair, this was apparently McNamee's first work of fiction, and it can take a lifetime to master that genre. McNamee certainly realized at some point that this story seemed fantastic, and modified it somewhat later in his Congressional deposition by adding the caveat that his locker "was the first locker as soon as you walked in and it was a little bit away from the players. It wasn't in the open. It was in the open but it was nobody around … no one was around to see it."[30] As the comedian Lily Tomlin famously squealed, "How convenient!"

McNamee, in fact, was a creative man. He cleverly turned the tedium of cardiovascular workouts for Clemens into fun games of tossing footballs while running, backpedaling, and slam-dunking a basketball into a lowered net at the pitcher's 7,000-square foot gymnasium.[31] He was probably also bored. According to the trial testimony of Yankees General Manager Brian Cashman, McNamee interfered with the job of the Yankees' pitching coach and tried to lecture pitchers on their throwing motions, obviously not the role of a strength-and-conditioning coach.[32] As we saw previously, pitching coach Mel Stottlemyre was particularly annoyed at McNamee for telling certain pitchers to adjust their mechanics.[33] Cashman also testified that McNamee was always promoting himself, wanting players to work with him, rather than with head strength coach Jeff Mangold.

What was not creative and was one of the weakest angles to his story was the one-way nature of the communications that made no sense if McNamee was Clemens' main guy and go-to friend. If Clemens and McNamee were best buddies and Clemens was receiving injections of anabolic steroids and human growth hormone, it stands to reason that McNamee would have told Clemens about his other clients: the "Olympic caliber athletes" McNamee supposedly trained, the Wall Street gym rats, teammates Chuck Knoblauch, Andy Pettitte, and Mike Stanton. Yet nowhere did McNamee claim that he and Clemens had talked about McNamee giving anabolic steroids or HGH to these other people. In fact, the only reference McNamee made at all to Clemens having knowledge of his drug-dealing world, and it was a small reference, was the claim that Clemens came to him and said, "You know a guy, right?" Assured he did, McNamee claimed Clemens said, "Sure, get it," presumably an order to get the illegal drugs. Even that little story was contradicted at trial when McNamee claimed Clemens *always* supplied his own steroids. When New York Mets clubhouse attendant Kirk Radomski was arrested and Clemens, at the prompting of his agents, asked McNamee if he knew Radomski, McNamee denied knowing him. Conversely, McNamee did tell a few people he was giving HGH to Clemens when he was trying to make a sale. It makes no sense that McNamee would confide in strangers about injecting Clemens and not confide in Clemens about others he injected. After all, McNamee thought Clemens would be his financial salvation. In contrast, McNamee did talk to Andy Pettitte about injecting others and he injected Andy Pettitte. But then again, Pettitte and McNamee were good friends, according to Pettitte, and Clemens and McNamee were not.

It was particularly telling that there existed no incriminating e-mails between Clemens and McNamee at the time of the alleged HGH injections when it was not banned from baseball and there would have been no reason to keep it quiet and secret. Clemens did admit during his Congressional testimony that he took Ephedra before it was banned.

The bigger issue in McNamee's constantly evolving story, however, surrounded two questions. First, how did he create his story and make it so believable to so many people? Second, how did he think he could get away with it? McNamee's story was credible to so many people, it can be argued, because he morphed it onto real events that he either knew about or were taken for granted by the wider public, such as Jose Canseco's confessed use of anabolic steroids. Parties he attended with the Blue Jays and Yankees, such as the much-discussed one at Canseco's Miami house, and details about the clubhouses, Clemens' apartments, a buttocks injury Clemens once suffered in Toronto, were all morphed onto his allegations of injecting Clemens with anabolic steroids and human growth hormone. McNamee also had something for sale that Congress, baseball writers, and many baseball fans desperately wanted to buy: the guilt of Roger Clemens.

McNamee's *posture* of the confessor also enhanced his credibility. The prosecution against Clemens was similar to the prosecution of Alger Hiss in 1948 when the State Department official was accused by a former Communist Party member, Whittaker Chambers, of having passed secret documents to Soviet agents in the 1930s. Hiss was convicted of perjury in 1950 on weak evidence and made a convincing case the rest of his life that he had been framed. McNamee and Chambers were convincing witnesses, at least before Congress, because, as America's greatest diplomatic historian, George Kennan, said of

Chambers, he played the "role of the 'repentant,' and therefore pure and courageous ... from which, by noble agony ... had now liberated himself, and for whom a devotion to the truth had left no other alternative than to expose and denounce his former comrade."[34]

Many people must have believed McNamee's narrative because it came with a specific time-line of injecting Clemens with performance enhancing drugs from 1998 to 2001. This book has already cast many doubts on when, where, and if McNamee discussed performance enhancing drugs with Clemens, and the trial presented contradictory testimony by McNamee himself on when he supposedly last discussed the various illegal drugs with Clemens.

Others were also impressed that McNamee put a number on the times he injected Clemens with the various performance enhancing drugs. Even the fact that he kept changing the number of times he injected Clemens sounded convincing because it did not challenge the underlying crime, that he had injected Clemens *at least once*. And only one illegal injection was necessary to put in motion the whole sequence of possessing anabolic steroids and hence committing perjury before Congress. The guess here is that since the numbers bandied about by both Clemens and McNamee were similar, with Clemens contending it was B-12 and McNamee anabolic steroids and HGH, that McNamee took his numbers from the same shots. In a similar fashion, McNamee claimed that while he injected Clemens with three to four weeks' worth of testosterone in 2000, "All I know is he didn't finish the kit." Such a tidbit of not finishing makes a compelling argument for the existence of the testosterone to begin with. But then McNamee being McNamee, he hedged some more, "I'm not sure how consistent he was with that."[35] All impossible to challenge or contradict, of course.

Why did McNamee choose 2001 as the year he claimed to have last injected Clemens? First, as a former cop, McNamee may have known that there was a six-year statute of limitations after which he could not be prosecuted for illegal distribution of drugs—and that six years, coincidentally, ran out in 2007, the year he first talked to federal prosecutors and George Mitchell. If not, he was certainly told that by his first lawyer *before* he tried out his tale of injections of Clemens for Mitchell and the federal prosecutors.[36] Technically the statute had approximately six months to run when he first talked to the government but again, as a cop, he may have realized that the statute of limitations would probably run out before he was ever indicted. Second, the year 2001 was a clever choice because it could never be challenged by forensic evidence based on tests conducted by Major League Baseball. Since the regular testing of major league players began in 2005, they were a matter of public record, and the positive tests were made public. Clemens had not tested positive in 2005, 2006, and 2007, and McNamee knew that. However, at the time that McNamee talked to federal agents and Mitchell, the 2003 random tests were sealed and therefore confidential, and were supposed to remain confidential forever. Nevertheless, if McNamee told them he injected Clemens in late 2002 or 2003, and the tests became public and did not show a positive test, he was screwed. In fact, that's exactly what happened. Clemens waived his privacy right to keep the 2003 random test confidential; it did become public and he was clean. The test results of certain other players were leaked to the baseball writers.

Not coincidentally, 2001 was also the year McNamee had saved medical waste from injecting Chuck Knoblauch and "other players." For some bizarre reason that McNamee never explained in his many versions of his tale, he mixed up the various independent injections together in one wholesale mess. The mess may have included materials from injecting Clemens with B-12, or perhaps injecting himself or, considering that he placed used needles from injecting his son into beer cans, materials from those injections as well. McNamee or someone helping him may, at some point, have thrown out some of the materials and saved others. This is particularly plausible because his wife testified at trial that she heard needles in a Bud Lite can, and he claimed all the materials were contained in a Miller Lite can that were offered into evidence to Congress and to the Federal District Court at trial. In addition, McNamee did not often work with Clemens after the Yankees fired McNamee at the end of the 2001 season, making it less likely he could inject Clemens with anything after 2001, particularly in New York City—McNamee claimed that most of the injections were performed at Clemens' Upper East Side condominium. Therefore, because he could not take the risk of either being prosecuted under the statute of limitations or being caught red-handed about lying concerning injecting Clemens in 2002 or 2003, I think McNamee settled on the year 2001.

And, as mentioned above, 2001 was the year McNamee injected Chuck Knoblauch, the man he probably feared the most.

Furthermore, McNamee could say he *injected* Clemens with HGH and get away with it because he knew there was no paper trail of evidence such as cancelled checks at the time he told his story to Mitchell and federal prosecutors. Moreover, in 2007, there was no test for HGH.

Selecting the year 1998 as the starting point of McNamee's illegal injections had benefits as well. First there was the logical fact that it was the year they first met and worked together. It sounded more logical that Clemens would want the performance help from illegal drugs only two years after Red Sox General Manager Dan Duquette had made the inaccurate, wise-ass comment that Clemens "was in the twilight of his career." McNamee may have realized that it would not sound as believable to claim Clemens walked into the clubhouse years later and suddenly got interested in performance enhancing drugs after they had worked together a long time. Third, 1998 was the only year they worked together in Canada, which, unlike the United States, did not prosecute end-users of illegal drugs, only distributors who did not have a government license. That is why McNamee always claimed he never bought any of the performance enhancing drugs in Canada, but rather Clemens did. Finally, the year together in Toronto came with the free benefit, so to speak, that confessed steroids user Jose Canseco played with the Blue Jays. McNamee guessed people would believe anything he said concerning anabolic steroids and Jose Canseco.

McNamee's story was also credible because he knew his audience: The "Macho Mac" Theory. McNamee understood that his male sports audience would identify with his theme of loyalty, his claim that he injected performance enhancing drugs against his will, and only out of deference to his clients, and that he had to do it for the manly reason of "supporting his family." And that he was contrite in a manly way, taking responsibility for his past failures. Indeed both his Congressional testimony and trial testimony were littered with these manly and contrite statements. "Trying to do what my client wanted."[37] "I got caught up in something that led me to have to tell the truth about my clients. I had no choice. It killed me."[38] "I wanted Roger to know I had his back, I wouldn't rat him out."[39] "I made a mistake. I wish I wouldn't have done it. I was young."[40] "I worked all the time. I hustled, I took care of my kids. I kept working with Clemens and other players."[41] McNamee claimed that his eight days spent with Clemens in Houston each year precluded him from taking his wife and children to water parks and on other family outings[42]—a claim that was contradicted by McNamee's wife at trial.

When Rusty Hardin asked McNamee why he brought the alleged materials home to his house after telling IRS Agent Jeff Novitzky that originally he was just going to throw them away, the strength and conditioning coach said, "I wanted to protect my wife, so kept her out of it. I told Congress I was worried Clemens would take me down.... I was just trying to keep my wife, the mother of my children, out of this."[43]

When Hardin asked McNamee, as we saw during the trial, when he decided to add his wife to his narrative of gathering and keeping physical evidence, McNamee admitted, "I did it for the trial." And then he insisted again,

> "I was trying to keep my wife out of it and protect my family."[44]
> HARDIN RETORTED: Why did you ever [keep the materials]? Did you think that was a good solution to your problem?
> MCNAMEE: It was a very good solution.
> HARDIN: She's worried you're going to be caught for a crime, and your solution was to bring evidence of that crime to your home?[45]

Yet possibly the main reason for McNamee's claim that he injected Clemens with performance enhancing drugs was that he thought he could get away with it without any negative consequences to himself, for he testified at trial,[46] as did Kirk Radomski, that George Mitchell promised him anonymity in the Mitchell Report if he cooperated and that Mitchell would not name players in the Report. Rusty Hardin asked, "You didn't know Mitchell would name names. Until December 5, you thought you'd be able to stay under the radar?"

McNamee responded, "True. I thought I could keep that in house."[47]

This contention is also supported by the proffer memo from Mitchell to Major League players, dated on September 6, 2007, wherein Mitchell said his Report would "honor any player request for confidentiality."[48] The memo did contain the following equivocation: "He does not pledge ... that any *information* [emphasis added] you provide will actually remain confidential and not be disclosed without your consent."[49] While that equivocation would reasonably suggest that the word "information" would include the allegation that McNamee was the injector of Clemens, a fair interpretation suggests McNamee would indeed not be publicly outed as the source of the claim and Clemens would not be named in the Report. While it was not clear that the Feds used the same language in talking to McNamee as Mitchell did in the memo to players, the language was routine enough, and covered all the legal issues appropriately enough, to suggest that it was a good possibility. Whether Mitchell actually made such a promise was beside the point. The issue was what McNamee believed because it was McNamee's motives under discussion, not George Mitchell's. It is therefore my opinion that McNamee sincerely believed that he could fulfill his legal obligations under his proffer agreement without any negative consequences to himself. It was certainly naïve to believe that a claim that Roger Clemens enhanced the second half of his career by taking performance enhancing drugs would not cause a firestorm of public attention. On the other hand, McNamee had just lived through more than a year of a published report that claimed the *Los Angeles Times* had seen testimony by Jason Grimsley, a pitcher then with the Arizona Diamondbacks, who had been a teammate on the Yankees with Clemens, implicating Clemens and several other players as users of PEDs, in an affidavit to search Grimsley's house. The story turned out to be false.[50] The affidavit, requested by Special IRS agent Jeff Novitzky, contained the names of players implicated on pages 13–15 of the affidavit, but were blacked out before they were made public.[51] Nevertheless, the *Los Angeles Times* implicated Clemens. Almost immediately after the story went public, Kevin Ryan, U.S. Attorney in San Francisco, stated that the *LA Times* story had "significant inaccuracies," and the paper eventually offered a public apology for its error.

As we saw in the first trial chapter, even star investigator Jeff Novitzky admitted that it was unclear to him whether Mitchell would name names in his Report. Novitzky said that none of them knew what was going to be in the Report, "including whether Mitchell would name names."

Furthermore, McNamee seemed sincerely to believe that by talking to Clemens' investigators after the release of the Mitchell Report, he could still be friends with Clemens and Pettitte, for he said, "I hope it salvages whatever relationship I had with Andy and Roger."[52] In conclusion, it was possible that McNamee thought he could get away with telling Mitchell he injected Clemens without any consequences since the Report would not name sources, and when Mitchell made it obvious that McNamee was the source of the information against Clemens and named Clemens publicly in the Report, McNamee simply decided to tough it out. And the blowback to him was brutal.

The biggest mistake in McNamee's story, as in most criminal inventions, may not have been a big issue but rather a small fact. McNamee made the mistake of stubbornly insisting he had never given Clemens B-12 after the star pitcher said on *60 Minutes* that he had received injections from him of B-12 and Lidocaine, but not HGH and anabolic steroids. Clemens must have told the truth because it clearly unnerved McNamee. Clemens had started taking B-12 in the pill form at his mother's insistence; it was, after all, a common, over-the-counter dietary supplement taken by millions of Americans, and Clemens had also taken it via injections throughout his baseball career. Furthermore, the 2012 trial revealed that Clemens actually had prescriptions for B-12 and Vioxx.[53] Vioxx was later outlawed, as was ephedra. Clemens, a law-abiding citizen, stopped taking both. The idea that McNamee gave Clemens Hydroxycut, Thermacore, testosterone, anabolic steroids, human growth hormone, vitamins and health drinks of all concoctions to address Clemens' aches and pains, several of them eventually codified in law as illegal, but not B-12, which Clemens had taken forever, was not believable. This conclusion is supported by McNamee's admission during the Clemens trial that he advised players to take vitamin B-12 instead of HGH[54] even though he did market his services, so to speak, as an injector of HGH. Because McNamee was a sometime marketer to players of HGH, and a consistent marketer to players of B-12, but not anabolic steroids, it made it even less likely that he injected Clemens with anabolic steroids.

At trial, Brian McNamee ran away like a scared rabbit from the issue of whether he actually injected Clemens with B-12 instead of steroids.

> RUSTY HARDIN: You didn't ask why one of the greatest ever wanted steroids?
> BRIAN MCNAMEE: No.
> HARDIN: How did you know he meant steroids?

McNamee: I just did.
Hardin: When Clemens said he wanted a booty shot, were you aware B-12 shots were given in the booty? To use the phrase?
McNamee: No.
Hardin: Where are B-12 shots given?
McNamee: The only B-12 shots I ever saw was in the arm.
Hardin: Tell me everything you remember he said in the "booty shot" conversation.
McNamee: I knew he was talking about steroids.
Hardin: How?[55]

Indeed, aided by team doctors who mostly suffered attacks of amnesia when grilled by the government concerning the injection of B-12 in baseball clubhouses, federal prosecutors, sportswriters, and Clemens-haters believed they had a winning issue against the star pitcher. The winning issue came to an abrupt end at the trial when the defense provided a veritable parade of witnesses in the form of ex players, trainers, a former manager, and a general manager, who verified Clemens' contention of widespread use of B-12 in the Major Leagues.

McNamee later claimed that it was Clemens' release of the tape of the telephone conversation where he mentioned his son was dying that made him angry enough to retrieve vials of blood and syringes from the basement of his house in Queens. This makes no sense because it was McNamee who told the outrageous lie about his son's impending death, not Clemens. Certainly McNamee was probably angry and embarrassed that his own lie was played on a tape recorder before a Houston news conference and heard around the world. The real truth—that McNamee's son was not dying, but rather had diabetes—was not earthshaking news. Indeed, the second trial revealed that McNamee himself had diabetes, and almost nobody noticed since it is so common in the U.S. population, despite McNamee's melodramatic antics to cover it up. That Clemens played the recording referring to the alleged terminal illness was not malicious on his part. To the contrary, it demonstrated Clemens' concern for McNamee's son. As it turned out at trial, it was not Clemens' idea to play the tape anyway, but that of his lawyer, Rusty Hardin.[56] Fortunately for McNamee, his bold-faced fabrication flew over the heads of the sports reporters after Clemens angrily ended the press conference over critical comments about him by the Houston press.

All this said, it may be that McNamee could not remember everything about his injections of Roger Clemens because he gave the pitcher so many painkillers and so many vitamins. While most people would say that forgetting whether you injected such a famous athlete as Roger Clemens with illegal drugs was impossible, perhaps it was not. The mind can play tricks on people when they desperately want to believe something for their own survival. In addition,

McNamee kept no records of *what* performance enhancing drugs he injected, or *when* he injected them into athletes or other clients, or *who* was injected. The evidence against McNamee turned over to George Mitchell by federal investigators took the form of cancelled checks subpoenaed from McNamee's bank records. Although the government attempted to soften the blow regarding McNamee's own steroids use, by offering it on direct examination at Clemens' trial, to give the impression he had been neither a long-time dealer nor user, and McNamee asserted that he did not begin injecting himself with steroids until after shoulder surgery in 2004 or 2005,[57] it was not clear how truthful that claim was. Yet it would have added to McNamee's confusion if he had to remember the time periods of his own use, interspersed with that of his clients. The fact that he could not even narrow down the time or year of his own injections of himself leads to the conclusion either that he was not telling the truth about his own first injection, or that he was genuinely confused about who, when, where, and how he had injected *everybody*.[58] This could also explain why McNamee could never give a definitive answer to the most basic questions of where the anabolic steroids came from and if and how much he was paid for allegedly injecting Clemens with performance enhancing drugs. It could also explain the "morphing" structure of his story, how it was essentially piggy-backed off of known facts, such as Jose Canseco's admissions of using steroids and what turned out to be a contusion on Roger Clemens' posterior.

One conclusion regarding Brian McNamee does seem fair to make without hesitation. Going to jail for from five to seven years and paying a quarter of a million dollar fine was never an option.

18

At Home in Houston

The one thing that everybody agreed on when it came to Roger Clemens was that he had done a terrific job in charity work. Even Congressman Henry Waxman, at the beginning of his disgraceful show trial, said, "I am also aware of the tremendous amount of good that Mr. Clemens has done through the Roger Clemens Foundation—and I thank you for helping so many children."[1]

After his more or less forced retirement from baseball upon the conclusion of the 2007 season in the wake of the Mitchell Report charges, Roger Clemens devoted himself mostly to charity work, not an uncommon second career for retired athletes who played golf to their heart's content and raised money for worthy social causes. Yet Clemens applied himself to his charities with the same fierce energy and attention to detail that he devoted to baseball. Probably due to his own traumatic home life, where he forced his natural father out of the household for beating his mother, and where his stepfather died of a heart attack when he was nine, he felt great comfort in the children he met. They were the focus of his Roger Clemens Foundation, created in 1992 when he still pitched for the Red Sox.[2]

Indeed, Clemens' first exposure to charity work came in his first big league season, 1984, with the city's Jimmy Fund, which raised money for the Dana-Farber Cancer Institute, the top-ranked cancer hospital in New England. It was the only cancer center in the nation ranked in the top four for both adult and pediatric cancer care. Clemens always jogged the mile from Fenway Park to the clinic. It is now a legendary story that on one visit, a little girl did not believe he was Roger Clemens because he was in street clothes. Whereupon he ran back to the baseball park, put on his Red Sox uniform, and returned. Thereafter he always wore his Red Sox uniform when visiting the children.[3] Clemens continued to support the Jimmy Fund. In 2014, for example, he pitched batting practice to fans and friends for one hour, where the minimum bid per batter started at $20,000, for the fund's benefit, and also participated in the yearly Radio-Telethon which raised more than $33 million.[4] Playing golf with

Clemens for $20,000 seemed a mainstay of his fundraising methods, for he used the same approach with his own foundation.

Joe Castiglione, the Red Sox announcer, said of Clemens on WEEI radio in August 2014, "I will tell you what the people at Dana Farber told me is that there has been no athlete in Boston who has ever given more of himself."

Clemens was inducted into the Red Sox Hall of Fame on August 14, 2014, with pitcher Pedro Martinez[5] and shortstop Nomar Garciaparra.

In Houston, where Clemens and his wife Debbie operated the Roger Clemens Foundation, they received 15 requests a day. It was probably a good thing that Debbie was an outstanding golfer who has won club championships, for they mainly raised money through golf tournaments and silent auctions. The Foundation supported educational, charitable, literary, scientific and religious activities for children, with a special emphasis on underprivileged and at-risk children, and children with specific needs. As of 2015, The Foundation had raised several million dollars, and 98 percent of it, according to Clemens, had gone directly to people and not to overhead. Much of the charity work, according to his wife Debbie, was done behind the scenes, not known publicly.

The Foundation gave money to the Cystic Fibrosis Foundation, Variety Clubs International, Boys and Girls Clubs of America, Make a Wish Foundation, Sunshine Kids, Periwinkle Foundation, the National Paralysis Foundation, and the Starlight Children's Fund of Canada. It also supported the Dystrophic Epidermolysis Bullosa Research Association, the Muscular Dystrophy Association, the Multiple Sclerosis Society, and the Mission of Yahweh, a Houston homeless shelter for women and children. Clemens also raised money for Cystic Fibrosis by running a baseball camp. He told the kids in his camp, "Don't go getting ticked off like I did when I was young."[6]

In order to support other charities, Clemens sold baseball memorabilia on the Foundation's website. He also donated some of the memorabilia, such as signed baseballs, for auctions and still made personal appearances in hospitals. Roger and Debbie also donated their time by coordinating the collection and distribution of donations for the Houston Food Drive.

Despite the obvious strain on the arm of Clemens, who turned 53 in August 2015, he continued to offer to pitch batting practice in Houston or anywhere people would pay him to do it for charity. He even paid half the cost of the plane trip (he owned his own plane) when he flew out of Houston to pitch. The going rate seemed to be $20,000, with half of the fee going to Roger's foundation and the other half to the charity of the other person's wish. He had the same arrangement in playing golf for charity.

An old-fashioned patriot, Roger Clemens was particularly generous of his time for the U.S. military, visiting troops in Middle East war zones and at bases across the United States. At home, in nearby Oklahoma, Clemens golfed for Folds of Honor, a charity providing scholarships for military families where a veteran had been killed or disabled on active duty.[7]

Helping out his hometown Houston Astros by working with the team's young pitchers, under a ten-year services contract, Clemens also held charity benefits at Minute Maid Park, the team's home field, such as the "Rocketman Celebrity Slam" in July 2014. It benefitted children's charities and military families. The celebrities included actor Lee Majors, country singer Toby Keith, Astros teammates Jeff Bagwell and Roy Oswalt, and Vince Young, quarterback on the national champion Texas Longhorns team of 2005 and for the Tennessee Titans. The man Yankees announcer Michael Kay once called "an evangelist for pitching" was an astute observer of the game, particularly the mechanics of young pitchers and their problems. He said of many he observed, "You also see guys come out now level shoulder. There's no tilt. Try to teach them to have a little tilt. Most of the guys who get hurt are level shouldered and it puts a lot of stress on the elbow."[8] Of his work with the young Astros pitchers, Clemens said, "I enjoy teaching. I don't coach, and there's a difference."

Clemens had gone into retirement in Houston after the 2003 season, but the team's signing of Yankees teammate and Houston native Andy Pettitte prompted him to pitch again, and he played from 2004 to 2006 in his hometown. Somehow the Astros played in their first World Series in the fall of 2005, despite exhibiting a team batting average of .256, 13th among the 16 National League teams. Their on-base percentage was an awful .322; they ranked 14th in hits, 11th in runs and ninth in home runs.[9] Lance Berkman, in his prime, hit .293 with 24 home runs, and 39-year-old Craig Biggio, at the end of a Hall of Fame career, knocked out 26 home runs and batted .264. Clemens' 36-year-old catcher, Brad Ausmus, batted .258 with

In 2005 Clemens pitched his hometown Astros to their only World Series appearance.

three homers. Ausmus would come to Clemens' defense when the Mitchell Report accusations were published. The team's strength derived from its pitching, with the 42-year-old Clemens going 13–8 with a league-best 1.87 ERA and 185 strikeouts. Roy Oswalt was the team ace, going 20–12 with a 2.94 ERA and 184 strikeouts. Andy Pettitte was also impressive, going 17–9 with a 2.39 ERA and 171 strikeouts. Brad Lidge saved 42 games. Set-up men Chad Qualls, Dan Wheeler and Russ Springer threw a respective 79⅔ innings, 73⅓ innings and 59 innings. The Astros, who had finished second in the NL Central and thus became a Wild Card team, beat the Atlanta Braves in the first round, three games to one, and defeated the St. Louis Cardinals in the championship series. Unfortunately, they played like a team with a .256 batting average in the World Series and were swept in four straight by the Chicago White Sox. Clemens, the once durable ace who had thrown 46 shutouts in his long career, had run out of gas.

While Roger and Debbie Clemens may not have exactly been a team in the sense of French writers and philosophers Jean Paul Sartre and Simone de Beauvoir, they were as close to a team as anyone could possibly get as a force in charity. Debbie Clemens was known as the "Needlepoint Queen" and designed jackets and hats for charity. She also wrote a cookbook back in 1991, entitled "Christmas Confection Collections." She donated the proceeds to charity.

They were as busy as ever with their charity work in 2015. In February 2015, they helped raise $100,000 at Tootsies, "Love's in Fashion," a runway show on behalf of a children's charity, Deck My Room. They helped raise $700,000 to help premature, NICU babies, for the Nicklaus Children's Hospital, by playing in Jack Nicklaus' Creighton Farms Invitational golf tournament in Leesburg, Virginia. In March 2015, they participated in Fashion Woodlands in suburban Houston to raise funds for a Veterans Memorial in Woodlands, Texas, in the northern sector of Houston. In April of that year they supported World Autism Awareness, a growing issue among American children.

19

Roger Clemens, Family Man

As with his charity work, there was universal agreement that Roger Clemens acted as a wonderful father to his children and an exemplary family man. As we have seen in this book, even his nemesis, Brian McNamee, extolled Clemens as a family man at every opportunity. In New York, McNamee testified, Clemens was acutely aware of the one-hour time difference with Texas in order to speak to his children before they went to bed if at all possible. Even during the time of his battles with the baseball establishment, Clemens' life always centered on his family, including a large, extended family, with close relations with his in-laws and his five siblings, three sisters and two brothers. Clemens was never a guy who spent a lot of time hanging out with the guys drinking or playing poker.

"It's really all about family, nurturing and supporting each other," his wife Debbie said.[1]

A 2013 profile of Clemens and his family said, "The Clemens crew can best be described in two words: Family Unity. All six stay busy with work, school" and extracurricular activity. "But they carve time out of hectic schedules to volunteer at the Roger Clemens Foundation and the Roger & Debbie Clemens Pediatric Wing at Children's Memorial Hermann Hospital."[2]

Clemens, a strikeout pitcher, was severely criticized for giving his four sons names that begin with K, the baseball symbol for a strikeout. He and Debbie named their first son Koby Aaron after Henry Aaron, not a pitcher, and Koby, which derives from Jakob or Jacob, one of Debbie's favorite names, presumably from the Bible. Koby was a minor league third baseman and catcher and became a baseball coach. In one famous incident in the minor leagues, he batted against his father, who was pitching on a rehab assignment, and hit a home run. The next time up his father hit him with the first pitch. Koby did not cry or complain or charge the mound or call for a federal investigation. He did what batters were supposed to do under such circumstances—he kept his mouth shut, accepted the gift of first base, and plotted his revenge of hitting another home run the next time up.

Their second son, Kory Allen, grew up with an artistic temperament and originally was thought to be contemplating a career as an artist. His artistry went into cooking instead of drawing, attending the Le Cordon Bleu French cooking school in Austin, Texas. He interned at the Taste of Texas Restaurant in Houston, learned his craft as a cook at Ragin' Cajun in Houston, and by 2015 was co-owner and cook of Katch 22, a sports bar/restaurant in that city. The name Katch 22 was a clever pun on the classic novel, *Catch-22*, by Joseph Heller, with a touch of salute to the number his father wore in the latter part of his major league career, 22. The fare at Katch 22 featured what you might expect in a sports themed eating establishment: lobster sliders, bone-in pork chops, Southern clam chowder, chicken wings, salad, gourmet burgers and, as it was Texas, steaks. Actually, the menu at Katch 22 sounds more upscale and exotic than most sports bars.[3] The restaurant's opening was attended by Derek Jeter.

Third son Kacy Austin presumably received his middle name in honor of the capital city of Texas, Austin. The CY in Kacy was derived from Cy Young, who is tied with Clemens for most wins among all Boston Red Sox pitchers. As of this writing, Kacy is a junior business major at his father's alma mater. Like his father, Kacy played baseball for the University of Texas Longhorns. Unlike his father, he did not look like a Major League prospect. In his freshman year he played mostly first base and batted .212 with one homerun and 21 runs batted in. He had a fielding percentage of .992. He mostly pitched in his sophomore year, won three, lost two, had an earned run average of 4.17, struck out 21 batters and walked 18 in a little over 45 innings. He had a perfect fielding average at first base, no errors in 143 chances, for a 1.000 percentage. He batted .204 with no extra-base hits or runs batted in.[4]

The youngest child was Kody Alec, a student at Houston Memorial High School. He does not even play baseball. Perhaps he took after his mother Debbie more because he is a golfer instead. Or perhaps he was traumatized away from baseball when the mob-like news media hounded him and his father when his Dad drove him to school during the PED frenzy.

On the issue of his family life, as in all other issues, Roger Clemens is practically unhittable, for when you think you have him figured out, when you think you can beat him, Clemens is a step ahead of you with the truth. Why is he such an extraordinary family man? Because he passed the most difficult test of any husband and father. He even gets along with his mother-in-law.

Summing up their life together, Debbie Clemens said, "We are thankful to people who have supported and prayed for us. We are blessed by our friends.

Our kids have grown up under a microscope and are grounded and rooted in faith. We've learned to tune out the negativity."

About baseball, Roger Clemens concluded, "It's what I did, but not who I am.... I didn't play the game to go to the Hall of Fame.... We love the Hall of Fame.... I played the game because it was an opportunity to take care of my family."[5]

Chapter Notes

Acknowledgments

1. Quentin Reynolds, *Courtroom: The Story of Samuel S. Leibowitz* (New York: Farrar, Straus and Giroux, 1950).

Introduction

1. www.m.mlb.com./news/article, May 6, 2007.
2. www.baseball-reference.com/players/c/clemero.
3. During Clemens' year at San Jacinto Junior College, his coaches discovered and corrected a defect in his pitching motion, thereby increasing the velocity of his fastball.
4. www.baseball-reference.com/players/c/clemens.
5. Reporters and cameramen even besieged Clemens like baying hounds as he drove his youngest son to school.
6. Committee on Oversight and Government Reform, U.S. House of Representatives, Washington, D.C., February 5, 2008, Deposition of William Roger Clemens, 82.
7. For the record, the House Committee on Oversight and Government Reform denied that the questioning of Clemens under oath was intended to set him up to be indicted for perjury by the United States government. One committee lawyer stated for posterity, "There may have been a suggestion that the signal coming from the committee or the chairman if somebody challenged the Mitchell Report that would be the basis for a criminal referral. There has been no such *statement* [emphasis added] by the chairman or the ranking member." Clemens' attorney, Rusty Hardin, used to showing deference toward judges—and the lawyer was essentially the judge during his questioning— and wanting to appear agreeable, backed down. "I take it back," Hardin said, "because I have no evidence that the chairman has said any such thing. I really was talking about a perception rather than actual quotes or positions of the committee." While it was literally correct that Waxman and Republican senior member Davis of Virginia had not officially made such a threat, sources on the committee did tell Hardin that Clemens would in fact face referral for prosecution if he denied taking performance enhancing drugs.
8. www.opensecrets.org/pac_2006_election_cycle.
9. Katie Thomas, "Once Bound for Cooperstown, Now Headed to a Courtroom," *New York Times*, August 19, 2010.
10. A source within the Clemens defense.
11. Gabe Feldman, "How Did Roger Clemens Walk?" www.grantland.com/the-triangle, June 19, 2012.
12. www.baseball-reference.com/players/c/clemero. There is some debate about Clemens' salary in his early years in Boston so this amount must still be considered an estimate.
13. Clarke Canfield, "F. Lee Bailey's Paper Proves OJ Simpson's Innocence," www.cnsnews.com, January 11, 2011.
14. Committee on Oversight and Government Reform, U.S. House of Representatives, Washington, D.C., Monday, February 4, 2008. Deposition of Andrew Pettitte, 20–24.
15. *Ibid.*
16. *Ibid.*, 25.
17. Clemens deposition, 70.
18. Pettitte said of McNamee in 2008, "He's become a friend of mine." Pettitte deposition, 8.
19. @TJQuinnESPN, May 31, 2012.
20. Clemens deposition, 54.
21. *Ibid.*, 58.
22. Don Amore, and David Heuschkel, "In-

side Clemens' Head, Few Hunt," *Hartford Courant,* July 16, 2000.

23. Committee on Oversight and Government Reform, U.S. House of Representatives, Washington, D.C., Thursday, January 31, 2008. Interview of James Joseph Murray IV, 24–27, 29–35, 36–52, 67–88, 111–115, 120–122, 126–136, 138–143.

24. Clemens deposition, 123.

25. www.newyork.cbslocal.com, May 31, 2012.

26. Clemens deposition, 188.

27. www.baseball-reference.com.

28. Peter Abraham, "Red Sox Agree to Deal with Pitcher David Price," *Boston Globe,* December 1, 2015.

29. Christian Red, "Doctor: Roger Clemens Is Clean," *New York Daily News,* February 12, 2008.

30. "Weighing the Committee Record: A Balanced Review of the Evidence Regarding Performance Enhancing Drugs in Baseball," Committee on Oversight and Government Reform, Tom Davis, Ranking Member, March 25, 2008, 21.

31. Committee on Oversight and Government Reform, U.S. House of Representatives, Washington, D.C., Monday, February 4, 2008, 20.

32. Harlan Levy, *And the Blood Cried Out: A Prosecutor's Spellbinding Account of the Power of DNA* (New York: Basic Books, 1996).

33. *60 Minutes,* CBS Television, May 27, 2003.

34. William C. Thompson, "The Potential for Error in Forensic DNA Testing," www.councilforresponsbiblegenetics.org.

Chapter 1

1. Opening Statement of William Roger Clemens, Preliminary Transcript, The Mitchell Report: The Illegal Use of Steroids in Major League Baseball, Day 2, Wednesday, February 13, 2008, House of Representatives, Committee on Oversight and Government Reform, Washington, D.C., 5.

2. *Ibid.*

3. Jeff Pearlman, *The Rocket That Fell to Earth: Roger Clemens and the Rage for Baseball Immortality* (New York: HarperCollins, 2009), 6–59. Pearlman's fanciful take on Clemens is relentlessly negative. It opens with the bizarre suggestion that Clemens was led to taking PEDS because his older brother did cocaine.

4. Kristie Rieken, "Roger Clemens Allows One Hit in Return to the Mound," AP, August 26, 2012.

5. Pearlman, *The Rocket That Fell to Earth,* 21.

6. Pat Jordan, "Late Innings; Roger Clemens Refuses to Grow Up," *New York Times Magazine,* March 4, 2001.

7. @TJQuinnESPN, May 29, 2012.

8. *Ibid.*

9. *Ibid.*

10. *Ibid.*

11. *Ibid.*

12. www.rocket_roger_clemens.tripod.com/bio.

13. Dave Sheinin, "Clemens Puts Off His Grief and Wins," *Washington Post,* September 15, 2005.

14. Lee Jenkins, "Clemens Pitches Hours After Mother Dies," *New York Times,* September 15, 2005.

15. Jimmy Connors, *The Outsider: A Memoir* (New York: HarperCollins, 2013).

16. Pearlman, *The Rocket That Fell to Earth,* 124–126. Pearlman apparently did not share Clemens' sense of team loyalty. In this book, Pearlman calls Clemens' decision "unparalleled self-centeredness."

17. Joe Holley, "Leading Texas Republican Anne Armstrong," *Washington Post,* July 31, 2008.

18. Annette Gordon-Reed, *The Hemingses of Monticello: An American Family* (New York: W. W. Norton, 2008).

19. Ivins was selected as a finalist for the Pulitzer Prize for commentary in 1985 and 1998.

20. Pearlman, *The Rocket That Fell to Earth,* 45.

21. Tyler Kepner, "Baseball, Clemens and Mets Are Ready to Complete a Circle," *New York Times,* June 27, 2008.

22. *Ibid.,* 7–8.

23. *Ibid.,* 29.

24. Susan Slusser, "The Slugger No One Wanted—Future Hall of Famer was 62nd-round Pick," *San Francisco Chronicle,* March 4, 2007.

25. www.baseball-reference.com/players/g/griffey. Griffey was an amazing hitter, slugging 630 home runs in his career. Coincidently, Griffey was born in Donora, Pennsylvania, the same town as Judge Reggie Walton, who presided over both Clemens trials.

26. Jonathan Mayo, *Facing Clemens: Hitters on Confronting Baseball's Most Intimidating Pitcher* (Guilford, CT: Lyon Press, 2008), 93–94.

27. Woody Booher, the stepfather who replaced Clemens' biological father, died of a heart attack when Roger was nine. Preliminary

Notes. Chapter 1

Transcript, The Mitchell Report: The Illegal Use of Steroids in Major League Baseball, Day 2, Wednesday, February 13, 2008, House of Representatives, Committee on Oversight and Government Reform, Washington, D.C., 114.

28. Bob Carter, "Clemens Thrives on Confrontation," www.espn.go.com/classic/biography/s/clemens_roger.html, accessed July 18, 2011.

29. Dan Barry, *Bottom of the 33rd: Hope, Redemption and Baseball's Longest Game* (New York: HarperCollins, 2011), 211.

30. Committee on Oversight and Government Reform, U.S. House of Representatives, Deposition of William Roger Clemens, 51.

31. www.rosstraining.com/blog/2010/09/14/hand-training-with-a-rice-bucket.

32. Mayo, *Facing Clemens*, 52.

33. The Mitchell Report: The Illegal Use of Steroids in Major League Baseball, 5.

34. Clay Coppedge, *Hill Country Chronicles* (Charleston, SC: History Press, 2010), 30–32.

35. Tyler Kepner, "Clemens Misses Another Start," *New York Times*, July 22, 2007.

36. Frederick C. Bush, "Roger Clemens," Society for Baseball Research, November 16, 2015.

37. Buster Olney, "Baseball; Clemens Gives All, Then the Yankees Give Out," *New York Times*, July 19, 2001.

38. Joe Torre and Tom Verducci, *The Yankee Years* (New York: Random House, 2008), 135.

39. Pearlman, *The Rocket That Fell to Earth*, 220.

40. Ibid.

41. Author's e-mail interview with Jeff Hearron, December 28, 2011.

42. Pearlman, *The Rocket That Fell to Earth*, 128.

43. Ibid., 196.

44. @TJQuinnESPN, May 10, 2012.

45. Ibid.

46. Pearlman, *The Rocket That Fell to Earth*, 196.

47. YES Network telecast, September 18, 2013.

48. Ibid.

49. Bob Carter, "Clemens Thrives on Confrontation," ESPN, www.espn.go.com/biography/s/Clemens_Roger.html.

50. Pearlman, *The Rocket That Fell to Earth*, 69. Clemens' wife Debbie, a health fanatic, would drive a car alongside him as he ran in the dark along the Boston streets.

51. Mike Cole, "John McNamara Recalls 1986 World Series, Stands by Claim That Roger Clemens Asked Out of Game 6," www.nesn.com, November 8, 2011.

52. Pearlman, *The Rocket That Fell to Earth*, 113–115.

53. Ibid.

54. Pearlman, *The Rocket That Fell to Earth*, 58.

55. Bob Carter, "Clemens Thrives on Confrontation," www.espn.go.com/classic/biography/s/clemens_coger.html.

56. Pat Jordan, "Late Innings; Roger Clemens Refuses to Grow Up," *New York Times*, March 3, 2001.

57. Don Amore and David Heuschkel, "Inside Clemens' Head, Few Hunt," *Hartford Courant*, July 16, 2000.

58. Robert W. Creamer, *Stengel: His Life and Times* (New York: Simon & Schuster, 1990), 197.

59. www.efootage.com/stock-footage/86695/casey_stengel_hall_of_fame_induction_speech_-_HD/.

60. Creamer, *Stengel: His Life and Times*, 21. Coincidentally, Creamer was comparing Stengel to another man named Clemens, Samuel Clemens, a.k.a. Mark Twain.

61. Ibid., 24.

62. Ibid., 35–36.

63. Pearlman, *The Rocket That Fell to Earth*, 49.

64. Ibid.

65. Creamer, *Stengel: His Life and Times*, 197.

66. Ibid., 258.

67. Ibid., 266.

68. Ibid., 270.

69. Clemens deposition, 113–114.

70. Creamer, *Stengel: His Life and Times*, 278.

Chapter 2

1. The college takes its name from the 1836 Battle of San Jacinto wherein Texas won its independence from Mexico.

2. Pearlman, *The Rocket That Fell to Earth*, 35.

3. Clay Coppedge, *Hill Country Chronicles* (Charleston, SC: History Press, 2010), 30–32.

4. Ibid., 60.

5. www.baseball-reference.com/teams/nym/.

6. Jimmy Breslin, *Can't Anybody Here Play This Game? The Improbable Saga of the New York Mets' First Year* (New York: Penguin, 1963).

7. www.baseball-reference.com/player/f/thomasfr.03.html. The Frank Thomas mentioned in the text, a player who was in the Majors from 1951 to 1966, should not be confused with Frank Thomas of more recent vintage. The latter Thomas, also known as the "The Big

Hurt," began his athletic career as a six-foot, five-inch Auburn fullback who opened holes for Bo Jackson, and hit 521 major league home runs, primarily as a designated hitter with the Chicago White Sox. The Big Hurt was elected to the Baseball Hall of Fame in January 2014.

8. www.baseball-reference.com/player/s/stuart.01/html. The nickname "Dr. Strangeglove" is a pun on a popular movie of that era, Stanley Kubrick's *Dr. Strangelove or: How I Learned to Stop Worrying and Love the Bomb*.

9. Alexsandr I. Solzhenitsyn, *The Oak and the Calf: Sketches of Literary Life in the Soviet Union* (New York: Harper & Row, 1979), 3–4.

10. Mayo, *Facing Clemens*, 27.

11. Tyler Kepner, "Baseball, Clemens and Mets Are Ready to Complete a Circle," *New York Times*, June 27, 2008.

12. Author's telephone interview with Cliff Gustafson, December 26, 2011.

13. Mayo, *Facing Clemens*, 27.

14. Gustafson had played his college baseball at the University of Texas.

15. Author's e-mail interview with Jeff Hearron, December 28, 2011; Author's telephone interview with Cliff Gustafson, December 26, 2011. See also: Anthony McCarron, "Catcher Tells Tall Tales of Longhorn Days," *New York Daily News*, June 1, 2003.

16. Bob Carter, "Clemens Thrives on Confrontation," www.espn.go.com/classic/biography/s/clemens_roger.html.

17. Pearlman, *The Rocket That Fell to Earth*, p. 45; author's telephone interview with Cliff Gustafson, December 26, 2011.

18. Author's e-mail interview with Steve Campbell, January 12, 2012.

19. Texas Baseball, 2010 Media Guide, Grfx.cstu.com/photos/schools.

20. TexasLonghornsBaseballHistory/Listrong.com, TexasLonghornsBaseballeNotes.com; Reference, www.texassports.com/genrel/110606; www.fanbase.com/texas-longhorns-baseball (1963).

21. www.fanbase.com/texas-longhorns-baseball1983.

22. Carey could have passed for Clemens in intensity, however, for he sulked after winning four gold medals at the Los Angeles Olympics because he was displeased with his times.

23. Author's e-mail interview with Jeff Hearron, December 28, 2011.

24. www.baseball-reference.com/players/b/brum/.

25. SeattleMariners.mlb.com/team/coaches.

26. Ok, so Bates was one for one. www.baseball-reference.com/players/b/batesbio.

27. Anthony McCarron, "Catcher Tells Tall Tales of Longhorn Days," *New York Daily News*, June 1, 2003.

28. Kirk Bohls, "Clemens Handcuffs Sun Devils," *Austin American Statesman*, March 21, 1983. Courtesy Mike Gustafson, College Baseball Foundation.

29. *Ibid*.

30. Mayo, *Facing Clemens*, 3–17. Thomas would later serve as the hitting coach of the Texas Rangers.

31. Martin Buber, *The Knowledge of Man* (New York: HarperCollins, 1965), 130.

32. www.e-yearbook.com/yearbooks/university_texas_cactus_yearbook/1983/page_283.html.

33. McDowell's major league career spanned seven seasons (1985–1990, 1994), including stints with the Texas Rangers, Cleveland Indians and Atlanta Braves.

34. Trent proved less successful in convincing a Michigan high school shortstop he entertained for that weekend, Barry Larkin, to play for Texas. Larkin decided to stay home and play for the Wolverines in Ann Arbor. Larkin proved more amenable to the request of the Baseball Hall of Fame in scenic Cooperstown, New York, where he was enshrined in 2012 after batting .295 over 19 seasons, winning the National League Most Valuable Player Award in 1995, and earning three Gold Glove Awards as the best defensive shortstop in the National League. All of those accomplishments came as a player with the Cincinnati Reds. www.baseball-reference.com/l/larkinba.

35. www.baseball-reference.com/players/c/clemerooz.shtml. Doyle, who signed Clemens for the Red Sox on June 21, 1983, caught briefly for the Red Sox in 1943. See Barry, *Bottom of the 33rd: Hope, Redemption and Baseball's Longest Game*, 39.

36. www.baseball-reference.com/players/s/shirca.

37. www.baseball-reference.com/players/c/capelmi.

38. Texas Baseball, 2010 Media Guide.

39. www.baseball-reference.com/minors/player.cyi.

40. www.baseball-reference.com/players/r/ruth.

41. www.baseball-reference.com/players/b/boggs.

42. Bill Koenig, "The Eyes Have It," *Baseball Weekly*, June 6, 1996.

43. www.baseball-reference.com/player/b/boggs.

44. www.baseball-reference.com/players/v/vaughn.
45. www.baseball-reference.com/players/g/garcino.
46. www.baseball-reference.com/players/d/damon.
47. Amy K. Nelson, "Pedro Exists in Quite the Hurry," www.espn.go.com/mlb/playoffs/2009/news/story.
48. www.baseball-reference.com/player/l/lester.
49. Tom Singer, "Splendid Splinter's Final at Bat Was Poetic End," www.mlb.com, September 26, 2010.
50. Andrew Mahoney, "Play-by-Play Announcers Enjoy Special Place in Red Sox Nation," *Boston Globe*, August 26, 2015.
51. Cited in Warren Buffett, *Berkshire Hathaway Letters to Shareholders: 1965 to 2012* (Mountain View, CA: Explorist Productions, 2014), 335.
52. He keeps a faded Cy Young autographed baseball in a dark place in his house so the signature will not be further damaged by light. See Pat Jordan, "Late Innings; Roger Clemens Refuses to Grow Up," *New York Times*, March 4, 2001.
53. YES television broadcast, August 5, 2011.
54. www.baseball-reference.com.
55. *Ibid.*
56. Ira Berkow, "33 Innings, 882 Pitches and One Crazy Game," *New York Times*, June 24, 2006.
57. Pat Jordan, "Late Innings; Roger Clemens Refuses to Grow Up," *New York Times Magazine*, March 4, 2001.
58. *Ibid.*
59. www.baseball-reference.com/players/p/price.
60. www.baseball-reference.com.
61. www.baseball-reference.com/players/c/clemero.
62. www.baseball-almanac.com/asgbox/yr2004.
63. www.baseball-reference.com/teams/hou/2005.
64. @TJQuinnESPN, May 31, 2012.
65. Lester Munson, "Report: Penn Professor's Findings Contradict Clemens' Analysis of Career Stats," www.espn.com, February 10, 2008.
66. www.baseball-almanac.com/players/player.clemens.
67. Nick Cafardo, "Clemens Strongly Defends Himself, Latest Book Release Continues to Put the Drug-Abuse Spot-Light on Former Pitcher," *Boston Globe*, May 17, 2009.
68. Michael S. Schmidt, "Clemens Lied About Doping, Indictment Charges," *New York Times*, August 19, 2010.
69. Alyson Footer, "Notes: Ausmus supports Clemens," www.mlb.com, February 14, 2008.

Chapter 3

1. Committee on Oversight and Government Reform, U.S. House of representatives, Washington, D.C., Thursday, February 7, 2008, Deposition of Brian Jerome McNamee, Sr., 56.
2. *Ibid.*, 56–57.
3. *Ibid.*, 57, 59.
4. *Ibid.*, 58.
5. No evidence was ever found to corroborate McNamee's claim that Clemens might have kept computer records of his illicit drug use.
6. Brian McNamee deposition, 61.
7. "Cashman: Clemens Pushed to Hire McNamee After Poor Payoff Outing," www.cbssports.com, May 10, 2012.
8. Brian McNamee deposition, 22.
9. *Ibid.*, 66.
10. The original Yankee Stadium opened in 1923. In 2009 the team opened its new facility directly across the street, demolishing the old structure. www.newyork.yankees.mlb.com/nyy/ballpark/newstadium.
11. Brian McNamee deposition, 13–21.
12. *Ibid.*
13. *Ibid.*, 37–38.
14. The testimony at Clemens' second trial by McNamee's wife that it was a Bud Lite can and not a Miller Lite can suggests that McNamee may have doctored the evidence, placing materials in a Miller Lite can to implicate Clemens, and tossing out the Bud Lite can with materials saved from injecting Chuck Knoblauch and other players.
15. Brian McNamee deposition, 39.
16. *Ibid.* (emphasis added).
17. *Ibid.* (emphasis added).
18. *Ibid.*, 40.
19. ESPN television dramatically exhibited those demonstrative photographs during its live coverage of the Waxman hearings.
20. Brian McNamee deposition, 41.
21. *Ibid.*, 76–77.
22. *Ibid.*
23. Criminal Code, R.S.C. 1985, C. c-46. C.R.C. c 870 Food and Drug Regulations.
24. New York Public Health Law, Section 3306(1) (h); New York Penal Law, Section

220.03 & 220.31. Under New York law, the sale of anabolic steroids is a Class D felony.
   25. www.baseball-reference.com/teams/tor/1997.
   26. www.baseball-reference.com/teams/tor/1998.
   27. Controlled Drugs and Substances Act (Canada) 1996, C. 19. Accessed at www.canlii.org.
   28. Brian McNamee deposition, 69. McNamee noted that Winstrol is highly toxic. Indeed, Winstrol is known to adversely affect the liver and can markedly raise serum cholesterol levels.
   29. Brian McNamee deposition, 70.
   30. *Ibid.*, 71.
   31. *Ibid.*, 72.
   32. *Ibid.*

Chapter 4

   1. Steven K. Brumer, "Baseball's Jose Canseco: More Money, More Problems—Including Bankruptcy," *Washington Times*, September 27, 2012.
   2. www.mlb.com/news/article, December 13, 2007 (*citing* CNN news report).
   3. Cited by AP, "Canseco: 'Steroid Use by Players at 85%,'" *Los Angeles Times*, based upon an interview with Fox SportsNet, May 18, 2002.
   4. Nick Cafardo, "Clemens Strongly Defends Himself, Latest Book Release Continues to Put the Drug-Abuse Spo-tLight on Former Pitcher," *Boston Globe*, May 17, 2009.
   5. The Mitchell Report: The Illegal Use of Steroids in Major League Baseball, 169–170.
   6. Brian McNamee deposition, 32.
   7. The Mitchell Report: The Illegal Use of Steroids in Major League Baseball, 169.
   8. Affidavit of Jose Canseco, Harris County, Texas, January 22, 2008, 3.
   9. www.mlb.com/news/article, May 17, 2009; ESPN.com, April 18, 2008.
   10. www.espn.com, June 3, 2010.
   11. The Mitchell Report: The Illegal Use of Steroids in Major League Baseball, 141–233.
   12. *Ibid.*, 146.
   13. The letter is dated September 6, 2007, and is appended to the Report. See The Mitchell Report: The Illegal Use of Steroids in Major League Baseball, Appendix B-9 and B-10.
   14. The Mitchell Report: The Illegal Use of Steroids in Major League Baseball, *Independence of the Investigation*, Appendix A.
   15. *Ibid.*, 309.
   16. *Ibid.*, Introduction, SR-10.
   17. *Ibid.*, 293.
   18. *Ibid*
   19. *Ibid.*, 54.
   20. Tony Blair, *A Journey: My Political Life* (New York: Random House, 2011), 153–154.
   21. *Ibid.*, 165.
   22. *Ibid.*, 168.
   23. James B. Stewart, *Disney Wars* (New York: Simon & Schuster, 2005), 403–412, 422–494. Stewart later wrote about Barry Bonds' steroid use in his 2011 book, *Tangled Webs: How False Statements Are Undermining America: From Martha Stewart to Bernie Madoff* (New York: Penguin Press, 2011).
   24. Committee on Oversight and Government Reform, U.S. House of Representatives, Washington, D.C., Tuesday, January 15, 2008, 40–41.
   25. *Ibid.*, 61.
   26. www.baseball-almanac.com/legendary/steriods/baseball.shtml.
   27. Selig's annual paycheck had reached $18.35 million by the time Mitchell actually released the report, and at a time when NFL Commissioner Roger Goodell made $11.2 million a year. With the belly-aching about baseball salaries, it should be noted that in 2007, Selig, the most fawned over commissioner since Kenesaw Landis among the baseball scribblers, made more money than all but four players: Alex Rodriguez, Derek Jeter, Roger Clemens, and Jason Giambi. See www.sportsbusinessdaily.com/journal, "Selig's Pay Climbs Past $18 Million."
   28. www.sports.jrank.org/pages/4376/selig-bud-heads-major-league-executive-council.html.
   29. www.forbes.com/mlb-valuation, March 27, 2013.
   30. Mark Townsend, "Bud Selig to Get $6M Annual Pension, Serve as Commissioner Emeritus," Yahoo.com, December 19, 2014.
   31. The Mitchell Report: The Illegal Use of Steroids in Major League Baseball, 9.
   32. www.baseball-almanac.com/legendary/steriods/baseball.shtml.
   33. Nathaniel Vinton, "In MLB, There Were No Positive Steroid Tests Out of 5,391 Samples," *New York Daily News*, November 29, 2013; Alex Hall, "MLB Releases 2013 Drug Testing Report," www.sbnation.com, November 29, 2013.
   34. The Mitchell Report: The Illegal Use of Steroids in Major League Baseball, SR-8.
   35. www.reuters/com/article/2007/12/14. Professor Tobin did suggest, however, that logical conclusions might be made but that the science was not there.
   36. www.gov.uk/government/uploads/

attachment_data/file/119133/anabolic-steroids-annexes.pdf.

37. Narcotics Educational Foundation of America, www.cnoa.org/nefa.

38. www.baseball-reference.com/players/a/rodrial.shtml.

39. Marc Carig, "Yankee Slugger Reportedly Goes to Germany for Knee Treatment," *Newark Star-Ledger*, December 28, 2011.

40. www.baseball-reference.com/players/r/rodrial.

41. www.baseball-reference.com/players/c/cabreme01.shtml.

42. The specific PED for which Ortiz tested positive in 2003 was never publicly disclosed by MLB, nor should it have been, as it was part of a confidential random test that was not supposed to be made public, via agreement between the Players' Union and Major League Baseball. In 2003, "Big Papi" (Ortiz) upped his homer total from the previous year with Minnesota from 20 to 31, increased his RBI total from 75 to 101, and slapped seven more doubles and seven more hits. www.baseball-reference.com/o/ortiz.

43. www.baseball-reference.com/o/ortiz.

44. Howard Bryant, "Different Messages from Hamilton, Ortiz: While Rangers' Slugger Offers a Human Response, Big Papi Toes the MLB Line on Steroids," www.espn.com, August 9, 2009.

45. "Barry Bonds 'Threatened to Tear Out My Breast Implants Because He Paid for Them,' Claims Slugger's Mistress in Steroid Abuse Case," *London Daily Mail*, March 29, 2011.

46. *Ibid.*

47. Michael Hurcomb, "Appeals Court Reverses Barry Bonds' Obstruction of Justice Conviction," www.cbssports.com, April 22, 2015.

48. *Ibid.*

49. www.baseball-reference.com/players/b/bonds.

50. www.mlb.com/mlb/official_info/official_rules/batters.

51. www.baseball-reference.com/players/b/bonds.

52. www.baseball-reference.com/players/j/jacks.

53. www.sports-reference.com/olympics/athletes/bo/rosie-bonds.

54. Lou Pavlovich, Jr., "The Baseball Vision of Barry Bonds," *Collegiate Baseball*, May 7, 2014.

55. Bill Koenig, "The Eyes Have It," *Baseball Weekly*, June 6, 1996.

56. www.si.com/vault/1990/06/25/122210/3030vision-pittsburgh-barry-bonds.

57. Although Caminiti did have an alcohol problem, the actual cause of his 2004 death was from a "speedball," a lethal cocktail of cocaine and heroin. See "Caminiti Died of Overdose," *Washington Post*, November 2, 2004.

58. The Mitchell Report: The Illegal Use of Steroids in Major League Baseball, SR-2.

59. www.baseball-almanac.com/hitting/histb.

60. *Ibid.*

61. *Ibid.*

62. Robert Mc G. Thomas, Jr., "Lyle Alzado, 43, Fierce Lineman Who Turned to Steroid Foe, Is Dead," *New York Times*, May 15, 1992.

63. Author's telephone interview with Cliff Gustafson, December 26, 2011.

64. The Mitchell Report: The Illegal Use of Steroids in Major League Baseball, 307.

65. *Ibid.*, SR-35.

Chapter 5

1. The Mitchell Report: The Illegal Use of Steroids in Major League Baseball, 149–167.

2. *Ibid.*, 167.

3. *Ibid.*, 147.

4. Defendant's Motion to Dismiss, *Clemens v. McNamee*, 4:08—CU-00471, March 4, 2008.

5. The Mitchell Report: The Illegal Use of Steroids in Major League Baseball, 168.

6. *Ibid.*

7. *Ibid.*

8. Brian McNamee deposition, 231–232.

9. Deposition conducted by John "Billy" Belk, 37.

10. The Mitchell Report: The Illegal Use of Steroids in Major League Baseball, 169.

11. @TJQuinnESPN, May 21, 2012.

12. *Ibid.*

13. The Mitchell Report: The Illegal Use of Steroids in Major League Baseball, 170.

14. Cooke won the Pulitzer Prize for her story about a young heroin addict. The *Washington Post* published "Jimmy's World" on September 28, 1980. It was a tale of drug addiction and depravity in Washington, D.C. Janet Cooke was then a 25-year-old novice reporter. The story offered vivid descriptions of the life of a poor, inner-city drug addict. The story was a fake. See www.pbs.org/newshour/bradlee/background_cooke.

15. The Mitchell Report: The Illegal Use of Steroids in Major League Baseball, 170.

16. www.indiemedia.ie/article/74119, February 6, 2006.

17. www.cbssports.com, May 10, 2012.

18. @TJQuinnESPN, May 18, 2012.
19. The Mitchell Report: The Illegal Use of Steroids in Major League Baseball, 172.
20. *Ibid.*
21. *Ibid.*, 173.
22. *Ibid.*
23. *Ibid.*
24. *Ibid.*, 175–176.
25. Jack Curry, "Jeter Declares His Independence from the Steroids Era," *New York Times*, February 19, 2009.
26. Author's telephone interview with Cliff Gustafson, December 26, 2011.
27. www.bizofbaseball.com.
28. "Minor League Suspensions in 2012," www.mlb.com/news/article, March 15, 2012.
29. These are updated numbers as of November 10, 2012. Originally, only six players were identified as having failed the 2005 tests. www.baseball-almanac.com/legendary/steroids_of_baseball.html.
30. www.espn.com, August 18, 2013.
31. See Nathaniel Vinton, "In MLB, There Were No Positive Steroid Tests Out of 5,391 Samples," *New York Daily News*, November 19, 2013. See also Alex Hall, "MLB Releases 2013 Drug-Testing Report," www.sbnation.com/mlb, November 29, 2013.
32. Brittany Ghiroli, "Davis Suspended Twenty-Five Games for Amphetamines," www.mlb.com, September 12, 2014.
33. *Ibid.*; Daniel Kramer, "Maybin Suspended Twenty-Five Games for Amphetamines," mlb.com, July 23, 2014.
34. "Minor League Suspensions in 2012," www.mlb.com/news/article, March 15, 2012.
35. Selena Roberts and David Epstein, "Sources Tell *SI* Alex Rodriguez Tests Positive for Steroids in 2003," si.com, February 7, 2009. Leaks to the press, apparently by federal prosecutors or Mitchell, have proved both accurate and inaccurate regarding the particular players who flunked the 2003 drug tests. A list published in 2009 with www.ickypeople.com in correctly implicated Alex Rodriguez, Jay Gibbons, David Ortiz, Manny Ramirez and Sammy Sosa. Yet there has been no credible evidence to surface that would implicate Nomar Garciaparra, Johnny Damon, Derek Lowe, Pedro Martinez, Alfonso Soriano, Aaron Boone, Vernon Wells, Sandy Alomar, Magglio Ordonez, Eric Chavez, Carlos Delgado, Bret Boone, Freddy Garcia, Todd Helton, Jason Schmidt, Ivan Rodriguez, Derek Lee, Bobby Abreu, Liván Hernández, Moises Alou, Mark Prior or Kerry Wood.
36. www.espn.com, March 8, 2012.

37. The Mitchell Report: The Illegal Use of Steroids in Major League Baseball, 285.
38. *Ibid.*
39. Defendant's Motion to Dismiss, *Clemens v. McNamee*, 4:08—CU-00471, March 4, 2008, 17–18.
40. Sources include Fox affiliate WTTG, Philadelphia, which offered both audio and video recordings of the exchange between Buck and McCarver. www/archive.or/details/WTTG-20110515_02000. Buck's comments were widely discussed on the Internet that night and the next day. Former MLB commissioner Fay Vincent took note of Buck's comments that same night on Twitter, @FayVincent.
41. Major League Baseball finally banned amphetamines in 2006, a year after it banned Human Growth Hormone.
42. The Mitchell Report: The Illegal Use of Steroids in Major League Baseball, 67.
43. www.mlb.com/news article, June 1, 2016.
44. Robert R. Dallek, *An Unfinished Life: John F. Kennedy, 1917–1963* (Boston: Little, Brown, 2003), 105.
45. "Debbie Clemens Contradicts Trainer," AP, http://www.espn.go.com/mlb/story/_/id/8025811/debbie-clemens-says-roger-clemens-there-hgh-shot, June 8, 2012.
46. *Ibid.* See also Lester Munson, "A Pretty but Costly Picture," www.espn.com, June 8, 2012.
47. In 2009, while this author was immersed in conducting research for this book, two Chicago attorneys, Dan Voelker and Paul Duffy, said they doubted the widely held belief that Shoeless Joe Jackson helped to throw the 1919 World Series—reputedly for $5,000. After examining historical records, including a report by private detectives hired by the owner of the White Sox, the pair concluded that there existed no evidence that Jackson had conspired with mobsters and gamblers to fix the games. *ABA Journal*, December 2009, 10.
48. The New York Yankees even offered a non-alcoholic beverage package for their luxury suites at the new Yankee Stadium. YES Network, April 16, 2014.
49. In 2001 the United States Supreme Court upheld an arbitration award based on the apparent collusion among Major League Baseball teams. The case involved Steve Garvey and the San Diego Padres. See *Major League Players Association v. Garvey*, 532 U.S. 504 (2001). The general rule of law is that random drug testing is unconstitutional. But the Supreme Court carved out an exception for railway workers in 1989 when it said their work involved safety-

sensitive functions that could cause "great human loss." See *Skinner v. Railway Labor Executives' Assn*, 489 U.S. 602 (1989). It is hard to fathom the safety-sensitive issues of baseball. Nevertheless, random drug testing laws are all over the place, including conflicting federal and state statutes. The rationale of random drug testing of major league players is based on an agreement between the Players' Association and Major League Baseball wherein the players waived their rights. However, the agreement does contain a "probable cause" section wherein Major League Baseball would have to show considerable evidence against a player should a suspension for a drug violation be challenged. As of 2012 only one player, Ryan Braun of the Milwaukee Brewers, had successfully challenged a suspension. And he was suspended the next year, 2013, for apparently buying banned substances from a Miami clinic. Alex Rodriguez was banned for the entire 2014 season after he too was implicated in making purchases from Miami's Biogenesis and Aging Clinic. Originally, only the federal government was held accountable for unconstitutional interference in a citizen's privacy. Subsequent court cases, particularly *Adamson v. California*, 332 U.S. 46 (1947), holding that the Due Process Clause of the Fourteenth Amendment applied to state criminal trials, and legislation have extended that prohibition to states and to the workplace.

50. @TJQuinnESPN.com, April 15, 2012.
51. Mitchell Report, p. 285.

Chapter 6

1. www.baseball-reference.com/players/h/hended. See also "Dave Henderson, Who Hit Famous Playoff Homer Against Angels, Dies at 57," AP, December 27, 2015.
2. www.baseball-almanac.com/box-scores/, April 29, 1986.
3. Ibid., citing *Boston Globe*, April 30, 1986.
4. www.baseball-reference.com/players/c/clemero.
5. Pearlman, *The Rocket That Fell to Earth*, 117–121.
6. Connery settled out of court with Broccoli and United Artists. The terms of that settlement agreement remain confidential. See Paul Scott, "Autographs? I Don't Get Paid for Them So I Don't Sign Them ... The Obsession with Money That Haunts Sean Connery," *London Daily Mail*, August 10, 2008.
7. Harold Clurman, Introduction to Henrik Ibsen, *The Master Builder* (New York: Penguin Classics, 1978), iv.
8. Nick Carfado, "Book Released; Clemens Won't Let It Go," *Boston Globe*, May 13, 2009.
9. Clemens ranks 14th, having hit 159 batters in his career. Nolan Ryan was right behind him with 158 victims, 15th all-time. Randy Johnson is tied for fifth with 190 and Tim Wakefield is seventh.
10. Evan Weiner, "The Baseball Writer v. Roger Clemens," www.baseballthinkfactory.org, June 21, 2012.
11. A New York jury in that case awarded the Plaintiff $11.6 million in damages. The parties are believed to have settled the matter for $11.5 million. The terms of the settlement agreement, however, remain confidential.
12. Mike Oz, "Barry Bonds, Roger Clemens See Small Rise in HOF Votes," Yahoo Sports, January 6, 2015.
13. George Will, *Men at Work: The Craft of Baseball* (New York: Macmillan, 1990).
14. Pat Jordan, "Late Innings; Roger Clemens Refuses to Grow Up," *New York Times Magazine*, March 4, 2001.
15. Lester Munson, "A Pretty but Costly Picture," www.espn.com, June 8, 2012.
16. Audrey Herkels, "Q&A: Covering the Beat with Law Alum Lester Munson," *Chicago Maroon* (May 14, 2010).
17. Quinn holds a Bachelor of Journalism degree from the University of Missouri.
18. Matt Snyder, "Report: Alex Rodriguez Admitted Steroid Use to DEA," www.cbssports.com, November 5, 2014.
19. Danny Knobler, "Happy Crawford Says of Boston: 'They Love It When You're Miserable,'" www.cbssports.com, March 7, 2013.
20. Dan Shaughnessy, "David Ortiz Rejects Talk of Steroid Use," *Boston Globe*, May 8, 2013. Ortiz responded in an interview by an ESPN Sports Radio affiliate in the Dominican Republic.
21. The designation of Boston as "the Athens of America" was apparently made in a Hebrew guidebook published in Berlin sometime after the American Civil War. Cited in Rachel Cohen, *Bernard Berenson: A Life in the Picture Trade* (New Haven: Yale University Press, 2013), 25.
22. Nick Cafardo, "Clemens Strongly Defends Himself; Latest Book Release Continues to Put the Drug-Abuse Spot-Light on Former Pitcher," *Boston Globe*, May 17, 2009.
23. Clemens deposition, 161–162.
24. Pat Jordan, "Late Innings; Roger Clemens Refuses to Grow Up," *New York Times Magazine*, March 4, 2001.

25. Ibid.
26. George Vecsey, "Wanting the Ball One Hearing Too Many," *New York Times*, February 17, 2008.
27. As far as can be ascertained, Clemens was ejected only twice.
28. Stewart Powell, "Debbie Clemens Set to Take the Blame," www.blog.chron.com/clemens/, June 7, 2012.
29. Clemens deposition, 86.
30. Ibid.
31. Email exchange between the author and George Vecsey, March 11, 2015.
32. George Vecsey, "Wanting the Ball One Hearing Too Many," *New York Times*, February 17, 2008.
33. www.economist.com/news/business/21583284, April 10, 2013.
34. Robert Caro, *The Years of Lyndon Johnson: The Passage of Power* (New York: Knopf Doubleday, 2012), 410.
35. Elizabeth Traynor, "Lead Clemens Lawyer Draws Judge's Ire," blog.chon.com/clemens/2012/6/lead-lawyer-draws-screaming-judge.
36. Ibid.
37. Ibid.
38. Ibid.
39. Jose Canseco, *Juiced: Wild Times, Rampant 'Roids, Smash Hits, and How Baseball Got Big* (New York: Regan Books, 2005), 162.
40. David Sweet, "Clemens Can Kiss Endorsements Goodbye," www.nbcnews.com, December 26, 2007.
41. Teri Thompson, Nathaniel Vinton, Michael O'Keeffe, and Christian Red, *American Icon: The Fall of Roger Clemens and the Rise of Steroids in America's Pastime* (New York: Knopf, 2009), 205.
42. Christian Red, "Lawyers Seek Testimony from Roger Clemens in Defamation Suit Filed by Former Trainer Brian McNamee," *New York Daily News*, June 10, 2014.
43. George Vecsey, "Reprieve of Sorts in a Costly Blunder, *New York Times*, p. B13, July 14, 2011.
44. Pat Jordan, "Late Innings; Roger Clemens Refuses to Grow Up," *New York Times Magazine*, March 4, 2001.
45. Transcript, "Mitchell's Report to Mold Baseball's Future," Tony Cox, host, National Public Radio, December 20, 2007.
46. Ibid.
47. Ibid.
48. Daniel Okrent, "The Public Editor; Weapons of Mass Destruction? Or Mass Distraction?" *New York Times*, May 30, 2004.

49. Although a Yankees fan, the author liked Piazza, and missed his first night of class for the bar exam to watch Piazza's first game for the Mets against the Los Angeles Dodgers.
50. David Waldstein, "A Big Hitter's Baseball Life, Without the Bombshells," *New York Times*, February 9, 2013.
51. Tim Dahlberg, "Column: Piazza Book Is a Bizarre Page Turner," www.timesnews.net, February 20, 2013.
52. The author rates Tim McCarver as the best color commentator television produced in any sport.
53. Michael S. Schmidt, "Lawyer Says 2003 Clemens Test Was Negative," *New York Times*, July 4, 2009.
54. Thompson, *American Icon*, 60–61, 81, 135, 160, 169, 209–210, 277–280, 324.
55. Michael S. Schmidt, "Clemens Lied About Doping, Indictment Charges," *New York Times*, August 19, 2010.
56. Thomas Boswell, "Baseball's Lie Comes Home to Roost," *Washington Post*, December 16, 2007.
57. www.chron.com/business/article/chron, May 11, 2012. See also www.abcas3.auditedmedia.com/ecirc, March 31, 2013.
58. Richard Justice, "Even If He Refutes It All, Clemens Is Under Same Cloud as Bonds," *Houston Chronicle*, December 14, 2007.
59. Teri Thompson, Christian Red, Nathaniel Vinton, and Michael O'Keeffe, "Roger Clemens May Have Joked About Wife's Chat with Jessica Canseco," *New York Daily News*, February 26, 2008.
60. Brian McNamee deposition, 27.
61. Brian McNamee deposition, p. 27.
62. Mike Fish, "Clemens Saga Weaves a Tangled Web in Houston," www.espn.com, May 21, 2008.
63. www.abcas3.auditedmedia.com/ecirc, March 31, 2013.
64. This was in marked contrast to *The Michael Kay Show* on ESPN radio, which had turned into frenetic improv theater by 2015.
65. Greg Doyel, "Clemens' Best Option: Misremember His Ego, Plead Guilty Now," www.cbssports.com, August 22, 2010.
66. Cited in Kinky Friedman, *Kinky Friedman's Guide to Texas Etiquette: Or How to Get to Heaven or Hell Without Going Through Dallas-Fort Worth* (New York: HarperCollins, 2001), 120.

Chapter 7

1. @TJQuinnESPN, May 17, 2012.

2. Clemens deposition, 82.
3. Ibid., 136.
4. Ibid.
5. Ibid.
6. @TJQuinnESPN, May 8, 2012.
7. @TJQuinnESPN, May 17, 2012.
8. www.baseball-reference.com/players/g/giambi.
9. Howard Bryant, "Friction and Fractures Erode Faith in Mitchell's Investigation," www.espn.com, December 11, 2007.
10. Ibid.
11. Ibid.
12. Ibid.
13. Ibid.
14. Ibid.
15. Ibid.
16. Ibid.
17. Ibid.
18. Ibid.
19. Ibid.
20. Ibid.
21. See Skinner v. Railway Labor Executives' Assn., 489 U.S. 602 (1989).
22. Howard Bryant, "Friction and Fractures Erode Faith in Mitchell's Investigation," www.espn.com, December 11, 2007.
23. Ibid. This is from whence the 5 to 7 percent usage rate was derived. The results were not necessarily accurate in all cases, and therefore some leeway was built into that estimate. Generally, a review of the challenges of DNA testing in the introduction is worth reviewing.
24. Howard Bryant, "Friction and Fractures Erode Faith in Mitchell's Investigation," www.espn.com, December 11, 2007.
25. Ibid. The law is unclear, however, as to whether former players would have been entitled to such representation.
26. www.reuters.com/article/2007/12/14.

Chapter 8

1. Michael O'Keeffe, "Guards at Roger Clemens Trial Under Investigation for Accepting Signed Baseballs from Rocket," *New York Daily News*, August 17, 2011.
2. Thompson, *American Icon*, 164.
3. Michael Feeney Callan, *Robert Redford: The Biography* (New York: Knopf, 2011), 359–360.
4. The author was employed as an account executive for a half-decade at a New York public relations firm before turning to the law.
5. Jonathan Mahler, "Why Clemens and Armstrong Aren't Worth Pursuing Anymore," *New York Times*, July 1, 2011.
6. Pat Jordan, "Late Innings; Roger Clemens Refuses to Grow Up," *New York Times Magazine*, March 4, 2001.
7. Clemens deposition, 102.
8. Ibid., 103.
9. Ibid.
10. Ibid., 103–104.
11. Ibid., 105.
12. Ibid.
13. Ibid., 175.
14. Ibid., 175–176.
15. Ibid., 176.
16. Ibid., 99–100.
17. Ibid., 100.
18. Ibid.
19. www.opensecrets.org/pac_2006_election_cycle.
20. The term "show trial" has traditionally been used to describe the sham trials conducted by Soviet Russia during the Cold War.
21. Preliminary Transcript, The Mitchell Report: The Illegal Use of Steroids in Major League Baseball, Day 2, Wednesday, February 13, 2008, House of Representatives, Committee on Oversight and Government Reform, Washington, D.C., 4–5.
22. Ibid., 12.
23. Ibid., 10.
24. Ibid., 14–15.
25. Ibid.
26. Ibid., 10.
27. Ibid.
28. www.opensecrets.org/pac_2006_election_cycle.
29. Steve Belcher, "Davis: Andy Pettitte Was Key," www.espn.com, August 21, 2010.
30. Day 2, February 13, 2008, 12.
31. Indeed, Congressman Cummings' statements wound-up spiking Clemens' first criminal trial as federal prosecutors tried to sneak into evidence Cummings' statement implying Clemens' guilt. The introduction of this rank, unfairly-prejudicial and inadmissible hearsay resulted in a mistrial.
32. Preliminary Transcript, The Mitchell Report: The Illegal Use of Steroids in Major League Baseball, Day 2, February 13, 2008, 38.
33. Ibid., 85.
34. Ibid., 39.
35. Ibid., 40.
36. Ibid. As it turned out, neither Pettitte nor Clemens was named in the Grimsley affidavit. The *Los Angeles Times* was forced, therefore, to issue a retraction. Clemens remembered this correctly because a reporter for the

paper did ask both players in October 2005 (in Atlanta, during a playoff series against the Braves) whether they had taken any performance enhancing drugs. Pettitte obviously lied because he denied such use to the reporter. Pettitte, as we saw earlier, also misremembered the interview as taking place in Kissimmee, Florida.

37. Preliminary Transcript, The Mitchell Report: The Illegal Use of Steroids in Major League Baseball, Day 2, February 13, 2008, 40–41. Cummings' thesis was wrongly premised. Clemens testified that he had discussed HGH in general terms with Pettitte. Furthermore, Clemens was on record as having said that the conversation to which Cummings alluded never occurred. Clemens insisted that the discussion between himself and Pettitte involved the use of HGH by Clemens' wife. Clemens' recollection was corroborated by Brian McNamee's testimony as well.

38. *Ibid.*, 41.

39. *Ibid.* Cummings' statement was problematic as well because Pettitte testified that he did not remember telling his wife about the discussion with Clemens.

40. *Ibid.*, 62.

41. *Ibid.*, 63.

42. *Ibid.*, 65.

43. *Ibid.*, 67.

44. *Ibid.*, 102. Clemens obviously knew that this question would be asked at the hearing. Yet he did not independently seek the answer ahead of his appearance, buttressing his credibility and suggesting that he was telling the truth.

45. *Ibid.*

46. *Ibid.*, 187–188.

47. *Ibid.*, 148.

48. *Ibid.*, 116.

49. *Ibid.*, 188. Waxman seemed somewhat oblivious to the fact that the accuser always bears the burden of proof. Thus, inconsistencies in the accuser's "story" are *always* particularly relevant.

50. Tom Davis, Minority Report, 13.

Chapter 9

1. www.baseball-reference.com/players/j/jackso.

2. The Mitchell Report: The Illegal Use of Steroids in Major League Baseball, 102.

3. *Ibid.*, 131–132.

4. *Ibid.*, 133.

5. *Ibid.*

6. The calendar was ruled inadmissible at trial because it was deemed not to have been exempted from the rule against hearsay as a business record. The court found that the calendar was not kept in the ordinary course of business and thus did not satisfy the requirements of Rule 803(6) of the Federal Rules of Evidence. For an easily understood explanation of Rule 803(6), *see* Michael H. Graham, *Federal Rules of Evidence in a Nutshell (8th ed.)* (Eagan, MN: West Publishing, West Nutshell Series, 2014), 466–478.

7. The Mitchell Report: The Illegal Use of Steroids in Major League Baseball, 150–152.

8. *Ibid.*

9. *Ibid.*, 265.

10. The seasons encompassed the period from 2002 to 2004.

11. Interestingly, the record for similar streaks—consecutive scoreless innings pitched and consecutive games pitched in relief—are also held by pitchers for the Los Angeles Dodgers. Orel Hershiser pitched 59 consecutive scoreless innings in 1988, and Mike Marshall pitched 13 consecutive games in relief in 1974. Dale Mohorcic of the Texas Rangers duplicated this feat in 1986.

12. The Mitchell Report: The Illegal Use of Steroids in Major League Baseball, 263.

13. Committee on Oversight and Government Reform, U.S. House of Representatives, Washington, D.C., Friday, February 1, 2008, Interview of Edward Charles Knoblauch, 6–8.

14. *Ibid.*, 9.

15. *Ibid.*, 10.

16. *Ibid.*, 11.

17. *Ibid.*, 12.

18. *Ibid.*, 13.

19. *Ibid.*, 14.

20. *Ibid.*, 14–15.

21. *Ibid.*, 15–16. It is unclear on what basis Schiliro premised this statement. Not one of the players who were subjected to a deposition made any statements that would have led Schiliro to reach that conclusion.

22. Edward Charles Knoblauch interview, 17.

23. *Ibid.*, 21.

24. *Ibid.*, 23.

25. *Ibid.*, 24.

26. *Ibid.*, 28.

27. *Ibid.*, 35.

28. *Ibid.*, 36.

29. *Ibid.*, 37.

30. *Ibid.*

31. Andrew Pettitte deposition, 13.

32. *Ibid.*, 14.

33. *Ibid.*, 15.

34. *Ibid.*, 16.

35. *Ibid.,* 17.
36. *Ibid.,* 18.
37. *Ibid.,* 19.
38. *Ibid.,* 36.
39. *Ibid.,* 37.
40. *Ibid.*
41. *Ibid.,* 38. This is what I call the D.O. or the "designated out," whereby pitchers in the National League are forced to bat. I think that this exercise in futility should be eliminated in the National League as it has been in the American League, where the Designated Hitter Rule has replaced it.
42. Andrew Pettitte deposition, 79.
43. *Ibid.,* 80.
44. *Ibid.,* 93.
45. *Ibid.*
46. *Ibid.*
47. *Ibid.*

Chapter 10

1. Brian McNamee deposition, 6.
2. *Ibid.,* 71–74, 77–78.
3. *Ibid.,* 87.
4. *Ibid.,* 193.
5. *Ibid.*
6. *Ibid.,* 181–182.
7. *Ibid.*
8. *Ibid.,* 87.
9. *Ibid.,* 135–136.
10. *Ibid.,* 181–189.
11. *Ibid.,* 192.
12. Clemens deposition, 60.
13. *Ibid.,* 182. McNamee testified, "I bit my tongue quite a bit, because I could have buried him, but I didn't."
14. *Ibid.,* 199.
15. Pat Jordan, "Late Innings; Roger Clemens Refuses to Grow Up," *New York Times Magazine,* March 4, 2001.
16. Brian McNamee deposition, 72.
17. *Ibid.,* 197–198.
18. *Ibid.,* 219.
19. *Ibid.*
20. *Ibid.,* 217.
21. Andrew Pettitte deposition, 37.
22. @TJQuinnESPN, May 21, 2012.
23. Christie Smythe, "Clemens Fails to Settle Trainer's Steroid Defamation Case," *Bloomberg Business,* April 29, 2014.
24. E-mail interview with author, August 5, 2016.
25. R. J. White, "Settlement Reached in Roger Clemens Defamation Lawsuit," www.cbssports.com, March 18, 2015.
26. "Defamation suit versus Clemens settled," ESPN.com, March 18, 2015.
27. Ibid.
28. Pat Jordan, "Late Innings; Roger Clemens Refuses to Grow Up," *New York Times Magazine,* March 4, 2001.
29. Interview of James Joseph Murray, IV, Committee on Oversight and Government Reform, January 31, 2008, 13–43.
30. *Ibid.,* 13.
31. *Ibid.,* 13, 21, 27–28, 30.
32. *Ibid.,* 40.
33. *Ibid.,* 39.
34. *Ibid.,* 39–40.
35. On December 12, 2007, Jim Yarbrough and John "Billy" Belk, investigators for Rusty Hardin's law firm, recorded and transcribed an interview with McNamee. Belk was a retired Houston cop. I refer to the transcribed interview in this book as the "Belk deposition." The Belk deposition is in the public record and is available online.
36. Belk deposition, 112.
37. Holmes Norton was the Congressional Delegate from the District of Columbia. The author notes that Holmes Norton was the recipient of a campaign contribution from Major League Baseball in 2006. See opensecrets.org/pacs/2006_election_cycle.
38. Committee on Oversight and Government Reform, Day 2, February 13, 2008, 125–126. In that same exchange, Clemens denied to Holmes Norton that he had obtained tickets for McNamee to the Springsteen concert.
39. Thompson, *American Icon,* 14.
40. "Clemens Prosecutors Sought to Preclude Evidence," AP, April 27, 2012.
41. *Ibid.* McNamee allegedly altered a crime scene by placing a beer can in the hand of the deceased victim.
42. Thompson, *American Icon,* 77.
43. Clemens deposition, 60.
44. Thompson, *American Icon,* 81.
45. See *Catholic Encyclopedia,* www.newadvent.org/cathen/08341a.
46. Clemens deposition, 86.
47. "Cashman: Clemens Pushed to Hire McNamee After Poor Playoff Outing," AP, May 10, 2012.
48. Thompson, *American Icon,* 42.
49. Jim Baumbach and Tom Brune, "McNamee Due to Take Stand at Clemens Trial," *Newsday,* May 13, 2012.
50. www.baseball-reference.com/players/gl/clemens2001.
51. www.baseball-reference.com/managers/stengca.

52. www.baseball-reference.com/managers/torrejo01.
53. www.baseball-reference.complayers/r/rivermo.
54. Mike Lupica, "Joe Torre, the First Manager to Fire the Yankees," *New York Daily News*, October 19, 2007.
55. www.baseball-reference.com/post season/2001_alcs.
56. Michael Powell, "In 9/11 Chaos, Giuliani Forged a Lasting Image," *New York Times*, September 21, 2007.
57. *Ibid.*, 42–46.
58. *Ibid.*, 45.
59. *Ibid.*, 43.

Chapter 11

1. Brian McNamee deposition, 157–158.
2. McNamee added testosterone to the list of drugs he claimed to have shot into Clemens.
3. Jim Baumbach and Tom Brune, "McNamee Due to Take Stand at Clemens Trial," *Newsday*, May 13, 2012.
4. Brian McNamee deposition, 158.
5. *Ibid.*, 159.
6. *Ibid.*, 160. McNamee sounded almost as if he were suffering from Stockholm Syndrome, whereby hostages are said to identify with their captors out of a sense of self-preservation and perhaps brainwashing.
7. Understandable because McNamee was crossing his own Rubicon, a point of no return, a departure from his past life, a recanting of his own story about Roger Clemens, an unknown future wherein his main purpose was to be used by the United States government to shoot down the Rocket.
8. Brian McNamee deposition, 161.
9. *Ibid.*, 162.
10. *Ibid.*, 164.
11. *Ibid.*, 165.
12. *Ibid.*, 167.
13. *Ibid.*, 168.
14. *Ibid.*, 169.
15. *Ibid.*, 171.
16. *Ibid.*
17. Belk deposition, 22.
18. *Ibid.*, 18–23.
19. *Ibid.*, 36.
20. *Ibid.*, 37.
21. Preliminary Transcript, Committee on Oversight and Government Reform, Day 2, 158.
22. *Ibid.*, 38.
23. *Ibid.*, 47.
24. *Ibid.*, 48.
25. *Ibid.*, 51.
26. *Ibid.*, 57.
27. *Ibid.*, 67.
28. *Ibid.*, 75.
29. *Ibid.*, 79.
30. *Ibid.*, 80.
31. Thompson, *American Icon*, 205.

Chapter 12

1. See Jeffrey Toobin, *A Vast Conspiracy* (New York: Random House, 2000), 297.
2. Graham, *Federal Rules of Evidence in a Nutshell* (8th ed.), 407.
3. The rule was set down in *Messler v. Simmons Gun Specialties, Inc.*, 687 P.2d. 121, 127 (S. Ct. Okla. 1984).
4. A motion *in limine* is pretrial motion requesting the court to prohibit opposing counsel from referring to or offering evidence on matters so highly prejudicial to moving party that curative instructions cannot prevent a predispositional effect on the jury. See Graham, *Federal Rules of Evidence in a Nutshell* (8th ed.), 33.
5. Trial Transcript, *United States v. Clemens*, CR 10–223 (DDC 2011), July 14, 2011, 47.
6. *Ibid.*, 34.
7. *Ibid.*
8. Motions *in limine* are covered under Federal Rule of Evidence 103(c). A motion *in limine* shields a jury from inadmissible evidence being presented as well as any unfair prejudice that could arise from the asking of a question and the making of an objection. "A motion *in limine* may be made either during pretrial or at trial in advance of the presentation of evidence." See Graham, *Federal Rules of Evidence in a Nutshell* (8th ed.), p. 19–20.
9. Trial Transcript, *United States v. Clemens*, CR 10–223 (DDC 2011), July 14, 2011, 36–37.
10. *Ibid.*, 37.
11. *Ibid.*, 38.
12. *Ibid.*, 39.
13. *Ibid.*, 40.
14. *Ibid.*, 41.
15. *Ibid.*, 43.
16. *Ibid.*, 44.
17. *Ibid.*, 45–46.
18. *Ibid.*, 46.
19. *Ibid.*, 47.
20. "Experts Say Clemens Likely to go on Trial Again," AP, July 24, 2011.
21. *Ibid.*
22. Davis & Hoss, PC, "What Jurors Will

Be Selected in the Trial of Roger Clemens?" www.athletesincourt.com, July 9, 2011.

23. David Fucillo, "Roger Clemens Trial: Perjury Case Begins Wednesday in Washington, D.C.," www.sbnation.com, July 6, 2011.

24. Ibid.

25. *Taylor v. Louisiana*, 419 U.S. 522 (1975).

26. www.quickfactscensus.gov/2010_census. The white percentage of D.C. was 34.8 percent compared to the national average of 63.7 percent. The Hispanic and Asian populations were lower than the national average as well, with 9.1 percent Hispanics in D.C. to 16.3 percent nationwide, and 3.5 percent Asian compared to 4.8 percent nationally.

27. Molly O'Toole, "Jury Selection at Clemens Trial Moves Slowly," Reuters, July 11, 2011.

28. "Jury Selected for Clemens Trial; Defense Reveals Strategy," www.cbssports.com, July 12, 2011.

29. Del Quentin Wilber, "Roger Clemens Jury Selected," *Washington Post*, July 12, 2011.

30. Both Clemens' attorneys and federal prosecutors obtained post-trial feedback from the first jury that was not available to the author. Investigators for Clemens violated court rules by contacting jurors without Judge Walton's permission, and the judge subsequently permitted the prosecutors to talk to the jurors. See "Roger Clemens Legal Team in Hot Water for Contacting Jurors in Violation of Court," *New York Daily News*, September 7, 2011.

31. A.J. Perez, "Clemens Jury Is Predominantly Women," www.foxsports.com, July 12, 2011.

32. www.quickfactcensus.gov.

33. A. J. Perez, "Clemens Jury Is Predominantly Women," www.msn.foxsports.com, July 12, 2011.

34. *New York Times v. Sullivan*, 376 U.S. 254 (1964).

35. *Citizens United v. Federal Election Commission*, 558 U.S. 310 (2010).

Chapter 13

1. Jonathan Mahler, "Why Clemens and Armstrong Aren't Worth Pursuing Anymore," *New York Times*, July 1, 2011.

2. Trial Transcript, *United States v. Clemens*, CR 10-223 (DDC 2011), July 14, 2011, 47.

3. Les Carpenter, "Another Clemens Trial Is Pointless and Wasteful," www.yahoo.com, September 2, 2011.

4. Charlie Savage, "Judge Reverses Suspensions of Prosecutors in Stevens Case," *New York Times*, April 7, 2013.

5. Kim Severson and John Schwartz, "Edwards Not Guilty on One Count; Mistrial on Five Others," *New York Times*, May 31, 2012.

6. James B. Stewart, *The Prosecutors: Inside the Offices of the Government's Most Powerful Lawyers* (New York: Touchstone Books, 1988).

7. Lester Munson, "Championship Effort in Clemens Trial: Detailed Questioning of DNA Experts Shows How Seriously Both Sides Taking Case," www.espn.com, May 25, 2012.

8. Richard A. Clarke, *Against All Enemies: Inside America's War on Terror* (New York: Simon & Schuster, 2004), 91.

9. www.justice.gov/jmd/2011summary/pfd/doj-budget-summary.

10. Lester Munson, "Roger Clemens Returns to Court for Retrial on Perjury Charges," www.espn.com, April 16, 2012.

11. Lester Munson, "A Long, Winding Road to Get Clemens," www.espn.com, June 11, 2012.

12. Lester Munson, "Roger Clemens Returns to Court for Retrial on Perjury Charges," www.espn.com, April 16, 2012.

13. Ibid.

14. Greg Doyel, "Clemens' Best Option: Misremember His Ego, Plead Guilty Now," www.cbssports.com, August 22, 2012.

15. Ibid.

16. Judge Walton said he allowed jurors to take notes because it kept them awake and prevented them from being bored during long trials. @TJQuinnESPN, April 15, 2012.

17. Graham, *Federal Rules of Evidence in a Nutshell* (8th ed.), 235–236.

18. Ibid. The use of the term "fairness doctrine" is meant to be descriptive and not to be taken literally. The Fairness Doctrine, once part of the Federal Communications Commission rules, no longer exists.

19. @TJQuinnESPN, May 14, 2012.

20. "Roger Clemens Judge Warns Lawyers," AP, May 8, 2012.

21. Pat Jordan, "Late Innings; Roger Clemens Refuses to Grow Up," *New York Times Magazine*, March 4, 2001.

22. @TJQuinnESPN, May 29, 2012.

23. @TJQuinnESPN, May 14, 2012.

24. "David Segui Testifies at Trial," AP, May 24, 2012. Despite evidence of his HGH use in the form of a cancelled check written to McNamee, Stanton denied the allegation.

25. "Judge Limits Andy Pettitte Testimony," AP, May 23, 2012.

26. Lester Munson, "A Most Uncomfortable Witness, Andy Pettitte Reluctantly Testifies Against Friend, Former Teammate Roger Clemens," www.espn.com, April 1, 2012.
27. Ibid.
28. Ibid.
29. @TJQuinnESPN, May 18, 2012.
30. Graham, *Federal Rules of Evidence in a Nutshell (8th ed.)*, 110–113.
31. @TJQuinnESPN, May 14, 2012.
32. Ibid.
33. "Prosecution Rests Clemens Case," AP, May 29, 2012.
34. Lester Munson, "A Most Uncomfortable Witness, Andy Pettitte Reluctantly Testifies Against Friend, Former Teammate Roger Clemens," www.espn.com, April 1, 2012.
35. Ibid. Munson used the phrase "clear and convincing" in a rhetorical sense, not in a legal-proof sense. "Clear and convincing" is the standard for considering evidence in a civil trial. The standard in a criminal trial is "beyond a reasonable doubt."
36. "Jurors See Physical Evidence in Trial," AP, May 13, 2012.
37. "Novitsky Testifies Clemens Wasn't Initially Targeted in Investigation," www.cbssports.com, May 7, 2012.
38. Ibid.
39. Belk deposition, 47.
40. Ibid., 51.
41. Ibid., 38.
42. Lester Munson, "Rough Day for Clemens Prosecutors," www.espn.com, May 2, 2012.
43. @TJQuinnESPN, April 14, 2012.
44. Ibid.
45. @TJQuinnESPN, May 8, 2012.
46. Kirk Radomski, *Bases Loaded: The Inside Story of the Steroid Era in Baseball by the Central Figure in the Mitchell Report* (New York: Hudson Street Press, 2009).
47. Lester Munson, "Big Day for Clemens Prosecutors," www.espn.com, May 8, 2012.
48. @TJQuinnESPN, May 17, 2012.
49. "Witness: Roger Clemens at Party," www.espn.com, May 22, 2012.
50. John Schlegel, "Judge Tells Lawyers to Speed Up Clemens Trial," www.mlb.com/news article, May 18, 2012.
51. Lester Munson, "Big Day for Clemens Prosecutors," www.espn.com, May 8, 2012.
52. Ibid.
53. Ibid.
54. Ibid.
55. Ibid.
56. Ibid.
57. Lester Munson, "Crucial Confrontation Coming, Star Witness Brian McNamee to Face Star Attorney Rusty Hardin in Clemens Trial," www.espn.com, May 13, 2012.
58. @TJQuinnESPN, May 14, 2012.
59. Joseph White, "Clemens Key Accuser: 'I Misspoke About Evidence,'" AP, May 18, 2012.
60. Lester Munson, "Can Familiar McNamee Story Hold Up?" www.espn.com, May 14, 2012.
61. Ibid.
62. Ibid.
63. @TJQuinnESPN, April 15, 2012.
64. Ibid.
65. "Brian McNamee Saved Waste," AP, May 15, 2012.
66. @TJQuinnESPN, April 15, 2012.
67. A "clubhouse" in baseball is what a locker room is called in other sports.
68. @TJQuinnESPN, April 15, 2012.
69. Ibid.
70. Ibid.
71. Ibid.
72. Ibid
73. "Brian McNamee Saved Waste," AP, May 15, 2012.
74. Ibid.
75. @TJQuinnESPN, April 15, 2012.
76. Ibid.
77. Ibid.
78. "Brian McNamee Saved Waste," AP, May 15, 2012.
79. @TJQuinnESPN, April 15, 2012.
80. Ibid.
81. Lester Munson, "Long and Drawn Out—but Successful, Prosecutors' Questions of Clemens' Former Trainer Draw Answers That Hurt Clemens," www.espn.com, May 15, 2012.
82. @TJQuinnESPN, April 15, 2012.
83. "Witness: Roger Clemens at Party," www.espn.com, May 22, 2012.
84. @TJQuinnESPN, May 21, 2012.
85. Ibid.
86. Ibid.
87. @TJQuinnESPN, May 21, 2012.
88. "Prosecution Rests Clemens Case," AP, May 29, 2012.
89. Ibid.
90. Ibid.
91. Ibid.
92. Ibid.
93. "Segui Backs McNamee Testimony, Helps Feds' Case in Clemens Trial," www.cbssports.com, May 24, 2012.
94. Lester Munson, "Clemens Jury Questions Illustrative," www.espn.com, May 24, 2012.

95. *Ibid.*
96. *Ibid.*
97. "Segui Backs McNamee Testimony, Helps Feds' Case in Clemens Trial," www.cbssports.com, May 24, 2012.
98. *Ibid.*
99. @TJQuinnESPN, May 25, 2012.
100. *Ibid.*
101. *Ibid.*
102. Gabe Feldman, "How Did Roger Clemens Walk?" www.grantland.com/the-triangle, June 19, 2012.
103. @TJQuinnESPN, May 25, 2012.
104. *Ibid.*
105. *Ibid.*
106. "Witness: Roger Clemens at Party," www.espn.com, May 22, 2012.
107. @TJQuinnESPN, May 21, 2012.
108. *Ibid.*
109. "Prosecution Rests Clemens Case," AP, May 29, 2012.
110. @TJQuinnESPN, May 21, 2012.
111. "Prosecution Rests Clemens Case," AP, May 29, 2012.
112. @TJQuinnESPN, May 21, 2012.
113. *Ibid.*
114. *Ibid.*
115. Lester Munson, "Championship Effort in Clemens Trial: Detailed Questioning of DNA Expert Shows How Seriously Both Sides Taking Case," www.espn.com, May 25, 2012.
116. *Ibid.*
117. *Ibid.*

6. Author interview, August 22, 2016.
7. Lester Munson, "Lawyers Annoying Each Other, Clearly Not Getting Along," www.espn.com, May 13, 2012.
8. *Ibid.*
9. *Ibid.*
10. Author interview, August 22, 2016.
11. Clemens deposition, 84.
12. Lester Munson, "Crucial Confrontation Coming, Star Witness Brian McNamee to Face Star Attorney Rusty Hardin in Clemens Trial," www.espn.com, May 13, 2012.
13. @TJQuinnESPN, May 14, 2012.
14. @TJQuinn, ESPN, May 16, 2012.
15. Lester Munson, "Clemens' Lawyer Draws Out McNamee," www.espn.com, May 16, 2012.
16. @TJQuinnESPN, May 15, 2012.
17. @TJQuinnESPN, May 17, 2012.
18. @TJQuinnESPN, May 18, 2012.
19. @TJQuinnESPN, May 17, 2012.
20. *Ibid.*
21. Lester Munson, "Another Withering Day for McNamee," www.espn.com, May 17, 2012.
22. *Ibid.*
23. *Ibid.*
24. *Ibid.*
25. *Ibid.*
26. *Ibid.*
27. *Ibid.*
28. "Jurors Doubted Brian McNamee," AP, June 28, 2012.

Chapter 14

1. David Ovalle, "Death Sentence for Defendant in Ana Maria Angel Murder Is Overturned," *Miami Herald*, June 24, 2010.
2. Lester Munson, "Championship Effort in Clemens Trial: Detailed Questioning of DNA Expert Shows How Seriously Both Sides Taking Case," www.espn.com, May 25, 2012.
3. www.rustyhardin.com/our-team/rusty-hardin.
4. The term "outside counsel" can have two meanings. Here it involves specialists brought in by Hardin for this particular case. In the more general usage, outside counsel consists of lawyers from large corporate firms, who are usually paid in billable hours, contrasted to "inside counsel," who are salaried lawyers of a corporation, and who are referred to as general counsel.
5. "Roger Clemens Trial Continues," AP, April 24, 2012.

Chapter 15

1. Affidavit of Jose Canseco, Harris County, Texas, January 22, 2008, 2–3.
2. Nathan Vinton and Christian Red, "Feds Asked Mindy McCready About Sex Life with Roger Clemens to Determine If Rocket Used Steroids," *New York Daily News*, March 30, 2010.
3. www.nydailynews.com, May 29, 2008.
4. "Country Star Has New Album and Sex Tape Released Same Week," www.richardhuntershow.com, March 29, 2010.
5. "Roger Clemens Erectile Dysfunction? Mindy McCready Says ED Plagued Pitcher," huffingtonpost.com, March 29, 2010.
6. "Clemens Viagra, Clubhouse Source," *New York Daily News*, May 10, 2008.
7. Anthony Miccio, "Mindy McCready Tells All About Relationship with Roger Clemens," www.vh1.com/celebrity, November 18, 2008.

8. Author Interview with Rusty Hardin, August 22, 2016.
9. Frederic J. Frommer, "Pettitte Says He May Have Misunderstood Clemens," AP, May 2, 2012.
10. Ibid.
11. Lester Munson, "Rough Day for Clemens Prosecutors," www.espn.com, May 2, 2012.
12. Ibid.
13. "Jurors See Physical Evidence in Trial," AP, May 3, 2012. The term "chain of custody" refers to the collection and retention of evidence by law enforcement and begins the moment the evidence is in their hands. From that moment on, they must be able to vouch for its integrity and whereabouts until the moment it is introduced at trial. See *Black's Law Dictionary (10th Edition)* (St. Paul: Thompson Reuters, 2015), 229.
14. T. J. Quinn and Lester Munson, "Juror Questions Show Skepticism: Questions of Prosecution Witness in Clemens Trial Indicate Trouble for Government," www.espn.com, May 10, 2012.
15. Ibid.
16. Ibid.
17. Ibid.
18. Belk deposition, 36.
19. Ibid., 37.
20. T.J. Quinn and Lester Munson, "Juror Questions Show Skepticism: Questions of Prosecution Witness in Clemens Trial Indicate Trouble for Government," www.espn.com, May 10, 2012.
21. Ibid.
22. Ibid.
23. "Cashman: Clemens Pushed to Hire McNamee After Poor Playoff Outing," www.cbssports.com, May 10, 2012.
24. @TJQuinnESPN, May 10, 2012.
25. "Cashman: Clemens Pushed to Hire McNamee After Poor Playoff Outing," www.cbssports.com, May 10, 2012.
26. @TJQuinnESPN, May 10, 2012.
27. Ibid.
28. Ibid.
29. Ibid.
30. Ibid.
31. Ibid.
32. Ibid.
33. @TJQuinnESPN, June 11, 2012.
34. Ibid.
35. "Eileen McNamee Expected to Testify in Clemens' Trial," *Houston Chronicle*, June 4, 2012. The Justice Department gave Eileen McNamee the same form of immunity her husband enjoyed, "use immunity," meaning she was exempt from federal prosecution for any criminal behavior that might occur during her testimony in this one case.
36. "Estranged Wife Takes Stand, Says She Didn't Nag Mac About Clemens," www.cbssports.com, June 6, 2012.
37. Elizabeth Traynor, "Wife of Chief Clemens Accuser Disputes Testimony," www.blog.chron.com/clemens, June 6, 2012.
38. Ibid.
39. Ibid.
40. Lester Munson, "Clemens' Actions in 2008 Costly: Vigorous Defense Against PED Use Gave Accuser Impetus to Bring Out Evidence," www.espn.com, June 7, 2012.
41. Ibid.
42. Ibid.
43. Ibid.
44. Ibid.
45. Ibid.
46. Lester Munson, "He Said, She Said, but She's Believable; Brian McNamee's Ex-Wife Credibly Contradicts His Testimony in Nearly Every Way," www.espn.com, June 6, 2012.
47. Ibid.
48. Ibid.
49. Ibid.
50. Ibid.
51. Ibid.
52. Ibid.
53. Ibid.
54. Ibid.
55. Ibid.
56. Ibid.
57. Ibid.

Chapter 16

1. Elizabeth Traynor, "Defense Scores Major Victory with Toxicology Testimony," www.blog.chron.com/clemens, June 5, 2012.
2. Ibid.
3. John Schlegel, "Toxicologist Testifies on Clemens Evidence," www.mlb.com, June 5, 2012.
4. Ibid.
5. Lester Munson, "An Aggressive, All-Out Defense: Clemens' Defense Team Leaves Nothing to Chance, Has Prosecutors Scrambling," www.espn.com, June 16, 2012.
6. Ibid.
7. Ibid.
8. Greg Sanders, "Clemens Expert: DNA Could Have Been Put on Needle," AP, June 6, 2012.
9. Stewart Powell, "Clemens DNA Witness,

Challenges Prosecutors' Claims," www.blog.chron.com/clemens, June 6, 2012.

10. @TJQuinnESPN, May 31, 2012. Ironically, this supports Brian McNamee's dismissive assertion that B-12 was merely a placebo.

11. *Ibid.*
12. *Ibid.*
13. *Ibid.*

14. Elizabeth Traynor, "Former Astros Masseur Discusses Clemens Training," *Houston Chronicle* www.blog.chron.com, June 6, 2012.

15. "Joe Angel, Mike Boddicker Testify," AP, June 5, 2012.

16. Elizabeth Traynor, "Former Astros Masseur Discusses Clemens Training," *Houston Chronicle* www.blog.chron.com, June 6, 2012.

17. *Ibid.*

18. Elizabeth Traynor, "Defense Rests in Roger Clemens Perjury Trial, Pitcher Declines to Testify," www.blog.chron.com/clemens, June 10, 2012.

19. "A "stipulation of facts" is an agreement wherein both sides specify that certain facts are to be taken as true.

20. Elizabeth Traynor, "Defense Rests in Roger Clemens Perjury Trial, Pitcher Declines to Testify," blog.chron.com/clemens, June 10, 2012.

21. "Former Blue Jays' Catcher O'Brien Backs Clemens on B-12 Claims," www.cbssports.com, May 30, 2012.

22. *Ibid.*
23. @TJQuinnESPN, May 30, 2012.
24. *Ibid.*
25. *Ibid.*
26. *Ibid.*

27. *Ibid.* The government objected to the word "reckless," and Judge Walton ordered the word stricken from the official record.

28. @TJQuinnESPN, May 31, 2012.
29. *Ibid.*
30. *Ibid.*

31. Lester Munson, "Garner Leads Clinic in Clemens Trial, Ex-Manager Enthralls Courtroom with Baseball Knowledge, Facts About Pitchers," www.espn.com, May 31, 2012.

32. *Ibid.*
33. *Ibid.*

34. Lester Munson, "An Aggressive, All-Out Defense: Clemens Defense Team Leaves Nothing to Chance, Has Prosecution Scrambling," www.espn.com, June 6, 2012.

35. *Ibid.*

36. Jane E. Brody, "Vitamin B-12 as Protection for Aging Brain," *New York Times*, September 6, 2016.

37. Lester Munson, "An Aggressive, All-Out Defense: Clemens Defense Team Leaves Nothing to Chance, Has Prosecution Scrambling," www.espn.com, June 6, 2012..

38. *Associated Press*, "Joe Angel, Mike Boddicker Testify," June 5, 2012. Clemens seldom drank alcohol, and if he did, it was more likely to be wine with dinner.

39. @TJQuinnESPN, May 31, 2012.
40. *Ibid.*
41. *Ibid.*

42. "Debbie Clemens Contradicts Trainer," AP, June 8, 2012.

43. *Ibid.*

44. Stewart Powell, "Prosecution Takes Aim at Debbie Clemens After Her Claim of Taking HGH," www.blog.chron.com/clemens, June 8, 2012.

45. "Joe Angel, Mike Boddicker Testify," AP, June 5, 2012.

46. @TJ QuinnESPN, May 30, 2012.
47. *Ibid.*
48. *Ibid.*

49. John Schlegel, "Jury Begins Deliberations in Clemens Trial: Prosecution Asks for Common Sense; Hardin Calls Trial 'Outrageous,'" www.mlb.com/news/article, June 12, 2012.

50. "Clemens Trial Nears End," AP, June 12, 2012.

51. "Jurors Doubted Brian McNamee," AP, June 28, 2012.

52. *Ibid.*
53. *Ibid.*
54. *Ibid.*
55. *Ibid.*

56. "Clemens Trial Nears End," AP, June 12, 2012.

57. Paul Courson, "Arguments Conclude in Roger Clemens Perjury Trial," www.cnn.com, June 12, 2012.

58. *Ibid.*

59. Elizabeth Traynor, "Government Rebuttal Seeks to Answer Defense's Barbs About Witness," www.blog.chron.com, June 12, 2012.

60. *Ibid.*

61. John Schlegel, "Jury Begins Deliberations in Clemens Trial: Prosecution Asks for Common Sense; Hardin Calls Trial 'Outrageous,'" www.mlb.com/news/article, June 12, 2012.

62. *Ibid.*

63. Paul Courson, "Arguments Conclude in Roger Clemens Perjury Trial," www.cnn.com, June 12, 2012.

64. Elizabeth Traynor, "Second Half of Defense's Closing Argument Pits Clemens Against McNamee," www.blog.chron.com/clemens, June 12, 2012.

65. *Ibid.*

66. Janet Macur, "After Contrasting Closing Arguments, Clemens Jurors Are 'Final Umpires,'" *New York Times*, June 12, 2012.

67. Elizabeth Traynor, "Second Half of Defense's Closing Argument Pits Clemens Against McNamee," www.blog.chron.com/clemens, June 12, 2012.

68. *Ibid.*

69. *Ibid.*

70. *Ibid.*

71. *Ibid.*

Chapter 17

1. Lester Munson, "Garner Leads Clinic in Clemens Trial, Ex-Manager Enthralls Courtroom with Baseball Knowledge, Facts About Pitchers," www.espn.com, May 31, 2012.

2. Roger Clemens Career Highlights, www.YouTube.com/watch, December 7, 2014.

3. www.baseball-reference.com/players/c/clemero.

4. Joe Halverson, "Roger Clemens' Decline in Boston Was Greatly Overstated," www.bleacherreport.com, June 20, 2012.

5. www.history.com/this-day-in-history/clemens-strikes-out-20-again.

6. "Clemens Becomes Free Agent," AP, November 6, 1996, cited in the *Victoria Advocate*.

7. "Clemens Signs Three-Year Deal with Blue Jays," *Reading Eagle*, December 13, 1996.

8. "Clemens Becomes Free Agent," AP, November 6, 1996, cited in the *Victoria Adocate*.

9. Jack Curry, "Yankees Make Call to Stanton While Aiming for Clemens," *New York Times*, December 11, 1996.

10. *Ibid.*

11. "Clemens Signs Three-Year Deal with Blue Jays," *Reading Eagle*, December 13, 1996.

12. www.baseball-reference.com/players/w/wellsda.

13. Scott McClellan, *What Happened: Inside the Bush White House and Washington's Culture of Deception* (New York: Public Affairs, 2008), 50.

14. Caro, *The Passage of Power: The Years of Lyndon Johnson, Vol. IV*, 275–303.

15. Kermit L. Hall, ed., *The Oxford Companion to the Supreme Court of the United States (Second Edition)* (New York: Oxford University Press, 2005), 382. See also Adam Liptak, "The Memo That Rehnquist Wrote and Had to Disown," *New York Times*, September 11, 2005.

16. See Ronald Collins, "The Roberts Court and the First Amendment," www.scotusblog.com, July 9, 2013.

17. Belk deposition, 36–37.

18. *Ibid.*, 75.

19. 394 U.S. 731 (1969). A suspect confessed to a murder after he was falsely told by police that his cousin had confessed, even though investigators lied to the suspect, claiming that a witness had seen his car in the alley where the victim had been raped, was held to be Constitutional. The issue of whether such confessions, obtained through lying by law enforcement officials, should be Constitutional, is beyond the scope of this book, but the Innocence Project makes the alarming claim that 25 percent of all overturned convictions involved confessions to the crime. See www.relentlessdefense.com/forensics/falseconfessions. One state, New York, was so concerned about the issue that its highest court, the Court of Appeals, was taking a look at it in January 2014. See James C. McKinley, Jr., "Court Weighs Police Role in Coercing Confessions," *New York Times*, January 14, 2014.

20. @TJQuinnESPN, May 15, 2012.

21. Lester Munson, "He Said, She Said, but She's Believable; Brian McNamee's Ex-Wife Credibly Contradicts His Testimony in Nearly Every Way," www.espn.com, June 6, 2012.

22. This obsession did not extend to the press, as Pettitte had lied to a *Los Angeles Times* reporter in October 2005 about his own use of HGH. See Ben Bulch, "Clemens, Pettitte Deny Use of Drugs," *Los Angeles Times*, October 2, 2005.

23. "Mindy McCready's Autopsy Confirms Death Was a Suicide," AP, February 20, 2013.

24. "Clemens on Death of Country Star McCready: 'Sad News,'" www.cbssports.com, February 18, 2013.

25. Patrick Read, "NY Daily News Refuted: McCready-Roger Clemens Report Bogus," bleacher report.com, May 7, 2008.

26. Telephone interview with the author, August 22, 2016.

27. TMZ Staff, "Mindy McCready's Porn Studio Slams Brakes on Sex Tape," February 19, 2013. www.tmx.com/2013/02/19-mindy-mccready sex tape.

28. Affidavit of Jose Canseco, Harris County, Texas, January 22, 2008, 2.

29. Brian McNamee deposition, 214.

30. *Ibid.*, 200.

31. Pat Jordan, "Late Innings; Roger Clemens Refuses to Grow Up," *New York Times Magazine*, March 4, 2001.

32. @TJQuinnESPN, May 10, 2012.
33. Ibid.
34. George F. Kennan, *The Kennan Diaries* (New York: W. W. Norton, 2014), 660.
35. Brian McNamee deposition, 22.
36. Belk deposition, 81.
37. @TJQuinnESPN, April 15, 2012.
38. Ibid.
39. @TJQuinnESPN, May 15, 2012.
40. @TJQuinnESPN, May 12, 2012.
41. @TJQuinnESPN, May 18, 2012.
42. "Brian McNamee Saved Waste," AP, May 15, 2012.
43. @TJQuinnESPN, May 17, 2012.
44. Lester Munson, "Another Withering Day for McNamee," www.espn.com, May 17, 2012.
45. @TJQuinnESPN, May 17, 2012.
46. "Witness: Roger Clemens at Party," www.espn.com, May 22, 2012.
47. @TJQuinnESPN, May 17, 2012.
48. Mitchell Report, Appendix B-9, B-10.
49. Ibid.
50. Christian Red, Michael O'Keeffe, and Teri Thompson, "Jason Grimsley Affidavit Unsealed, Roger Clemens Not Mentioned," *New York Daily News*, December 20, 2007.
51. Ibid. See also Affidavit of Jeff Novitzky in support of an application for search warrant in Case No. 06–7142MP; United States District Court for the District of Arizona, 13–15.
52. Belk deposition, 130.
53. @TJQuinnESPN, May 30, 2012.
54. @TJQuinnESPN, April 15, 2012.
55. @TJQuinnESPN, May 16, 2012.
56. Lester Munson, "Clemens' Actions in 2008 Costly: Vigorous Defense Against PED Use Gave Accuser Impetus to Bring Out Evidence," www.espn.com, June 7, 2012.
57. @TJQuinnESPN, April 15, 2012.
58. This reinforces the fact that this book is a "theory" of what happened between Clemens and McNamee, and does not purport to be an account of what necessarily, or actually, happened. Furthermore, since the author was not privy to their conversations or interactions, he only quotes other sources using the term "liar" for either man, and only uses the term

himself in the hypothetical and theoretical senses.

Chapter 18

1. Preliminary Report: The Illegal Use of steroids in Major League Baseball, Day 2, 12.
2. www.rogerclemensfoundation.org/about.
3. www.jimmyfund.org/aboutus/boston-redsox/players/.
4. www.nesn.com/2014/08/charitable-roger-clemens-offering-one-of-a-kind-auction-item-at-fenway-park.
5. Martinez, but not Clemens, was elected to the Major League Baseball Hall of Fame in Cooperstown, New York, in 2015.
6. Nick Cafardo, "PED Accusations Still Costing Roger Clemens," *Boston Globe*, July 12, 2014. Once again, Clemens' penchant for invoking ancient, outdated expressions such as "ticked off" is particularly amusing—and charming.
7. The author was a beneficiary of a similar program for disabled veterans as an undergraduate.
8. Nick Cafardo, "PED Accusations Still Costing Roger Clemens," *Boston Globe*, July 12, 2014.
9. www.baseball-reference.com/teams/hou/2005.

Chapter 19

1. Melanie Saxton, "Catching Up with the Clemens Family," www.houstonlifestyles.com/catching-up-with-the-clemens-family, 2013.
2. Ibid.
3. Greg Morago, "Kory Clemens: Cooking Up a Hit Restaurant?" *Houston Chronicle*, June 5, 2013.
4. www.Texassports.com/cumestats.
5. www.sports.espn.go.com/boston/mlb/news/story, August 20, 2010.

Bibliography

Barry, Dan. *Bottom of the 33rd: Hope, Redemption, and Baseball's Longest Game*. New York: HarperCollins, 2011.
Blair, Tony. *A Journey: My Political Life*. New York: Random House, 2011.
Breslin, Jimmy. *Can't Anybody Here Play This Game? The Improbable Saga of the New York Mets First Year*. New York: Penguin, 1963.
Buber, Martin. *The Knowledge of Man*. New York: HarperCollins, 1965.
Buffett, Warren. *Berkshire Hathaway Letters to Shareholders: 1965–2012*. Mountain View, CA: Explorist Productions, 2014.
Callan, Michael Feeney. *Robert Redford: The Biography*. New York: Knopf, 2011.
Canseco, Jose. *Juiced: Wild Times, Rampant Roids, Smash Hits, and How Baseball Got Big*. New York: Regan Books, 2005.
Caro, Robert. *The Years of Lyndon Johnson: The Passage of Power*. New York: Knopf Doubleday, 2012.
Clarke, Richard A. *Against All Enemies: Inside America's War on Terror*. New York: Simon & Schuster, 2004.
Clemens, Roger with Peter Gammons. *Rocket Man*. Lexington, Massachusetts: The Stephen Greene Press, 1987.
Clurman, Harold. *Introduction to Henrik Ibsen: The Master Builder*. New York: Penguin Classics, 1978.
Cohen, Rachel. *Bernard Berenson: A Life in the Picture Trade*. New Haven: Yale University Press, 2013.
Connors, Jimmy. *The Outsider: A Memoir*. New York: HarperCollins, 2013.
Coppedge, Clay. *Hill Country Chronicles*. Charleston, SC: History Press, 2010.
Creamer, Robert W. *Stengel: His Life and Times*. New York: Simon & Schuster, 1990.
Dallek, Robert R. *An Unfinished Life: John F. Kennedy, 1917–1963*. Boston: Little & Brown, 2003.
Friedman, Kinky. *Kinky Friedman's Guide to Texas Etiquette: Or How to Get to Heaven or Hell Without Going Through Dallas-Fort Worth*. New York: HarperCollins, 2001.
Graham, Michael H. *Federal Rules of Evidence in a Nutshell*. Eagan, MN: West Publishing, 2014.
Hall, Kermit L., ed. *The Oxford Companion to the Supreme Court of the United States*. New York: Oxford University Press, 2005.
Kennan, George F. *The Kennan Diaries*. New York: W. W. Norton, 2014.
Levy, Harlan. *And the Blood Cried Out: A Prosecutor's Spellbinding Account of the Power of DNA*. New York: Basic Books, 1996.
Mayo, Jonathan. *Facing Clemens: Hitters on Confronting Baseball's Most Intimidating Pitcher*. Guilford, CT: Lyon Press, 2008.
McClellan, Scott. *What Happened: Inside the Bush White House and Washington's Culture of Deception*. New York: Public Affairs, 2008.

Pearlman, Jeff. *The Rocket That Fell to Earth: Roger Clemens and the Rage for Baseball Immortality.* New York: HarperCollins, 2009.
Radomski, Kirk. *Bases Loaded: The Inside Story of the Steroid Era in Baseball by the Central Figure in the Mitchell Report.* New York: Hudson Street Press, 2009.
Reynolds, Quentin Q. *Courtroom: The Story of Samuel S. Leibowitz.* New York: Farrar, Straus & Giroux, 1950.
Solzhenitsyn, Alexsandr I. *The Oak and the Calf: Sketches of Literary Life in the Soviet Union.* New York: Harper & Row, 1979.
Stewart, James B. *Disney Wars.* New York: Simon & Schuster, 2003.
_____. *The Prosecutors: Inside the Offices of the Government's Most Powerful Lawyers.* New York: Touchstone, 1998.
_____. *Tangled Webs: How False Statements are Undermining America: From Martha Stewart to Bernie Madoff.* New York: Penguin, 2011.
Thompson, Teri, and Nathaniel Vinton, Michael O'Keefe, Christian Red. *American Icon: The Fall of Roger Clemens and the Rise of Steroids in America's Pastime.* New York: Knopf, 2009.
Toobin, Jeffrey. *A Vast Conspiracy.* New York: Random House, 2000.
Torre, Joe, and Tom Verducci. *The Yankee Years.* New York: Random House, 2008.
Vecsey, George. *The Subway Series: A Year of New York Baseball.* New York: Bishop Books, 2000.
Will, George. *Men at Work: The Craft of Baseball.* New York: Macmillan, 1990.

Index

Adams, Gerry 69
Alexander, Grover Cleveland 40
Anderson, Greg 118
Andrews, Dr. James R. 131
Angel, Joe 202
Ankiel, Rick 55
Armas, Tony 33
Armstrong, Jack 63
Attanasio, Michael 75, 152, 150, 175, 187, 197
August, Steve 8, 202
Ausmus, Brad 40, 225–226

B-12 10, 111–112, 125, 167, 174, 191–200, 201, 204, 217, 220–221
Babcock, Chip 131
Bagwell, Jeff 225
Baichu, Rohan 197
Bailey, F. Lee 6, 185
Balco Lab 54
Barnett, Phil 106–109
Barrett, Marty 16, 33
Bates, Billy 25
Beckham, David 83
Belk, Billy 132
Belk Deposition 140, 145, 170, 190, 311
Bell, Mike 109
Berkman, Lance 225
Berra, Yogi 32
Bigbie, Larry 66
Biggio, Craig 225
Blair, Prime Minister Tony 56
Boddicker, Mike 201, 204
Boggs, Wade 3, 27–28, 32, 33
Bonds, Barry 4, 26, 54, 59, 61–62, 64, 74, 93, 118, 189
Bonds, Bobby 62
Bonds, Rosie 62
Boswell, Thomas 95
Boyd, Oil Can 17, 32, 90
Bradley, Phil 78
Brady, Tom 82

Braley, Congressman Bruce 114
Breuer, Lanny 98
British Government Study on Anabolic Steroids 59–60
Brosius, Scott 137
Brown, Kevin 119
Brumley, Mike 25
Bryant, Bear 13
Bryant, Howard 99–100, 101, 157
Buck, Joe 72
Buckley, Jerry 77
Buckner, Bill 33
Bud Lite can 10, 192, 194, 217
Bugli, Bill 90
Bush, Pres. George W. 74
Bush, Gov. Jeb 176
Butler, Daniel 152, 156, 160, 168
Byrd, Marlon 71, 73
Byrd, Paul 55

Cabrera, Melky 60
Cameron, Mike 71
Caminiti, Ken 62, 63, 64
Canseco, Jessica 96
Canseco, Jose 4, 7, 52–54, 67, 71, 91, 96, 98, 99, 116–117, 145–146, 171, 186, 190, 199, 202, 211, 214, 218, 222
Capel, Mike 12, 23
Carey, Rick 25
Carreon, Mark 66
Carter, Joe 47
Cashman, Brian 16, 69, 134, 190–191, 214
Castiglione, Joe 31, 224
Castor, Steve 42, 44, 46
Chain of Custody 46
Clemens, Bess 13–14, 21, 83
Clemens, Debbie 35, 73, 83, 86, 96, 106–108, 111–115, 127, 130, 169–171, 201–202, 204, 208, 226, 227–229
Clemens, Kacy Austin 228
Clemens, Koby Aaron 227

Clemens, Kody Alec 228
Clemens, Kory Allen 228
Clemens, William 14
Clinton, Pres. Bill 55
Coleman, Vince 63
Connery, Sean 79
Cooke, Janet 68
Corso, Anthony 171–172
Craig, Tommy 167
Crawford, Carl 85
Cummings, Congressman Elijah 112–113, 148–152
Cust, Jack 66
Cy Young Award 1–2, 36, 40

Damon, Johnny 29
Dana Farber Cancer Institute 223
date rape drug GBH 10, 162
Davis, Chris 71
Davis, Congressman Tom 5, 112, 115
Death, Taxes and Mac 178
Denaro, Black Jack 176
Denaro, Joel 176
Dershowitz, Alan 152
Di Maggio, Joe 74
DNA evidence 5
Donnells, Chris 66
Doyle, Danny 23
Drumheller, Andy 177
Duquette, Dan 7, 208–209, 217
Durham, Steven 148, 156, 159, 160, 163, 178–179, 189, 196, 198, 201
Dykstra, Lenny 66

Edwards, Senator John 159
Eisner, Michael 56
Emery, Richard 45, 130–131, 164, 186
Epstein, Theo 30
Evans, Dwight 33, 78
evidence tampering 46

Federal Bureau of Investigation (FBI) 42, 54, 66, 89
Fehr, Donald 55, 102
Feldman, Gabe 5
Fifth Amendment (U.S. Constitution) 4, 118
Flaherty, John 16
Fletcher, Darrin 40, 48, 198
Flood, Curt 99
Fourth Amendment (U.S. Constitution) 57, 102
Francesa, Mike 89
Franco, Julio 22
Franco, Matt 66
Franklin, Ryan 71
Frazier v. Cupp 211

Gabilanez, Fanny 201
Gagne, Eric 119
Gammons, Peter 95
Garciaparra, Nomar 29, 207
Garner, Phil 4, 8, 199–200, 207
Gedman, Rich 2, 33, 40, 79
Giambi, Jason 4, 37, 54, 99, 100, 118
Girardi, Joe 210
Giuliani, Rudolph 137
Godfrey, Craig 202
Goldberger, Dr. Bruce 195
Goodhand, David B. 160
Gordon, Michael 44, 122, 126, 141
Gordon-Reed, Annette 13
Gorman, Lou 79, 87
Gowdy, Curt 31
Graham, Wayne 20–21
Greenwell, Mike 33
Grimsley, Jason 122, 219
Guerrero, Gil 37, 167, 198–199, 203, 205
Guillen, Jose 71
Gustafson, Cliff (Coach Gus) 2, 21, 22–26, 64, 70, 197

Hamm, Mia 29
Hardin, Rusty 4, 9, 12, 88, 90, 94, 98–99, 112, 130, 135, 148–157, 221
Harrison, Dr. Bill 62
Haselman, Bill 207
Hearron, Jeff 3, 16, 22, 25, 92
hearsay evidence 148–153
Henderson, Dave 77, 78
Henderson, Rickey 63
Hendricks, Alan 122
Hendricks, Randy 8, 122, 131, 210
Hendricks Agency 8, 94, 131
Hollingsworth, Derek S. 177
Holmes, Delegate Eleanor Norton 204
Holmes, Justice Oliver Wendell 117
Hooten, Burt 110
Houk, Ralph 3, 32
House Committee on Oversight and Government Reform 5, 57
Howey, Todd 12
Hundley, Todd 66
Hurst, Bruce 30, 32

Jackson, Reggie 62
Jackson, Shoeless Joe 74, 118
Jerome, Saint 133
Jeter, Derek 37, 70, 83, 135, 228
Jim Crow Laws 118
Jimmy Fund 223
John, Pope XXIII 136
Johnson, Randy 79, 137
Johnson, Walter 40
Joplin, Janis 13

Jordan, Pat 92, 105
Junction Boys 13
Jury Pool (District of Columbia) 5
jury selection 153–156
Justice, Richard 95

Katch 22 restaurant 228
Kay, Michael 16, 85, 97
Keel, Alan 173
Kennan, George 216
Kennedy, Kevin 208
Key, Jimmy 209
Killingworth, Kirk 26
Knoblauch, Chuck 4, 9, 45, 70, 111, 119–122, 131, 139, 148, 161, 212, 217

Landis, Judge Kenesaw Mountain 117
Laveroni, Jerry 197
Lester, John 30
Levy, Harlan 9
Likover, Dr. Larry 196, 204
Lo Duca, Paul 119
Los Angeles Times 219
Lowrey, Alexander 171
Lupica, Mike 89
Lynn, Fred 33

Magadan, Dave 26
Maiorana, Charlie 11
Major, Prime Minister John 56
Mangold, Jeff 214
Mantle, Mickey 18
Manuele, Anthony 173
Maris, Roger 74
Martin, Ned 31
Martinez, Pedro 14, 29, 224
Martinez, Tino 17, 135, 137
Martinez, Victor 1
Mason, Perry 6
Matsui, Hideki 30
Maybin, Cameron 71
McCarthy, Sen. Joseph 109
McCarver, Tim 72
McCready, Mindy 186–187, 213
McDonough, Sean 31
McDowell, Oddibe 26
McGuiness, Martin 69
McGwire, Mark 59, 63, 93, 124
McKay, Dave 63
McNamara, John 16
McNamee, Brian, Jr. 133, 192, 221
McNamee, Eileen Taylor 10, 46, 133, 169, 192, 193–194, 212
Mejia, Jenrry 71
Mercker, Kent 109
Mica, Congressman John 114
Miller Lite 173; can 7, 10, 192, 194

Mitchell, Sen. George 5, 55–56, 98, 100, 101, 146–147, 170, 195, 216, 219, 222
Mitchell Report 2, 52–76, 192, 219
Monahan, Gene 167
Morris, Hal 66
Morris-Kukoski, Cynthia 174, 191
Moss, Charlie 167
Mota, Guillermo 71
Munson, Lester 83–84, 159, 160, 164–168, 170–172, 174–175, 176, 178–179, 184–185, 190, 193–194, 196, 200
Murray, Jim 8, 94, 131, 170

Neagle, Denny 109
Nicol, Hugh 63
Nipper, Al 32, 78, 208
Novitzky, Jeff 44, 54, 98, 141–143, 189–190, 192, 212, 218, 220

O'Brien, Charlie 3, 40, 48, 197, 204
O'Malley, Dr. Bert 9, 96
Ortiz, David 3, 60–61, 64, 85
Orza, Gene 102
Oswalt, Roy 225–226
Owen, Spike 22–23, 33, 77–78

Palmeiro, Rafael 71
Parrella, Matt 142
Paterno, Joe 81
Pearlman, Jeff 16, 23, 85–87, 90, 92
Pedroia, Dustin 33
Perez, Neifi 71
Pettitte, Andy 7, 35, 45, 53, 70, 75, 111, 122–125, 130, 131, 132, 135, 141, 146, 147, 158, 161, 187, 188–189, 203, 205, 225
Pettitte, Laura 149–150, 152
Piazza, Mike 14, 32, 93–94
Pokorak, Eric 174
Pollack, U.S. Magistrate Judge Cheryl 130
Posada, Jorge 3, 40, 135
Price, David 9, 30, 35
Price, Jeremy 173
Proffer Agreement 145

Quinn, TJ 37, 84, 170–171, 179, 190

Radomski, Kirk 6, 8, 49–50, 54, 66–67, 89, 99, 116, 119, 140, 166–167, 169, 212, 215
Ramirez, Manny 3, 37, 60, 64, 66, 71
Redfern, Cheryl 197
Redford, Robert 104
Republican Minority Report 68
Reyes, Jose 33
Reynolds, Pamela 173
Reynolds, RJ 62
Rice, Jim 27, 33
Rickey, Branch 118

Index

Ripken, Cal, Jr. 3, 15
Rivera, Mariano 135–136, 209
Roberts, Brian 66
Robinson, Jackie 118
Rodriguez, Alex 37, 60, 64, 71, 84
Roger Clemens Foundation 223–226
Rowe, Jim 167
Ruth, Babe 8, 27–28, 74
Ryan, Kevin 219
Ryan, Nolan 15, 40, 60, 78, 79

Safavian, Jennifer 107
Saleski, Courtney 5, 173–174, 175, 193, 204–205
San Jacinto College 20
Schiliro, Phil 120–121
Schilling, Curt 85, 137
Schwartz, Fred 96, 105
Scully, Vince 31
Seaver, Tom 33
Segui, David 46, 119, 139, 172
Selig, Bud 54, 56, 58, 71, 101, 110
Shiraldi, Calvin 3, 22–23, 26, 33
Showalter, Buck 133
Sirbaugh, Jennifer Ryan 213
Sixth Amendment (U.S. Constitution) 148, 154
Smoltz, John 210
Sosa, Sammy 59, 63
Spring Branch High School 11
Springsteen, Bruce 132
Stanley, Bob 33
Stanley, Cody 71, 73
Stanton, Mike 43, 148, 210, 212, 214
Steinbrenner, George M. 1, 88, 191, 208–209
Stengel, Casey 3, 17, 19, 135
Sterkel, Jill 25
Stevens, Sen. Ted 159
Stewart, Dave 134
Stockton, Dick 31
Stottlemeyer, Mel 191
Strain, Lily 96
Stuart, Dick 21
Sugar Land, Texas 11

Tartabull, Danny 77, 78
Tartabull, Jose 77

Taylor, Marc 196
Tejada, Miguel 71, 99, 101, 213
Thomas, Clint 26
Thomas, Frank 54, 100
Thomas, Isiah 80
Tiant, Luis 8
Tierney, Congressman John F. 113
Tobin, Prof. Robert 59
Torre, Joe 15, 135–136, 209
Trammel, Alan 208
Trent, Mike 26
Trump, Pres. Donald 83

Ueberroth, Peter 79

Varitek, Jason 29
Vaughn, Mo 16, 28, 109
Vecsey, George 17, 87–88, 92

Wakefield, Tim 79
Waldman, Suzy 1
Wall Street gym rats 10, 133
Wallace, Mike 91
Walton, Judge Reggie 75, 90, 148–156, 161, 158–192, 212
Ward, Earl 130, 146, 166
Waxman, Congressman Henry 5, 58, 74, 100–115, 118, 223
Waxman Committee 68, 74, 89, 102, 108, 110, 119, 141
Weiner, Michael 55
Wells, David 88, 209–210
Westmoreland, Congressman Lynn 146
Wetteland, John 209
White, Rondell 66
Will, George 83
Williams, Ted 3–4, 27, 30–32, 84
Wilson, Mookie 33
Wonsowicz, Charlie 134, 137–139
Wood, Kerry 208

Yarbrough, John 132
Yastrzemski, Carl 27
Young, Cy 30, 32, 40, 128, 208

Zaun, Gregg 109

www.ingramcontent.com/pod-product-compliance
Ingram Content Group UK Ltd.
Pitfield, Milton Keynes, MK11 3LW, UK
UKHW041933140426
5217IPUK00014B/448

9 781476 665764